MEDICAL LIBRARY
ASSOCIATION *Guides*

Introduction *to* Reference Sources in the Health Sciences

Fifth Edition

Compiled and Edited By

JEFFREY T. HUBER

JO ANNE BOORKMAN

JEAN BLACKWELL

NEAL-SCHUMAN PUBLISHERS, INC.

NEW YORK   LONDON

Published by Neal-Schuman Publishers, Inc.
100 William St., Suite 2004
New York, NY 10038

Printed and bound in the United States of America.

The paper used in this publication meets the minimum requirements of American National Standard for Information Sciences—Permanence of Paper for Printed Library Materials, ANSI Z39.48-1992.

Library of Congress Cataloging-in-Publication Data

Introduction to reference sources in the health sciences / [edited by] Jeffrey T. Huber, Jo Anne Boorkman, Jean C. Blackwell. — 5th ed.
    p. ; cm.
    Includes bibliographical references and index.
    ISBN 978-1-55570-636-4 (alk. paper)
    1. Medicine—Reference books—Bibliography. 2. Medicine—Bibliography.
3. Medicine—Information services. I. Huber, Jeffrey T. II. Boorkman, Jo Anne.
III. Blackwell, Jean C.
    [DNLM: 1. Medicine—Abstracts. 2. Medicine—Resource Guides. 3. Information Services—Abstracts. 4. Information Services—Resource Guides. 5. Reference Books—Abstracts. 6. Reference Books—Resource Guides. ZWB 100 I62 2008]

Z6658.I54 2008
[R118.6]
016.61072—dc22
                                                    2007047819

Contents

List of Figures
and Appendices

Figures

Appendices

Foreword

The first edition of *Introduction to Reference Sources in the Health Sciences* was developed due to my frustration with having no textbook for use in my health sciences classes at the University of North Carolina. Jo Anne Boorkman was on the staff of the UNC Health Sciences Library at the time, and she agreed to work with me on producing a textbook that would be a selective guide to the major reference materials in the health sciences. Our model was William Katz's *Introduction to Reference Sources*, which was the standard text for general reference courses. We developed a plan for the book and presented it to the Medical Library Association's Books Panel. It was accepted, we went to work, and the first edition was released in 1980. Jo Anne and I have been overwhelmed and gratified by the reception that first edition and subsequent editions have received.

The heart and soul of each of the editions to date, and for those to come, has been and will be the chapter contributors. We attempted to identify those individuals in the profession who had great expertise in the topics that needed to be covered. The list of contributors reads like a veritable who's who of the profession and of the Medical Library Association. Jo Anne and I are profoundly grateful to each and every one of them for sharing their expertise with several generations of library school students.

A comparison of the latest edition with the first edition will show the tremendous changes that have occurred in health sciences reference. The first edition had only print sources. In later editions we added special chapters on electronic sources. Now *IRSHS* is a fully integrated publication with print and electronic sources together.

My association with the publication ended with the fourth edition and my retirement. Jo Anne and I invited Jeff Huber to join us as a co-editor, and he and Jo Anne have continued the tradition with this new edition. Jeff proved to be the right person at the right time! The new team of Boorkman and Huber, along with Jean Blackwell, has created a fine new edition, again with a stellar group of contributors. *Introduction to Reference Sources in the Health Sciences* is in good hands, and I shall watch subsequent editions with great interest.

I want to pay tribute to Jo Anne Boorkman. Working with her has been a joy, and I want to thank her for her good judgment, her industriousness, her knowledge of the area, and, most of all, for her friendship over the years. She has been the glue that held our endeavors together!

I am grateful for the opportunity that the Medical Library Association gave us in the early days of the publications program. It has been a wonderful experience for me, both personally and professionally!

Fred W. Roper
Dean Emeritus
School of Library and Information Science
University of South Carolina

Preface

Today's librarians must be prepared to handle a wide variety of health reference requests, drawing upon an ever-expanding range of resources. They may be called upon to assist a medical student in determining the best evidence related to a particular diagnosis, help a consumer answer a drug question, find a good definition of a medical term for a patron, demonstrate the differences among point of care resources to a group of residents, or show a graduate student which databases to search for information on a research topic. Informed and competent reference work is essential to helping clients locate relevant, accurate, and timely information.

Introduction to Reference Sources in the Health Sciences, Fifth Edition, explores the nature of reference work and offers the authors' selections of some of the most important resources for answering questions in this area. The chapters in this guide identify and describe both general titles for answering bibliographic questions and authoritative works specific to the health sciences, which librarians can use to assist their patrons in finding information on medical topics. The recommendations highlight the best works available for answering questions from health professionals, students, researchers, and consumers.

Introduction to Reference Sources in the Health Sciences attempts to include a broad cross-section of the types of information that are available today. This fifth edition includes even more Web resources than previous editions, but print sources are still an important component of the library collection and the librarian's toolkit. Many people hold the misconception that most information is available and accessible via the Web; they use general-purpose search engines even when searching for health information. The informed librarian can guide users to the more specialized Web sites, databases, or print information that will truly address their questions.

Since no consensus exists as to what constitutes "basic works," the materials included here represent the authors' candidates for such a list. We have chosen those tools that librarians may use on a daily basis in reference work in the health sciences—those that may be considered foundation or basic works. Some major specialized works have also been included when appropriate. Emphasis is placed on U.S. publications, although we have also attempted to address Canadian publications and needs. For certain groups of sources (e.g., technical report literature), materials that are considerably broader in scope than the health sciences field alone have been included to help the reader toward a clear understanding of the use of these sources in reference work in the health sciences.

Arrangement of the Material

Each chapter contains a discussion of the general characteristics of the type of source being considered, followed by examples of the most important tools in the area. The annotations have been thoroughly updated to reflect changes since the last edition, and many new listings have been added. Citations indicate the availability of electronic access to print works in addition to listing electronic-only resources.

The book is organized into three parts: "The Reference Collection," "Bibliographic Sources," and "Information Sources." In Part I, "The Reference Collection," Chapter 1, "Organization and Management of the Reference Collection," discusses the nature of reference and the practicalities of working with this type of collection. It explores methods of organizing and weeding the collection and the criteria the authors consider relevant for selecting both print and electronic resources.

Part II, "Bibliographic Sources," includes recommendations that will help the reader verify, locate, and select high-quality works in different formats. Chapter 2, "Bibliographic Sources for Monographs," focuses on books, while Chapter 3, "Bibliographic Sources for Periodicals," addresses journals, serials, and magazines.

The significantly expanded Chapter 4, "Indexing, Abstracting, and Digital Database Resources," examines the rich array of databases now available in the health sciences, providing the author's perspective on primary and secondary databases. Chapter 5, "U.S. Government Documents and Technical Reports," highlights the breadth of health information available in government documents and technical reports, while Chapter 6, "Conferences, Reviews, and Translations," illuminates less familiar but vital categories of information.

Part III, "Information Sources," offers recommendations that may form the foundation of a health sciences reference collection. Chapter 7, "Terminology," lists a wide range of medical dictionaries. Chapter 8, "Handbooks and Manuals," contains scientific data books and compendia as well as popular resources for laboratory methods and clinical decision-making. Chapter 9, "Drug Information Sources," guides librarians and health care professionals through references on this complex topic. Chapter 10, "Consumer Health Sources," discusses what has become an important area of collecting and service in many libraries. Chapter 11, "Medical and Health Statistics," explains the types of statistics that are collected and where readers can find them. Chapter 12, "Directories and Biographical Sources," explores ways to unearth information about people and organizations, while Chapter 13, "History Sources," introduces more than thirty new places to find historical facts and knowledge. The final Chapter 14, "Grant Sources," provides grantsmanship guides, directories, and indexes for health care professionals seeking funding.

The need for health sciences reference work is as great as ever. With the continuing growth of the health care industry and of the number and types of information sources available, librarians will face new opportunities and new issues in health reference.

We hope that this fifth edition of *Introduction to Reference Sources in the Health Sciences* will help guide readers in navigating the maze of print and electronic health sciences resources and in the challenges of building and maintaining a current reference collection.

A Brief History of *Introduction to Reference Sources in the Health Sciences*

In 1979, Fred Roper approached the Medical Library Association's publications program about writing a text to support a course in health sciences reference that he taught at the University of North Carolina-Chapel Hill's School of Library Science, with the idea that it would be useful for others teaching similar courses at other library schools. The Medical Library Association expressed interest and suggested that there would be a broader audience for such a text among practicing health sciences librarians and for supporting MLA's CE course in reference resources. At that time, Jo Anne Boorkman was head of public services and head of reference at the Health Sciences Library at UNC-Chapel Hill. Fred asked her to join him as a coeditor in this endeavor. They invited several librarians, some of whom were relatively new to the field and others with a wealth of experience, to participate in this publishing venture. This mix of contributors proved to be a successful collaboration.

In 1980, the first edition appeared and was met with enthusiasm. It became a familiar text for both library school courses and MLA CE courses. It also gained a broader audience than the authors expected among practicing librarians from general academic and public libraries as well as health sciences libraries. The second edition followed four years later and continued to receive acceptance and recognition. With major career moves for both of them to different parts of the country, their goal of regular updates slipped, and the third edition did not appear until 1994. And it was a full ten years later that the fourth edition was published. With the fourth edition being completed as Fred prepared for retirement, Jeff Huber was invited to serve as one of the editors.

The reception of the first four editions of *Introduction to Reference Sources in the Health Sciences* has been most gratifying. It was the editors' intention to begin work on a fifth edition soon after publication of the fourth edition, to keep the publication up to date to reflect the changes brought on by the growth of the Web and expansion of electronic reference resources. Jo Anne's plans to retire provided further impetus to complete the fifth edition in a timely fashion. To assist with preparation of the fifth edition, Jean Blackwell was invited to serve as one of the editors and with the hope that she would continue with future editions of this book. A different mix of authors was invited to contribute to this edition for another successful collaboration that is in keeping with the idea originally promoted by Fred and MLA almost thirty years ago.

Many people have played important roles in the production of this fifth edition. The chapter authors have all shared their expertise, experience, and enthusiasm for their respective topics. New authors have revised several chapters from the fourth edition. These authors are indebted to Fred Roper, Jerry Perry, David Howse, Joan Schlimgen, and Amy Butros for the excellent groundwork that they laid for this edition in preparing the chapters in the fifth edition. Their contributions are gratefully acknowledged.

Jeffrey T. Huber
Jo Anne Boorkman
Jean C. Blackwell

PART I

The Reference Collection

CHAPTER 1

Organization and Management of the Reference Collection

Jean C. Blackwell, Jo Anne Boorkman, and Anneliese Taylor

Previous editions of *Introduction to Reference Sources in the Health Sciences* have covered in great detail the organization and management of print reference collections. The explanations of various types and formats of materials, the components of collection development policies, and the physical arrangement of reference collections presented in those editions continue to be relevant and useful. While the fourth edition (2004) gave significant attention to the evolution of electronic resources and their use in health sciences libraries, this edition will focus on the impact of e-resources on reference services and, by extension, reference collections. In preparation for writing this chapter, the authors surveyed health sciences librarians in March 2007 to gather data on current trends in reference services and collections. A copy of the Health Sciences Reference Collections Survey is included in Appendix 1-1.

There is no question that the rapid proliferation of electronic information resources has literally transformed how librarians do reference. When we operate from libraries without walls, and the ability to search full text turns every collection of electronic information resources into a potential reference collection, it is impossible to separate reference from everything else—and some will argue that it is pointless to try.

How, then, can libraries balance the need for collecting important print publications, while at the same time responding to the increasing availability of and demand for electronic resources? If books are online, do we still need them in print? Should they still be labeled reference? How much can print reference collections be streamlined without being eviscerated? Will librarians continue to be responsible for selecting and organizing the highest quality resources, when many of them are freely available on the Web and our clients are finding them on their own?

This chapter will examine the changing nature of reference today and what it means to the organization and management of reference collections. It will review selection and weeding criteria and the importance of a reference collection development policy. It will report how health sciences librarians are responding to changing patterns of library use and to dramatic shifts in methods of providing resources and services. Decisions related to the duplication of formats will be addressed, including costs, print cancellations, and the presentation and management of online reference collections. Finally, the chapter will look at the impact of developing trends such as information portals, metasearching, and book digitization projects.

What Is Reference?

Reference as a place with a sign saying "Reference" is a nineteenth-century development, and the term "reference work" first appeared in the index to *Library Journal* in 1891 [1]. In addition to giving directions, finding facts, and verifying bibliographic citations, reference librarians provide assistance in literature searching and the use of myriad print and electronic information sources. Nowadays, they also field technical questions with increasing frequency.

Reference collections evolve and develop from the nature of reference work, and the tools used most frequently to answer these questions comprise the Reference Collection. Reference sources are consulted for specific and immediate information rather than being read from beginning to end. They typically include these categories of materials: dictionaries, manuals and guides, almanacs and statistical compilations, subject handbooks and data books, drug lists, directories of organizations, biographical directories, geographic atlases, encyclopedic works, library information, serial information, book catalogs, and lists of meetings and translations [2].

Decisions about what materials to include in the Reference Collection should be guided by a reference collection development policy that is developed as a document parallel to the overall collection development policy of the library. As a guide to this process, *Collection Development and Management*

for Electronic, Audiovisual, and Print Resources in Health Sciences Libraries
[3] provides samples of collection development policies from a range of
health sciences and hospital libraries.

Elements of a Collection Development Policy

   I. Statement of objectives indicating purpose and focus of policy
  II. Location of collection
 III. Scope of coverage/breadth of collection
 IV. Format of materials collected
  V. Electronic reference sources
 VI. Subject descriptions in terms of library's classification scheme
VII. Types of reference materials
VIII. Library unit's local selection responsibilities
 IX. Criteria for selection, updating, and weeding
  X. External relationships [4]

A collection development policy serves several purposes. In a time of
limited resources, it helps define the scope of the collection for selection con-
sistency and wise use of resources. It can be used to train new staff and orient
them to the nature of reference work in a particular library. It can be used for
evaluation of current and future needs based on clients' queries, new curriculum
and research demands, and new technology. The reference collection policy
can also be useful in defining areas of cooperative collection building with
other libraries. As freely available online resources become increasingly
important components of reference service, defining their place in the reference
collection development policy can facilitate integration into the collection [5].

Along with a collection development policy for reference, there should
be sensible guidelines for the weeding and retention of materials. Weeding is
the process of removing materials from the active collection. A weeding
policy can be written as a separate document or incorporated into the overall
collection development policy.

Reference collections need regular weeding to maintain relevancy and
currency. Establishing standing orders for regularly published works, such
as annual statistics and directories, helps assure that the latest editions of
these resources are added to the collection. Libraries may choose to get rid
of reference materials that are no longer current or appropriate, or they may
move selected resources to the circulating collection. Other options are to put
these materials in compact shelving or in storage at a less-accessible place.

Questions to Consider before Weeding

1. Is the content still pertinent?
2. Is it duplicated in the collection?
3. Is it available elsewhere?
4. Is it valuable or rare or both?
5. Has it been superseded by a new edition?
6. Was it selected originally in error?
7. Is it cited in standard abstracting or indexing tools?
8. Is it listed in a bibliography of important works?
9. Does it have local relevance?
10. Does it fill a consortial agreement or regional need?
11. If available in electronic format, is continued access to retrospective files ensured? [6]

The disposition of outdated materials will depend on the type of library; a hospital library may want to keep only the most recent edition of a work, while an academic health sciences library may need to retain earlier editions for historical and research purposes.

As electronic resources replace books on the shelf, and users express strong preference for information in digital formats, many libraries are reducing their print reference collections at a rapid pace. Ideally, libraries conduct a complete review of the reference collection on a set schedule following the guidelines in the collection policy—for example, every two years or every five years. In reality, it usually takes an event such as a library renovation or the loss of space for other purposes to bring about a comprehensive evaluation and updating of the collection.

A thorough weeding project requires a huge amount of time to plan and implement. In *Fundamentals of Collection Development and Management*, Peggy Johnson suggests that planning such a project should include comparing the costs of the effort with the costs of doing nothing. Costs associated with weeding include staff time to review materials, revise catalog records, move materials, educate library users, and retrieve materials from somewhere else if they are requested later. Costs associated with doing nothing include ongoing maintenance, such as re-shelving, shifting collections, and maintaining catalog records; dealing with a shortage of shelf space; and providing outdated and possibly inaccurate information [7].

A written collection development policy is as important today as it ever was—perhaps even more so. As the number of new resources increases exponentially and libraries struggle to keep pace with rising demand, it is imperative to document the policies and procedures that guide collection decisions; otherwise, libraries risk building collections that lack depth and comprehensiveness and do not serve the needs of their constituencies.

Selection Tools

There is a variety of selection tools to assist librarians in making decisions about what to add to their collections. For almost forty years, health sciences and hospital librarians depended heavily on the Brandon/Hill Selected Lists (www.mssm.edu/library/brandon-hill/) for guidance in choosing books and journals, with the "minimal core" titles serving as a particularly helpful list from which to make reference selections. That all changed when Dorothy Hill retired in 2004, and the lists that she and the late Alfred Brandon had created, updated, and offered as a free service were no longer being published. Doody Enterprises soon filled the vacuum with *Doody's Core Titles in the Health Sciences (DCT)*, produced annually and available by subscription only. *DCT* combines Web-based services with the expert opinion of content specialists and library selectors to identify books and software that constitute the core body of literature for a health sciences library [8].

Other selection aids available to health sciences librarians include reviews in library journals, reviews in medical and allied health journals, publisher and vendor notifications, approval plans, standing orders, and holdings lists of other libraries. Respondents to the authors' survey listed publisher/vendor notifications (85 percent), reviews (83 percent), and standing orders (49 percent) as the selection tools they prefer to use in identifying new print reference materials. *DCT* was the most frequently mentioned source of evaluative reviews, along with those in journals such as *Medical Reference Services Quarterly*, *Journal of the Medical Library Association*, and *JAMA*. Many librarians noted that they found recommendations from faculty to be helpful, because they knew the resources would be used.

The Collection Development Section of the Medical Library Association (colldev.mlanet.org/index.html) provides a forum for communication and cooperation among health sciences librarians responsible for selection of library materials. It maintains a newsletter and a discussion list and has a section on resources for librarians, which includes a list of vendors, lists of subject-based resources, a methodology for comparing approval plans, and other useful information.

Evaluation Criteria for New Material

Criteria for evaluating new materials include the following, which can also be used for maintaining and weeding the reference collection [9]:

1. Significance and usefulness of the resource to the library's clientele
2. Intended audience: readership level, language
3. Overlap with existing reference resources
4. Demand for resource by clientele
5. Authority and reputation of the author, publisher or database producer
6. Age and currency of the contents
7. Favorable reviews in the professional literature
8. Inclusion of the resource in reference guides
9. Price of the publication or database in relation to
   a. Availability of the information contained within the resource
   b. Quality and physical production of the resource, and
   c. Amount of anticipated use
10. Space required
11. Appropriate format (print vs. microform vs. electronic)

When looking at specific reference tools, librarians use a combination of measures for evaluation, with a definite focus on the materials' usefulness to *their* particular library's collection and clientele. Because budgets are frequently limited, librarians often look for new tools that will fill the gaps in their collection [10].

Reference Collections in the Electronic Environment

The Reference Collection has traditionally been separated from circulating collections, placed in an area easily accessible to librarians and library users, and made noncirculating to assure that the materials are available for immediate and short-term use. Although this tradition is being challenged in the electronic environment, as it is becomes more and more difficult to separate reference works from everything else, libraries are not doing away with their print reference collections. All of the respondents (n=64) to the authors' 2007 survey said that they continue to maintain a separate reference collection. More than 60 percent of the respondents reported that the size of their print reference collections has shrunk during the past five years—about half of the collections by 25 percent, and 12 percent of the collections by 50 percent or more. A few libraries are finding they no longer need to maintain a separate "Ready Reference" collection, since much of this type of information is more conveniently found online. If there is no electronic equivalent of heavily used books—for example, the *AHA Guide to the Health Care Field* and the *Publication Manual of the American Psychological Association*—they can be merged into the reference collection [11].

Libraries at large institutions are often better equipped to offer a wide variety of electronic resources than are smaller libraries. A respondent to the authors' survey commented that libraries in small hospitals and nonprofit organizations have difficulty purchasing extensive electronic collections due to budget restraints. She noted that in these libraries, print reference collections are still vital.

In 2005, Nancy and Susan Clemmons interviewed health sciences librarians and library directors about the biggest changes and challenges for medical reference in the twenty-first century. They were following up on a similar survey conducted five years earlier. One librarian responded that collection development for print reference books is increasingly a challenge: "Books we used to use daily, especially directories, are rarely used anymore.... Given how stretched our budgets are, it's difficult to justify purchasing expensive reference books 'just in case,' or only for archival purposes." Another added, "The use of the print reference collection continues to decline largely due to the 'Googleization' of online information. Another side effect of the declining use of the print collection could be that our skills with using the print reference collection have deteriorated" [12].

A study of trends in reference usage statistics at the Library of the Health Sciences (Peoria) of the University of Illinois at Chicago found that directional questions and mediated searching had decreased between 1990 and 2005, but in-depth reference and consultations had increased, implying that users have become more sophisticated information seekers and require more instructional and in-depth assistance rather than traditional ready refer-ence [13]. This trend is reflected in other locations, where librarians are spending much less time at the reference desk and more time conducting consultations, giving instruction to individuals and classes, creating online materials, and doing outreach. The authors of the UIC study concluded, "The physical reference desk has had many different incarnations, but in the midst of continued changes in users' needs, expectations, and habits, it remains a central facet of public service in the health sciences library" [14].

Since libraries' Web sites have come to serve as an extension of reference, offering a menu of full-text electronic resources in every conceivable format and arrangement, the current challenge is how to organize and present these e-resources so that the maze of information can be easily navigated. As James Shedlock describes, "We are trying to design tools that give the user more direct contact with the primary literature, and trying to do this before they even ask for it" [15]. In an article tracing the evolution of reference collections, Margaret Landesman noted, "In the past, a reference simply pointed the way. Now users expect to be taken there" [16].

Selection Criteria for Electronic Resources

Most librarians agree that the selection criteria for e-resources should be essentially the same as those for print materials, with the emphasis being on authoritativeness and value of a resource to the defined community of users. Indeed, the U.S. National Library of Medicine's *Collection Development Manual* states, "When considering electronic resources for selection, the Library's intent is to apply the same criteria for scope, depth of coverage, and authoritativeness as for publications in other formats" [17].

While some criteria apply to all formats, additional criteria need to be considered for digital formats. The authors' survey respondents rated these evaluation criteria for electronic reference resources, in order from most to least important:

- Audience
- Cost
- Accessibility (vendor licensing restrictions)
- Scope (subjects covered)
- Technology support requirements
- Reviews and recommendations
- Authority of publisher/producer
- Ease of use (layout, navigation)
- Frequency of updates
- Output options (PDF, PDA, exporting)
- Uniqueness of presentation (video, sound)

The Collection Development Policy for Electronic Resources at Johns Hopkins University Welch Medical Library offers a concise, yet thorough policy that could serve as a model for large or small libraries (www.welch. jhu.edu/about/ecdpolicy.html). It addresses questions of vision, scope, selection criteria, multiple formats, retention, licensing, funding models, and implementation and review of e-resources. It also has a section delineating library staff responsibilities related to e-resources, including: (1) evaluation, selection, acquisition, and renewal; (2) presentation and management of e-resources; (3) technical support and maintenance; (4) staff and end-user training; and (5) publicity and marketing.

Doing a trial is a useful method to help evaluate digital resources before committing to a purchase. Based on survey responses, 96 percent of libraries run trials on at least selected e-resources. The most common trial period is 30 days, however, trials of 60 and 90 days are not unusual. Because online resources represent recurring costs, getting feedback about the usefulness and quality of the resource after a trial can be crucial. A popular method is to target relevant and specific clientele for feedback. The library can also put up a brief Web-based questionnaire to be filled out after the user logs out from the resource on trial.

Duplication of Formats in a Reference Collection

These days many reference resources are available in multiple formats: print, CD-ROM, and Web-based. The multitude of choices puts us into what John Morse refers to as a publishing "Age of Also," where print and electronic formats will continue to coexist, and perhaps flourish, for the next 10 to 15 years [18]. The benefit of having the same resource in both the trusted print and the newer online formats means that libraries can gradually adjust to the reliability of the online version, while keeping the print version in addition if desired. Many libraries decide to purchase only the online, not wanting to spend precious funds on two formats of the same resource.

Health sciences reference resources on the Web consist of both the e-versions of established print products, as well as new resources that were never available in print. The challenge is to maintain accuracy and comprehensiveness while weighing the relative efficiency and cost-effectiveness of print and electronic resources, says Gary McMillan. In an article examining the evolving information marketplace, he recommends a core list of both free and fee-based medical reference sources on the Web [19]. Under pressure to add more electronic content, libraries have sometimes been willing to accept publishers' products without seriously evaluating quality. "The challenge for libraries is to ensure that collection development tools are applied to the acquisition of electronic textbooks as they are to the acquisition of print textbooks, and to work with publishers in creating standards of publication for Web-based textbooks" [20].

Differences between Print and Electronic Resources

Despite the benefits of digital versions of reference resources compared to print—more frequent updates, sophisticated search capabilities, more convenient access—there are additional aspects that need to be considered:

1. *The cost for online resources is often much higher than print resources* since publishers can charge prices that bear no relation to print. For example, *Harrison's Online* costs ten times as much as the print *Harrison's Principles of Internal Medicine.*
2. *Online subscriptions typically require a yearly renewal and payment,* even for content that has not been updated or has been only partially updated. This ongoing commitment eliminates the possibility for the library to extend its reference budget by purchasing a regularly updated resource only every couple of years or editions.
3. *Online subscriptions are a form of leasing content rather than owning it.* Most online reference resources are only accessible as long as they are renewed, and the content remains in the hands of the provider rather than the subscriber.
4. *Online content is ephemeral.* When a new edition of a reference work such as *Nelson Textbook of Pediatrics* is available, the publisher removes the old edition and provides the new content online.
5. *License agreements* must be reviewed, negotiated, and signed for most Web-based resources. These licenses can be time consuming for both the library and the vendor, and can delay the beginning of the subscription until the wording meets both parties' licensing criteria.
6. Libraries have to take into account the *extra staff time* required to install and troubleshoot CD-ROMs. Technology is becoming less of an issue with Web-based resources, although platforms and browser versions may be problematic.

Deciding between Formats

Because so many electronic reference sources also have print counterparts, a decision must be made whether to duplicate formats. Libraries have plenty of evidence that once a resource is online, the print counterpart does not get used. We know this based on:

- Anecdotal reports and direct observations of dwindling use of the print reference collection by our clients
- Usage statistics for print vs. online resources
- Librarians' own practice of using online instead of print to answer reference questions

We know that most of our clientele prefers the online version, yet librarians still strongly favor providing access to both print and electronic versions (80 percent of survey respondents). There are many situations where it makes sense for libraries to duplicate print and online formats, or to only purchase the print version.

Duplicate print and online counterparts are often purchased to fulfill the archival mission of the library (mainly academic research libraries) and provide a record of reference sources for future research. Some online resources are not as complete as their print counterparts. For example, Doctor Finder, the e-version of *AMA's Directory of Physicians in the United States*, does not provide the same level of detail about physicians as the print. For a core directory such as this one, maintaining print editions may be important.

There are also still users who prefer the searchability of the print compared to online. In this situation the library may wish to provide access to both formats to meet the needs of different clients. Still other resources have unique features in both print and online. Clients may take advantage of multiple formats for the same resource depending on the situation. Dictionaries are a good example of this scenario—particularly the Merriam-Webster dictionary, as outlined by John Morse [21]. Undeniably, librarians often maintain both versions because they are familiar with time-honored print and do not feel comfortable letting it go completely.

Print Only

The cost of online resources often makes a subscription untenable. This is especially true with reference collections, where a sizeable percentage of libraries' collections are still print only. To transfer so many resources to an online format at one time is simply not affordable for many libraries. Priorities have to be determined and choices made for key resources to be purchased online.

Licensing restrictions, access restrictions, and poor design and navigation of online resources may also convince a library to stick with the print version only. Some types of resources are also still more practical in print format than online. When they are well designed, single-volume handbooks, dictionaries, and some statistical texts can be easier to use in print rather than online.

Online Only

The resource type that most libraries prefer to have online only is indexing and abstracting databases. Multivolume resources such as *Chemical Abstracts* and large encyclopedias such as the *McGraw-Hill Encyclopedia of Science and Technology* are widely accepted online only since they can be updated frequently, free up large amounts of shelf space, and can be searched much more easily than flipping through multiple print volumes. Once these resources were put online, clients stopped using the print, making it easy for libraries to migrate to online only.

Some government publications and small press publications have already ceased being printed and are now online only, e.g., *Index Medicus* and *Vital Statistics of the United States*. In some cases the resource has become freely available online, such as *Linscott's Directory of Immunological & Biological Reagents*. The benefit of such a move is that the Web format makes it possible for a publisher to provide a free resource through paid advertising; however, this business model is not completely reliable. It is safe to assume that publishers will move in the direction of pushing their resources in a single format: Web-based.

Today's Print Reference Collection

As online reference resources become more numerous and the print collection continues to get less use, libraries must reflect on how large their print reference collection needs to be. Christopher Nolan warns of diminished use and value of reference collections that are too large and carry "deadwood"— unused and outdated materials that make it harder to find the useful sources [22]. The deadwood effect was true of print collections before digital came along, and is even more of a problem in light of clients foregoing print in favor of online resources.

An informal survey by Margaret Landesman revealed that library users have begrudgingly thought of the reference collection as "the books that the librarians lock up and won't let me take home" [23]. Landesman questioned whether print reference collections would continue to exist at all considering that, once digitized, it's difficult to distinguish what is and isn't a reference resource.

As mentioned earlier, the trend is for libraries to reduce and revamp their print reference collections according to current needs for answering reference questions. The authors' own libraries have significantly reduced their print collections and have adapted their collection policies to reflect a "leaner and meaner" reference collection. The size of today's reference collection will be determined by the needs of each individual library; however, the following guidelines could apply to any situation.

General Guidelines

- Currency is vital in order to encourage use and give a better overall impression of the collection.
- Selection of fewer, key resources that get used is more meaningful than a collection of indiscriminate scope and depth.
- The needs of the current library clientele should guide the selection of resources.
- Resources should truly be used for reference, and not be meant to be read cover to cover.

With respect to online resources, print resources should:

- Be supplementary or complementary to the online
- Provide access to resources that work better in print than online
- Provide a selection of resources to satisfy clients still wedded to the print
- Serve an archival function where the need exists

Budget Considerations

Multiple factors are driving the trend toward smaller print reference collections. In the authors' survey, librarians reported that the primary reasons for the reduction of their collections have been decline in use by their clientele (52 percent), print is not needed when an online equivalent is available (60 percent), and budgets can no longer support a large print collection (30 percent). Clearly, budgetary considerations often dictate choices. The Health Sciences Library at the University of North Carolina–Chapel Hill evaluated their reference collection asking "Electronic, Print, or Both?" The following criteria were used [24]:

- Compare the cost of each format (sometimes electronic is free!)
- Arrange for trial access before purchasing an electronic product
- Consider both user and librarian demand for a particular format
- Test the ease and speed of use of electronic vs. print
- Compare the ability to search and to browse for information
- Compare the currency of the information in each format
- Consider the labor involved in print loose-leaf services
- Monitor the use of print copies of electronic titles and stop purchasing those that are seldom used, except for titles of archival value
- Evaluate the archival value of print in your collection

Usage statistics can be helpful in making transition decisions about which titles need to be retained in print and electronic versions. Re-shelving statistics can indicate when a print resource is still important to reference librarians and clientele. On the other hand, use of the print version may drop significantly with the availability of the online version, a circumstance that is especially notable with indexing and abstracting resources [25]. Online use statistics for traditional Ready Reference resources, such as dictionaries, encyclopedias, and directories, are useful in determining whether a license is a reasonable option, given the difference in costs and the relative use of these resources. For this type of resource, a limited (one to two) concurrent user license may be appropriate or the only option when funding is tight.

One library eased the transition from print to electronic only by retaining the earlier print edition in reference and tagging it with a sticker placed above the call number reading, "Now on the Web." This sticker alerted reference stack browsers to Web availability of the more current resource and provided a bridge from print to electronic [26].

Surveys conducted for earlier editions of this chapter consistently indicated estimates that 5 to 9 percent of the collections budget is spent on reference materials, regardless of library size. Few libraries maintain a separate budget for reference materials, with the serial publications for reference funded most often through the library's serials budget. Many libraries also fund electronic resources through the serials budget as well. Sources other than the regular acquisitions budget (grants, gifts, and endowments) are frequently used to fund expensive electronic resources.

In larger institutions, where electronic resources are shared across disciplines and budgets, funding of electronic resources is shared by several budgets, or a pooled budget is created for the purchase of electronic resources. Consortial agreements among groups of libraries have also become a way of sharing costs for expensive online resources. Additional funding outside the acquisitions budget must be sought to purchase and maintain the equipment needed to use electronic sources. Funding sources vary among libraries. Some are able to fund such purchases from regular equipment budgets, while other libraries must seek alternative funding, such as capital requests, grants, and gifts and endowments. Many libraries use a combination of funding sources.

As libraries have made more decisions to cut print resources and rely on electronic access only, publishers have substantially increased the costs for electronic licenses and changed the business models for these licenses. This is especially evident for journals. Academic journal publishers increasingly look to library subscriptions, now electronic licenses, to sustain their organizations' activities, not just their publications. Pricing models for access to electronic resources are shifting as publishers seek to sustain a defined level of income for their organizations. As libraries have moved to electronic access only, these electronic costs to libraries that negotiate institutional and remote access for their primary clientele have increased significantly, due in part to publishers' lost revenue from (real and/or anticipated) loss of individual subscriptions and reduced income from sale of advertisements.

Publishers have also begun to expand their offerings of electronic books. Many of these have been traditionally found in reference collections, such as handbooks and encyclopedias. Different pricing models are emerging, such as outright purchase of an electronic edition (Wiley), purchase with annual access fees (Gale) and annual licensing for titles with continuous updates (CRCnetBASE and *Harrison's Online*), or access to the latest edition online (MDConsult texts and STAT!Ref titles). Direct purchase of an online edition of a book allows a library to control its budget or take advantage of one-time funding to acquire selected online resources. However, the trend appears to be for publishers to offer online packages of resources, necessitating a shift to ongoing annual subscriptions or licensing agreements to maintain online access. Publishers' pricing models are also being challenged by the open access initiative. Several large university libraries have partnered with Google or Microsoft/Yahoo! to digitize their collections. If nothing else, this initiative will highlight the existence of print resources available in these libraries.

Difficult choices will need to be made as health sciences libraries and their institutions address meeting their obligations to provide the most current health information resources to their clientele. In the area of reference selection, librarians will need to make hard choices. Using the criteria listed above, comparing and evaluating resources for best value and at times being very selective, librarians will need to allocate dollars judiciously.

Fortunately for health sciences libraries, as the shift in use and availability of reference resources from print to online grows, there is a wealth of reliable reference resources freely available on the Web that can also be "selected" for access via the library's OPAC and Web pages. These can augment the traditional print reference collection and reduce pressure on the tightest collections budget. These include a wide array of reference resources provided by the federal government, such as PubMed and *Vital and Health Statistics*. MedlinePlus provides easy access to a number of directories, encyclopedias and dictionaries. Later chapters in this book will highlight the availability of many free reference resources that librarians can use to create virtual reference collections on their library's Web pages or provide access through their libraries' OPACs.

Presentation of Reference Resources Online

The vast majority of libraries provide links to electronic reference resources on the Web, separate from the OPAC. There is no standard cataloging or terminology such as medical subject headings or Library of Congress call numbers, for categorizing online resources. The Web makes it possible to organize e-resources in any number of arrangements, and libraries are doing just that. Some sites use an A to Z arrangement, while others lists sources by subject, by discipline, by format, or by audience (clinicians, nurses, students, faculty, etc.). Common nomenclature for groupings includes:

- Subject Guides
- Reference Shelf
- Resources
- Research Links

Library Web sites frequently include a "Reference" category of sorts; however, there may also be categories listed alongside it such as "Statistical Sources" that would traditionally be thought of as reference resources in the print world. Steven Sowards' study of academic and public library Web sites found that 75 percent of sites visited had a "Reference" category [27]. Just over half (55 percent) of respondents to the authors' survey of health sciences libraries used this category. The authors found that the resources fitting into the reference category on library Web sites tend to be what would traditionally be considered ready reference resources—dictionaries, thesauruses, directories, encyclopedias, and style manuals.

As discussed earlier in this chapter, the term "reference" has lost much of its meaning in the online arena. This change is not surprising, since earlier usability studies have revealed that library terminology such as reference, reserves, databases, and resources are lost on many of our clients [28]. The flexibility of Web technology can be used to libraries' advantage; powerful search tools can help get clients to the information they need, and e-resources can be organized in ways that are most useful to the local clientele, using intuitive language that they understand.

By default, all online resources have a potential reference function in that they allow full-text searching and can provide a concordance for the content of the resource. With new technologies such as metasearch that search multiple resources simultaneously, the location and classification of the resource are irrelevant. Indeed, after several years of making resources available via their Web pages, many libraries are rethinking how they list these resources and are accommodating their presentation to clients' information-seeking patterns.

Elsevier's pamphlet, "How to Design Library Web Sites to Maximize Usability," offers these guidelines [29]:

- Organize information in multiple ways—e.g., by format and by subject.
- Cross-link different types of information, e.g., provide a link from the OPAC to bibliographic databases.
- Get clients to resources with as few clicks as possible. Direct links from the top page to frequently-used databases are especially popular.
- Emphasize access points to research resources above all else, since getting to these resources is the number-one priority for clients at all institutions.

The issue of currency requires a different, more diligent approach for reference resources that are available online. Keeping up-to-date descriptions of resources and current links to Web sites can be a chore, especially for resources that are not used regularly. Link resolver tools can assist in identifying old links; however, staff intervention to reestablish the proper links is an ongoing workload. Often the problem links are only identified when trying to answer a reference question or when a user has difficulty accessing a resource.

Minimizing the frequency of these awkward and inconvenient occurrences is a challenge that often involves the assistance of others, including technical support staff (library or institution) and the vendor/publisher technical staff. Maintaining current Web pages that are easy to navigate requires librarians to continue to hone their technical and design skills.

Putting Technology to the Task

The technology behind the World Wide Web offers an endless number of methods for organizing resources, searching through data, and presenting results. Since most online bibliographic databases ignore encyclopedia articles, book chapters, and other nonjournal research material, these resources often gather dust on the reference shelves or are overlooked by users among all the other links on the library's Web page. Many clients go to a bibliographic database or a Web search engine only and thus miss out on the other valuable e-resources libraries provide. Several innovative tools can be used to help promote all of the library's resources and provide clients with a richer pool of results.

Portal Technology

A portal is an information space where multiple resources are gathered and organized in a single space. Typically clients must create a login and can then customize the space according to what resources and links they want to view upon logging in. Portal software runs on the Web site and may include tools for collaboration among clients. MyLibrary@NCState (www.lib.ncsu.edu/mylibrary/about.html) was one of the first and most successful library portal initiatives. Began in 1999, it offered authenticated users a space to link to selected library resources, borrowing account information, and links to help. The service has recently been modified and now focuses on pulling together various library resources and services that can be personalized by individual clients.

James Beattie and Kevin Messner argue that libraries should partner with enterprise-wide portals instead of creating separate portals for library resources. Libraries already face information management competition from outside businesses, such as Google. They maintain that it is more efficient to develop a portal to be used throughout the institution for various purposes, rather than have portals for different factions within the institution. Institutional portals are also better poised to meet the clients' desire for one-stop shopping [30].

Subject Guides, Toolkits, and Pathfinders

Another way to promote library reference resources is to use librarians' skills at sifting through the plethora of available resources and highlighting the best among them in organized collections. There is significant variation in what these collections are called—subject guides, pathfinders and toolkits are frequently used. The idea is to present a set of highly authoritative e-resources that will provide users with an overview of the research area or help them get started with their research. While some groupings are very extensive, it is best to moderate the number of resources included to avoid overwhelming the researcher. Colleen Cuddy and Patricia Tomasulo reviewed library Web sites for all 142 AAMC medical schools and found that 59% had one or more collections of resources [31].

The following collections provide some interesting examples of ways to bring together and present resources:

1. The University of California, Davis Health Sciences Library collaborated with the UC Davis Center for Health and Technology in putting together the Clinical Resources Center (ecrc.ucdmc.ucdavis.edu/c/). This site, which has restricted access, links to both library and non-library sites and resources. It organizes links in categories such as Library Resources and Library Services, as well as Decision Support, Drug Reference, and Medical Coding.

2. The Harvard College Library includes print reference resources alongside the electronic on its Subject Guides. Resources such as *Stedman's Medical Dictionary* list the call number and library location, followed by a link to the online version (hcl.harvard.edu/research/guides/subject.html).

3. The Welch Medical Library at Johns Hopkins University has created Information Suites (www.welch.jhu.edu/services/information_suites.html), aimed at "providing efficient, professional information resources and services for patrons where they work." Information Suites can be a virtual collection or a physical location that promotes collaboration between information professionals and faculty, staff and students.

   Welch's Information Suite for the Basic Sciences presents:
   - A digital library of targeted resources
   - A suite in a building with computers and consultation space
   - A librarian available on site and for consultations

Databases of Resources

Another popular tool used by the library today is a searchable database of its electronic resources. This "database of databases" does not search the content of the databases, but rather descriptions of the resources themselves in order to guide users to relevant tools. Each resource has its own record with searchable data fields entered by the library. The library creates a customized template so that each record looks the same. Entries include a description of the resource's content and the research areas included in the database. The user can then run a search by title for a known resource, or search for all resources by subject, keyword or category.

Since the data is stored in a database, when a client runs a search, the results are dynamically generated and up to date. The library needs to only add, update and delete individual records as necessary. This kind of tool eliminates the inefficiency of updating static Web pages with lists of resources. Creating such a database does require work and is somewhat duplicative of the library catalog; however, it is a valuable tool for informing users about the variety of e-resources that are available.

The screen shots in Figure 1-1 show the search screen for the University of Toronto Library's database of databases, as well as the list of the library's selected resources for the subject Medicine.

Figure 1-1a. University of Toronto Libraries E-Resources Page

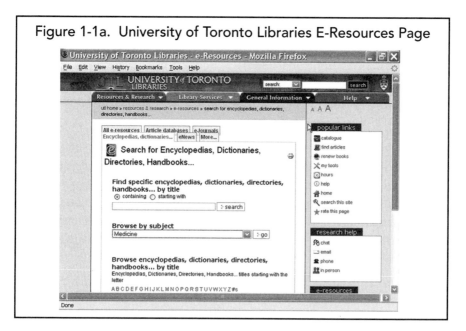

Figure 1-1b. University of Toronto Libraries Best Research Resources for Medicine Page

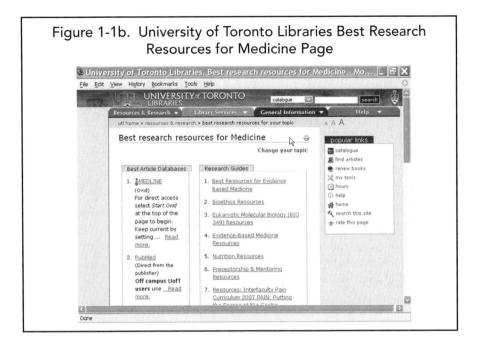

Metasearching

Metasearching can be defined as the practice of searching the content of multiple online databases simultaneously. It is also known as integrated, simultaneous, cross-database, parallel, broadcast, and federated searching [32]. Use of metasearching applications is become increasingly popular as libraries try to ease the burden of resource selection and to provide one-stop shopping for their clients. Approximately 17 percent of respondents to the authors' survey (*n*=52) have a metasearch tool in their library. There are several commercial metasearch applications available, and libraries can build their own as well. *Library Journal*'s 2006 Automation System Marketplace tracks the top metasearch vendors, lists sales, and provides company profiles [33].

Cross-database searching is made possible through the use of the Z39.50 standard, which translates data fields between disparate databases and presents search results in a uniform format. So long as a database uses Z39.50, it can be included in a metasearch, meaning that library catalogs, proprietary databases, and public search engines can all be searched simultaneously. The researcher benefits by having only one place to type in a search for multiple databases. The results from all resources included in the metasearch are presented on the same screen and users can easily select which results they wish to view. They may find results from a resource they previously would not have thought to use.

Lane Medical Library at Stanford University built its own metasearch tool for searching over 150 clinical resources with one search. The search results screen shows the number of hits from specific electronic books, journals, drug resources, and other reference sources. Preliminary results are shown right away, and a status bar lets the user know that the search is still running. When the search is completed, all results are shown (Figure 1-2).

Though cross-database searching has significantly improved since its earliest days in the 1980s, there are limitations that prevent metasearching from achieving its full promise. The Z39.50 standard accommodates a wide variety of record formats and search syntaxes, but this broadness often results in inaccurate results and less sophistication than popular Web search engines. Due to the time it takes to retrieve records from multiple vendors over a network, the program displays the first-retrieved results immediately. Some programs limit the number of records retrieved; others require the client to initiate viewing additional results. To the client, it may mistakenly appear that the first results are the only or the best results. Libraries, e-resource vendors, and

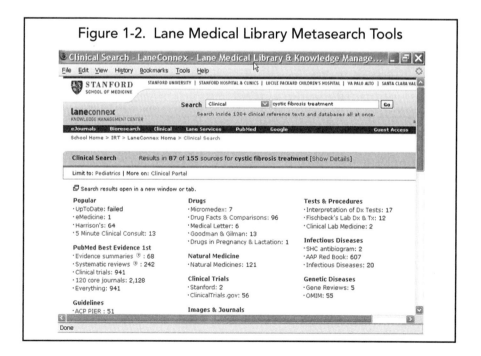

Figure 1-2. Lane Medical Library Metasearch Tools

information technologists are working together to solve these problems by improving indexing and search syntaxes [34].

Large-scale Digitization

Two major, large-scale digitization projects that began in 2005 may have a significant impact on libraries. In late 2004, Google announced its Book Search: a project with the goal of scanning entire book collections from several public and academic libraries. All books—both in the public domain and still under copyright—are being scanned, making the full text searchable. The Open Content Alliance (OCA) is a similar project run by the Internet Archive and Yahoo! that is scanning only public domain materials and copyrighted materials with publisher permissions.

The advantage to researchers of having full-text searching capability of millions of previously undigitized books will no doubt be significant. Scanning these books essentially turns them into reference tools for identifying which books contain specific pieces of information. While there is concern in the library world that clients will no longer find any reason for coming into the library once the last print materials are fully digitized, the scans may in fact serve as a finding aid that leads clients to the library to retrieve the physical books.

Conclusion

Finding ways to help users navigate today's rapidly expanding information universe presents new opportunities and challenges for health sciences librarians. In the past, librarians sifted through available information, selected what was appropriate for their users, organized it, and made it available on library shelves, "just in case" it was needed. More recently, advances in information technology have allowed libraries to provide "just-in-time" resources and services at the point of need, including access to thousands of e-books and journals and to online reference services via e-mail, chat, or instant messaging. The development of even more sophisticated technology has been accompanied by growing expectations for customized information services. Specialized information portals, federated search tools, and subject-specific toolkits are being designed to help our users deal with the mind-boggling array of information choices. Libraries are making steady progress toward "just-for-you" services by offering clients the ability to personalize options for information retrieval and delivery, in much the same way as commercial models such as

Google and Amazon. Along the continuum from print to electronic, from people to technology, from bricks-and-mortar to virtual libraries, our users will still need "reference collections." These collections should serve as a window to the larger information world, offering the best, the most authoritative, the most dependable resources—and presenting them in a way that quickly connects users to the information they need.

References

1. Landesman M. Getting it right—the evolution of reference collections. *Ref Lib* 2005; 44(91/92):5–22.
2. Boorkman JA. Organization and management of the reference collection. In: Boorkman JA, Huber JT, Roper FW, eds. *Introduction to reference sources in the health sciences.* 4th ed. New York, NY: Neal-Schuman, 2004.
3. Walton L, et al., eds. *Collection development and management for electronic, audiovisual, and print resources in health sciences libraries.* 2nd rev. ed. Chicago, IL: Medical Library Association, 2004.
4. Perez AJ. Checklist for writing a reference collection development policy. In: Perez AJ, ed. *Reference collection development: a manual.* 2nd ed. Chicago, IL: American Library Association, 2004:1–2.
5. Boorkman, op. cit.
6. Johnson P. Managing collections. In: Johnson P. *Fundamentals of collection development and management.* Chicago, IL: American Library Association, 2004:141–2.
7. Ibid.
8. Shedlock J, Walton LJ. Developing a virtual community for health sciences library book selection: Doody's Core Titles. *J Med Lib Assoc* 2006; 94(1): 61–6.
9. Boorkman, op. cit.
10. Ibid.
11. Delwiche F, Guitar C. Building a practical bridge between print and web-based reference sources. *J Hosp Lib* 2004; 4(1):105–8.
12. Clemmons NW, Clemmons SL. Five years later: medical reference in the 21st Century. *Med Ref Serv Q* 2005 Spring; 24(1):1–18 (p. 7).
13. De Groote SL, Hitchcock K, McGowan R. Trends in reference usage in an academic health sciences library. *J Med Lib Assoc* 2007; 95(1):23–30.
14. Ibid., p. 27.
15. Clemmons, op. cit., p. 4.
16. Landesman, op. cit., p. 19.

17. National Library of Medicine. *Collection development manual of the National Library of Medicine.* [Web document], 2004. Available: www.nlm. nih.gov/tsd/acquisitions/cdm/. Accessed: 13 June 2007.
18. Morse JM. Reference publishing in the Age of Also. *Ref Lib* 2005; (91/92): 69–81.
19. McMillan GA. Medical reference sources on the internet: an evolving information forum and marketplace. *Ref Lib* 2005; (91/92):197–209.
20. Stewart DC. Electronic textbook vendors: an evaluation. *J Elec Res Med Lib* 2004; 1(3):1–11 (p. 11).
21. Morse, op. cit.
22. Nolan CW. *Managing the reference collection.* Chicago, IL: American Library Association, 1999.
23. Landesman, op. cit.
24. McGraw K, McKenzie D, Hayes B. *The evolving reference collection: examining turbulent waters.* Poster presented at the Medical Library Association Annual Meeting, San Diego, CA, May 2–5, 2003.
25. Tannery NH, Silverman DL, Epstein BA. Online use statistics. *Med Ref Serv Q* 2002 Spring; 21(1):25–33.
26. Delwiche, op. cit.
27. Sowards SW. Structures and choices for ready reference web sites. *Ref Lib* 2005; (91/92):117–38.
28. Jasek C. *How to design library websites for maximum usability*, Library Connect Pamphlet #5. San Diego, CA: Elsevier, 2004.
29. Ibid.
30. Beattie JW, Messner KR. Exploring partnerships with institution portal initiatives. *J Elec Res Med Lib* 2004; 1(2):1–8.
31. Cuddy C, Tomasulo P. Toolkit use in health sciences libraries. *J Elec Res Med Lib* 2004; 1(4):45–58.
32. Sadeh T. The challenge of metasearching. *New Lib World* 2004; 105(3/4): 104–12.
33. Breeding M. Reshuffling the deck [Automation System Marketplace 2006]. *Lib J* 2006 April 1; 131(6):40, 6, 48, 50, 52, 54. Available: www.libraryjournal. com/article/CA6319048.html. Accessed: 13 June 2007.
34. Sadeh, op. cit.

Appendix 1-1

A Web-based survey of health sciences librarians was conducted in March 2007 to ascertain trends in current reference collection development practices. Librarians on the AAHSL, MEDLIB-L and SLA Biomedical and Life Sciences Division listservs were invited to participate in the survey. A total of 67 responded during the designated survey period. Respondents were from: 55 percent (37) academic libraries, 25 percent; (17) hospital libraries; 9 percent (6) corporate libraries; 3 percent (2) government libraries; and 7.5 percent (5) identified themselves as other—associations, nonprofits, or research institutes.

Health Sciences Reference Collections Survey

Thank you for taking part in this survey, which will be used as background information for the revision of the first chapter of the upcoming fifth edition of *Introduction to Reference Sources in the Health Sciences.*

This survey consists of 29 questions in 6 parts. Your answers are anonymous and confidential.

1. What type of library do you work in?

    Academic   Public
    Hospital   Government
    Corporate   Other (please specify)

2. Overall size of your library's collection in volumes

    under 50,000   500,000–999,999
    50,000-99,999   1,000,000 or above
    100,000–499,999

3. Overall annual acquisitions budget

    under $100,000 $1,000,000–$1,499,000
    $100,000–$499,000 $1,500,000 and above
    $500,000–$999,000

4. Does your library maintain a separate print reference collection?

    ☐ Yes   ☐ No

5. What is your preferred format for reference resources?

    Stand-alone CD-ROM   Print and Electronic
    Networked CD-ROM   Print and Web-based
    Web-based   Other (please specify)
    Print

6. Approximately what percentage of current reference resources in your library is:

    Available only on the Web   CD-ROM/DVD
    Available in print and on the Web   Print only
    Available on an Intranet or limited local network   Don't know

7. What selection tools do you prefer to use to identify new print reference materials? (choose all that apply)

    Publisher/Vendor Notifications   Holdings lists of other libraries
    Reviews   Other (please specify)
    Standing Orders

8. Which source(s) are most helpful and why?

9. How important are the following criteria for evaluating new electronic resources for the reference collection?

Criteria	Very Important	Important	Somewhat Important	Not Important
Audience				
Cost				
Authority (publisher/producer)				
Scope (subjects covered)				
Accessibility (vendor licensing restrictions)				
Ease of use (layout navigation)				
Frequency of updates				
Output options (PDA, PDF exporting)				
Technology support requirements				
Uniqueness of presentation (video, sound)				
Reviews & recommendations				

10. For electronic resources do you arrange for trial access before subscribing?
    ☐ Yes, always   ☐ Yes, for selected resources   ☐ No

11. What is the usual trial period?
    30 days
    60 days
    90 days

12. Who participates in the trial? (choose all that apply)
> Library staff
> Clientele
> Review Committee
> Other (please specify)

13. How do you elicit feedback? (choose all that apply)
> Feedback button when user logs out, with brief questionnaire
> Follow-up with invited participants
> Demo/ usability study with invited groups
> Other (please specify)

14. For networked electronic resources how do you provide access? (choose all that apply)
> IP address authentication
> Log-in and password
> Remote access for authenticated clientele
> Other (please specify)

15. How likely are these factors to prevent you from licensing an electronic resource?

Factor	Definitely will prevent	Very likely to prevent	Somewhat likely to prevent	Not likely to prevent	N/A
Log-in/password required					
Cost is too high					
Remote access not allowed					
General licensing restrictions					
Standard evaluative criteria not met					
Poor design or navigation					
Already have similar content					
Has pervasive advertising					

16. Which resource types do you prefer to receive in *print only*? You may list specific resource titles in the Other category.

Dictionaries	Handbooks
Directories	Indexes
Drug Compendia	Statistical Sources
Encyclopedias	Other (please specify)

17. Which resource types do you prefer to receive in both *print and electronic* formats? You may list specific resource titles in the Other category.

Dictionaries	Handbooks
Directories	Indexes
Drug Compendia	Statistical Sources
Encyclopedias	Other (please specify)

18. Which resource types do you prefer to receive in *electronic format only*? You may list specific resource titles in the Other category.

Dictionaries	Handbooks
Directories	Indexes
Drug Compendia	Statistical Sources
Encyclopedias	Other (please specify)

19. How has the size of your print reference collection changed in the past 5 years?

Stayed the same	Eliminated entirely
Decreased by 25%	Increased by 25%
Decreased by 50%	Increased by 50% or more
Decreased by 75% or more	

20. What are the major factors that have caused the size of your print reference collection to *decrease*? (choose all that apply)

    Has not decreased (skip to #21)
    Decline in use by clientele
    Decline in use by reference librarians
    Print not needed when online equivalent is available
    Budget can not support a large collection
    Some subjects no longer need to be covered
    Loss of space for non-reference purposes
    Other (please specify)

21. What are the major factors that have caused the size of your print reference collection to *increase*? (choose all that apply)

    Has not increased (skip to #22)
    Decline in use by clientele
    Decline in use by reference librarians
    Print not needed when online equivalent is available
    Budget can not support a large collection
    Some subjects no longer need to be covered

Loss of space for non-reference purposes
Other (please specify)

22. What criteria do you use for removing items from the print reference collection? (choose all that apply)
    Duplicated by electronic resource   Usefulness of subject for reference
    Publication date   Space limitations
    Condition of material   Other (please specify)

23. Do you provide links to electronic reference resources on your library Web site outside of the OPAC?
    ☐ Yes   ☐ No

24. Do you include free Web resources in this online reference collection?
    ☐ Yes   ☐ No   ☐ Not Sure

25. How do you present electronic reference resources on your Web site?
    Resources are listed in a distinct Reference category.
    Reference resources are mixed in with other e-resources in different
       categories or subject groupings, but are not called Reference.
    Resources are included in a distinct Reference category as well as in other
       categories in different sections of the site.
    Other (please specify)

27. If yes, which product or software do you use? (such as Metalib, Ovid SearchSolver, homegrown)

28. How has the availability of electronic reference resources both licensed and free changed the way reference services are offered at your library?

29. How do you envision both reference services and reference collections changing in the next 5 years?

30. Please feel free to make additional comments here.

PART II

Bibliographic Sources

CHAPTER 2

Bibliographic Sources for Monographs

Jeffrey T. Huber

Historically, monographs have played a significant role in the dissemination of health sciences information. "The seventeenth century saw the culmination of medical bibliography predicated on the publication of medical works in monographic form and the first appearance of bibliographies taking into account publication of advances in medicine in periodicals" [1]. While periodicals grew to become the preferred biomedical and scientific communication forum for current research and opinion, monographs continued to serve as an important means for conveying "gold standard" information. This trend remains true today, whether the monograph be in print or electronic format. Like the monograph itself, materials used for bibliographic control of monographs continue to serve as an integral component of a reference collection.

Over time, bibliographies have been developed to bring order out of chaos by providing information that identifies works within a particular discipline or group of disciplines [2–3]. These bibliographies serve as verification, location, and selection tools. *Verification* refers to standard information contained in bibliographical citations, such as author, title, edition, and place of publication. It may be necessary to consult multiple sources in order to verify all of the needed information about a particular monograph, often moving from a general source to a particular one with a more narrow subject area. *Location* indicates which library or other information agency owns a particular title or the vendor from which it may be purchased. Location also specifies where a title can be found in a particular library or information agency. Online bibliographic databases are the primary resources for identifying institutional holdings. Trade bibliographies, available in both print and electronic formats, are used to determine basic purchasing data. Since collection development is an essential function within a library or information setting, the *selection* function presupposes bibliographies that indicate the availability of titles within a particular subject domain, by a specific author, or in a given format.

Bibliographies in the health sciences often fulfill more than one of these three functions and typically contain entries for multiple types of materials (e.g., monographs, periodicals, government documents, etc.).

Current Sources

While print resources historically have been a mainstay for bibliographic data, the generic growth in electronic information resources is reflected in current sources for monograph information. Many print bibliographic resources for monograph titles have been replaced by electronic ones.

The U.S. National Library of Medicine (NLM) is the leading authority concerning current coverage of health science monographs.

2.1   *LocatorPlus*. Bethesda, MD: U.S. National Library of Medicine. Available: www.locatorplus.gov/

2.2   *NLM Catalog*. Bethesda, MD: U.S. National Library of Medicine. Available: www.ncbi.nlm.nih.gov/entrez/query.fcgi?DB=nlmctalog

LocatorPlus is the NLM's online catalog accessed on the Internet. In 1999, LocatorPlus replaced NLM's telnet-based online catalog, LOCATOR, and replaced the catalog databases CATLINE, SERLINE, and AVLINE. Prior to 1999, CATLINE was a primary bibliographic source for monograph records. LocatorPlus is updated continuously and includes over 1.2 million catalog records for books, audiovisuals, journals, computer files, and other materials in NLM's collections. Records from the CATLINE, SERLINE, and AVLINE databases are available via LocatorPlus. LocatorPlus contains links from catalog records to Internet resources when available and appropriate. LocatorPlus includes circulation status information for materials, including those on order or in process at the Library. The LocatorPlus interface allows users to find unknown author or organization names if unsure about the exact name, view or use bibliographic records in MARC format, and view or use authority records for names and titles. Through its "Search Other Resources" menu, LocatorPlus provides direct access to additional free resources, such as NLM databases (including PubMed/MEDLINE), consumer health information and MedlinePlus, history of medicine databases, NLM Catalog, PubMed Central, TOXNET and toxicology databases, health services research and *HSTAT*, and catalogs of other U.S. medical and consumer health libraries. LocatorPlus contains only records that are available in machine readable format. Users may need to consult retrospective sources for early works covering the biomedical sciences. LocatorPlus is available free of charge.

The NLM Catalog is an alternative search interface to NLM bibliographic records for journals, books, audiovisuals, computer software, electronic resources, and other materials using the NCBI Entrez system. The NLM Catalog links to LocatorPlus for access to NLM holdings information. The NLM Catalog provides access to over 10,000 citations. The interface allows users to explore on MeSH headings, identify or search primary subjects, find a known name of an author or organization, find a known item, and view or use bibliographic records in XML format.

NLM's cataloging records are also available from other vendors, such as Online Computer Library Center (OCLC).

2.3   *WorldCat*. Dublin, OH: Online Computer Library Center (OCLC).
       Available: www.oclc.org/worldcat/

OCLC Online Computer Library Center provides shared cataloging records and bibliographic descriptions through its international network system. Cataloging records are included for a variety of materials, including monographs, in all subject domains. In addition to NLM, sources of cataloging information include the Library of Congress, National Agriculture Library, British Library, and member libraries. OCLC is a major source of bibliographic information for monographs. It also provides location information, since cataloging records indicate the holding libraries for items included in its databases.

Founded in 1967, OCLC Online Computer Library Center is a nonprofit computer library service and research organization, serving a membership of more than 52,000 libraries in 112 countries and territories worldwide. The WorldCat database serves as the core for all OCLC services. WorldCat includes more than 82 million bibliographic records and 1 billion individual holdings contributed by libraries around the world.

In July 2006, RLG—a membership-based, nonprofit information organization, originally founded by the New York Public Library, Columbia University, Harvard University, and Yale University—merged operations with OCLC. RLG Programs is part of OCLC's Programs and Research division. RLG

Programs consists of some 150 research libraries, archives, museums, and other cultural memory institutions. The RLG Union Catalog is available as part of the WorldCat database.

2.4   *Doody's Book Reviews.* Chicago, IL: Doody Enterprises, Inc. 1993–. Continues *Doody's Health Sciences Book Review Journal.* Oak Park, IL: Doody Publishing, 1993–2002. Bimonthly. Cumulated with additional reviews in *Doody's Health Sciences Book Review Annual.* Oak Park, IL: Doody Publishing, 1993–1995/96. Annual. *Doody's Health Sciences Book Review Journal* absorbed *Doody's Rating Service: A Buyer's Guide to the 250 Best Health Sciences Books.* Oak Park, IL: Doody Publishing, 1993–1997. Annual.

2.5   *Doody's Core Titles in the Health Sciences [electronic resource].* Chicago, IL: Doody Enterprises, Inc., 2004–. Annual. Available: www.doody.com/dct/

Doody's earlier print resources, such as *Doody's Health Sciences Book Review Journal, Doody's Health Sciences Book Review Annual,* and *Doody's Rating Service: A Buyer's Guide to the 250 Best Health Sciences Books,* have been replaced with electronic counterparts (see www.doodyenterprises.com/). Doody's products and other general bibliographic sources, such as the *National Union Catalog* and *American Book Publishing Record,* are useful tools for verifying health science monograph information as well as identifying their location. However, these sources are not likely to be available in many health sciences libraries, particularly those outside of large academic settings.

Founded in 1993, Doody Enterprises, Inc. is a medical publishing company devoted to producing information products for health care professionals. At the core of Doody's clinical information database are the Doody's Book Reviews, which evaluate books and electronic resources across a wide range of specialty areas, including basic sciences, clinical medicine, nursing, and the allied health disciplines. Doody Enterprises maintains a database of more than 90,000 health sciences titles with over 20,000 reviews. In addition, each review is accompanied by a Doody's Star Rating. The expert reviews and star ratings are available electronically as part of Doody's Book Reviews database and distributed via *Doody's Review Service.* Doody commissions original expert reviews for approximately 3,000 books and electronic resources from over 250 publishers each year. About 2,000 of those titles are reviewed each year by a network of more than 5,000 academic-affiliated health care professionals. Reviews feature the byline of the reviewer and consist of a general description of the book, intended audience, purpose, features, assessment, and a star rating. Doody's star rating is derived from a questionnaire completed by the expert reviewer during the course of completing a review. Bibliographic and descriptive information is contained in each entry for in-print and forthcoming books. Access to the database is available via the Web.

In mid-2004, Doody's began publishing *Doody's Core Titles in the Health Sciences* to serve as a replacement for the Brandon/Hill Selected Lists, which had been discontinued. This electronic resource is designed to serve as a collection development tool for health sciences libraries of all sizes. This resource rates core titles in more than 120 specialty areas in health sciences, basic sciences, clinical medicine, allied health, associated health sciences, and nursing.

Originally published in the *Journal of the Medical Library Association* (formerly titled *Bulletin of the Medical Library Association*), the Brandon/Hill Selected List of Print Books and Journals for the Small Medical Library, Brandon/Hill Selected List of Print Books and Journals in Allied Health, and Brandon/Hill Selected List of Print Books and Journals in Nursing are widely recognized collection development tools. The selected lists were created by Alfred N. Brandon, who first published the Selected List of Books and Journals for the Small Medical Library in 1965. The selected list for nursing followed in 1979 and the selected list for allied health in 1984. The 2002/2003 lists are available electronically via the Web at www.mssm.edu/library/brandon-hill/. Each list is categorized by subject. An author/editor index is included for book entries. Daggers and asterisks are used to designate level of significance for purchase.

2.6   *National Union Catalog. Books*. Washington, DC: Library of Congress, 1983–2002. Monthly. Microfiche.

2.7   *American Book Publishing Record*. New York: R.R. Bowker, 1960–. Monthly; annual cumulation with quinquennial cumulations.

2.8   *Publishers Weekly*. New York: F. Leypoldt, 1873–.

Published by the Library of Congress, the *National Union Catalog (NUC)* provides a cumulative record of materials cataloged by LC and participating libraries for imprints published 1956 and later. The *NUC* is a vast bibliography that is frequently consulted, since its holdings represent the broad scope of the world's output of monographs and other types of materials.

The microfiche *NUC. Books* was published in multiple sections using a register/index format. The five sections of *NUC. Books* include the register, name index, title index, LC series index, and LC subject index. Item records include all bibliographic elements traditionally found on LC printed cards. Since entries appear in *NUC* only if a participating library has acquired and cataloged a title, *NUC* serves as a location source as well as a verification tool.

The *American Book Publishing Record* cumulates the listings in *Publishers Weekly*. This ongoing resource provides bibliographic information about English-language publications in all subject areas. The primary goal of this bibliographic resource is to list books that can be purchased from publishers and to provide enough information to order any given title. This resource is important to health sciences librarians because the health science arena is impacted by disciplines outside of health and biomedicine. In addition, the *American Book Publishing Record* and *Publishers Weekly* provide an historical account of books published in the United States.

2.9   *Books in Print.* New Jersey: R.R. Bowker, 1948–. Annual. *Books in Print Supplement.* New Providence, NJ: R.R. Bowker, 1972/73–. Annual. *Subject Guide to Books in Print.* New York: R.R. Bowker, 1957–. Annual. Available: www.booksinprint.com/

2.10 *Medical and Health Care Books and Serials in Print.* New York: R.R. Bowker, 1985–, 2 vols. Annual. Continues *Medical Books and Serials in Print.* New York: R.R. Bowker, 1978–1984. Annual.

2.11 *Canadian Books in Print. Author and Title Index.* Toronto: University of Toronto Press, 1975–2006. Annual. Continues *Canadian Books in Print.* Toronto: University of Toronto Press, 1967–1975.

2.12 *GlobalBooksInPrint.com.* New York: R.R. Bowker, 2004–. Available: www.globalbooksinprint.com

An ongoing task for a librarian is to determine the availability of a given title for purchase. The librarian must first identify whether or not a title is still in print and subsequently if it is for sale. The following resources are designed to assist with this process.

Books in Print (BIP) is a broad resource that covers all subject areas. *Books in Print* is indexed by *Subject Guide to Books in Print, 1957–1987/88* and *Books in Print. Subject Guide, 1988/89–. BIP* is kept updated by the annual publication of *Books in Print Supplement, 1972/73–.* Each entry includes bibliographic elements, cost information, and source(s) from which the book can be purchased. Although the print version of *BIP* remains useful, Web access is becoming more common. Bowker's Books In Print Web site provides the same resources as the print version but with many enhanced features. For example, the Web site includes resource guides, publisher spotlights, and new features. Whereas the print version supports author and title access, the Web site allows for keyword, author, title, and ISBN/UPC access. The Web site also allows the user to browse by subject area or by index whereas the print version requires purchasing the annual *Subject Guide to Books in Print* to accommodate searching by subject headings. BooksInPrint.com includes the full *Books in Print* database of U.S. titles as well as *Books Out-of-Print* and *Forthcoming Books*.

Also produced by R.R. Bowker, *Medical and Health Care Books and Serials in Print* continues *Medical Books and Serials in Print*. This title serves as an index to literature in the health sciences and is of obvious interest to health sciences librarians. *Medical and Health Care Books and Serials in Print* lists more than 109,000 books under 6,000 health and medical subject areas, including some 3,500 new titles. Ordering and publisher information is included in each entry to facilitate acquisitions.

Canadian Books in Print. Author and Title Index continues *Canadian Books in Print*. This work serves as a companion resource to *Books in Print* and *Whitaker's Books in Print* (formerly *British Books in Print*). *Canadian Books in Print. Author and Title Index* includes entries for English-language titles produced by Canadian publishers. It ceased publication in 2006.

In 2004, R.R. Bowker debuted its new GlobalBooksInPrint.com. The Web resource features over 14.8 million English and Spanish-language titles from 43 markets. It allows users to search by author, title, keyword, ISBN, and/or market. GlobalBooksInPrint.com also allows user to browse by general subject area or by index. It includes out-of-print, in-print, and forthcoming titles.

2.13   *Amazon.com*. Seattle, WA: Amazon.com Inc. Available: www. amazon.com

2.14   *Barnes&Noble.com*. New York, NY: Barnes & Noble, Inc. Available: www.barnesandnoble.com

Commercial Internet vendors such as Amazon.com and Barnes& Noble.com have become recognized bibliographic information sources. Their customer rating and related purchases features are useful collection development tools.

Amazon.com is perhaps one of the most popular Internet vendors. Originally focusing on the book and music markets, Amazon.com has grown to include books, music videos, DVDs, magazine subscriptions, office products, apparel, electronics, toys, games, housewares, hardware, home and garden supplies, gift items, and registries among its retail offerings. To locate monograph titles, users may perform a keyword search or browse by subjects. Records may be sorted by featured title, bestsellers, customer ratings, price, publication date, or alphabetically. Monograph records include bibliographic elements, ordering information, and purchase availability. Records also include customer ratings and reviews as well as published editorial reviews. Links are provided to authors of similar works that were purchased by individuals who purchased a particular title. Amazon.com supplies new and used books.

Another popular Internet vendor of books, textbooks, music, videos and DVDs, Barnes&Noble.com offers many of the same features as Amazon.com. Users may search for monograph titles by keyword or browse by subject. Titles may be sorted by bestsellers. Entries include ordering information and note title availability for purchase. Customer reviews with ratings are included, as are notes from the publisher. Records also indicate related titles purchased by individuals who purchased a particular book.

Retrospective Sources

Using clay tablets, papyrus, parchment, and, ultimately, paper, man has sought to record information for future reference. Development of the printing press in the fifteenth century forever changed the communication process. Society moved farther away from oral tradition to the printed word. Subsequently, the printed book reigned as the primary source of information until the mid-nineteenth century. By that time, the periodical had grown in use and popularity as the preferred means for disseminating scientific information.

Prior to the mid-nineteenth century, bibliographies containing entries for medical works were published, but they were not all inclusive in subject coverage. In addition, these bibliographies were primarily concerned with medical works in monographic form. For a detailed account of early medical bibliography, the reader should consult *The Development of Medical Bibliography* by Estelle Broadman [1]; for a detailed account of medical bibliography since World War II, the reader should consult *Medical Bibliography in an Age of Discontinuity* by Scott Adams [4].

2.15   *Index-Catalogue of the Library of the Surgeon-General's Office.* Ser. 1–5. Washington, DC: U.S. Government Printing Office, 1880–1961, 61 vols. *IndexCat.* Available: http://indexcat.nlm.nih.gov

2.16   *Index Medicus.* Ser. 1–3. Various publishers, 1879–1927, 45 vols.

John Shaw Billings, librarian of the Surgeon General's Library (forerunner of the National Library of Medicine) is considered the founding father of medical bibliography. Billings was responsible for the creation of the *Index-Catalogue of the Library of the Surgeon-General's Office* as well as the original *Index Medicus.* These two publications marked the beginning of a systematic attempt to provide bibliographic coverage of medical works worldwide.

First published in 1880, the *Index-Catalogue* contained a list of all monographic and periodical literature received by the Library of the Surgeon-General's Office (which became the Army Medical Library, the Armed Forces Medical Library, and, ultimately, the National Library of Medicine).

The *Index-Catalogue* was published in five series from 1880 to 1961, with a total of 61 volumes. Each series was intended to contain author and subject entries in dictionary form within a single alphabet. Monographic entries were listed under authors' names as well as under subject headings; entries for periodical articles were listed only under subject headings. Publication of the fourth series contained only alphabetical entries A through M, and the fifth series did not include subject entries. Despite omissions, the *Index-Catalogue* was more comprehensive in coverage than any previous medical bibliography. Items were included as they were acquired by the library rather than by date of publication. Therefore, older items may be found in more recent series of the *Index-Catalogue.* Since the *Index-Catalogue* is comprised of only those items acquired by the library, it is not a comprehensive bibliography of medical works. However, the extent of the library's collection—a collection that eventually became the National Library of Medicine—makes the *Index-Catalogue* the most comprehensive listing of medical literature of the period. The *Index-Catalogue* continues to serve as a valuable retrospective bibliography and historical source. Digitizing the *Index-Catalogue* was completed in 2004, resulting in the National Library Medicine's *IndexCat.*

IndexCat is the digitized version of the *Index-Catalogue of the Library of the Surgeon-General's Office.* The content of *IndexCat* reflects the bibliographic citations in the original publication of approximately 3.7 million references dated from the fifth century to the first half of the twentieth century. Some 616,000 references to monographs (books, pamphlets, and reports) are included, as well as 470,000 dissertations and theses.

Given that the *Index-Catalogue* was published as a series over many years, Billings developed the *Index Medicus* as a bibliographic updating tool. The *Index Medicus* was published from 1879 to 1927, with publication suspended from May 1899 to 1902. It was published monthly from 1879 to 1920 and then quarterly from 1921 to 1927. Entries for books and journal articles were arranged by subject with an author index. Further discussion of *Index Medicus* appears in Chapter 4.

Since the original *Index Medicus* ceased publication in 1927 and the *Index-Catalogue* contained entries for only those works purchased by the library, users should consult multiple resources in locating monograph titles published between 1927 and 1948 when the Army Medical Library *Catalog* began publication. These sources should not be limited to those specifically covering the health sciences, but should also include more general ones, such as those compiled by the Library of Congress.

2.17 National Library of Medicine (U.S.). *Catalog.* Washington, DC: Library of Congress, 1956–1960/65. Issued annually with quinquennial cumulation (1955–59) and a sexennial cumulation (1960–65). Continues Armed Forces Medical Library (U.S.). *Catalog of the Army Medical Library*, 1952–1955. Continues Army Medical Library (U.S.). *Catalog*, 1948–1951.

From 1948 to 1965, these volumes were published as supplements to the printed catalogs published by the Library of Congress. They also serve as a bridge to *Index-Catalogue* series as well as the *National Library of Medicine Current Catalog*, which began publication in 1966. Each volume contains bibliographic information for monographs cataloged during this period, regardless of date of publication.

2.18 *National Union Catalog, Pre-1956 Imprints.* Chicago: Mansell, 1968–1980, 685 vols. *Supplement*, 1980–1981, vols. 686–754.

National Union Catalog, Pre-1956 Imprints, compiled and edited with the cooperation of the Library of Congress and the National Union Catalog Subcommittee of the Resources and Technical Services Division of the American Library Association, is a centerpiece for verification of books and other materials prior to 1956. This work is also used to verify serials titles that closed prior to 1956. *Pre-1956 Imprints* consists of an alphabetical listing of materials published prior to January 1, 1956, that have been cataloged by the Library of Congress or by one of the *NUC* participating libraries.

2.19   *The American Book Publishing Record Cumulative, 1876–1949. New York: R.R. Bowker, 1980, 15 vols. The American Book Publishing Record Cumulative, 1950–1977, 1978,* 15 vols.

2.20   Health Science Books, 1876–1982. New York: R.R. Bowker, 1982.

Essentially, the two *American Book Publishing Record Cumulative* works contain bibliographic data for every book published and distributed in the United States between 1876 and 1977. More than 1.5 million titles, with full bibliographic and cataloging information, are included in these resources.

Health Science Books, 1876–1982 contains bibliographic and cataloging information from the Library of Congress for more than 133,000 titles published and distributed in the United States between 1876 and 1982. All areas of the health sciences are represented in this work.

References

1. Broadman E. *The development of medical bibliography*. Baltimore: Medical Library Association, 1954:53.
2. Katz WA. *Introduction to reference work*. 8th ed. New York: McGraw-Hill, 2002.
3. Gaskell P. *A new introduction to bibliography*. New York: Oxford University Press, 1972.
4. Adams S. *Medical bibliography in an age of discontinuity*. Chicago: Medical Library Association, 1981.

CHAPTER 3

Bibliographic Sources for Periodicals

Feili Tu

Periodicals, in both printed and electronic formats, are one of the major components of the collections of health sciences (HS) information settings. In general, they are the most used resources in many HS libraries [1]. According to the "Online Dictionary for Library and Information Science," a periodical is "a serial publication with its own distinctive title, containing a mix of articles, editorials, reviews, columns, or other short works written by more than one contributor issued more than once, generally at regular stated intervals of less than a year" [2]. Scientific journals began in the seventeenth century with the French *Journal des Savants* and the British *Philosophical Transactions of the Royal Society* [3].

The words *periodical*, *journal*, and *serial* are used interchangeably. Usually, the periodical's editor or editorial board is responsible for its content. The categories of periodicals include magazines, sold by subscription and at newsstands; journals (also called serials), sold by subscription and/or distributed to members of scholarly societies and professional associations; and newsletters. The publishers of periodicals include, but are not limited to, scholarly societies, university presses, professional associations, trade organizations, commercial publishers, and nonprofit organizations. Many HS periodicals are scholarly journals; therefore, they are peer-reviewed publications. The peer-review process means that an article is chosen to be published based on evaluations by the journal editor and a panel of experts on the subject. These experts, known as referees, are responsible for determining if the subject of the article falls within the scope of the publication and for evaluating originality, quality of research, clarity of presentation, etc. [4].

Medical journals play a significant role in the support of health care, education, and research. These resources affect how physicians provide patient care as well as how public health professionals develop policies and take action [5]. Currently, many health care providers (including physicians, nurses, and allied health professionals) are required to integrate evidence-based medicine (EBM) models into their practices. Physicians and clinicians must have rapid access to relevant evidence (usually journal articles) when critical clinical decisions are to be made [6]. Due to the increasing use of full-text journals in electronic format, many HS information settings are currently maintaining subscriptions to printed journals and acquiring substantial collections of full-text journals in electronic format [7].

Bibliographic Sources for Periodical Selection and Development

HS information professionals use a variety of aids for the selection of periodical titles. Some librarians look at what other libraries have in their collections to help them decide what to include in their own journal collections. In addition, the information regarding electronic journal aggregators provided by vendors is also a useful tool for deciding what information systems should be included in a library's e-collections. The following describes several useful tools for finding information on current HS periodical titles.

3.1   *LocatorPlus*. Bethesda, MD: U.S. National Library of Medicine.
      Available: http://locatorplus.gov

The National Library of Medicine (NLM) is a well-known guiding force for health sciences libraries worldwide. Currently, the NLM acquires, licenses, and processes over 22,000 print, nonprint and electronic serial titles. According to the NLM's collection development policy, the Library's priority is to collect "scientific or scholarly journals containing signed papers that report original research from all countries and in any language; clinical and other practice journals emphasizing those of interest to U.S. health professionals; review journals summarizing and sometimes analyzing recent research in a field; current awareness periodicals providing cursory summaries that are of particular interest to U.S. health professionals" [8]. LocatorPlus is the NLM online catalog and a comprehensive source to search for information on periodical publications. It can be accessed for free on the Internet. LocatorPlus is continuously updated and includes [9]:

- over 1.2 million catalog records for books, audiovisuals, journals, computer files, and other materials in the NLM collections
- holdings information for journals and other materials
- links from catalog records to Internet resources, including online journals
- circulation status information for materials, including those on order or in process at the NLM

In 1999, the NLM retired AVLINE, CATLINE, SERLINE and LOCATOR databases and began to use one integrated information system, LocatorPlus, to include all the catalog records of the NLM collections.

3.2   *NLM Catalog.* Bethesda, MD: U.S. National Library of Medicine. Available: www.ncbi.nlm.nih.gov/entrez/query.fcgi?db=nlmcatalog

The NLM Catalog is an alternative search interface to NLM bibliographic records for journals, books, audiovisuals, computer software, electronic resources, and other materials using the NCBI Entrez system. The NLM Catalog links to LocatorPlus for access to NLM holdings information.

3.3   *Ulrich's Periodicals Directory.* New Providence, NJ: R.R. Bowker LLC, 1932–. Ann Arbor, MI: ProQuest-CSA LLC. Available: www. ulrichsweb.com/ulrichsweb/

Since 1932, *Ulrich's Periodicals Directory* has been the preferred source of information about periodical publications worldwide. The 45th edition, a four-volume set, was published in 2007. It includes over 201,330 regularly and irregularly issued serials classified under 906 subject headings; 6,910 serials on CD-ROM; over 51,440 serials available exclusively online or in addition to hard copy; and over 5,000 daily and weekly newspapers. *Ulrich's Periodicals Directory* was first published in 1932 by R.R. Bowker under the title *Periodicals Directory: A Classified Guide to a Selected List of Current Periodicals Foreign and Domestic.* This title continued through the third edition, published in 1938. A title change to *Ulrich's Periodicals Directory: A Selected Guide to Current Periodicals, Inter-American Edition* occurred in the Fourth edition in 1943. The next change, to *International Periodicals Directory*, was in the 11th edition, published in 1965. The current title has been the same since 2000, with the publication of the 39th edition [10].

Ulrich's Periodicals Directory is available in both printed and online formats. The electronic edition, *Ulrichsweb*, is available at ulrichsweb.com. The publisher is ProQuest-CSA LLC. This electronic resource also includes information on open-access journals and the contents of both *Magazine for Libraries* and *Irregular Serials and Annuals in Printed Format* [11].

3.4 *Medical and Health Care Books and Serials in Print*. New Providence, NJ: R.R. Bowker LLC, 1985–.

The 2007 edition of this title has two volumes. *Medical and Health Care Books and Serials in Print* lists more than 109,000 books and more than 22,600 U.S. and foreign serials—organized in 6,000 medical and health subject areas, including medicine, dentistry, veterinary medicine, psychiatry, psychology, behavioral science, and more. The serial titles in this item are included in the *Ulrichsweb* database.

3.5 *Periodicals for the Health Sciences*. Birmingham, AL: EBSCO Information Services, 2007.

Many HS libraries and information centers use subscription services to manage their periodical collections. EBSCO, a periodicals subscription vendor, publishes *Periodicals for the Health Sciences* as a tool for ordering serials subscriptions. This directory contains ordering information on more than 2,500 publications as well as descriptions of many titles. A medical subject classification based on categories from the *List of Journals Indexed for MEDLINE* is also provided.

3.6 *The Standard Periodical Directory*. New York, NY: Oxbridge Communications, Inc.

The *Standard Periodical Directory* is a directory listing 58,000 U.S. and Canadian magazines, journals, newsletters, and newspapers. It is published every two years and is known for listing many trade publications not listed elsewhere.

3.7 Nobari N, ed. *Books and Periodicals Online*. New York, NY: Library Technology Alliance, Ltd. Available: www.booksandperiodicals.com/

Books and Periodicals Online is known as BooksandPeriodicals.com, and it lists publications that can be searched electronically through information providers such as Gale and ProQuest. This site serves as a directory providing sources for global news and business, legal, scientific and medical information available online through hosting services such as Cambridge Scientific Abstracts, Factiva, and Westlaw.

3.8 *PubList.com, the Internet Directory of Publications.* Wilton, CT: PubList, Inc. Available: www.publist.com/search_title.html

PubList.com is an electronic yellow pages for over 150,000 domestic and international print and electronic publications including magazines, journals, e-journals, newsletters, and monographs. The Web site provides several types of searching functions.

3.9 *Collection Guide: Newsletters and Periodicals.* Toronto, Canada: Consumer Health Information Service, Toronto Reference Library. Available: www.torontopubliclibrary.ca/uni_chi_guide_newsletter.jsp

This list is one of the resources recommended by the Medical Library Association's Consumer and Patient Health Information Section as a collection development aid for building a consumer health collection. This list can serve as a general guide to useful materials for consumer health collections. Canadian materials are included along with U.S. standard medical and health titles. The list is expanded and updated by Consumer Health Information Service staff of the Toronto Reference Library.

Electronic Databases' Periodical Lists

3.10 *List of Serials Indexed for Online Users.* [Web document]. Bethesda, MD: U.S. National Library of Medicine. Available: www.nlm.nih.gov/tsd/serials/lsiou.html

This list provides bibliographic information for all journals ever indexed for MEDLINE. It includes titles that ceased publication, changed titles, or were deselected. The entire list is available in Portable Document Format (PDF) and can be downloaded through ftp at this address: ftp://nlmpubs.nlm.nih.gov/online/journals/lsiweb.pdf.

3.11 *List of Journals Indexed for MEDLINE.* [Web document]. Bethesda, MD: U.S. National Library of Medicine. Available: www.nlm.nih.gov/tsd/serials/lji.html

This list is available in PDF and can be downloaded at ftp://nlmpubs.nlm.nih.gov/online/journals/lsiweb.pdf. The information is also available in the html format at this address: www.nlm.nih.gov/bsd/journals/online.html. The 5,164 journals being indexed for MEDLINE as of January 2007 are listed in four sections: (1) alphabetic listing by abbreviated title, followed by full title; (2) alphabetic listing by full title, followed by abbreviated title; (3) alphabetic listing by subject field; and (4) alphabetic listing by country of publication. Both the *List of Journals Indexed for MEDLINE* and the *List of Serials Indexed for Online Users* are updated annually. The new versions are generally available by February of the edition year.

3.12   *EMBASE Journal Lists.* [Web document]. New York: Elsevier B.V. Available: http://info.embase.com/embase_suite/content/journals/ embase_ priority.pdf

EMBASE is an international bibliographic database, concentrating on the drug and biomedical literature. This journal database contains over 11 million records from 1974 to present. The title list indexed in this database is available in PDF and can be downloaded online.

3.13   *BIOSIS Previews Serials List.* Philadelphia, PA: Thomson Scientific. Available: http://scientific.thomson.com/support/products/previews/ bp-serials/

BIOSIS Previews is a comprehensive reference database in the life sciences. This database covers 5,000 international serials from *Biological Abstracts*. The full serial list of this database is available online. *BIOSIS Serial Sources* includes a listing of 5,000 current titles, as well as the 13,000 archival titles reviewed by BIOSIS. This resource provides an indicator for each of the approximately 2,300 serials from *BIOSIS Previews* and *Biological Abstracts* that were indexed cover-to-cover in 2001. *BIOSIS Serial Sources* is available in printed format through Thomson Scientific.

3.14   *List of Journal Titles Currently Indexed in the CINAHL Database.* [Web document]. Glendale, CA: CINAHL Information Systems. Available: www.cinahl.com/library/library.htm

CINAHL provides an extensive index for issues related to nursing and allied health. It covers more than 2,900 journals, including complete coverage of English-language nursing journals and publications from the National League for Nursing and the American Nurses' Association. A list of journal titles currently included in the CINAHL database is available in PDF format and can be downloaded on the Internet.

3.15   *Health & Wellness Resource Center Journal Title Lists.* Farmington Hills, MI: Thomson Gale. Available: www.gale.com/tlist/sb5117.doc

This database provides a collection of general interest and fitness magazines, medical and professional periodicals, reference books and pamphlets. The resources indexed cover more than 900 medical journals and newsletters. Health-related articles from 2,200 general interest publications are also included. The journal titles listed can serve as an aid for building a consumer health collection.

3.16   *CAplus Core Journal Coverage List.* Columbus, OH: American Chemical Society. Available: www.cas.org/expertise/cascontent/ caplus/corejournals.html

Chemical Abstracts Service (CAS) monitors, indexes, and abstracts the world's chemistry-related literature and patents. SciFinder Scholar is the online version of CAS and includes the CAplus database, the CAS REGISTRY file and MEDLINE, as well as information on chemical substances and reactions. This database covers nearly 9,500 major scientific journals worldwide. Among them, there is cover-to-cover coverage for more than 1,500 key chemical journals in many scientific disciplines, including biomedical sciences, chemistry, engineering, materials science, agricultural science, and others. Though it is not a searchable site, the entire current journal list is available online.

3.17   *Scopus: Complete List of Titles.* [Web document]. New York, NY: Elsevier B.V. Available: http://info.scopus.com/docs/publisher_list. xls.

Scopus is a citation database of peer-reviewed literature and Web resources. This database covers more than 15,000 peer-reviewed journals in science, technology, medicine and social sciences from over 4,000 international publishers, which includes over 1,000 open access journals. The entire publication list can be downloaded in Microsoft Excel format at this address: http://info.scopus.com/docs/publisher_list.xls.

3.18   *Thomson Scientific Master Journal List.* Philadelphia, PA: Thomson Scientific. Available: http://scientific.thomson.com/knowledgelink/ frames/frameset-journallist/

This Web-based resource provides the entire list of journal resources indexed by the Thomson Scientific ISI Web of Knowledge database family. The Web site is searchable, and the entire journal listing is also available for browsing in alphabetical order.

Periodical Holdings Information

For many HS libraries, the need for efficient and widespread access to resources not owned by the libraries is crucial because of the escalating cost of books and journals and the need to meet users' demands [13]. Currently, the NLM has one of the largest collections of biomedical literature in the world. NLM's interlibrary loan (ILL) and document delivery services make these resources available to U.S. and international libraries. This resource-sharing arrangement is through a network system, the National Network of Libraries of Medicine (NN/LM).

The member libraries of the NN/LM provide health information and resource exchanges through eight regional networks. The U.S. members of the NN/LM and selected Canadian and Mexican libraries input their serial holdings statements for biomedical serial titles to the NLM's SERHOLD database. The ILL requests are sent to DOCLINE, the NLM's automated ILL request routing and referral system. The SERHOLD module provides the information used by DOCLINE's automatic routing feature, and the linking journal holdings are able to route the requests to potential lending libraries on behalf of the borrower.

3.19   *SERHOLD*. Bethesda, MD: U.S. National Library of Medicine. [Web document]. Available: www.nlm.nih.gov/pubs/factsheets/serhold. html

As of November 2006, the SERHOLD database includes over 1.4 million holdings statements for 55,013 serial titles from 3,024 health sciences libraries in the United States, Canada, and Mexico. The major function of SERHOLD is to facilitate the network arrangements of ILL services. In addition, the serial holding statements from various types of HS information settings are great resources for helping libraries modify their periodical collections. However, only DOCLINE participants have access to SERHOLD via the DOCLINE Serial Holdings module.

Sources of Electronic Journals on the Internet

Technology has made fundamental changes in the services provided by HS libraries and librarians. Today, most users in health-related information settings are technology savvy, spending a great deal of time searching for information from various sources, including the Internet. Most scientific literature is now created in digital form and is available in nearly every discipline [14]. The increasing access to electronic journals in HS information settings has shown their widespread acceptance in major library collections. Several of these electronic journals are open-access materials which are available free of charge on the Internet. Following are several centralized sources of information that can assist users in locating electronic journals on the Internet.

3.20   *MedicalStudent.com: MEDLINE and Medical Journals.* Available: www.medicalstudent.com/#MEDLINE

This Web site was created and is curated by Michael P. D'Alessandro, M.D., to serve as a digital library of authoritative medical information designed to help students of medicine. It includes a group of links to free medical journals in full-text format available on the Internet.

3.21   *Free Medical Journals.* Paris: Flying Publisher. Available: www.free medicaljournals.com/htm/index.htm

The Free Medical Journals site was launched in late February 2000 by Flying Publisher. The purpose is to promote free access to full-text medical journals on the Internet. Most articles from the journals listed at Free Medical Journals are available one to six months after publication. This site does not provide searching functions. Users are able to browse the journal titles.

3.22   *Free Medical Journals.* Iowa City, IA: Hardin Library for the Health Sciences–The University of Iowa Libraries. Available: www.lib.uiowa. edu/hardin/journals.html#free

This is a selected list of sources of information of the free full-text medical journal aggregator Web sites. Direct links to sites such as PubMed, BioMed Central, and Public Library of Science Central, are included. No searching function is available; users can browse the titles of the Web sites.

3.23   *Free Medical Journals: PubMed Search.* Iowa City, IA: Hardin Library for the Health Sciences–The University of Iowa Libraries. Available: www.lib.uiowa.edu/hardin/md/ej.html

This is an interface to access the full-text resources available from the PubMed journals provided by the Hardin Library. The subjects are selected because they are popular with the library's user community. Users are able to click on each subject and view the free full-text resources related to the subject on the PubMed site.

3.24   *HighWire Press: Free Online Full-text Articles.* Palo Alto, CA: HighWire Press, The Board of Trustees of the Leland Stanford Junior University. Available: http://highwire.stanford.edu/lists/free art.dtl

HighWire Press, a division of the Stanford University Libraries, has high-impact, peer-reviewed content with 1,053 journals and 4,346,060 full-text articles from over 130 scholarly publishers. HighWire Press began in early 1995 with the online production of the weekly *Journal of Biological Chemistry* (JBC). Users are able to access some full-text articles free of charge on the HighWire Free Online Full-text Articles Web site, while some can only be accessed through pay-per-view. In addition, the site provides searching functions.

3.25   *MedWeb.* Bethesda, MD: Emory Health Sciences Center Library. Available: www.medweb.emory.edu/MedWeb/

MedWeb is a catalog of biomedical and health-related Web sites maintained by the staff of the Robert W. Woodruff Health Sciences Center Library at Emory University. Users are able to browse the journal titles by subjects, and the site also provides searching functions.

3.26   *Electronic Journals and Open Access.* Bethesda, MD: National Network of Libraries of Medicine. Available: http://nnlm.gov/rsdd/ejournals/

This NN/LM Web site provides information about methods of gaining access to free full-text information as well as collaborative projects that are ongoing such as Scholarly Publishing and Academic Resources Coalition (SPARC) and Public Library of Science.

Abbreviations

Many electronic information systems supply journal title abbreviations in their bibliographic records. As the NLM points out, abbreviations are useful both online and in printed lists of references. The NLM provides journal title abbreviations in all their journal databases. Decoding periodical title abbreviations and identifying the full names of these titles are difficult tasks, and one of the most frequently asked questions of HS information professionals is the identification of periodical titles included in the reference bibliographies. Currently, a massive number of periodicals are published by national and international publishing companies. There is a lack of standards for regulating the construction of title abbreviations used by periodicals publishers and database producers. The NLM is collaborating with the International Committee of Medical Journal Editors (ICMJE) with regard to the format of references in bibliographies for journal articles. The NISO/ANSI Z39.29.-2005 Bibliographic References has been adopted for the construction of journal title abbreviations [15]. Following are several print and electronic resources that can be used to identify and verify the proper names of periodical titles.

3.27   *Acronyms, Initialisms & Abbreviations Dictionary*. 38th ed. Farmington Hills, MI: Thomson Gale, 2007.

This is a multivolume resource arranged alphabetically; users can consult the dictionary to decode an acronym and to identify the accepted truncation for a given term. The content coverage of this resource includes journal abbreviations.

3.28   *All That JAS: Journal Abbreviation Sources—Abbreviations.com*. Fair Lawn, NJ: STANDS4 LLC. Available: www.abbreviations.com/ jas.asp

This resource is a categorized registry of Web resources that list or provide access to the full title of journal abbreviations or other types of abbreviated publication titles (e.g., conference proceedings titles). In addition, it includes select lists and directories that provide access to the *unabbreviated* titles of serial publications.

3.29   *Periodical Title Abbreviations: By Abbreviation*. 17th ed. Farmington Hills, MI: Thomson Gale, 2006.

This volume lists, in a single alphabetical sequence, abbreviations commonly used for periodicals together with their full titles.

3.30   *Journals Database*. Bethesda, MD: U.S. National Library of Medicine. Available: www.ncbi.nlm.nih.gov/sites/entrez?db=journals

This is a direct source for looking up journals cited in any of the Entrez databases, including PubMed.

Conclusion

Developing a core periodical collection is an important task for HS professionals and requires a thorough understanding of the user community and the environment. Since every environment is different, the selection of periodical titles varies, based on the user communities, needs and purposes, health-related specialties, services provided, setting sizes, missions of the parent organizations, consortial agreements, and other factors [16]. Presently, a major challenge is to build a solid collection of full-text periodicals in electronic format, maintain subscriptions to printed journals, and increase access to various online databases to augment the scope of full-text journal access.

Periodical publications change frequently as new titles appear, old ones disappear, and names are changed. Information professionals must be aware of the most recent information regarding periodical publications. In addition, there must be careful bibliographic control to ensure that the periodical information recorded in the library resource databases is current and accurate. That is the only way to guarantee that library OPACs will provide their users with the information they need and expect.

References

1. Shaw-Kokot J. Using a journal availability study to improve access. *Bull Med Libr Assoc* 2001; 98(1):21–8.
2. Reitz JM. *Online dictionary for library and information science*. [Web document]. Westport, CT: Libraries Unlimited, 2004–6. Available: http://lu.com/odlis/odlis_p.cfm. Accessed: 30 May 2007.
3. Smith R. The trouble with medical journals. *J R Soc Med* 2006; 99:115–9.
4. Reitz, op. cit.
5. Smith, op. cit.
6. Alper B, et al. How much effort is needed to keep up with the literature relevant for primary care? *J Med Libr Assoc* 2004; 92(4):429–37.
7. De Groote SL, Dorsch JL. Measuring use patterns of online journals and databases. *J Med Libr Assoc* 2004 Apr; 91(2):231–40.
8. U.S. National Library of Medicine. *Collection development manual: journals*. Bethesda, MD, 2004. Available: www.nlm.nih.gov/tsd/acquisitions/cdm/formats29.html#1027134. Accessed: 1 May 2007.
9. U.S. National Library of Medicine. *LocatorPlus fact sheet*. [Web document]. Bethesda, MD, 2005. Available: www.nlm.nih.gov/pubs/factsheets/ locatorplus.html. Accessed: 16 July 2007.
10. ProQuest-CSA LLC. *About Ulrichsweb.com*. Ann Arbor, MI, 2007. Available: www.ulrichsweb.com/ulrichsweb/ulrichsweb_news/ulrichsinsideabout.asp. Accessed: 1 May 2007.
11. Cassell KA, Hiremath U. *Reference and information services in the 21st Century: an introduction*. New York: Neal-Schuman, 2006.

12. Nobari N., Ed. *Books and periodicals online*. [Web document]. New York, NY: Library Technology Alliance, Ltd. Available: www. booksandperiodicals. com. Accessed: 1 May 2007.
13. Holst R., Phillips, SA. *The Medical Library Association guide to managing health care libraries*. New York, NY: Neal-Schuman, 2000.
14. Johnson RK. Will research sharing keep pace with the Internet? *J Neurosci* 2006; 26(37):9349–51.
15. U.S. National Library of Medicine. *FAQ: the use of journal title abbreviations in NLM databases*. [Web document], Bethesda, MD, 2007. Available: www.nlm.nih.gov/services/pm_title_abbrev.html. Accessed: 30 June 2007.
16. Thompson LL, Toedt LJ, D'Agostino FJ. Zero-based print journal collection development in a community teaching hospital library: planning for the future. *J Med Libr Assoc* 2005; 93(4):427–30.

CHAPTER 4

Indexing, Abstracting, and Digital Database Resources

Laura Abate

In 2006, Tang and Ng published an article in the *British Medical Journal* showing that 58 percent of a set of clinical cases were correctly diagnosed using the Google search engine [1]. The previous year, HighWire Press, an electronic platform for scholarly publishers, reported that Google and Google Scholar accounted for 60 percent of the referrals from Web sites to HighWire hosted journals, while the PubMed database provided only 9 percent of referrals [2].

Given the seeming ability of Google to correctly identify diagnoses and its popularity, particularly when compared to a standard research tool such as PubMed, users might conclude that publicly accessible search engines such as Google have supplanted other medical research databases in usefulness. This hypothesis, however, confuses the ability of Google to suggest possible diagnoses for "mystery illnesses" with the ability of professional-level databases to identify high-quality information targeted to the specific breadth and depth required by an individual user. As Tang and Ng emphasize in a reply to their original study, Google works well to spur diagnosticians to consider conditions which are rarely seen in clinical work and whose signs and symptoms may not be immediately recognized, but most clinical questions can be answered using databases such as PubMed, the Cochrane Library, or UpToDate [3].

Google's proven abilities, while important to note, do not equate with the stringent quality standards intrinsic to many health information databases or the capacity for honing a search based on the varying depths of information required by health care providers, researchers, and students. While Google and its academic counterpart, Google Scholar, are excellent research tools for identifying information by topic, these search engines do not differentiate among the different types of health sciences information required by students, practitioners, and researchers. For example, a health sciences student needing information on the pathophysiology of asthma would do well to consult a database that includes introductory or background information, such as AccessMedicine or STAT!Ref, while a researcher needing the latest research on this topic would identify recent journal articles using a database such as MEDLINE, and a health care provider might consult concise, evidence-based information by accessing ACP PIER or DynaMed. While Google or Google Scholar users can efficiently identify information by topic or keywords, users of these search tools must browse results in order to locate the type of information that they seek.

A hypothesis that assumes the dominance of Google and other widely used search tools over other health professional databases might also confuse the needs of the general public, who use the World Wide Web for health information searches in astounding numbers, with the needs of health professionals. While health information searches constitute an impressive proportion of information searches on the World Wide Web, comprising an impressive 4.5 percent of all searches [4], the needs of general consumers differ greatly from those of health care professionals. Consumers frequently search for background information on diseases, but more than half of consumers evaluate health information Web sites by checking source, date, or privacy information "only sometimes" [5, 6]. Whereas health care professionals might not fare much better when queried on their evaluation habits, health sciences databases intended for health care professionals use quality measures to screen information so that health care professionals have some idea of the type and source of information that they are retrieving. Quality measures built into health sciences databases include focusing on peer-reviewed literature (e.g., MEDLINE), synthesizing medical evidence and establishing levels of evidence (e.g., Clinical Evidence, FirstConsult, etc.), and providing independent review of research results (e.g., ACP Medicine, Faculty of 1000).

This chapter will describe the indexing, abstracting, and digital database resources which are most important to health sciences students, researchers, and practitioners. Particular attention will be paid to the evolving technologies permitting the integration of multiple information sources and the blurring of boundaries between traditional indexes and newer full-text information resources. Issues of special interest to health sciences librarians, including vendors, licensing, and pricing and access issues, will also be covered.

Contemporary Practice

As indexes have evolved from print to electronic tools and as database searching has changed from librarian-mediated to being accomplished by the individual, user expectations have shifted. Many of today's users cannot fathom an information world where only an "expert" conducts searches. Most users have grown accustomed to or have only known an environment in which searches are conducted by the individual. Users may still rely on librarians for assistance in getting started on a project or for advice on locating materials which are proving difficult to identify, but few will request searches primarily through a librarian. In 2007, De Groote, Hitchcock, and McGowan published data showing that mediated searches declined from 2,157 searches in 1990–1991 to 18 searches in 2004–2005 [7].

As part of their experience as database searchers, today's users have high expectations for the information tools at their disposal. Both users who have accessed the Web from their earliest school years and those who began using it later in their educational or professional careers may have expectations that are not based on the reality of a library environment. The seamless delivery of full text via open-linking systems, whether a user is searching *Google Scholar* or *PubMed*, may lead users to believe that all information is free and freely accessible. This perception may leave users ignorant of the business of subscriptions and license agreements, and of the value of the resources that the library provides. The ability to type keywords into a Web search tool may make it difficult for users to understand the use, impact, and possible advantages of indexing schemes versus full-text searching. Finally, users' ability to harness the breadth of the Web to find *some* information on virtually *any* topic, may leave them poorly prepared to identify the best information resource for their needs and to evaluate information retrieved for quality and merit.

As the onus of searching has shifted from the librarian to the individual user, the role of the librarian has changed. While librarians remain expert searchers due to their knowledge of information tools and their practiced skill with individual resources, librarians must now redouble their efforts as instructors to enable users to locate information effectively and efficiently. In their role as instructors, librarians should educate users on the contents and prospective uses of information resources in both in print and electronic formats, the structure and design of the data resources, and the search strategies that work best for each resource. This education will occur in a variety of settings according to the library environment, availability of professional staff, and the needs of the users. Educational sessions will vary from informal to formal settings (e.g., from Reference Desk inquiries to prepared remarks at Grand Rounds), from general topics to specific resources (e.g., from Natural Medicines to MEDLINE), and from sessions with an individual to classes of several hundred students.

Finally, while users expect immediate and direct access to electronic information resources, librarians must remain knowledgeable and skilled in locating information in print resources. Some indexes remain accessible only in print format, and the information available in print indexes may not be accessible through online search tools. In 2007, the MEDLINE database changed its coverage dates, extending coverage back from 1966 to 1950. While this change added sixteen years of data to the MEDLINE database, indexing data from MEDLINE's various precursors extends even further back, into the nineteenth century. Users who rely exclusively on searching MEDLINE online may miss relevant information that is available in print indexes.

As database coverage years shift and electronic resources evolve, librarians need to maintain their knowledge of both print and electronic indexes in order to select the most appropriate research tools. Librarians should monitor coverage dates for relevant databases as the coverage years continue to change and be able to identify corresponding print indexes which can be used when searches need to be extended to earlier year spans. Librarians are also advised that comprehensive literature searches will likely require the use of print indexes. In the fourth edition of this book, Perry, Howse and Schlimgen produced an extensive table describing key print abstracts and indexes which serves as a valuable reference tool for identifying relevant print indexes [8]. In the third edition of this book, Boorkman provided additional detail on the history of medical indexes including the titles and coverage years of MEDLINE's predecessors [9]. For detailed information on print indexes and their coverage, readers should refer these editions.

From Indexing and Abstracting to Full Text

As the electronic environment has evolved, users' perceptions about databases have shifted. Initially, literature databases mirrored their previously published print counterparts and organized articles by author and topic. Early online users were grateful for the convenience and speed with which a literature search could be conducted to identify all articles by a particular author or to identify all articles on one or more topics. However, even as early users appreciated the newfound convenience of online searching, users and librarian expectations were changing. Users were no longer satisfied with a printout of citations and abstracts, but began to seek and expect to access full-text articles online.

In contrast to previous decades when print indexes provided the key to locating pertinent journal articles, contemporary databases offer a range of full-text content. Indexing and abstracting resources such as MEDLINE still echo their print counterparts by recording who/what/where data about journal articles. However, these indexing sources are now frequently integrated with linking systems which allow users to jump from indexing information describing who wrote an article, what it is about, and where it can be found, to a full-text copy of the actual article. Link resolvers such as SFX, 1Cate, and ArticleLinker maintain databases of information about a library's electronic journal titles and their coverage dates, and serve as an intermediary by connecting an article's record in an online index to an electronic full-text copy of the article.

In contrast to the above example, where users continue to search an indexing and abstracting source and link from that database to a full-text document, some databases provide all or part of their content in full-text format. For example, MDConsult provides a range of document types, including journal articles, practice guidelines, drug information, and textbooks. Much of the information in MDConsult is available in full-text format, while indexing and abstracting information alone persists in other areas. MDConsult users who search books, *Clinics of North America* articles, or drug information will find that the search system has retrieved possible matches by searching the full text of documents, while MDConsult users who search the journal articles will find that the search system retrieves possible matches from whatever data is available. For some articles in MDConsult, indexing and abstracting data alone is available and searched, while for other articles MDConsult attempts to locate term matches in the full-text document as well as the indexing and abstracting data.

Continuing on the spectrum of full-text availability are databases that are full text in their entirety. Databases in this category include resources containing the online equivalent of traditional textbooks such as AccessMedicine or STAT!Ref, collections of full-text reviews such as the Cochrane Database of Systematic Reviews, and full-text point-of-care databases such as eMedicine and UpToDate. While items from these databases may occasionally be indexed in traditional indexing and abstracting sources (as in the Cochrane Database), more frequently these databases stand on their own as individual knowledge sources.

Presently, totally full-text databases do not provide access to the original research published in scholarly journals, but provide background information and synthesize or analyze the original research in some fashion. For example, an entirely full-text database is unlikely to contain the full text of a recent article from *JAMA* that published the findings of a randomized controlled trial on treating hypertension. However, a full-text database may provide background information on the definition and classification of hypertension, analyze all evidence previously published on a specific treatment option, or provide concise information on differential diagnosis and how to evaluate a hypertensive patient.

While full-text availability is popular with users, it is important to remember that full-text availability is not a quality measure. Depending on a user's research needs, a partial, hybrid, or completely full-text database may be appropriate, or a more traditional indexing and abstracting tool may better meet a user's information needs. A user who needs to review recent evidence on treating a particular condition may be satisfied by an information resource containing some level of full text, while a user who needs a comprehensive search will likely need to use information resources which provide full text, as well as those that do not.

While customer service and satisfaction are important, librarians should not be cowed by user expectations. User expectations may not be in accord with a user's information needs. Librarians can sympathize with users needs and should work to improve search tools and skills, but should also remain vigilant in trying to assure that the best search is conducted and that the best information tools are identified and used. Librarians possess vital information about the current availability of information and the architecture of information resources, as well as information on user needs and expectations, and can use these bodies of knowledge to enhance database content, structure, and interface for future users.

Primary Research Databases

Primary research databases form the backbone of medical research. These databases index and abstract original research as it is published in scholarly journals. As such, primary research databases contain the latest information available by publishing news articles, research reports (e.g., clinical trials results), recommendations (e.g., practice guidelines), and opinion pieces (e.g., letters, editorials). Primary research databases are integral to comprehensive information searches as they provide an ongoing record of information as it is made available to the public.

Primary research databases are generally citation and abstract databases, though they increasingly provide some mechanism for linking to full-text documents. Indexing systems and standards vary by database, but some generalizations can be made. Indexing usually contains some subject classification system which can range from an informal collection of author-provided keywords to a highly structured, consistently applied thesaurus of terms. Primary research databases also frequently provide additional information about the article including type of publication (e.g., Meta Analysis, Peer-Reviewed Journal Article), language, and date, as well as information about the research subjects (e.g., human, rabbit), patient characteristics (e.g., gender, age, ethnicity), and research locale (e.g., Taiwan, California).

4.1   *MEDLINE*. Bethesda, MD: U.S. National Library of Medicine. Available: www.pubmed.gov

MEDLINE is the premier biomedical research database in the world. It is produced by the U.S. National Library of Medicine, which provides free access to MEDLINE via the PubMed Web interface. The National Library of Medicine also leases MEDLINE data to commercial database vendors and Web sites who may provide free access to MEDLINE, or who may sell access to MEDLINE via proprietary search interfaces. Even as the availability of information on the Web and the number of databases has proliferated, MEDLINE has likely maintained its position as the most important research tool in the health sciences; it serves as a baseline for health sciences research against which other literature databases are measured.

MEDLINE is highly valued as a research resource for a number of reasons: breadth of medicine and health sciences topics covered; quality standards applied to journals selected for indexing; expanding year coverage; variety of languages and geographic span of journals indexed; a consistent and evolving indexing scheme; and wide accessibility. MEDLINE indexes about 5,000 publications, primarily scholarly journals. MEDLINE covers medicine and health sciences broadly including "the life sciences, behavioral sciences, chemical sciences and bioengineering needed by health professionals and others engaged in basic research and clinical care, public health, health policy development, or related educational activities" [10].

Journals selected for MEDLINE indexing undergo a stringent review process through which they are evaluated for scope and coverage, quality of content, quality of editorial work, production quality, audience, and types of content [11]. In 2007, MEDLINE expanded its year coverage to 1950 through the present by incorporating data that was previously included in OLDMEDLINE [12]. Although MEDLINE is produced by the U.S. National Library of Medicine, it covers journals published worldwide. Currently, MEDLINE includes journal articles written in 37 languages and historically has included articles in 60 languages [10].

Journal articles are indexed for MEDLINE using a controlled vocabulary called MeSH (Medical Subject Headings). The power of MeSH indexing lies in its consistent application and ongoing adaptation to new concepts and terminology in health sciences. MEDLINE's consistent and detailed indexing can be used to retrieve and sort items to answer specific research questions. Indexers assign MeSH terms to describe the topics of each article, the publication type (e.g., controlled clinical trial, editorial), and geographics (e.g., continent, region, country, state, etc.) [13]. MeSH terms can also contain qualifiers or subheadings to further specify the type of information contained in an article (e.g., Economics, Epidemiology, Enzymology, etc.). Multiple MeSH terms may be applied to sufficiently describe an article. For example, an article on assessing a chickenpox vaccination program in Brazil might contain the following MeSH terms:

Brazil
Chickenpox / Prevention & Control
Chickenpox Vaccine / Administration & Dosage
Child
Humans
Immunization Programs/Organization & Administration
Journal Article
Review

Part of MEDLINE's influence as a research tool undoubtedly lies in its broad accessibility. Free access to MEDLINE is provided via PubMed (www.pubmed.gov), and numerous additional free and fee-based sources of MEDLINE are available. PubMed is a popular tool for searching MEDLINE, as it offers a flexible search environment that is navigable both by novice searchers and that can be harnessed by experienced users for complex searches. In addition to MEDLINE data, PubMed contains records for "In Process" citations, which are generally waiting for the addition of MeSH terms. "In Process" citations include those that were published prior to a journal's being officially indexed in MEDLINE, those that are not within the scope of MEDLINE though other articles from these sources are indexed, and citations to articles available in the PubMedCentral full-text archive but not indexed in MEDLINE [14].

4.2   *CINAHL*. Glendale, CA: Cinahl Information Systems. Available: www.cinahl.com

CINAHL is the Cumulative Index to Nursing & Allied Health Literature, a bibliographic database that provides access to the nursing and allied health literature going back to 1982. While MEDLINE covers health sciences broadly, CINAHL focuses specifically on the numerous and varied disciplines of nursing (e.g., Anesthesia Nursing, Gerontologic Nursing, Private Duty Nursing, etc.), as well as allied health care fields, including athletic training, physical therapy, physician assistants, nutrition & dietetics, and respiratory therapy, among others [15]. Presently, CINAHL indexes approximately 1,750 journals, over half of which are not indexed in MEDLINE [16].

CINAHL's primary focus is journal articles, but unlike MEDLINE, CINAHL also indexes other sources of information. In CINAHL, users can find references to books, audiovisuals, pamphlets, software, dissertations, and research instruments. In CINAHL, the "Publication Types" field describes the format of the original item (i.e., book, journal article, pamphlet, etc.), as well as aspects of information within that document. For example, research results may be indexed to multiple entries under publication type to reflect that the publication was a journal article, and also that it included tables or charts and included a questionnaire or scale. CINAHL also uses several unique publication types which are useful to nursing and allied health personnel, including Clinical Innovations, Accreditation, Legal Cases, Drugs, and Research Instruments [15].

CINAHL is indexed using CINAHL Subject Headings which are modeled after MeSH. CINAHL's indexing terms include a subject heading to which a subheading can be added in order to specify the type of information presented on a specific topic (e.g., Emergency Nursing /Legislation and Jurisprudence). While many of CINAHL's Subject Headings reflect its focus on nursing and allied health literature and so echo the terminology used in these professions, other portions of the CINAHL thesaurus are drawn directly from MeSH.

While CINAHL is primarily a bibliographic database, some full-text publications are incorporated. The selected full text in CINAHL includes research instruments, critical paths, standards of practice, government publications, and patient education materials, among others. Also, a version of CINAHL which provides the full text of more than 500 of the indexed journals is now available.

In October 2003, Ebsco Publishing announced that it had completed the acquisition of CINAHL from the Glendale Adventist Medical Center. Ebsco Publishing provides access to CINAHL as a fee-based subscription through several online vendors.

4.3   *International Pharmaceutical Abstracts.* Philadelphia, PA: Thomson Scientific. Available: scientific.thomson.com/products/ipa/

The International Pharmaceutical Abstracts (IPA) database provides in-depth coverage of pharmacy and pharmacology literature. Whereas MEDLINE covers health sciences literature broadly and CINAHL focuses on information relevant to a subset of health sciences professions, IPA provides deep coverage of a specific discipline within the health sciences. In addition to its exhaustive topical coverage of pharmacy and pharmacology, IPA's coverage is geographically extensive and indexes journals published worldwide.

IPA is a bibliographic database that began as a print index in 1964. IPA became an electronic index in 1970, and the database generally covers from 1970 through the present, although a backfile covering 1964–1969 has been digitized and is available from some vendors. From its inception until 2005, IPA was produced by the American Society of Health Systems Pharmacists. IPA was acquired from this group in 2005 by Thomson Scientific, a company that now makes IPA commercially available through several database vendors.

To complement the authority of its exhaustive coverage of pharmacology literature, IPA is indexed using seven indexes to provide detailed information on the topics of each article, including pharmacy and pharmacology topics and specific drugs or compounds discussed. In 2002, Wolfe described IPA's indexing scheme, which incorporates the IPA thesaurus of pharmacy-related principles; MeSH terms; AHFS Therapeutic Classification System to provide the drug class name, a code number for the specific drug, and the drug's generic name; Drug Trade Names; USAN to supply generic names for drugs; CAS Registry Numbers to link the specific chemical compound(s) in a drug; and IPA's Natural Products Index document plants and other naturally occurring agents [17].

While IPA is a valuable research tool for pharmacy-related research, it does not entirely supplant MEDLINE as a research tool in this area. In 1996, Fishman, Stone, and DiPaula showed that both research tools are valuable for pharmacy information searches and that there is very little overlap between the two databases [18].

4.4   *PsycINFO*. Washington, DC: American Psychological Association. Available: www.apa.org/psycinfo

PsycINFO differs from MEDLINE, CINAHL, and IPA in both its content coverage of the behavioral sciences and mental health and in its broader coverage of item types. While journal records account for 78 percent of the database content, PsycINFO also indexes entire books, book chapters, and dissertations [19]. This diversity in item types lends to the depth of PsycINFO, as it permits users to identify items not only by subject but by format. For example, users in need of an introduction to a particular topic might limit a search in PsycINFO to book chapters or review articles, while users seeking the latest scholarly research might limit their search to peer-reviewed journals and original journal articles.

In terms of subject, PsycINFO covers the breadth of topics related to psychology, including the behavioral sciences and mental health. PsycINFO's subject coverage tends to be inclusive, pulling relevant materials from other disciplines as their topics intersect with psychology. For example, PsycINFO is useful for health sciences users when researching the behavioral causes and effects of disease and the behavioral treatment of disease, among other topics. While PsycINFO has considerable overlap with MEDLINE, its specific focus on psychology-related research, and its coverage of additional item types support its importance as a health sciences database.

PsycINFO indexes about 1,100 journals in their entirety, and another 1,100 selectively for relevance to PsycINFO's scope. While coverage from several print indexes which contributed to PsycINFO extends back into the nineteenth century, indexing using the controlled vocabulary provided in the *Thesaurus of Psychological Index Terms* begins with records dating from 1967 and continues through the present. A particular strength of PsycINFO is its extensive indexing beyond topical coverage to permit users to focus searches by methodology (empirical studies, field studies, literature reviews, etc.) and auxiliary material (data sets, video, workbook/study guide, etc.), and to identify other valuable information about studies including identification of tests and measures used and sources of financial support.

PsycINFO is produced by the American Psychological Association, which also produces several related products including PsycARTICLES (full-text articles from 50 journals), PsycFIRST (the most recent three years of PsycINFO data), and PsycSCANs (subsets of PsycINFO targeting a specific discipline or area of study).

4.5   *Scopus*. Amsterdam: Elsevier B.V. Available: www.scopus.com

The inclusion of Scopus in a list of primary research databases in the health sciences may be controversial, as this is an interdisciplinary database rather than primarily a health sciences tool. However, Scopus's coverage of the health sciences and its strength as an interdisciplinary resource in the intersecting disciplines of basic sciences, clinical sciences, and public health demonstrate its merit as a health sciences research tool. Broadly, Scopus covers the life sciences, health sciences, physical sciences, and social sciences, and indexes the same journal titles as are covered in MEDLINE. However, because of Scopus's broad topical coverage and ability to link articles by cited and citing information, users can call upon a deeper pool of research and find connections between research studies which may not have been otherwise apparent.

While Scopus is primarily a citation and abstract database, Scopus records contain additional information on citing and cited research. For articles published from 1996 through the present, Scopus provides a list of the documents that are cited in the original article's bibliography. This allows users to work backwards in time to locate the research findings upon which the articles author or authors relied. Scopus also provides information on citing articles. Drawing on the same data regarding articles cited, Scopus links individual articles to subsequently published items that cite them. This function also allows users to work forward in time to locate research that drew on and cited a particular article.

In addition to its broad and interdisciplinary topical coverage, Scopus has a more international focus than MEDLINE or CINAHL. Produced by Elsevier B.V., which is based in Amsterdam, over 60 percent of the journals indexed in Scopus originate from outside of the United States [20]. Scopus's year coverage runs from 1966 through the present, and expanded information is available for journal articles published from 1996 through present. Scopus lacks a systematically applied subject thesaurus and tracks publication types at a limited level, but its flexible search interface and methods of linking between articles makes it a powerful research tool.

Secondary Research Databases

While the primary research databases can be differentiated by important differences in content and format, these databases are similar in that they are primarily citation and abstract databases, and they cover overlapping segments of the original health sciences research. In contrast, the secondary research databases vary widely in format, scope, and representation of original research.

Many of the secondary research databases contain records which are similar to that of the primary research databases. These databases contain citation and abstract information describing original publications and may link to or contain selected full-text documents. However, certain secondary research databases demonstrate the ability of databases to provide access to information in other formats. Images.MD and Entrez's PubChem Compound, among others, provide images as well as textual information. As databases continue to evolve, librarians should remain open to databases that provide information in nontextual formats and innovations in the format of information.

The secondary research databases tend to be more specialized in scope and to provide more comprehensive information on specific topics. While the primary research databases cover a wide range of topics, the secondary research databases cover narrow fields of research in even greater depth than is available in the primary databases. The secondary research databases may focus on a particular population; for example, AgeLine focuses on the geriatric population, and the Native Health Research Database covers health-related information on Native Americans. Secondary research databases may focus on information relevant to specific health professional fields; for example, AMED provides information relevant to a spectrum of allied health professions. And certainly, secondary health databases can focus on a specific discipline; for example, TOXNET provides toxicology information via a number of different databases, and SPORTDiscus focuses on the field of sports medicine.

While some of the secondary research databases mimic the primary research databases in that they also contain citations and abstracts to original research, other databases provide information on diverse phases of the research process. Citations and abstracts in MEDLINE and other primary research databases generally describe completed research. The projects described have usually been designed, funded, executed, and analyzed before entering the databases. Some secondary research databases can be used to identify research at earlier phases in this process, as well as to find commentary on previously published research. CRISP can be searched to identify research that has been funded but not necessarily completed, and ClinicalTrials.gov and PDQ can be used to identify clinical studies which may be ongoing and still accruing patients. HaPI can be used to identify research instruments in relationship to the studies in which they were deployed. The Faculty of 1000 databases can be used to locate commentary on original research, and to identify what may be the most important research articles published in specific disciplines.

The following list of secondary research databases is not meant to be exhaustive, but rather representational of the types of databases currently available. Indeed, as database development has accelerated in recent years, it would be nearly impossible to accurately maintain a comprehensive list of health sciences databases. Librarians can use this list both as a guide to the most valuable current resources, and as a reminder to investigate additional databases which may contain information relevant to a specific research question.

Several subsets of databases have been intentionally omitted from this list. Drug information databases are discussed more completely in Chapter 9, "Drug Information Sources." Several online directories are cited here, but in-depth discussion can be found in Chapter 12, "Directories and Biographical Sources." Consumer health databases are discussed in a subsequent section of this chapter, as well as in Chapter 10, "Consumer Health Sources."

4.6   *AgeLine*. Washington, DC: AARP. Available: www.aarp.org/ research/ageline

Scope: Professional and selected consumer information related to aging and gerontology.
Record Type: Indexing and abstract
Coverage: 1978–present; selected coverage 1966–1977
Availability: Free

4.7   *AMED—Allied and Complementary Medicine Database*. London: Health Care Information Service, British Library. Available: www.bl. uk/collections/health/amed.html

Scope: Complementary medicine and allied health professions, including physiotherapy, occupational therapy, rehabilitation, podiatry, palliative care, and speech and language therapy.
Record Type: Indexing and abstract
Coverage: 1985–present
Availability: Vendor

4.8   *Biological Abstracts.* Philadelphia, PA: Thomson Scientific. Available: scientific.thomson.com/products/ba

> Scope: International coverage of life sciences, including biochemistry, biotechnology, microbiology, neurology, pharmacology, public health, and toxicology.
>
> Record Type: Indexing and abstract
>
> Coverage: 1969–present; archives 1926–1968
>
> Availability: Vendor

4.9   *ClinicalTrials.gov.* Bethesda, MD: U.S. National Library of Medicine. Available: clinicaltrials.gov

> Scope: Clinical trials sponsored by the U.S. federal government and private industry, occurring in the United States and worldwide.
>
> Record Type: Full-text information on purpose, eligibility, location(s), and contact information on recruiting and closed clinical trials
>
> Coverage: Open and closed clinical trials
>
> Availability: Free

4.10   *Cochrane Central Register of Controlled Trials (CENTRAL).* Oxford: Cochrane Collaboration. Available: www.cochrane.org

> Scope: Controlled trials identified by Cochrane Collaboration authors and by hand-searching the medical literature.
>
> Record Type: Indexing and abstract
>
> Coverage: No dates specified
>
> Availability: Vendor

4.11   *CRISP (Computer Retrieval of Information on Scientific Projects).* Bethesda, MD: National Institutes of Health and the Department of Health and Human Services. Available: crisp.cit.nih.gov

> Scope: Project descriptions for federally funded biomedical research projects.
>
> Record Type: Indexing and abstract
>
> Coverage: 1972–present
>
> Availability: Free

4.12   *Database of Abstracts of Reviews of Effects (DARE).* York, England: Centre for Reviews and Dissemination. Available: www.york.ac.uk/inst/crd/crddatabases.htm#DARE

> Scope: Summaries of systematic reviews which evaluate health care interventions.

Record Type: Indexing and structured summary of original article
Coverage: 1994–present
Availability: Free

4.13   *DIRLINE (Directory of Information Resources Online)*. Bethesda, MD: U.S. National Library of Medicine. Available: dirline.nlm.nih.gov

Scope: Online directory of health sciences information resources including organizations, research resources, projects, and databases.
Record Type: Directory
Coverage: Current
Availability: Free

4.14   *EMBASE*. Amsterdam: Elsevier B.V. Available: www.elsevier.com/wps/product/cws_home/523328

Scope: Broad bibliographic database including medical and pharmacology information published worldwide.
Record Type: Indexing and abstract
Coverage: 1974–present
Availability: Vendor

4.15   *Entrez*. Bethesda, MD: National Center for Biotechnology Information (NCBI). Available: www.ncbi.nlm.nih.gov

Scope: Search interface for multiple databases including *PubMed (MEDLINE)*, *PubMed Central*, *OMIM* (Online Mendelian Inheritance in Man), molecular biology databases (nucleotide, protein, genome, etc.), and the *NLM Catalog*.
Record Type: Varies by database
Coverage: Varies by database
Availability: Free

4.16   *Faculty of 1000*. London: Biology Reports Ltd. Available: www.facultyof1000.com

Scope: Faculty members worldwide select and evaluate what they consider to be the most important articles to be included in the Faculty of 1000 Biology or the Faculty of 1000 Medicine.
Record Type: Indexing and abstract plus full-text user comments
Coverage: 2002–present (Biology); 2006–present (Medicine)
Availability: Vendor

4.17   *Global Health.* Wallingford, England: CABI Publishing. Available: www.cabi.org/datapage.asp?iDocID=169

    Scope: International coverage of public health documents including journal articles, books, reports, and conferences.

    Record Type: Indexing and abstract

    Coverage: 1973–present; archive 1910–1973

    Availability: Vendor

4.18   *Health and Psychosocial Instruments (HaPI).* Pittsburgh: Behavioral Measurement Database Services (BMDS). Available: www.ovid.com/site/products/ovidguide/hapidb.htm

    Scope: Index to research instruments including questionnaires, interview schedules, tests, checklists, rating and other scales, coding schemes, and projective techniques.

    Record Type: Indexing and abstract

    Coverage: 1985–present

    Availability: Vendor

4.19   *images.MD.* Philadelphia, PA: Current Medicine Group LLC. Available: images.md

    Scope: Collection of 50,000+ medical images including photographs, charts, tables, diagrams, microscopy images, and illustrations.

    Record Type: Images with indexing and abstracts

    Coverage: Current

    Availability: Vendor

4.20   *IndexCat.* Bethesda, MD: U.S. National Library of Medicine. Available: indexcat.nlm.nih.gov

    Scope: Online version of the *Index-Catalogue of the Library of the Surgeon General's Office* which indexed monographs and periodical literature.

    Record Type: Indexing

    Coverage: 1880–1961

    Availability: Free

4.21   *Native Health Research Database.* Albuquerque, NM: Indian Health Service and the the University of New Mexico Health Sciences Library and Informatics Center. Available: hscapp.unm.edu/nhd/nhrd_search.cfm

    Scope: Health-related information on American Indians, Alaska Natives, and Canadian First Nations.

Record Type: Indexing and abstract
Coverage: 1966–present
Availability: Free

4.22   *OSH-ROM (Occupational Safety and Health)*. New York: SilverPlatter International. Available: www.ovid.com/site/catalog/DataBase/ 2578.jsp

Scope: Database incorporating seven bibliographic databases covering occupational health and safety information including *OSHLINE, CISDOC, HSELINE, MEDLINE:* Occupational and Environmental Medicine (*MOEM*), *MHIDAS* (Major Hazard Incident Data Service), *NIOSHTIC* and *NIOSHTIC-2*, and *RILOSH* (Ryerson International Labour Occupational Safety and Health) Index.

Record Type: Indexing and abstract
Coverage: 1966–present
Availability: Vendor

4.23   *PDQ*. Bethesda, MD: National Cancer Institute. Available: www. cancer.gov/cancertopics/pdq/cancerdatabase

Scope: Cancer information summaries for health professionals and patients, cancer clinical trials registry, directory of health professionals and organizations involved with cancer.

Record Type: Full-text articles; full-text clinical trials information; directory
Coverage: Current; open, and closed clinical trials
Availability: Free

4.24   *POPLINE (POPulation information onLINE)*. Baltimore, MD: Information & Knowledge for Optimal Health (INFO) Project. Available: db.jhuccp.org/ics-wpd/popweb

Scope: Index to scholarly articles, reports, and books on reproductive health information including population and family planning

Record Type: Indexing and abstract
Coverage: 1970–present
Availability: Free

4.25   *Rare Disease Database*. Danbury, CT: National Organization for Rare Disorders (NORD). Available: www.rarediseases.org/search/ rdbsearch.html

Scope: Information on symptoms, causes, and standard and investigational therapies for rare diseases.

Record Type: Full-text articles

Coverage: Current

Availability: Vendor

4.26 *REHABDATA*. Lanham, MD: National Rehabilitation Information Center. Available: www.naric.com/research/rehab

Scope: Articles, reports and books on disability and rehabilitation topics.

Record Type: Indexing and abstract plus select full-text articles

Coverage: 1956–present

Availability: Free

4.27 *SPORTDiscus*. Ottawa, Canada: Sport Information Resource Centre (SIRC). Available: www.sirc.ca/products/sportdiscus.cfm

Scope: Sport and exercise science including education, therapy, psychology, and law.

Record Type: Indexing and abstract

Coverage: 1975–present; theses 1949–present; selected 1609–present

Availability: Vendor

4.28 *TOXNET (TOXicology Data NETwork)*. Bethesda, MD: U.S. National Library of Medicine. Available: toxnet.nlm.nih.gov

Scope: Extensive toxicology database incorporating thirteen distinct toxicology datasources including *ChemIDPlus*, *HSDB* (Hazardous Substances Data Bank), *TOXLINE* (Toxicology Literature Online), *CCRIS* (Chemical Carcinogenesis Research Information System), *DART* (Developmental and Reproductive Toxicology Database), *GENE-TOX* (Genetic Toxicology), *IRIS* (Integrated Risk Information System), *ITER* (International Toxicity Estimates for Risk), *LactMed* (Drugs and Lactation), *TRI* (Toxics Release Inventory), *Haz-Map*, Household Products Database, and *TOXMAP*.

Record Type: Varies by database

Coverage: Varies by database

Availability: Free

Clinical Reference and Evidence-based Medicine Databases

Clinical reference and evidence-based medicine tools developed in response to information overload. Information overload is the situation where practitioners are faced with exponentially increasing quantities of new information which they are unable to assimilate into clinical care. Clinical reference and evidence-based medicine tools have evolved to help health care providers identify the most useful information, to evaluate information, and to synthesize information in order to make clinical care decisions. The databases in this section use diverse methods to identify, evaluate, and synthesize the most recent and highest quality information, in order that clinicians can apply that information to the care of individual patients.

As the databases in the section are intended for use by clinicians primarily at the point of care, the intention is that these databases represent the current state of knowledge in the health sciences and reflect the highest quality information available. Users assume that new data are integrated into these sources immediately upon its release, and that it is carefully evaluated and appropriately included in or excluded from information resources. However, as users rarely have the time or expertise to evaluate the information tools that they use, librarians must be vigilant in their evaluations to ensure that health care providers have access to the highest quality information and most useful information tools. As librarians evaluate the resources in this section, as well as new resources which provide clinical reference and/or evidence-based medicine information, several specific criteria should be considered: quality of information/levels of evidence, currency, and format.

For some resources (e.g., MDConsult), evaluation can mimic that of a print environment as the components of the electronic resource are digital counterparts of resources which have been traditionally available in a print environment. However as information resources have evolved, new information resources for which no print counterpart exists have developed. For many of these clinical reference tools, the use and application of levels of evidence can form an important evaluation criterion. Level of evidence refers to the quality of the information on which a particular statement or recommendation is being made. The levels of evidence being used in a particular database may be specific to that resource or publisher, or may be based on a system developed for wider use such as the Oxford Centre for Evidence-based Medicine Levels of Evidence [21]. Whichever system is employed, librarians should ensure that it provides adequate information to end users so that they can interpret the information they are presented, and the levels of evidence can be easily referenced to their definitions.

As users will assume that the resources in this section represent the current state of knowledge in the health sciences, librarians should try to select resources that have regular update schedules and systematic methods for assuring that the information is up to date. Librarians should be prepared to elicit specific information from vendors regarding their update process, including the methods and timing of new information being identified, as well as the methods and timing of existing information undergoing review. In the case where a print counterpart is also available, librarians should determine if the online component is merely a digital copy or incorporates ongoing updates and refinements to the original publication.

While the resources in this section are all intended for clinical care, each of the resource has distinct methods of preparing and displaying the information. Some resources may provide information in a textual format that reflects a print counterpart, be it a textbook or journal article. Other resources will synthesize and summarize multiple information sources and provide the data in a range of formats from a brief bulleted list containing only the most essential pieces of information, to a format which displays the available data in brief paragraphs and provides some details of the underlying evidence and the rationale for a statement or recommendation. Librarians evaluating this aspect of clinical reference and evidence-based medicine tools must take into account their specific environment in terms of information need and application, as well as the preferences of the user population they serve.

4.29   *ACP PIER*. Philadelphia, PA: American College of Physicians. Available: pier.acponline.org/index.html

    Scope: Information modules containing brief, evidence-based information on diseases and conditions, ethical and legal issues, procedures, alternative and complementary medicine topics, and screening and prevention information for specific conditions.

    Record Type: Full text; brief bulleted information

    Availability: Vendor

4.30   *Clinical Evidence*. London: BMJ Publishing Group. Available: www.clinicalevidence.com

    Scope: Decision-support tool providing details of evidence for treatments of conditions commonly seen in clinical care. Background information on conditions including definition, incidence, etiology, and prognosis is provided in brief textual format. Evidence on individual therapies is ranked on a scale from "Beneficial" to "Likely to be Ineffective or Harmful," and summarized, including separate sections on possible benefits and harms. All evidence is fully referenced to original studies, and links to practice guidelines are presented.

Record Type: Full text; brief paragraph-format

Availability: Vendor

4.31   *Clinical Queries.* Bethesda, MD: National Center for Biotechnology Information. Available: www.ncbi.nlm.nih.gov/entrez/query/static/clinical.shtml

Scope: Search filters available in PubMed and other MEDLINE interfaces. Search filters work to identify articles by clinical studies category (e.g., etiology, diagnosis, therapy, etc.); to locate systematic reviews; and to conduct medical genetics searches by category (e.g., diagnosis, management, genetic counseling, etc.).

Record Type: Search filters

Availability: Free/Vendor

4.32   *Cochrane Database of Systematic Reviews.* Oxford, England: Cochrane Collaboration. Available: www.cochrane.org

Scope: Systematic reviews describing the evidence available on the effectiveness and appropriateness of treatments of specific conditions. Represent exhaustive and in-depth review of information currently available. Also includes protocols, which are outlines of reviews still being researched and written. Originates from the Cochrane Collaboration, a well-regarded organization devoted to the creation and dispersal of evidence-based information for health care.

Record Type: Full text; lengthy review articles

Availability: Vendor

4.33   *DynaMed.* Ipswich, MA: EBSCO Publishing. Available: www.ebscohost.com/dynamed/

Scope: Clinical topic summaries containing very brief, bulleted information on specific conditions. Topic summaries organized into sections including causes and risk factors, complications, history, physical, diagnosis, prognosis, treatment, and pre-vention/screening. Data is referenced and a list of reviews and practice guidelines is also provided.

Record Type: Full text; brief bulleted information

Availability: Vendor

4.34   *eMedicine*. Omaha, NE: eMedicine.com. Available: www.emedicine.com

Scope: Disease-based review articles including sections on: Introduction (Pathophysiology, Frequency, Morbidity/Mortality, Race, Sex, Age), Clinical (History, Physical, Causes), Differentials, Workup, Treatment (Medical, Surgical, Consultations, Diet, Activity, etc.), Medication, and Follow-Up (In Patient, Out Patient, Patient Education, etc.). Also includes images.

Record Type: Full text; structured review articles

Availability: Free (text information); vendor (also includes images and PDA downloads)

4.35   *FirstCONSULT*. Oxford, England: Elsevier Limited. Available: www.firstconsult.com

Scope: Evidence-based clinical information database. Medical condition files provide information on Background, Diagnosis, Treatment, Outcomes, Prevention, and Resources; evidence is described, ranked by strength (levels of evidence), and fully cited. Differential Diagnosis section works from primary sign/symptom to display possible diagnosis by patient age and in order of descending incidence. Also provides patient education handouts in English and Spanish, and step-by-step information on medical procedures.

Record Type: Full text; bulleted information

Availability: Vendor

4.36   *InfoRetriever with InfoPOEMs*. Hoboken, NJ: John Wiley & Sons. Available: www.infopoems.com/

Scope: Search interface for InfoPOEMs and additional EBM resources which organizes search results by topic (e.g., Over-view, Treatment, Diagnosis, Screening and Prevention, etc.), as well as by the type of information (e.g., practice guideline, InfoPOEM, 5-Minute Clinical Consult, etc.). InfoPOEMs are summary and commentary on recent research studies to identify clinically relevant research and evaluate its validity (InfoPOEMs). EBM resources integrated in InfoRetriever search include Cochrane Database of Systematic Reviews abstracts, practice guidelines, 5-Minute Clinical Consult, and decision-support, history and physical, and diagnostic calculators.

Record Type: Full text; brief paragraph-format (InfoPOEMS); also contains selected full text and links to full-text documents on other Web sites

Availability: Vendor

4.37 *MDConsult.* St. Louis, MO: Elsevier Inc. Available: www.mdconsult.com

Scope: Provides full-text access to collection of textbooks, journals, the Clinics of North America, and practice guidelines, as well as drug information and patient education handouts. Search interface permits users to search by topic or resource type, and search results are sorted by information type (e.g., Reference Books, Images, etc.). Available as Core Collection or in specialty editions (e.g., Pain Medicine, Respiratory and Critical Care Medicine, etc.)

Record Type: Full text; varies by document type

Availability: Vendor

4.38 *National Guideline Clearinghouse.* Rockville, MD: Agency for Health Care Research and Quality. Available: www.guideline.gov

Scope: Database of clinical practice guidelines which are based on systematic research; written reviewed or revised in the past five years; and are published in English. Guidelines can be accessed in numerous formats including Brief Summary, Complete Summary, XML View, Full Text, Palm Download, MS Word, and Adobe PDF.

Record Type: Lengthy structured abstracts; links to full-text documents

Availability: Free

4.39 *UpToDate.* Waltham, MA: UpToDate. Available: www.uptodate.com

Scope: Full-text topic reviews primarily covering conditions and interventions in internal medicine, obstetrics and gynecology,

and pediatrics. Topic reviews are extensively referenced and include images.
Record Type: Full-text review articles
Availability: Vendor

Textbooks Online

As databases that track the primary literature have evolved from indexing and abstracting tools to repositories providing various methods to access full-text documents, textbooks have also evolved. Long-standing standard library resources, textbooks have changed from discrete static volumes, issued periodically, to interconnected dynamic information resources. In both print and online formats, textbooks continue to serve as essential sources of background information for health care students and professionals alike.

Librarians evaluating online textbook databases should consider quality criteria which are specific to the online environment, in addition to using standard methods of evaluating textbooks. Because of their interconnected nature, textbook collections may need to be evaluated both as individual items and as a whole. That an online textbook should be up to date is evident, but librarians and users should also be aware of the difference between accessing a static digital version of a print edition and a dynamic digital document that is updated as new content becomes available.

4.40   *AccessMedicine*. New York, NY: McGraw-Hill Education. Available: www.accessmedicine.com

   Scope: Full-text collection of McGraw-Hill textbooks including the Lange Educational Series. Complementary products include AccessSurgery.

4.41   *Books@Ovid*. New York, NY: Ovid Technologies. Available: www. ovid.com/site/products/books_landing.jsp

   Scope: Full-text access to textbooks purchased by edition or leased by year. Titles may be selected individually or by collection.

4.42   *MDConsult*. St. Louis, MO: Elsevier Inc. Available: www.mdconsult. com

   Scope: Provides full-text access to collection of textbooks, and integrated access to selected full-text journals, the *Clinics of North America*, practice guidelines, drug information, and patient education handouts. Available as Core Collection or in specialty editions (e.g., Pain Medicine, Respiratory and Critical Care Medicine, etc.).

4.43   *R2 Library*. King of Prussia, PA: Rittenhouse Book Distributors. Available: www.rittenhouse.com

> Scope: Full-text access to textbooks that are purchased by edition and form an ongoing part of the library's collection.

4.44   *STAT!Ref Electronic Medical Reference Library*. Jackson, WY: Teton Data Systems. Available: www.statref.com

> Scope: Full-text access to textbooks selected individually. Also provides access to evidence-based medicine database *ACP PIER*.

Consumer Health Databases

As the Web has evolved, consumer health information has emerged as one of the primary types of information which individuals seek on the Web and comprises a substantial portion of all Web searches [22]. While librarians do not need to be familiar with every consumer health database and Web site, they should be able to identify several high-quality consumer health information portals, and readily be able to evaluate unfamiliar Web sites for authority, quality, and currency.

The U.S. government has several authoritative Web portals that link users to high-quality sources of consumer health information. The most extensive of these Web portals is MedlinePlus, which covers a wide range of diseases, conditions, and other health-related topics by linking users to information provided by the National Institutes of Health, other health-related U.S. government entities, and health organizations and associations. Additional federal government Web portals also target specific age groups (e.g., NIHSenior Health.gov), diseases (e.g., AIDSinfo), and ethnic groups (e.g., Asian American Health).

4.45   *MedlinePlus*. Bethesda, MD: U.S. National Library of Medicine. Available: www.medlineplus.gov

Numerous commercial Web sites also provide consumer health information. These health information Web sites are widely used and range from the well-known and reliable (e.g., MayoClinic.com) on a continuum to misleading and biased health information. Librarians and consumers alike must be vigilant in evaluating these Web sites before using the information to avoid obtaining health information that is biased, incomplete, or simply incorrect.

4.46 *MayoClinic.com*. Rochester, MN: Mayo Foundation for Medical Education and Research. Available: www.mayoclinic.com

> Scope: Extensive Web site with consumer information on diseases and conditions, drugs, and healthy living.

4.47 *Medem Medical Library*. San Francisco, CA: Medem, Inc. Available: www.medem.com/medlb/medlib_entry.cfm

> Scope: Library of patient education information from Medem's partner medical societies, including the American Academy of Pediatrics, the American College of Obstetricians and Gynecologists, the American Medical Association, and the American Psychiatric Association.

Vendors: Licensing, Pricing, and Access Issues

As the number and variety of information resources on the Web have exploded, librarians have learned to select resources that will best meet the information needs of their users. Readers will note that some databases described in this chapter are available for free. These resources are frequently provided by a government agency or educational institution which follows a mission of information distribution. Other databases are available through a single or multiple vendors. Wherever possible, the chapter author has made an effort to distinguish the information from the interface, as different libraries will evaluate the interface as well as the license, price, and access issues through the lens of their specific environment. In assessing databases for potential license or purchase, librarians must work cooperatively with vendors in order to acquire licensing terms by which librarians and library users can and will abide, pricing which the library can fiscally support, and access which reflects the library's environment and the needs of the users.

Conclusions

While Google can provide simple answers to simple questions, the range of databases available to health sciences librarians contributes to a more complex landscape. Librarians should be familiar with major research databases such as MEDLINE and Scopus; databases that target a specific type of information (e.g., clinical trials), population (e.g., Native Health Research Database), or discipline (e.g., AMED—Allied and Complementary Medicine Database); databases that serve as clinical information resources; databases that digitize health sciences textbooks; and databases that provide consumer health information. And librarians should keep their eyes on the horizon to identify and follow changes in the patterns of how information is stored and accessed. The number and type of databases and electronic resources will continue to grow and change as non-textual information including images, videos, and audio files are integrated into educational, clinical, and research environments. Changes in the use and acquisition of information will likely be wrought as interactive functions such as collaborating, commenting, and tagging are integrated into existing information resources or evolve into new resources altogether.

References

1. Tang H, Ng JHK. Googling for a diagnosis—use of Google as a diagnostic aid: Internet based study. *Br Med J* 2006; 333(7579):1143–5.
2. Steinbrook R. Searching for the right search—reaching the medical literature. *N Engl J Med* 2006; 354(1):4–7.
3. Tang H, Ng JHK. Use of Google as a diagnostic aid: authors' reply to responses. *Br Med J* 2006; 333(7581):1270.
4. Eysenbach G, Kohler C. What is the prevalence of health-related searches on the World Wide Web? Qualitative and quantitative analysis of search engine queries on the Internet. *AMIA Annu Symp Proc* 2003:225–9.
5. Morahan-Martin JM. How Internet users find, evaluate, and use online health information: a cross-cultural review. *Cyberpsychol Behav* 2004; 7(5): 497–510.
6. Fox S, Rainie L. *Vital decisions: how Internet users decide what information to trust when they or their loved ones are sick* [Web document]. Washington, DC: Pew Internet & American Life Project, 2002. Available: www.pewinternet.org/pdfs/PIP_Vital_Decisions_May2002.pdf. Accessed: 27 June 2007.
7. De Groote SL, Hitchcock K, McGowan R. Trends in reference usage statistics in an academic health sciences library. *J Med Libr Assoc* 2007; 95(1):23–30.
8. Boorkman JA, Huber JT, Roper FW. *Introduction to reference sources in the health sciences.* 4th ed. New York: Neal-Schuman, 2004.
9. Roper FW, Boorkman JA. *Introduction to reference sources in the health sciences.* 3rd ed. Chicago, IL; Metuchen, NJ: Medical Library Association; Scarecrow Press, 1994.

10. *Fact sheet: MEDLINE.* U.S. National Library of Medicine. Available: www.nlm.nih.gov/pubs/factsheets/medline.html. Accessed: 11 December 2006.

11. *Fact sheet: Journal selection for MEDLINE.* U.S. National Library of Medicine. Available: www.nlm.nih.gov/pubs/factsheets/jsel.html. Accessed: 25 August 2006.

12. OLDMEDLINE data. U.S. National Library of Medicine. Available: www.nlm.nih.gov/databases/databases_oldmedline.html. Accessed: 16 March 2007.

13. *Fact sheet: Medical subject headings (MeSH).* U.S. National Library of Medicine. Available: www.nlm.nih.gov/pubs/factsheets/mesh.html. Accessed: 27 June 2007.

14. *Fact sheet: PubMed: MEDLINE retrieval on the World Wide Web.* U.S. National Library of Medicine. Available: www.nlm.nih.gov/pubs/factsheets/pubmed.html. Accessed: 11 December 2006.

15. *The CINAHL database.* CINAHL Information Systems. Available: www.cinahl.com/prodsvcs/prodsvcs.htm. Accessed: 27 June 2007.

16. *Seize the power with the CINAHL database.* CINAHL Information Systems. Available: www.cinahl.com/prodsvcs/prodsvcs.htm. Accessed: 27 June 2007.

17. Wolfe C. International pharmaceutical abstracts: what's new and what can IPA do for you? *Am J Health Syst Pharm* 2002; 59(23):2360–1.

18. Fishman DL, Stone VL, DiPaula BA. Where should the pharmacy researcher look first? Comparing International Pharmaceutical Abstracts and MEDLINE. *Bull Med Libr Assoc* 1996; 84(3):402–8.

19. *PsycINFO database information.* American Psychological Association. Available: www.apa.org/psycinfo/products/psycinfo.html. Accessed: 27 June 2007.

20. *Scopus in detail: what does it cover?* Elsevier B.V. Available: www.info.scopus.com/detail/what/. Accessed: 27 June 2007.

21. Oxford Centre for Evidence-Based Medicine levels of evidence, May 2001. Available: www.cebm.net/index.aspx?o=1047. Accessed: 27 June 2007.

22. Eysenbach, op. cit.

CHAPTER 5

U.S. Government Documents and Technical Reports

Melody M. Allison

Government Documents

Typically government information is seen as synonymous with lawmaking, and indeed this is a major function of our government. In addition, the three branches of federal government each have their own operations with documents that relate to their activities. The federal government is an immensely rich source of information related to activities that are funded by its branches, offices, institutes, agencies, and other entities. It invests billions of dollars into research and development in the sciences, making it an important if not essential source of information for a variety of scientific areas. There are no better examples than those that relate to health care.

Each year the U.S. Department of Health and Human Services (HHS) supports biomedical research through nearly 75,000 grants totaling approximately $250 billion [1–2]. A great deal of health care information can be located from the Web sites of those governmental entities that supported the research. Examples of the types of health information resources that can be accessed from these sites are government-funded research report summaries and technical reports (see "Technical Reports" section that follows this section), health topic fact sheets, topic summaries, newsletters, listservs, bibliographies and other compilations, bibliographic indexes and databases, research summaries, and in some cases the complete full text of research and legislative/regulatory publications. But this does not entail all the information output produced by public monies. Currently much of the publicly funded re-search is disseminated through scholarly journal publication. Private publish-ers take the submitted work of researchers/authors, including ownership (copyright), and distribute through a fee-based publication system. A large constituency of library, academic, and consumer organizations have joined forces to advocate for free access to publicly taxpayer-funded research, through such proposed legislation as the Federal Research Public Access Act [3]. Public access advocacy groups feel that free public access is a right of taxpayers who fund research, and that it will promote wider dissemination, and use, of the latest research by anyone, not just those who can afford the price of publications. There are a number of issues concerning the viability of this model of research dissemination, and it remains to be seen if this will become the standard in the future.

Another important source of government information is the U.S. Govern-ment Printing Office (GPO), which is "the Federal Government's primary centralized resource for gathering, cataloging, producing, providing and pre-serving published information in all its forms" [4]. Official information from all three branches of government, such as the *Congressional Record, House Journal, U.S. Code, Congressional Serial Set*, and *Code of Federal Regulations*, is distributed by the GPO, which provides electronic access to a growing amount of these information products via its online *GPO Access* at: www.gpoaccess.gov/service [5–6]. Official government records can be an important source of health care information. For instance, access to information about legislation, such as the Medicare prescription drug benefit program or the inclusion of women in biomedical research and drug analysis by the U.S. Food and Drug Administration, can be important for both health care consumers and professionals. In partnership with the GPO, the Federal Depository Library Program (FDLP), a program of the GPO Office of Information Dissemination (SuDocs), provides free access to our government's information through by disseminating "information products from all three branches of the Government to over 1,250 [Federal depository] libraries nationwide" [7–8].

The federal government has historically been concerned with distribution of government information to its constituents. The early founders of the United States felt that it was necessary for citizens to know what the govern-ment was doing in order for them to fully and knowledgably participate in their democracy. The Act of 1813 was the first directive for Congress to provide copies of its documents to "to each university and college, and to each incorporated historical society in each state" [9]. Distribution to depository sites was carried out by various governmental entities until 1969 when the Superintendent of Documents position was expressly created to oversee the program [10]. By the latter 1850's each state was authorized to have one depository library; this was increased to two per congressional district by the Depository Act of 1962 [11].

The federal government's Depository FDLP collects, maintains, preserves, and assists users with federal government information through depository libraries across the nation [12]. There are over 1,300 federal depository libraries around the country administered by the GPO's Superintendent of Documents. The depository libraries are found in various types of libraries: academic, public, law, community college, federal agency, state, state and federal court, special and military service libraries [13]. There are two types of depositories— selective and regional. Both types receive free FDLP publications, including a core collection of titles, which they must make available to the public. In addition each type has different responsibilities to their collections. Selective depository libraries collect titles based on local needs and interests; these titles can be selected at any percentage of the total number available [14] and must be retained for at least five years [15]. Regional libraries (currently 53) must collect all FDLP titles and keep them permanently [16]. They also must provide additional public services, such as training and consultation [17].

Originally created in 1860 to print congressional papers, the GPO evolved into its current framework when the Printing Act of 1895 expanded the distribution of depository documents to include all government printing, and its Office of the Superintendent of Documents was moved to the GPO [18–19]. Although the GPO has the "largest information processing, printing, and distribution facility in the world" and produces very important information products such as the *Congressional Record* and the *Federal Register*, the majority of products are printed through arrangements with private sector printers from all 50 states [20].

The Government Printing Office Electronic Information Access Enhancement Act of 1993 (P.L. 103–40) required the GPO Superintendent of Documents, under the direction of the GPO Public Printer, "to establish in the Government Printing Office a means of enhancing electronic public access to a wide range of Federal electronic information," including to:

1. maintain an electronic directory of Federal electronic information;

2. provide a system of online access to the *Congressional Record*, the *Federal Register*, and, as determined by the Superintendent of Documents,

other appropriate publications distributed by the Superintendent of Documents; and

3. operate an electronic storage facility for Federal electronic information to which online access is made available under paragraph [21].

This Act prompted the monumental metamorphosis of government publications from print to online distribution and culminated in the creation of GPO Access [22].

Because currently over 60 percent of new depository items are provided online, the Federal Library Council, a group that advises on FDLP policy concerns, has explored the future role of the FDLP in federal government information provision including the possibility of a virtual depository library [23–25]. Although there are well-established methods of organizing and disseminating print materials in the FDLP, there are no such consistent standards and central infrastructure for organizing and disseminating the federal government's ever-expanding electronic information resources [26]. One response to this dilemma is the GPO's Future Digital Information System (FDsys), which is expected to be fully operational in late 2007. This system will contain all known print and digital federal government documents within the FDLP scope. Mechanisms for creation, submission, authentication, management, dissemination, migration, and preservation of content will be done using consistent methods and standards. It will also use "'smart' search" technologies to retrieve results that are accurate and relevant [27].

Government information is a challenge to deal with for several reasons. Standards and methods for information organization and location vary considerably from entity to entity. One cannot extrapolate the content organization from one entity Web site to another, making it necessary to learn how to find similar kinds of content type from site to site. Although Web sites such as USASearch.gov allow a federated search of multiple government sites, a search of the individual entities is the prudent thing to do for a comprehensive inventory of related information topics from more than one government source.

In addition, the names of federal government entities can be very confusing, sometimes seem redundant, and even have the same name abbreviation. For instance, there is the Office on Women's Health (OWH), the Office of Research on Women's Health (ORWH), and Office of Women's Health (OWH). If the sponsoring agent is not provided, it can take considerable finesse to find out who it is. In this example they are respectively the Department of Health and Human Services (HHS), the National Institutes of Health

(NIH), and the Food and Drug Administration (FDA). Not knowing the exact wording, including preposition, can make a significant difference in accessing information from each source [28–30].

The terms used for government information types can be no less confusing. In one place a title may be called a "document" and a similar title elsewhere may be called a "publication." Many times they are used interchangeably in the same publication or from the same source. Exactly what is the difference between a government document, government publication, and government information? "Government publication" is defined by Title 44—Public Printing and Documents, Chapter 19—Depository Library Program as "informational matter which is published as an individual document at Government expense, or as required by law" [31]. The Title 44 title refers to "documents" but does not include a definition of "document." Instead it defines "Government publication" which is referred to as a "document."

International and European entities such as the United Nations (UN) and the European Union (EU) adhere to a strict interpretation of what a document is. For instance, the United Nations define a document as "a text submitted to a principal organ or a subsidiary organ of the United Nations for consideration by it, usually in connection with item(s) on its agenda," and a UN publication as "any written material which is issued by or for the United Nations to the general public, normally under the authorization of the Publications Board" [32]. The UN Official Document System (ODS) includes parliamentary documentation and official records, such as meeting records, resolutions, and reports; it does not include sales publications, press releases, or public information materials [33–34]. The European Union refers to legislation, proposals, communications, reports, and green and white papers as documents [35] and asserts that access to documents should not be confused with access to information [36].

The American Heritage Dictionary of the English Language (4th ed.) defines "publication" as the "1) act or process of publishing printed matter; 2) an issue of printed material offered for sale or distribution; or 3) communication of information to the public" [37]. "Document" is defined as the "1) written or printed paper that bears the original, official, or legal form of something and can be used to furnish decisive evidence or information; 2) something, such as a recording or a photograph, that can be used to furnish evidence or information; or 3) a writing that contains information" [38]. The concept "document" can become even more confusing with regard to electronic information, where the term "document" can be used to refer to electronic files of any type, or for specific application types, such as "Word document" [39].

The more exacting interpretation of "document" will guide the content selection for this chapter. That is to say, resources that point to legislation, regulations, court decisions, reports, and other formal unclassified documents from the three branches of the federal government will be included. Government information and publications such as fact sheets, topic summaries, newsletters, listservs, bibliographies and other compilations, and bibliographic indexes and databases will be covered in appropriate chapters of this book. For instance, government statistics are covered in Chapter 11, "Medical and Health Statistics," and health information from the diverse and many agencies and offices of the U.S. Department of Health and Human Services (HHS) is covered in Chapter 10, "Consumer Health Sources."

Knowledge about how our government is organized and what information products are produced will bring considerable order to what may seem to be overwhelming chaos. In addition to a growing amount of full-text government information directly available online, there are many bibliographic resources to bring order and control over the vast amount of government information that is created. On those occasions when success is limited, or remains elusive or overwhelming, assistance is as close as contact with a federal depository librarian.

5.1   Hernon P, Relyea HC, Dugan RE, & Cheverie JF. *United States Government Information: Policies and Sources.* Westport, CT: Libraries Unlimited, 2002.

5.2   Maxymuk J. *Government Online: One-Click Access to 3,400 Federal and State Web Sites.* New York: Neal-Schuman, 2001.

5.3   Morehead J. *Introduction to United States Government Information Sources.* 6th ed. Englewood, CO: Libraries Unlimited, 1999.

5.4   Robinson JS. *Tapping the Government Grapevine: The User Friendly Guide to U.S. Government Information Sources.* 3rd ed. Phoenix, AZ: Oryx Press, 1998.

5.5   Sears JL, Moody MK. *Using Government Information Sources: Electronic and Print.* 3rd ed. Phoenix, AZ: Oryx Press, 2001.

In addition to identifying basic federal government information sources, the *United States Government Information: Policies and Sources* covers government information policies, all within a historical framework. Coverage includes information about all three branches of government, agencies, information finding aids, privacy protection, the Freedom of Information Act, government publishing, depository library programs, paperwork reduction, and electronic government. Although very limited coverage of health related topics (e.g., Health Insurance Portability and Accountability Act [HIPAA] and heath statistics), this work is extremely valuable in understanding how the federal government is organized and works, past and present. This important work was created as a tool to help make the vast wealth of government information, which has publications on most every topic, more accessible and thus more utilized by the public and professionals. A CD-ROM is included which contains reprints of key documents cited in print volume, digital copies of select historical out-of-print documents, tutorials, examples of concepts from print volume, exercises, and questions and answers about government information.

Government Online provides a very good overview of policy and legislative history concerning the Government Printing Office (GPO), Federal Depository Library Program (FDLP), and National Technical Information Service (NTIS) including the affects of the Internet on these entities. There are several chapters on government information sources from specific subject areas. A Health and Medicine chapter begins with an Agencies Web site Map which lists the government entities hierarchically. The names and URLs are provided for each entry along with a brief narrative followed by a list of Web site highlights. Entities are provided from the legislative and executive branches of the federal government; the Departments of Agriculture, Energy, Health and Human Services, Labor, and Veterans Affairs; as well as interagency sites. This title is somewhat dated (2001) but still useful.

Introduction to United States Government Information Sources, 6th ed., is an important guide to details about government information. A concise history of the Government Printing Office, the Federal Depository Library Program, and the transformation of government information from print to online distribution is presented. Information about finding aids and reference sources that includes current and retrospective bibliographies, catalogs, and indexes is provided. The legislative process is described and related to congressional documents and publications, as are activities emanating from the Executive Office and the federal court system. Additionally statistical sources are covered as well as intellectual property sources for patents, trademarks, and copyright. A small number of federal departments and agencies are discussed, including the National Technical Information Service (NTIS) but no specific health-related ones. Although health related information cannot be found directly in this title, one can certainly get informed about government processes and resources in general and search for health-related information using this knowledge. Time has marched on since this edition was published in 2002, but there is much of value here about basic governmental workings and information resources.

Tapping the Government Grapevine, 3rd ed., is a highly regarded work that covers all aspects of government information resources. A detailed introduction and overview is presented, including information about the Government Printing Office (GPO), Federal Depository Library Program (FDLP), and National Technical Information Service (NTIS). Specific resources are described along with illustrations, search and access tips, further readings, and other useful information. Coverage of health-related government resources is weak in this work. What health-related biomedical information that is available can be found in the "Scientific Information" chapter. Here one can find references to databases (mostly MEDLINE) from the National Library of Medicine (NLM), a few clearinghouses (Healthfinder.gov, National Health Information Center, and the Combined Health Information Database), the Congressional Information Service's *Index to Health Information*, and the National Institute for Occupational Safety and Health. Although this guide provides essential reading to get oriented to the universe of government information resources, it is in need of update. A *great deal* of change has happened since 1998 and will make for considerable revision. Sections concerning government publications relating to health care could easily take up an entire chapter or more in the next edition.

Using Government Information Sources: Electronic and Print, 3rd ed., not only provides basic and important sources of government information, it also delivers search strategies to research and locate other information. Each of the 53 chapters is based on a topic and particular search strategy—subject, agency, statistical, or special techniques—on a variety of topics. Checklists give the user a number of commonly used resources for the topic. The "Health" chapter provides checklists of common resources and discussions for general health sources, general health statistics sources, and sources on diseases, alcohol, drugs, smoking, mental health, children, aging, and disability. Although this work would benefit from being updated, it is still a valuable tool to locate a wide range of government information.

5.6   *Catalog of U.S. Government Publications (CGP)*. Washington, DC: U.S. Government Printing Office, 1976–. (Electronic counterpart of the *Monthly Catalog of the United States Government Publications*). Available: catalog.gpo.gov/F

5.7   *Monthly Catalog of the United States Government Publications.* Washington, DC: U.S. Government Printing Office, 1895–. Monthly; annual cumulative indexes.

The *Catalog of U.S. Government Publications (CGP)* is "the finding tool for electronic and print publications from the legislative, executive, and judicial branches of the U.S. government," both current and historical. (Welcome) The CGP contains more than 500,000 records dating from July 1976. Updates are daily. For records from original issue in 1895 to 1976, the print version entitled *Monthly Catalog of United States Government Publications* must be used. (Welcome) Links to online versions of documents are provided when available.

A principal component of the CGP is the *National Bibliography of U.S. Government Publications* [40]. Since 1976, over 337,000 records for federal publications have been contributed to OCLC WorldCat, "resulting in a de facto national bibliography for U.S. Government publications" [41]. Due to a number of access concerns, including multiple records for the same resource and inability to limit just to federal government information, and in keeping with its statutory requirements, the GPO made the decision to create the *National Bibliography of U.S. Government Publications*, a comprehensive catalog of unclassified U.S. government information [42]. The *National Bibliography of U.S. Government Publications* is comprised of publications from the CGP, and includes "any information product, regardless of form or format, that any U.S. Government agency discloses, publishes, disseminates, or makes available to the public, as well as information produced for administrative or operational purposes that is of public interest or educational value" [43].

National bibliographic standards such as *Anglo-American Cataloguing Rules*, 2nd ed.; *Library of Congress Rule Interpretations*; MARC21; CONSER; OCLC's *Bibliographic Formats and Standards*, 2nd ed.; and *GPO Cataloging Guidelines* are used to create CGP records. Catalog records include: title, publisher information, SuDoc number, item number, variation in title, edition, description, abstract, system details, subject, and subjec—LC, holdings, OCLC number, and system number.

The CGP can be searched using either Basic or Advanced Search features. The Basic Search allows keyword, title, author, and subject searches. The Advanced Search provides three concept boxes, each of which can be limited to one of many record fields. This search can be limited by year(s), format, and language. The Help page provides guidance to searching subsets and library locations, including: *Congressional Serial Set Catalog* (July 1976–), *Congressional Publications Catalog* (July 1976–), *GPO Access Publications* catalog (1994–), *Internet Publications* catalog (July 1976–), *Periodicals* catalog (1976–), and *Serials* catalog (1976–). Links to electronic versions are provided when available. Also a "Locate in a Library" feature can be used to find a Federal depository library with a hard copy of the title or to locate assistance.

5.8   *U.S. Government Bookstore.* Washington, DC: Government Printing Office, 2007. Available: bookstore.gpo.gov/

The U.S. Government Bookstore is the "official online bookstore for U.S. Government publications for purchase from the U.S. Government Printing Office." Items from the *Catalog of U.S. Government Publications (CGP)* that are not available electronically, or when a personal copy is desired, can be purchased here. The Bookstore can be searched by subject, keyword, stock number, or title; or browsed by subject. Health-related subjects include aging, cancer, diseases, health care, mental health, nutrition, physical fitness, physically challenged, safety, and substance abuse. Orders can be submitted via online, fax, phone, or mail.

5.9   *U.S. Government Accountability Office Reports and Testimony.* Washington, DC: U.S. General Accounting Office, 1971–. Available: www.gao.gov/

The Government Accountability Office (GAO), formerly General Accounting Office, is an independent, nonpartisan agency that evaluates audits, investigates, and provides legal decisions and opinions regarding government policies and procedures, operations, and other activities for Congress to use in their oversight role. This includes research about health topics and issues. Reports and congressional testimony of these endeavors can be searched by keyword or report number in a search box on the upper right corner of any GAO Web page. Once this is done, Advanced Searches becomes an option. There are four search boxes with the title, keyword, summary, subject field options as well as limits for date(s). Reports and testimonies can be browsed by date, topic (e.g., Health), or agency (e.g., Department of Health and Human Services).

GAO Reports from 1993 to the present can also be searched from GPO Access search engine at http://www.gpoaccess.gov/gaoreports/index.html. A

Quick Search can be done for reports from 2006. A Simple Search can be done limited by topic category and date(s). An Advanced Search can be done limited by topic category, issue date, report number, report title, and subject terms.

5.10   *THOMAS*. Washington, DC: Library of Congress. Available: www. thomas.gov

THOMAS is a free Library of Congress service that provides federal legislative information to the public, such as bills/resolutions, congressional activity, access to the *Congressional Record*, schedules/calendars, and committee information. Bill texts and Public Laws can be searched by Congress (101–present) or browsed by sponsor. Appropriations Bills can be browsed by year (1998–present). Links to information about current legislative activities is accessible from the homepage.

Technical Reports

The federal government sponsors a vast amount of research and development (R&D) through universities, corporations, and other organizations. Outlays for the conduct of non-defense research and development total nearly 50 billion dollars, including nearly $30 billion expended by the National Institutes of Health; almost a half of a million dollars of the total non-defense outlays goes to grants [44]. Reports that include technical details are generated to document progress and results of this research, as well as to account for these expenditures of public monies. Technical reports may be comprehensive in coverage about the research or brief summaries; they may cover preliminary, progress, or final results. Publications may not be easily recognized as technical reports; contract/grant number and accession/report series codes can be bibliographic indicators [45].

In recognition of the public's need, and right, to have access to unclassified information that it financially supports, the federal government through *U.S. Code 15 USC Sec. 3704b-2: Transfer of Federal Scientific and Technical Information* mandates that executive departments and agencies provide R&D results to the National Technical Information Service (NTIS) for dissemination to the public [46–47]. Although this code mandates that information about research supported by executive branch agencies is to be provided to NTIS, a GAO report found that this is not always done [48]. At the time of the report GAO found 19 percent of NTIS technical reports could also be acquired from the issuing agency, Google.com, FirstGov.gov, or the GPO, with 37 percent of these available for free the organization's Web site [49]. This likelihood increased exponentially since 1988, particularly for availability of technical reports from their issuing organization [50]. These actualities have raised questions about whether a central, self-sustaining repository is the suitable way for dissemination of technical reports to the public, which has implications for the relevance and future of NTIS [51]. The National Commission on Libraries and Information Science (NCLIS) concluded in a study that the NTIS should be retained for "fail-safe" permanent access and proper bibliographic control of research results [52]. They additionally recommended that rather than be self-sustaining, the NTIS should be funded by Congress to acquire, maintain, and provide free access to the full text to these reports [53–54].

Locating technical reports is still not a "one-stop shopping" venture. As "the largest central resource for government-funded scientific, technical, engineering, and business information available today," the NTIS is *the* clearinghouse for related technical reports and the first place to begin searches [55]. Although the goal of the NTIS is to fulfill its legislative mandate to be the clearinghouse for government-funded research information, there are a variety of reasons that relevant reports do not find their way to NTIS. As part of a comprehensive search strategy, it is also important to "consider the source." Government agencies may provide access to technical reports for research that they have sponsored, sometimes without charge. Other stops along the journey include portals such as CRISP (Computer Retrieval of Information on Scientific Products), Federal R&D Project Summaries, GrayLIT Network, and Information Bridge as well as bibliographic databases such as PubMed. Although it is not a major source of technical reports, the Government Printing Office (GPO) may have selected technical reports from federal agencies and thus be indexed in the *Catalog of U.S. Government Publications (CGP)* and available through the federal depository libraries system [56]. Depository librarians are nonetheless important resources to assist in locating technical reports using their expertise and knowledge about government resources as well as their access to NTIS Database subscription via commercial vendors. Current advocacy for public access to results from publicly financed research, such as the National Institutes of Health (NIH) *Policy on Enhancing Public Access to Archived Publications Resulting from NIH-Funded Research (Public Access Policy)*, along with technological advancements, holds great anticipation for improved access to technical reports and other government information [57].

5.11   *CRISP (Computer Retrieval of Information on Scientific Projects).* Bethesda, MD: Office of Extramural Research, National Institutes of Health, Department of Health and Human Services, 2007. Available: crisp.cit.nih.gov/

The CRISP database contains records (1972–present) for biomedical R&D support to universities, hospitals, and other research institutions by government agencies within the Department of Health and Human Services (HHS). The CRISP search engine allows a great deal of flexibility with multiple field and limits options. Although full text of technical reports is not available, the project details can be used for further investigation and inquiries.

5.12   *DTIC Public STINET (Scientific & Technical Information Network).* Ft. Belvoir, VA: Defense Technical Information Center (DTIC), 2007. Available: stinet.dtic.mil/

Defense Technical Information Center's (DTIC) Technical Reports Collection on "Public STINET" provides access to unclassified report citations and several full text reports from the Department of Defense (DOD). The U.S. Department of Defense (DOD) research interests encompass a number of areas outside military science, including biological and medical sciences. Quick, guided, or advanced searches can be performed. Limited or classified information requires registration by eligible entities, as does ordering printed documents. Unregistered public users can order DTIC unclassified, unlimited documents from the National Technical Information Service (NTIS) (see NTIS "Customer Service at a Glance" at: www.ntis.gov/help/cs_ov.asp). Minimal fees are charged for DTIC technical reports.

5.13   *Federal R&D Project Summaries.* Oak Ridge, TN: Department of Energy, Office of Scientific and Technical Information, 2007. Available: www.osti.gov/fedrnd/

This portal allows searching of over 750,000 records from databases at the Department of Energy, the National Institutes of Health, the National Science Foundation, the Environmental Protection Agency, the Small Business Administration, and the U.S. Department of Agriculture. Agency databases can be searched individually or in any combination. Records contain research project information such as grant number, project title, primary investigator details, research site, abstract, thesaurus terms, project dates, and agency sponsor. Although complete full text of technical reports are not available through these databases, the project details can be used for further investigation and inquiries.

5.14 *GrayLIT Network: A Science Portal of Technical Reports*. Oak Ridge, TN: Department of Energy, Office of Scientific and Technical Information, 2007. Available: www.osti.gov/graylit/

The GrayLit Network is "the most comprehensive portal to Federal gray literature" providing access to over 100,000 full text technical reports. The Department of Defense (DOD)/Defense Technical Information Center (DTIC), Department of Energy (DOE), Environmental Protection Agency (EPA), and National Aeronautics and Space Administration (NASA) are participating in this DOE Office of Scientific and Technical Information (OSTI) endeavor; expansion to additional participants is anticipated. Federated searching allows searches of individual or multiple collections.

5.15 *Information Bridge: DOE Scientific and Technical Information*. Oak Ridge, TN: U.S. Dept. of Energy (DOE), Office of Scientific and Technological Information (OSTI); and Washington, DC: U.S. Government Printing Office (GPO), 2007. Available: www.osti.gov/bridge/

Information Bridge provides access to research report citations and full text Department of Energy (DOE) and related documents in physics, chemistry, biology, environmental cleanup, energy technologies, and other topics from 1994 to the present.

5.16 *NASA Technical Reports Server (NTRS): Search NTRS*. Washington, DC: National Aeronautics and Space Administration, 2006. Available: ntrs.nasa.gov/search.jsp

The National Aeronautics and Space Administration (NASA) Technical Reports Server (NTRS) is a database of NASA's technical literature. NTRS includes the NACA (1915–1958), NASA (1958–present), and NASA Image eXchange (NIX) (1900–present) collections. Searches can be limited to technical reports by clicking on "Technical Report" and then using the search options to enter search terms and other navigation options. Links are included to full text pdfs when available. In addition to technical reports, lots of different types of materials are indexed, including images/photos, NACA reports, preprints, theses, dissertations, conference papers, NASA Reports, and movies.

5.17   *National Technical Information Service (NTIS).* Springfield, VA: U.S. Department of Commerce, Technology Administration. Available: www.ntis.gov/

The National Technical Information Service (NTIS) with its 3,000,000+ products (publications, technical reports, computer products, databases, and other product types) is the "largest central resource for government-funded scientific, technical, engineering, and business related information," which includes health-related areas such as biomedical technology and health care. The Department of Health and Human Services is one of over 200 federal agencies that NTIS collects information from. NTIS responsibilities include collecting and distributing unclassified government-sponsored research as well as assuring its archival via a permanent repository.

NTIS is a self-sustaining agency and recoups its costs through fees for its products and services. Information for over 600,000 publication products since 1990 can be searched and, when available, purchased from the NTIS Web site. Many purchased publication products may be downloaded via a link from the online item record. Formats vary from paper, CD, microfiche, multimedia, downloadable products (1997–present), and other format types. When an item requires a phone order, a contact phone order number is provided. More ordering, payment, and other related information is provided on the Web site. Links to free full-text publication from the source agency's Web site may be found on selected records. Covered by NTIS reports are anatomy; behavior and society; biochemistry; biomedical instrumentation and bioengineering; biomedical technology and human factors engineering; bionics and artificial intelligence; clinical medicine; cytology; genetics, and molecular biology; government inventions— biology and medicine; health and safety; several health care categories; medicine and biology; medicine and biology electrophysiology; occupational therapy, physical therapy, and rehabilitation; physiology; psychiatry; psychology; public health and industrial medicine; radiation shielding, protection, and safety; radiobiology; tissue preservation and storage; surgery; and toxicology.

A "Health and Safety Collection" is accessible from the NTIS Web site from the "Product Families" link under "Products We Offer." This collection of over 20,000 federal agency publications on health and safety topics from 1990 to present can be searched by category topic and/or keywords.

With over 2 million bibliographic records, the NTIS Database is *the* resource for identifying U.S.-sponsored research from 1964 to the present. The NTIS Database receives federally-funded scientific, technical, and engineering information within ten days of public availability. It also contains titles from state and local governments, academic institutions, private sector organizations, foreign governments, and international organizations. NTIS leases the NTIS Database through several commercial vendors. Update frequency of this database depends on the commercial vendor although NTIS provides updates weekly to the vendors. NTIS Database document requests can be made by phone, fax, e-mail, or Web site (see NTIS Web site). A free NTIS Database Search Guide can be accessed via the NTIS Web site.

5.18   *NSCEP/NEPIS—EPA's Gateway to Free Digital & Paper Publications.* U.S. Environmental Protection Agency, 2007. Available: www.epa.gov/ncepihom/

Through its many research programs, the EPA is an important source of health information related to the effects of pollution on health. Over 24,000 free electronic Environmental Protection Agency (EPA) titles, including technical reports, are available from the EPA's National Environmental Publications Internet Site (NEPIS) database. Caveat: In the current database version, limiting to a particular publication type, such as technical reports, is possible in only the broadest of senses through a phrase search using the term "technical report." No other concepts can be added to this phrase in a Boolean or other type of search, so the search results contain all items within the selected date ranges. With time and patience, locating technical reports may be achievable by browsing a regular search or submitting a known technical report title. Publications and other information of regional and state EPAs can be found via the site's "Where You Live" link. When electronic full text publications are not available, they can be ordered from the National Center for Environmental Publications (NSCEP) online, by phone, by fax, or by mail.

5.19   *PubMed.* Bethesda, MD: U.S. National Library of Medicine. Available: pubmed.gov.

PubMed provides access to technical report citations for a wide-range of biomedical topics using its "Publication Type" Limit: "Technical Report." Topics, both keyword and Medical Subject Headings (MeSH), are used with Boolean search techniques to define types of technical reports that are being sought. As with periodical titles of all publication types indexed in PubMed, there may be access to full text of technical reports available via the free digital biomedical literature archive PubMed Central (PMC) or via the local institution's e-journal subscriptions which are linked to PubMed citations. There may be additional related "Publication Types" such as "Research Support, Non-U.S. Gov't" and "Evaluation Studies" in addition to "Technical Report."

References

1. U.S. Department of Health and Human Services. *Welcome to GrantsNet*. [Web document]. The Department. Available: www.hhs.gov/grantsnet/Intro Welcome.htm. Accessed: 23 March 2007.
2. U.S. Department of Health and Human Services. *About HHS Grants*. [Web document]. The Department. Available: www.hhs.gov/grantsnet/FundAbout. htm. Accessed: 23 March 2007.
3. The Alliance for Taxpayer *Access. ATA*. [Web document]. The Alliance, 2007. Available: www.taxpayeraccess.org/frpaa/. Accessed: 23 Mar 2007.
4. U.S. Government Printing Office (GPO). *GPO facts: FAQ (frequently asked questions)*. [Web document]. Washington, DC: The Office, 2007. Available: www.gpo.gov/factsheet/index.html. Accessed: 23 March 2007.
5. Ibid.
6. U.S. Government Printing Office (GPO). *About GPO Access*. [Web document]. Washington, DC: The Office, 2007. Available: www.gpoaccess.gov/about/index.html. Accessed: 23 March 2007.
7. U.S. GPO. *GPO facts*. Op. cit.
8. U.S. Government Printing Office (GPO). *About the Federal Depository Library Program (FDLP)*. [Web document]. Washington, DC: The Office, 2007. Available: www.gpoaccess.gov/fdlp.html. Accessed: 23 March 2007.
9. Kling RE. *The Government Printing Office*. New York: Praeger Publishers, 1970:11.
10. Ibid.
11. U.S. Government Printing Office (GPO). *Keeping America informed: Federal Depository Library Program*. [Web document]. Washington, DC: The Office, 2007.Available: www.gpo.gov/su_docs/fdlp/pr/keepam.html. Accessed: 23 March 2007.
12. U.S. Government Printing Office (GPO). *About the FDLP*. [Web document]. Washington, DC: The Office, 2007. Available: www.access.gpo.gov/su_docs/fdlp/about.html. Accessed: 23 March 2007.
13. U.S. GPO. *Keeping America informed*. Op. cit.
14. Robinson JS. *Tapping the government grapevine*. 3rd ed. Phoenix, AZ: Oryx Press, 1998.
15. McGarr SM. *FDLP Desktop: Snapshots of the Federal Depository Library Program*. [Web document]. Washington DC: U.S. Government Printing Office, 2000. Available: www.gpo.gov/su_docs/fdlp/history/snapshot.html. Accessed: 23 March 2007.

16. Ibid.
17. Robinson JS, op. cit.
18. McGarr SM, op. cit.
19. U.S. GPO. *Keeping America informed*. Op. cit.
20. U.S. GPO. *GPO facts*. Op. cit.
21. Government Printing Office Electronic Information Access Enhancement Act of 1993. (P.L. 103–40 [S. 564]), United States Public Laws. 103rd Cong., 1st sess., June 8, 1993.
22. Depository Library Council. *The federal government information environment of the 21st Century: towards a vision statement and plan of action for federal depository libraries*. Discussion Paper. [Web document]. The Council, 2005. Available: www.gpo.gov/su_docs/fdlp/pubs/dlc_vision_09_02_2005.pdf. Accessed: 23 March 2007.
23. Rawan, A, Malone CK. A virtual depository: the Arizona project. Government Printing Office's transition to a more electronic format and its impact on the collection and reference services. *Ref Libr* 2006; 45(94): 5–18.
24. Depository Library Council. *Responses to recommendations. Depository Library Council, Fall 2001*. [Web document]. The Council, 2001. Available: www.access.gpo.gov/su_docs/fdlp/council/rfa01.html. Accessed: 23 March 2007.
25. Depository Library Council. *Knowledge will forever govern: a vision statement for Federal Depository Libraries in the 21st Century, Final Version*. [Web document]. The Council, 2006. Available: www.access.gpo.gov/su_docs/fdlp/pubs/proceedings/06fall/vision-document.pdf. Accessed: 23 March 2007.
26. Ibid.
27. U.S. Government Printing Office, FDsys Team. *Future digital information system (FDsys)*. [Web document). Washington, DC: The Team, 2007. Available: www.gpo.gov/projects/fdsys.htm. Accessed: 23 March 2007.
28. Office on Women's Health, U.S. Department of Health and Human Services. *About Us.* [Web document]. Washington, DC: The Office. Available: www.4women.gov/OWH/about. Accessed: 23 March 2007.
29. Office of Research on Women's Health, National Institutes of Health. *About ORWH*. Bethesda, MD: The Office. Available: http//orwh.od.nih.gov/about. Accessed: 23 March 2007.
30. Office of Women's Health, U.S. Food and Drug Administration. *About the FDA and its Office of Women's Health*. [Web document]. Rockville, MD: The Office. Available: www.fda.gov/womens/programs. Accessed: 23 March 2007.
31. Federal Depository Library Program. *FDLP Desktop: Title 44—Public Printing and Documents, Chapter 19—Depository Library Program*. [Web document]. The Program, 2000. Available: www.gpo.gov/su_docs/fdlp/pubs/title44/chap19.html. Accessed: 23 March 2007.

32. United Nations Secretariat. *Index to administrative issuances. [New York]: UN, 2006, quoted in United Nations Dag Hammarskjöld Library. United Nations documentation: research guide document symbols: United Nations documentation.* [Web document]. The Library. Available: www.un.org/Depts/dhl/resguide/symbol.htm#records. Accessed: 23 March 2007.

33. United Nations Dag Hammarskjöld Library. *United Nations documentation: research guide document symbols: United Nations documentation.* [Web document]. The Library, 2007. Available: www.un.org/Depts/dhl/resguide/symbol.htm#records. Accessed: 23 March 2007.

34. Ouedraogo, L-D. *From the Optical Disk System to the Official Documents System (ODS): status of implementation and evaluation. JIU/REP/2003/3.* [Web document]. Geneva: United Nations System Joint Inspection Unit, 2003. Available: www.unjiu.org/data/reports/2003/en2003_3.pdf. Accessed: 23 March 2007.

35. European Union. *European Union documents.* [Web document]. The Union. Available: http://europa.eu/documents/index_en.htm. Accessed: 23 March 2007.

36. European Union. *Access to European Parliament, Council and Commission documents: a user's guide.* [Web document]. Luxembourg: Office for Official Publications of the European Communities, 2002. Available: www.europarl.europa.eu/opengov/pdf/2001_1834_en.pdf. Accessed: 23 March 2007.

37. "publication." *The American Heritage dictionary of the English language, fourth edition.* [Web document]. Boston: Houghton Mifflin Company, 2004. Available: http://dictionary.reference.com/browse/publication. Accessed: 23 March 2007.

38. "document." *The American Heritage dictionary of the English language, fourth edition.* [Web document]. Boston: Houghton Mifflin Company, 2004. Available: http://dictionary.reference.com/browse/document. Accessed: 23 March 2007.

39. "document." *The free on-line dictionary of computing.* [Web document]. Available: http://dictionary.reference.com/browse/document. Accessed: 23 March 2007.

40. U.S. Government Printing Office (GPO). *The national government publications: initial planning statement.* [Web document]. Washington, DC: The Office, 2004: 3. Available: www.gpoaccess.gov/about/reports/natbib0604.pdf. Accessed: 23 March 2007.

41. Ibid.

42. Ibid.

43. Ibid.

44. Office of Management and Budget. Table 9.8—Composition of Outlays for the Conduct of Research and Development: 1949–2008 (in millions of dollars). In: *Budget of the United States government: 2008 historical tables.* [Web document]. Washington, DC: The Office, 2007. Available: http://frwebgate2.

access.gpo.gov/cgi-bin/waisgate.cgi?WAISdocID=26925331697+3+0+
0&WAISaction=retrieve. Accessed: 17 May 2007.

45. Office of the Law Revision Counsel, U.S. House of Representatives. *U.S. Code:
    transfer of federal scientific and technical information. 15 USC Sec. 3704b-2.
    (Source: Pub. L. 102-245, title I, Sec. 108, Feb. 14, 1992, 106 Stat. 13.).* [Web
    document]. Washington, DC: The Office. Available: http://uscode.house.gov/
    uscode-cgi/fastweb.exe?getdoc+uscview+t13t16+2405+132++%28%29%20%
    20AND%20%28USC%20w%2F10%20%2815% 2063%203704b-2%29%29%
    3ACITE%20%20%20%20%20%20%20% 20%20. Accessed: 17 May 2007.

46. Ibid.

47. National Technical Information Service, Technology Administration, De-
    partment of Commerce. *National Technology Preeminence Act: responsibil-
    ities of federal agencies for the transfer of scientific, technical, and
    engineering information to the National Technical Information Service
    (NTIS) under the American Technology Preeminence Act (ATPA).* [Web doc-
    ument]. Public Law 102-245, Section 108, American Technology Preemi-
    nence Act of 1991, (15 U.S.C. 3704b-2). Springfield, VA: The Service.
    Available: www.ntis.gov/pdf/ATPA.pdf. Accessed: 17 May 2007.

48. U.S. General Accounting Office. *Report to congressional requesters: infor-
    mation management: dissemination of technical reports.* [Web document].
    GAO-01-490. Washington, DC: U.S. GAO, May 2001. Available:
    www.gao.gov/new.items/d01490.pdf. Accessed: 17 May 2007.

49. Ibid.

50. Ibid.

51. Ibid.

52. Ibid.

53. Ibid.

54. U.S. National Commission on Libraries and Information Science. *A compre-
    hensive assessment of public information dissemination final report: execu-
    tive summary.* [Web document]. Washington, DC: The Commission, 26
    January 2001. Available: www.nclis.gov/govt/assess/assess.execsum.pdf.
    Accessed: 17 May 2007.

55. National Technical Information Service, U.S. Department of Commerce
    Technology Administration. *Welcome to NTIS.* Springfield, VA: The Service.
    Available: www.ntis.gov/about/index.asp?loc=6-0-0. Accessed: 17 May 2007.

56. Morehead J. *Introduction to United States government information sources.*
    6th ed. Englewood, CO: Libraries Unlimited, 1999.

57. Office of Extramural Research, National Institutes of Health. *NIH Public
    Access.* Bethesda, MD: National Instituted of Health, Department of Health
    and Human Services, 2005. Available: http://publicaccess.nih.gov/policy.htm.
    Accessed: 17 May 2007.

CHAPTER 6

Conferences, Reviews, and Translations

Dell Davis, Beatriz Varman,
and Mary Jackson

Conferences

Professional development activities such as conferences and seminars continue to provide health science professionals and researchers with a venue for professional growth. Several reputable publications exist only to identify such events and continue to be a reliable source for conference particulars, such as date, location, conference theme, sponsoring organization and contact information. Many health science serial publications devote sections or complete issues to meeting and conference information in an attempt to augment the reader's experience with upcoming related events of interest. The events represented in these publications are routinely scheduled by well-established health-centered organizations, educational institutions and health-based commercial concerns. The publications annotated on the next several pages have become a reliable source of information for planning conference attendance.

Over the last 15 years, an increasing number of conferences are available in the virtual world. Virtual conferences, such as Webinars or Webcasts, are oftentimes not listed in traditional publications. Rich in content, credibility and authority, there are an overwhelming number of health-related professional development opportunities available online. The ease at which these meetings are identified continues to grow in complexity as more conference organizers are loading and pushing programming in to the virtual world. It has now become a challenge for librarians to identify these virtual offerings and make them available to interested health professionals.

Virtual meetings began in the business world and were born as a result of increasing travel expenses coupled with technological advances in communication. This business model has been embraced by the medical and health science community, as the same concerns are prevalent. A critical look at overall costs for conference travel encouraged a move toward virtual meetings high in content, sometimes eliminating the need for professional travel. Many conference organizers now offer quality content in the virtual environment available to the participant in a variety of electronic formats ranging from a downloadable file for an ipod—to be accessed at the convenience of the participant— to a live satellite telecast with two-way communication capabilities.

Whatever the system of delivery, the librarian's role in identifying these offerings requires familiarity with the traditional printed resources and effective search strategies to use online. Evaluation of retrieved content is just as important as it is with any Internet resource. Retrieval can include unfamiliar sponsors, but that does not necessarily mean poor content. Not only are good search strategies important, but a working list of blogs, discussion lists, and special-interest forums can also be beneficial sources for conference information.

Many critics question the real value of virtual conferences. Webcasts and Webinars viewed from the privacy of an individual's computer are thought to be limiting, in the sense that they compromise the core value of conference attendance: networking with colleagues.

Calendars

Printed sources remain a useful and reliable source to use to locate conferences. In the health sciences, journals such as the *Journal of the American Medical Association (JAMA)* list meetings of generic interest to most health professionals. *JAMA*, along with the publications listed with it, are good points of reference for physicians and researchers who are seeking information about upcoming health science meetings.

Other major health professional and research-oriented periodicals should also be consulted for listings of meetings and conferences in their specific areas of interest. The amount of information about each event will vary.

Calendars can also be found online. One advantage to visiting a Web-based source to plan meeting attendance is that the information on a Web site can be more comprehensive. For instance, it is common to obtain an entire program of events, presentations, and presenters' bios online. Another advantage is that content is easily updated and links to important peripheral information can also be just a click away (travel, lodging, transfers, maps, conference center floor plans, etc.).

6.1   *JAMA: the Journal of the American Medical Association.* Chicago, IL: American Medical Association, 1960–. Weekly. Continues: *Journal of the American Medical Association.* Chicago, IL: American Medical Association, 1883–1960. Continues: *American Medical Association. Transactions.* Chicago, IL: American Medical Association, 1848–1883. Available: http://jama.ama-assn.org/

6.2   *JAMA & ARCHIVES Journals Calendar of Events.* Chicago, IL: American Medical Association. 2007. Available: http://pubs.ama-assn.org/cgi/calendarcontent

6.3   *World Meetings: United States and Canada.* New York: Macmillan, 1963–. Quarterly.

6.4   *World Meetings: Outside United States and Canada.* New York: Macmillan, 1968–. Quarterly.

6.5   *World Meetings: Medicine.* New York: Macmillan, 1978–. Quarterly.

6.6   *MInd: The Meetings Index.* InterDok Corporation. Available: www.interdok.com/mind

6.7   *Scientific Meetings.* San Diego, CA: Scientific Meetings Publications, 1957–. Quarterly.

6.8   *International Congress Calendar.* Brussels, Belgium: Union of International Associations, 1960–. Quarterly.

Since 1848, *JAMA* has published "Meetings Outside the United States" twice a year in January and July and "Meetings in the United States" in the first issue of each month. Meetings are announced up to one year in advance of the scheduled date.

JAMA & ARCHIVES Journals Calendar of Events is an online resource that lists upcoming events. It can be searched by topic, location, sponsoring organization, and date. Conference organizers can also submit events to be considered for inclusion in the Calendar using an online form.

World Meetings publications, as noted in their Prefaces, "provide information on meetings of international, national, and regional interest in the sciences, applied sciences and engineering, social sciences, and professions." *World Meetings: United States and Canada* and *World Meetings: Outside United*

States and Canada represent the most comprehensive listings available for future meetings in the sciences. Both of these publications are quarterly. Their entries include such information as: restrictions on attendance, availability of papers, paper submission deadlines, and technical session descriptions. Entries are updated in succeeding issues as more information becomes available.

World Meetings: Medicine is formatted in the same manner as the aforementioned *World Meetings* publications. The only difference is that the focus of this publication is specifically medical meetings/conferences from all over the world.

MInd: The Meetings Index is an online complementary service to InterDok's *Directory of Published Proceedings* and offers access to information on future conferences, congresses, meetings and symposia. Subjects supported in this resource include Science/Technology, Medical/Life Sciences, Pollution Control/Ecology and Social Sciences/Humanities.

Scientific Meetings is an international directory of upcoming scientific, technical, and medical organizations. Meetings are arranged alphabetically by sponsoring agency. A chronological index and subject index also provide access points to content. Many meetings are announced as much as 15 months in advance.

The Union of International Associations comprises three independent resources: the *International Congress Calendar*, the *Guide to Global Civil Society Meetings*, and *Future International Conferences and Meetings*. Over 15,000 entries are included annually. Four volumes are published each year, in January, April, July, and October. Each volume is divided into three sections: Geographical, Chronological, and Title/Subject. This resource uses the same identification numbers for international organizations as the Yearbook of International Organizations for easy cross-referencing. The Union of International Associations resources are available online at www.uia.org/meetings/pubcalen.php.

Meeting Previews

6.9   *Meeting Previews.* Philadelphia, PA: Thomson Scientific & Healthcare. Available: http://scientific.thomson.com/free/meeting previews/

Thomson Scientific maintains a Web site that features previews of upcoming conferences and meetings. Primarily focused on pharmaceutical research and development, *Meeting Previews* provides an overview of the planned event and highlights featured lectures and poster and paper presentations.

Previews generally appear on the Web site just prior to the meeting and remain online for at least six months after the event.

Conference Publications

For those individuals seeking information regarding conference publications from past meetings, retrospective tools may be of use. The following listing contains publications which index meetings that may have produced publications.

6.10 *Congresses: Tentative Chronological and Bibliographic Reference List of National and International Meetings of Physicians, Scientists and Experts.* Washington, DC: U.S. Government Printing Office, 1938. Supplement to Index Catalog, 4th series, 2nd supplement.

6.11 *Council for International Organizations of Medical Sciences. Bibliography of International Congresses of Medical Sciences.* Springfield, IL: Charles C Thomas, 1958.

6.12 *International Congresses, 1681 to 1899, Full List.* Brussels, Belgium: Union of International Associations, 1960. Documents, no. 8: Publication no. 164.

6.13 *International Congresses, 1900 to 1919, Full List.* Brussels, Belgium: Union of International Associations, 1964. Publication no. 188.

6.14 *Biosis Previews : Meetings and Conference Reports.* Philadelphia, PA: Thomson Scientific. Available: http://scientific.thomson.com/products/bp/

Congresses: Tentative Chronological and Bibliographic Reference List of National and International Meetings of Physicians, Scientists and Experts, a supplement to the *Index-Catalogue* in 1938, provides information on 17,000 congresses which were available in the Army Medical Library (now the U.S. National Library of Medicine). Content varies from basic information (name of congress and date) to more detailed information including resulting publications. The *Index-Catalogue* lists those congresses that are of peripheral interest to health science researchers as well as those that are directly related to the field.

The *Bibliography of International Congresses of Medical Sciences* was published under the auspices of the Council for International Organizations of Medical Sciences. It includes congresses directly related to the medical field. The basic arrangement is a chronological listing by subject.

The Union of International Associations prepared two lists of international congresses covering all subject areas from 1681 to 1899 and from 1900 to 1919. Each list provides a chronological approach to content. Listings include the name of the congress, location and date. *International Congresses, 1900 to 1919, Full List* includes a subject index for both volumes. *International Congresses Calendar* maintains an electronic counterpart which has been available since 2004. It is a fee-based resource, available at www.uia.org/meetings/mtonline.php.

Biosis Previews contains a subset database entitled *Meetings and Conference Reports*. Indexing over 165,000 conference reports, this database is searchable from the Biosis Previews platform. Abstracts are provided in each record as well as the sponsoring institution and source of publication.

Papers Presented at Meetings

Locating papers presented at meetings often poses a challenge for the health science librarian. It is becoming common for presented papers to be self-published on the Web or exist in a digital commons at an associated academic institution. Traditionally, papers presented at meetings are published as conference proceedings. Because papers represent the current trends and hot topics in the field, they are often sought after by health professionals and researchers.

Cruzat [1] has identified six forms of presentation for the proceedings of meetings.

1. A multivolume work encompassing the total proceeding of a conference or meeting.
2. A monograph or report with a specific title and editor.
3. A supplement, special number, or entire issue of an established journal (from either an official publication of the sponsoring society or agency or an unaffiliated publication that the society elects because of the subject content of the symposium or conference).
4. Selected papers or abstracts published in a journal because it is the official organ or because of subject content.
5. Reports of a meeting or conference in a journal that has a special section devoted to "congress or conference proceedings."
6. Dual publication as both an issue or part of a journal and as a monograph or report.

Individual papers are sometimes submitted to journals as a separate publication. These papers will be included by indexing and abstracting services that index journals. Revised papers published under a different title are also somewhat difficult to track. Expert database searches using controlled vocabulary, authors' names, and unique keywords can possibly aid in the location of these resources.

6.15   *Conference Papers Index.* Bethesda, MD: Cambridge Scientific Abstracts, 1973–. Monthly. Formerly: Current Programs. Available: www.csa.com/csa/factsheets/cpilong.shtml

6.16   *PapersFirst.* Dublin, OH: OCLC. Available: www.oclc.org/support/documentation/firstsearch/databases/dbdetails/details/PapersFirst.htm

Conference Papers Index (CPI) provides a listing of all papers presented at meetings, whether or not the paper appeared in a published format. This source includes scientific meetings and is prepared from programs or abstract publications of the conferences. Although published since 1973, emphasis on the life sciences, environmental sciences, and aquatic sciences first began in 1995. The *Index* is arranged by topic and is unique in that it supplies the name and address of individual presenters. An electronic counterpart is available through Cambridge Scientific Abstracts (CSA) and includes coverage from 1982 to the present, at www.csa.com/factsheets/cpi-set-c.php.

PapersFirst, an OCLC product, indexes papers presented at conferences worldwide. PapersFirst contains almost six million records and is updated semimonthly. Each of the papers contained in the database from 1993 forward are available through the British Library Document Supply Centre.

Current Bibliographies of Published Proceedings

Published proceedings of meetings may either include the full-text of papers presented or just an abstract. Depending upon the organization, some proceedings are relatively comprehensive. Proceedings also serve as a valuable resource to those who were not able to attend a particular conference or have an interest on a level that did not warrant attendance at an event. Many of these proceedings can be located online, through organizational websites, the official conference website, or identified using databases such as OCLC's ProceedingsFirst.

The following resources list published proceedings in the sciences.

6.17   *Index to Scientific and Technical Proceedings.* Philadelphia, PA: Institute for Scientific Information, 1978–. Monthly, annual cumulation. Available: www.isinet.com/isi/products/citation/wos/wosproceedings

6.18   *Directory of Published Proceedings: Series SEMT—Science/Engineering/Medicine/Technology.* Harrison, NY: InterDok, 1965–. Ten issues per year, annual cumulation. *Cumulated Index Supplement.* Harrison, NY: InterDok. Quarterly, annual cumulation.

6.19   *Directory of Published Proceedings: Series MLS—Medica/Life Sciences.* Harrison, NY: InterDok, 1990–. Annual.

6.20   *Directory of Published Proceedings: Series PCE—Pollution Control/Ecology.* Harrison, NY: InterDok, 1974–. Annual.

6.21   *Proceedings in Print.* Halifax, MA: Proceedings in Print, Inc., 1964–1997. Six issues per year; annual cumulative index.

6.22   *Biological Abstracts/RRM.* Philadelphia, PA: BioSciences Information Service, 1980–. Semimonthly. Online database Biological Abstracts/RRM via Biosis.

6.23   *ProceedingsFirst.* Dublin, OH: OCLC. Available: www.oclc.org/support/documentation/firstsearch/databases/dbdetails/details/Proceedings.htm

6.24   *IEEE Proceedings Order Plans (POP).* [database]. Washington, DC: IEEE. Available: www.ieee.org/products/onlinepubs/prod/pop_overview.html

Index to Scientific and Technical Proceedings (ITSP), produced by the Institute for Scientific Information (ISI), covers proceedings in all of the sciences. Proceedings, regardless of the format (book, journal issue, report, etc.) must contain complete papers to be listed. While many indexing services include only proceeding volumes, this resource indexes the individual papers. Published monthly, *ISTP* is one of the fastest printed means of access to proceedings literature. *ISTP* provides complete bibliographic information for published proceedings. Bibliographic entries contain titles of papers, authors, and the address of the first author in cases of multiple authorship. Other access points include a sponsors index, an author/editor index, a corporate index, a meeting location index, and subject access via category and permuterm subject index. *ISTP* is available on the Internet through the ISI Proceedings database and through DIMDI (Deutsche Institut fuer Medizinische Documentation und Information [German Institute for Medical Documentation and Information]). The ISI Proceedings database is updated weekly and indexes papers published since 1990 from more than 7,000 conferences per year.

The *Directory of Published Proceedings: Series SEMT*, produced by InterDok, provides basic bibliographic information for proceedings in the science, engineering, medical, and technology fields. Since 1964, this resource has provided monthly information on preprints and published proceedings of international congresses, conferences, symposia, meetings, seminars, and summer schools. Arranged chronologically by date of meeting, entries include meeting focus, sponsor, location, and editor.

InterDok produces two additional publications, *Directory of Published Proceedings: Series MLS—Medical/Life Sciences* and *Directory of Published Proceedings: Series PCE—Pollution Control/Ecology*. These publications are issued annually and are prepared from the entries in *Series SEMT* and a companion publication, *Series SSH—Social Sciences/Humanities*.

Proceedings in Print is broader in scope than the above titles. This resource, published from 1964 to 1997 covered all subject areas. An alphabetical index provides conference identification.

With well over 2.5 million records, *Biological Abstracts/RRM* provides the most comprehensive coverage of worldwide meeting literature, reviews, and books in the life sciences. It complements *Biological Abstracts* by supplying unique coverage of these increasingly important sources of information. Serving as the essential nonjournal literature resource, the database includes citations to biological and biochemical meeting papers presented at over 1,500 meetings, symposia, and workshops.

ProceedingsFirst is an OCLC database. It indexes worldwide conference proceedings received from the British Library Document Supply Centre. Database coverage is from 1993 to the present. The database contains more than 169,000 records and is updated twice a week.

IEEE Proceedings Order Plans (POP) is the resource of choice for identifying published and unpublished proceedings in biomedical technology. The online resource contains more than 590,000 conference proceedings from its 39 technical societies.

The resources above confirm that a particular conference occurred or that proceedings from these events exist. To actually locate the proceedings, the following sources provide holdings information for libraries that own them.

6.25   *Index of Conference Proceedings*. Boston Spa, U.K.: British Library Document Supply Centre. No. 69–, June 1973–. Monthly. *Index of Conference Proceedings*. Annual Cumulation. 1988–. Continues: *Index of Conference Proceedings Received*. Annual Cumulation. 1985–1987.

6.26   *Index of Conference Proceedings 1964–1988*. London: Saur, 1989.

The British Library Document Supply Centre owns one of the most comprehensive collections of unrestricted reports available for public use in the world. The collection of reports, conferences, and theses numbers 4.9 million. Conference papers alone number more than 400,000, with approximately 16,000 added each year. The printed publication was monthly and arranged by keywords taken from publication titles and organizers. The British Library Document Supply Centre supports a fee-based online delivery service. A new searching and ordering service is available for those who only search the database occasionally.

The *Index of Conference Proceedings 1964–1988* is a cumulation of the proceedings identified during this 25-year period.

It may be a good idea to also consider using WorldCat and LocatorPlus for papers or proceedings treated like monographs. For conference papers that get published as journal articles, PubMed is also a good resource.

Reviews

Reviews are secondary documents designed to provide the health information seeker with an overview of a detailed concept. In the health sciences, reviews are written by experts in the field to provide a synopsis, evaluation, or analysis of a documented research topic. Reviews are also written to cover health science information resources. Reviews range in complexity from fact sheets prepared for lay audiences to evidence-based systematic reviews for health-related intervention decisions.

MedlinePlus is the database of choice for consumer health information. At a minimum, reviews (fact-sheets) can contain a brief definition of a diagnosis, causes, symptoms and treatment options. Specifically created for the lay audience by the National Library of Medicine, the MedlinePlus database provides links to reputable organizations' prepared data as well. MedlinePlus is discussed in more detail in Chapter 10, Consumer Health Sources.

Health science professionals will seek a more detailed and professional account of health-related research. Their interest in a review may be to become acquainted with a health-related topic, update their existing knowledge base, or gather key information to aid in patient care decisions or research plans.

Monographs

Review articles published in monographic series are generally used by health science professionals to update their knowledge base. Titles such as

Annual Reviews, Reviews in Biochemical Toxicology, Concepts in Biochemistry, Clinical Reviews in Allergy and Immunology, and *State-of-the-Art Reviews* publish reviews in a series of monographs. Treated as books by some libraries and serial publications by others, these resources provide high-level content and include extensive bibliographies for additional support information. OCLC's WorldCat can provide the user with physical volume holdings in most libraries.

Articles

Review articles published in journals exist primarily in the form of literature reviews, systematic reviews, meta-analyses, and overviews (sometimes referred to as tutorials). In addition to these most popular forms, several different types of review articles can be identified in indexes and databases.

Literature reviews are built with the intent to provide the reader with a brief overview of a topic supported by an extensive bibliography of reputable articles in a specific area of health research. Composed of findings from currently published articles, literature reviews are excellent sources as they consider and report findings based on all items listed in the bibliography. These reviews will also typically contain the titles of the databases or indexes used to identify the sources, dates searched, and the search strategies used.

Systematic reviews are a synopsis of several clinical trials that have been compared and contrasted by experts in the field. The framework by which this document rests is usually consistent so that the information seeker can rely on this arrangement to locate specific areas within the systematic review. Lengthy in many cases, the systematic review can be considered a living document. It is updated periodically to include additional clinical trials of "like" subject matter as they are completed. As additional data is integrated into a systematic review, the conclusions and results may change over time. Evidence-based content is used to develop a systematic review so they are considered to contain the best evidence regarding interventions for direct patient care or research. Systematic reviews are often used as a primary support piece for practice guidelines in medicine.

Meta-analysis is a quantitative method for analyzing data included in independent experimental and clinical studies collectively. In the interest of validating data and providing another resource for evidence-based information, articles published summarizing these findings are published as reviews known as meta-analyses.

Review articles published as overviews or tutorials have been an excellent source of information in a compressed manner. Depending upon the primary source of information, review articles can provide the reader with a synopsis of a detailed research or experimental study, an overview of a case study, or an overview of a health-related concept.

Relatively new on the scene are point-of-care resources. UpToDate, MD Consult, InfoPOEMS, and MD on Tap are just a few. These resources contain reviews subdivided into small bits of quality information for bedside patient care for physicians. These electronic resources can be accessed using hand-held devices.

The U.S. National Library of Medicine has been instrumental in providing bibliographic management of reviews in the health sciences. Today, many commercial vendors are creating and maintaining products that provide the same type of service online, but may augment their scope to contain resources not indexed by National Library of Medicine resources.

6.27   *Bibliography of Medical Reviews.* Bethesda, MD: U.S. National Library of Medicine, 1955–. Annual, 1955–1967. Monthly, 1968–1977, separately and in *Index Medicus.* Monthly, 1978–2000. Only in *Index Medicus.* Weekly, 1978–. *PubMed.*

6.28   *Index to Scientific Reviews.* Philadelphia, PA: Institute for Scientific Information,1974–. Semiannual.

6.29   *PubMed Clinical Queries.* Bethesda, MD: National Library of Medicine, 1950–. Available: www.ncbi.nlm.nih.gov/entrez/query/static/clinical.shtml

6.30   *Cochrane Database of Systematic Reviews.* Boston, MA. The Cochrane Collaboration. Available: www.cochrane.org/index.htm

6.31   *EMBASE Excerpta Medica.* Bridgewater, NJ: Elsevier. Available: www.ovid.com/site/catalog/DataBase/61.jsp

6.32   *Biological Abstracts/RRM (Reports/Reviews/Meetings).* (See 6.22).

The publications and databases above identify reviews in the health and general sciences.

The Bibliography of Medical Reviews (BMR) first appeared in 1955 as an annual publication; a six-year cumulation in 1961 represents review articles from the 1955–1959 *Current List of Medical Literature* and the 1960 *Cumulated Index Medicus (CIM).* It continued as an annual publication through 1967. In January 1968, it began being published as a part of the monthly *Index Medicus (IM)* with an annual cumulation in *CIM.* It was also published as a separate monthly publication from 1968 through 1977. From 1978 to

2000, *BMR* appeared in print only as a separate section of the paper *Index Medicus*. Reviews are now published in the PubMed database.

BMR follows the same format as *IM* and provides subject access to citation of reviews. In 1988, NLM expanded its definition of medical reviews to include categories of materials that were previously excluded from *BMR*. The definition now includes articles such as academic reviews, subject reviews, epidemiologic reviews, and state-of-the-art reviews. Online access to reviews found in the print *BMR* is provided through PubMed and other vendors offering access to the MEDLINE database.

Since 1974, the Institute for Scientific Information (ISI) has published the *Index to Scientific Reviews (ISR)* to provide separate bibliographic coverage of the world's scientific review literature. *ISR* provides comprehensive coverage of the review literature for all of the sciences and covers the same disciplines as Science Citation Index (SCI).

Index to Scientific Reviews serves both as a source of bibliographic information for the reviews currently being published and as a citation index to these articles. The main section of *ISR* is the research front specialty index, which provides bibliographies of current reviews in identified areas of intense research activity. The *Index to Scientific Reviews* can be searched in print and online through Science Citation Index via the Web of Science.

In 1980, *Biological Abstracts/RRM (BA/RRM)* succeeded the BioSciences Information Services (BIOSIS) publication *BioResearch Index*. *Biological Abstracts/RRM* covers the nontraditional forms of literature in the life sciences with particular attention to reports, reviews, and meetings. *Biological Abstracts/RRM* can be searched online.

It has become quite common in the health science field to find databases and indexes which provide bibliographic control of reviews. Many databases have provided value-added limits to aid the end-user in specifying the type of review sought. As mentioned above, some indexes, databases, or subsets of databases are dedicated to providing an avenue for identifying reviews in the health sciences.

Translations

A Review of Online Products for Language Translation

The demand for high-quality reliable language translation services has been growing steadily in recent years. In addition to traditional human-centered translation centers, there has been a rapid growth in translation software products and online machine translation tools available via the Web.

Translating arbitrary documents from one language to another is not an easy task. In addition to requiring proficiency in the source and destination languages, accurate translation requires domain knowledge of the subject area of the original document as well as sensitivity to cultural nuances of the languages. Machine Translation (MT) is the use of computers to translate from one language to another. Machine translation has the advantage of being cheaper and faster than professional translation by a trained human specialist. This provides a tremendous advantage in situations such as online Web browsing, where Web pages that were created in one language must be translated and displayed in the reader's language in real time.

Currently, there are several general-purpose search engines and specialized Web sites that provide machine language translations. None of these however, can claim 100 percent translation accuracy, since a "machine" is doing the work. For simpler translation needs, such as words, phrases, nontechnical text, and even complete Web pages, these resources may be adequate. In more discipline-specific contexts these resources are a helpful starting point, providing an easy and cost-effective method to filter content for relevance. However, to have a reliable translated document in a specific discipline, human translation is currently the right choice.

Computer programs for language translation have been around for about 40 years or more. One of the earliest applications of machine translation still used today is to translate high-level human-oriented programming languages to more primitive languages understood by the computer hardware. Translation of natural languages, however, is considerably more difficult due to their richness, complexity, and underlying ambiguities in meaning. Over the years, machine translation programs have become increasingly sophisticated, providing both greater accuracy and a larger repertoire of languages. The typical quality of translation from English to languages like Japanese, Russian, or Chinese has improved considerably, and the numbers of pairs of languages that can be mutually translated has increased greatly. Historically most of the translation software programs and search engines have been for applications in the business field. However, the last few years have seen a growing increase in applications in other disciplines.

This section of the chapter provides an overview of some of the most popular free online machine-translation tools available via the Web. The products were identified by literature review of two databases—Library Literature and Information Full Text and Library Information Science and Technology Abstracts—and by searching the Web. (For a discussion of print translation resources no longer published, please see the fourth edition of *Introduction to Reference Sources in the Health Sciences*.)

Online language translation products come in two main categories: dictionaries and translators. Dictionaries provide translation of single words or short phrases. Translators provide two different functions: translation of Web sites or general text translation. The former enable a Web page created in one language, say in English, to be translated and displayed in the browser in a different language just by typing in its URL. Individuals can then surf the Web in their own language by using the Web translators to convert foreign-language Web pages.

Text translators can be used to translate arbitrary user text between different languages. Here too, two flavors of usage can be found. The most common mode is to provide a text box on a Website into which the user can type the text to be translated. The translated text will usually be displayed in a separate textbox on the Web page as well. Free Web translators usually limit the number of characters or words allowed in a single transaction. In some cases they may also limit the total number of transactions allowed, thereby limiting the maximum size of the text that can be translated without registration and payment. The average size tends to be in the range of 800 words. Some sites allow more sophisticated and flexible machine translations for a fee, and offer instant human translation at somewhat higher rates as well.

The second mode of text translation is to download software from the Web site into the client computer. The downloaded software provides greater flexibility and ease of use. For instance the source text can be chosen from a preexisting document by merely highlighting the desired sections in an editor like Microsoft Word or other Microsoft Office application. Products differ in the number of languages supported and the combinations of language pairs which can be mutually translated. The actual translation is still done by the translation engine at the Web site.

Some sites provide additional tools to supplement the translation process. For instance multilingual spell-checkers and virtual keyboards with non-English or accented characters greatly facilitate the input of text for translation, while automatic simultaneous retranslation of the translated text back into the original source language provides quick feedback on the fidelity of the translation. In addition, some Web sites provide a facility to directly e-mail or print the translated text merely by selecting the appropriate command on the page. Some of the Web sites are powered by their own translation engines, while others are merely consolidators with links to the free services provided by the primary translation service Web sites.

Free Online Translation Tools in the Internet

Several language translation products available on different Web sites are discussed below. A comparative summary is presented in the table at the end of this section. The author of this section is a native Spanish speaker and chose to translate text from English to Spanish using some of the free online tools to assess their accuracy.

6.33 *Babel Fish*, by AltaVista. Sunnyvale, CA: Overture Services, 2006. Available: http://babelfish.altavista.com

AltaVista was the pioneer in using multilingual search capabilities on the Internet. Babel Fish by AltaVista is a machine translation software powered by Systran. This site can translate up to 800 words of text at one time, as well as translate entire Web sites from English to twelve different languages. It also has the capability of translating among 19 pairs of languages, such as French to Spanish or Spanish to French. The site's FAQ has very good information on searching Babel Fish and tips on how to get the best results.

Translating using Babel Fish and then following up with a human translator will produce a very accurate document. For translations of scientific documents it is necessary to use a human translator in order to have adequate accuracy.

6.34   *Babylon*. Munich, Germany: Babylon, Ltd. 1997. Available: http:// babylon.com

This site supports both translation and dictionary software powered by LEC Translation. The Babylon text translator translates up to 320 characters (including spaces and punctuation marks) from English to 17 other languages: French, German, Spanish, Italian, Portuguese, Japanese, Hebrew, Chinese (Traditional), Chinese (Simplified), Dutch, Russian, Korean, Turkish, Arabic, Farsi, Polish, and Ukrainian. The software also translates directly between any pair of these languages.

Babylon requires downloading the software for a trial period of about four weeks. Once downloaded it is not necessary to cut and paste the text to be translated into the Babylon translation window. One can just use the CTRL Right click of the mouse from any Microsoft application like Word, PowerPoint or Outlook, and a Babylon translation window will pop up with options to translate the text to the desired target language.

Babylon software can be purchased from their Web site; a free trial is also available. It is not a freeware, and once the trial period has expired, one needs to purchase the software. The cost depends on the features added or the type of subscription selected.

6.35   *elmundo.es Traductor.* Madrid, Spain; Mundinteractivos, SA. Available: www.elmundo.es/traductor/

This site can be used to translate short text and Web pages between English and Spanish, French, or German. Special characters are available below the translation box. The translation service uses various software programs, including the Reverso Internet/PITS translation software (see description of Reverso below).

6.36   *Foreignword.com.* Alicante, Spain: Foreignword. 2000. Available: www.foreignword.com

This is a comprehensive Web site with links to word and text translators and language guessers; it offers help in locating a professional translator as well as a free translation wizard called Xanadu, which is available for download. It includes links to dictionaries in more than 50 languages. See below for a detailed explanation of Xanadu.

For word translations Foreignword uses DictSearch, a global dictionary that can search more than 200 other dictionaries and language portals. The site gives an explanation of each, and provides a URL when clicking on the information icon. Depending on the language, different dictionary options are available. For instance, when translating a word from English to Spanish or to German, there is a choice of using any of 18 or 21 different dictionaries respectively, while translations from Chinese to English offer one or two specialized dictionaries. DictSearch supports 73 languages, including more unusual languages, such as Esperanto. It is also available for WAP mobile phones. To search DictSearch one simply selects a source and target language and enters the term to be translated.

For text translations, Foreignword uses Translate Now!, a one-stop access to different translation products available via the Web. It provides 28 different machine translation tools; for example, translation from English to Spanish uses only one machine translator, but when translating text from English to French there are nine choices, using some of the search engines already mentioned earlier.

6.37   *FreeTranslation.com.* England: SDL International, 2000. Available: www.freetranslation.com

FreeTranslation.com translates both text and Web pages using Enterprise Translation Server, an automatic translation engine. It translates to and from English, Spanish, French, German, Italian, Dutch, Portuguese, Russian, and Japanese. It also translates from English to Norwegian and Chinese (simplified and traditional).

Their Web site offers the option to use either free machine translation, limited to 750 words at a time, or a fee-based human translation service. If one is not satisfied with the results of the free translation, one can on click on the button labeled "Human Translation"; another screen will pop up with the cost of translating the text.

More accurate translations by using advanced translation options (up to 10,000 words each time) and specialized dictionaries are available for a fee. Specialized software such as SDLDesktop Translator, SDL Chat Translator and SDLClipboard Translator are also available for a fee.

The help section and FAQs on the Web site contain very good information. It also offers helpful information on how to enter accented characters used in other languages. FreeTranslation.com is owned by SDL International, with headquarters in the United Kingdom and offices in North America, Asia, Europe, and the Middle East.

6.38   *Google Language Tools.* Mountain View, CA: Google. Available: www.google.com/language_tools?hl=en

This search engine can translate words, text, and Web pages. It also has the capability to search for foreign language Web pages in 35 different languages, including Arabic, Catalan, Icelandic, Latvian, and Turkish. To do so, one simply selects the preferred language from the pulldown menu in the "Search Specific Languages or Countries" section. Google translation software can translate Web sites published in Italian, French, Spanish, German, and Portuguese into English.

By setting preferences in the section "Use the Google Interface in Your Language," Google homepage, site messages, and buttons can be displayed in any of 117 different languages, including Cambodian, Hindi, Quechua, or Swahili. If someone's preferred language is not listed on the Web site, Google encourages volunteering for their translator program.

6.39   *ImTranslator.net.* Irvine, CA: Smart Link Corporation, 2003. Available: http://imtranslator.net/

A product of Smart Link Corporation and powered by PROMT Internet Translator, this site offers free translations between any pair of nineteen languages. The site includes a translator and a dictionary, as well as a suite of tools like Spellink, an eight-language spell checker, a virtual keyboard, and a decoder.

The translator can translate up to 1,000 characters at a time. It translates to and from twenty pairs of languages. Using the software is easy: from the translator window one can choose from the icons displayed for editing functions (copy, cut, paste, and delete) and various tools (virtual keyboard, dictionary, spelling, decode, print, and e-mail). The Web site has three different window frames on the right side of their Web page. The top window is where the original text can be typed, the middle window is the result of the translation, and the bottom window labeled "back translation" has the capability of retranslating the translated text back to the original language. However, don't expect the twice-translated text to match the original exactly!

Spellink can check the spelling of words in English, French, German, Italian, Portuguese, Russian, and Spanish. It has the capability to proof 500 characters at one time. The spell-checking dialog will flag misspelled words in red and provide a list of suggestions. There is also a dictionary available.

The virtual keyboard has the option of entering accent marks making it easy to deal with special characters in languages like Russian, Turkish, German, and French. Decoder helps with incorrect display of Russian characters in emails, Web pages or applications. Decoder identifies the encoding of a Russian text, and converts it, if needed, into the Windows standard encoding (Cyrillic Windows) using a sophisticated algorithm.

At the time of this review, the iMTranslator Web site was being updated. A new display is available on their Web site but still includes the same features mentioned above.

6.40 *NEWSTRAN. Free newspaper translations.* NEWSTRAN.COM. Humanitas-International.org, 1996. Available: www.humanitas-international.org/newstran/index.html

This is a free site that translates more than 5,000 major newspapers and magazines from 11 different countries. Major U.S. newspapers like the *New York Times* or *USA Today* can be translated from English to 11 different languages. NEWSTRAN also provides a text and Web translator into 28 different languages, and links to an extensive number of free foreign language dictionaries. This is a free service of the Humanitas-International Organization, a nonprofit human rights organization.

6.41   *PROMT Online Translator.* St. Petersburg, Russia: PROMT Ltd., 2003. Available: www.online-translator.com/text.asp#tr_form

This free online software translates text, Web sites, and e-mails in six languages. WAP (Wireless Application Protocol) translations for GSM phones with WAP support are offered in English and Russian only. Translated text can be saved or printed directly. A virtual keyboard is also available. The software can translate up to 500 words. Additional services like text and e-mail translations of up to 2,000 words, and specialized dictionaries are available free of charge for registered users.

6.42   *Reverso.* Paris, France: Softissimo, 2004. Available: www.reverso. net/text_translation.asp?lang=EN

This site provides software powered by Sofitissimo, for online translation between English and French, German, Italian, Spanish, and Russian, as well as between French and German, Italian and Spanish. Only the text translator is free. The Reverso Web page can be displayed in English, French, German, Italian, Russian, and Spanish.

6.43   *SYSTRAN.* Paris, France: Systran, 2007. Available: www.systransoft. com

SYSTRAN provides language translation software products for desktops, servers and online services. The desktop products include the capability to translate text or Web pages from the user's desktop, or Microsoft office applications. The server products are offered to larger companies to be accessed from their Intranet or LAN. Subscribers to the online service have real-time multiple language translations delivered directly to their personal computers without having to download the software. The software translates Web pages and text from English to any of 13 languages, including Arabic, both traditional and simplified Chinese, German, Dutch, Italian, Japanese, Korean, Portuguese, Russian, and Swedish. SYSTRAN will allow five free uses of the text translation service; after this one will have to purchase the software.

6.44   *WorldLingo.* Las Vegas, NV: World Lingo Translations, LLC, 2007. Available: http://www2.worldlingo.com/en/products_services/ worldlingo_translator.html

Three different translation choices in 15 different languages are available at this Web site: free text translator, e-mail translator and Web site translator. Human translation services are also offered for a fee.

There are some restrictions on the free services: the free translator and the e-mail translator will only translate the first 150 words of the input text. One can however use it repeatedly to copy and translate successive batches of 150 words of text. The Web site translator has a limit of 500 words. By clicking on the advanced options in the text and e-mail translators, "special character" boxes are displayed to enter accents and other foreign symbols. When sending or receiving a translated e-mail message via WorldLingo e-mail translator, the Web site will automatically register you and provide access to a secured page that offers an overview of fee-based WordLingo translation products. There is no need to access this page if only free available translations are sought.

The site claims their automated translations are approximately 70 to 75 percent accurate. If the text requires a higher accuracy rate, professional translators are available for a fee. The company offers professional translations, also known as human translations, in more that 141 languages.

6.45   *Xanadu*. In Foreignword.com. Alicante, Spain: Foreignword, 2000. Available: www.foreignword.biz/software/Xanadu/default. aspx

Xanadu is free language translation software offered by Foreignword. It has three sections to choose from: Translate, Locate, and Inform. Translate has the capability to translate words, terms, and text, and has links to professional translator services anywhere in the world. Locate will help in identifying specialized glossaries, and search for the meaning/definition of foreign words on the Web using search engines such as Google, AltaVista, Yahoo, Lycos, etc. Inform is an international news channel with news related to language topics, books or publishers; it may not be updated daily. Inform includes links to other Foreignword products, dictionaries, feedback, and suggestions for glossaries.

Once the software has been downloaded, one can choose from six languages for the user interface and help files: English, French, German, Spanish, Italian, or Portuguese. Xanadu translates words, terms, phrases, or texts from/to over 60 languages, and uses approximately 200 free online dictionaries or text translation systems. Several dictionaries, specialized glossaries, and keyboard shortcuts enable one to instantly translate terms selected in any Windows application (e.g. Word, PowerPoint, Outlook, etc.). Another feature of Xanadu is that there is a Wireless Application Protocol (WAP) translation for global system communication (GSM) users.

Search Engines

The following two sites provide links to several translation sites. Any of the hosted translators (e.g., Babel Fish, Google, WorldLingo, etc.) may be invoked to translate the input text.

6.46   *Free automatic translators—machine translations.* In NEWS TRAN.COM. Humanitas-International.org., 1996. Available: www. humanitas-international.org/newstran/more-trans.htm

Sponsored by NEWSTRAN, this Web site offers links to some of the translations sites discussed in this chapter. This is a free service of the Humanitas-International Organization, a nonprofit human rights organization.

6.47   *Mezzofanti translations.* Glenn Ellyn, IL: Mezzofanti.org., 2004. Available: www.mezzofanti.org/translation/index.html

This site is a compilation of free links to Web translators, dictionaries, and other language resources on the Internet. Mezzofanti.org is a nonprofit organization dedicated to the diffusion of foreign languages. Some of the links to Web translators were found to be obsolete.

Dictionaries and Specialized Translation Sites

There is a vast variety of translation dictionaries available via the Web. The list below is only a small sample of the available resources.

6.48   *Dictionary.com Translator.* Long Beach, CA: Lexico Publishing Group, 2007. Available: http://dictionary.reference.com/translate/

Powered by SYSTRAN this site can also translate phrases and long sentences from English and ten other languages, including Japanese, Korean, and Chinese.

6.49   *Globalgate.* Tokyo, Japan: Amikai Enterprise, 2006. Available: http://tool.nifty.com/globalgate/

Globalgate provides English-Japanese translations of text and Web sites.

6.50   *Glossary of Medical Terms. Multilingual lemmas.* Italy: UniPlan Software, 2007. Available: www.salus.it/voca4/language.html

This site includes an alphabetical list of medical terms and a glossary in English, Spanish, German, Danish, Dutch, Italian, French, and Portuguese.

Begin at the URL listed above to select the preferred language. After the language has been selected, one is directed to the appropriate medical glossary.

6.51 *Majstro Translation Dictionary.* Netherlands: Majstro Aplikaĵoj, 2002. Available: www.majstro.com/Web/Majstro/sdict.php

This dictionary translates to 36 languages, including Esperanto, Swahili, and Catalan. More advanced version button includes the use of virtual keyboards in Latin, Cyrillic, Greek, and Thai characters.

6.52 *Multilingual Thesaurus on Health Promotion in 12 European Languages.* NIGZ Netherlands Institute for Health Promotion and Disease Prevention, 2001. Available: www.hpmulti.net

The thesaurus is available to download in PDF or text format. This is not an interactive Web site. The languages supported are Danish, Dutch, English, Finnish, French, German, Greek, Italian, Norwegian, Portuguese, Spanish, and Swedish.

6.53 *Word2Word.com.* San Jose, CA: Bigben, 1995. Available: www. word2word.com//dictionary.html

This Web site includes links to a vast array of dictionaries in almost 200 languages, as well as links to other free translators. It also offers links to language courses, alphabets of the world, language learning podcasts, and forums for translators. This is a good site to visit for a comprehensive list of translation resources.

6.54 Kellog M. *WordReference.com.* McLean, VA: 1999. Available: www.wordreference.com

WordReference.com translates words in Spanish, French, Italian, and Portuguese. The site provides links to other dictionaries in these languages as well as links to language forums where questions about language usage can be answered by native speakers.

6.55 *YourDictionary.com.* Burlingame, CA: yourDictionary.com, Inc., 2007. Available: www.yourdictionary.com/translate/translate.html

This site includes word definitions in French, German, Italian, and Spanish. It also has links to Eurocosm UK dictionary of most common phrases. The dictionary displays several phrases in all four languages.

Summary

This section of the chapter is intended to inform and provide a brief introduction to some of the free online translation resources available. There are certainly many more free search engines and online dictionaries available via the Web. Also note that the sites are continually evolving, and it is worthwhile to visit the sites to see the latest services being offered.

To achieve high accuracy in translating documents, whether scientific or in some other discipline, human translation should be considered. Most machine translations simply recognize characters and words, and, based on these, translate the text literally without the capability to infer higher-level semantics or contextual information. When using machine translation it is worthwhile to follow the tips suggested on individual Web sites to achieve the best results. The Web site Mezzofanti.org also provides useful hints for getting good translations.

List of Features of Text and Web Translators

Babel Fish

- Translates between an extensive set of language pairs
- Limited number of characters in each transaction
- Good documentation and ease of use
- Translates text and Web sites only

Babylon

- Translates between an extensive set of language pairs
- Limited number of transactions
- Paid machine software translation of larger documents available
- Translates from highlighted text in Microsoft Office documents or within text
- Multilingual dictionary
- Translates text only
- Need to download software
- Only available for free on a trial basis period

elmundo.es traductor

- Translates only between English and a few other languages
- Paid machine software translation of larger documents available

- Translates text and Web sites only
- Virtual keyboard for special characters

Foreignword.com

- Translates between an extensive set of language pairs
- Limited number of characters in each transaction
- Paid human translation accessible from site
- WAP and PDA support
- Multilingual dictionary
- Translates text only

Free Automatic Translators—Machine Translations

- Provides access to several translation engines

FreeTranslation.com

- Translates between an extensive set of language pairs
- Limited number of characters in each transaction
- Paid machine software translation of larger documents available
- Paid human translation accessible from site
- Good documentation and ease of use
- Translates text and Web sites only
- Virtual keyboard for special characters

Google Language Tools

- Translate between an extensive set of language pairs
- Translates text and Web sites only
- Can display the Web site in five or more different languages or translate online newspapers into different languages

iMTranslator.net

- Translates between several pairs of major European languages (e.g., English, Spanish, French, German, etc.)
- Limited number of characters in each transaction
- Paid machine software translation of larger documents available
- Spell-checkers
- Multilingual dictionary
- Automatic retranslation to original source language
- Translates text only

- Virtual keyboard for special characters
- Provides option to print or email translated results

Mezzofanti Translations

- Provides access to several translation engines

NEWSTRAN Free Newspaper Translations

- Translates only between English and a few other languages
- Good documentation and ease of use
- Translates text only
- Can display the Web site in 5 or more different languages or translate online newspapers into different languages

PROMT Online Translator

- Translates between several pairs of major European languages (e.g., English, Spanish, French, German, etc.)
- Limited number of characters in each transaction
- Limited number of transactions
- Paid machine software translation of larger documents available
- WAP and PDA support
- Spell-checkers
- Translates text, Web sites, and e-mail
- Virtual keyboard for special characters

Reverso

- Translates between several pairs of major European languages (e.g., English, Spanish, French, German, etc.)
- Paid machine software translation of larger documents available
- Translates text and Web sites only
- Virtual keyboard for special characters
- Can display the Web site in five or more different languages or translate online newspapers into different languages

SYSTRAN

- Translates between an extensive set of language pairs
- Limited number of transactions
- Paid machine software translation of larger documents available
- Translates text and Web sites only

WorldLingo

- Translates between an extensive set of language pairs
- Limited number of characters in each transaction
- Paid machine software translation of larger documents available
- Paid human translation accessible from site
- Translates text, Web sites, and e-mail
- Virtual keyboard for special characters

Xanadu

- Translates between an extensive set of language pairs
- Translates from highlighted text in Microsoft Office documents or within text
- Spell-checkers
- Multilingual dictionary
- Translates text only
- Need to download software
- Can display the Web site in 5 or more different languages or translate online newspapers into different languages
- Provides option to print or email translated results

References

1. Cruzat GS. Keeping up with biomedical meetings. *RQ* 1967 Fall; 7:12–20.

PART III

Information Sources

CHAPTER 7

Terminology

Michelle L. Zafron

Understanding medical terminology is crucial to gaining competency with the literature of the health sciences. Reference tools that define terms or that provide insight into how such terms are formed are essential to learning medical terminology. Fortunately, there are a number of reference sources extant to assist with just this goal. These have been organized below in the following categories: general medical dictionaries; specialized dictionaries, which can be used to locate etymologies or abbreviations; subject dictionaries; foreign-language dictionaries; and compilations of syndromes, eponyms, and quotations.

General Dictionaries

General medical dictionaries may be divided into two categories: unabridged and abridged. A good medical dictionary should be updated to keep up with the discoveries, treatments, procedures, techniques, and advances that occur in the field of medicine and the health sciences with each passing day. Unabridged medical dictionaries are necessary because they are comprehensive in nature. There are two major unabridged medical dictionaries used in the United States.

7.1   *Dorland's Illustrated Medical Dictionary*. 30th ed. Philadelphia, PA: W.B. Saunders, 2003.

7.2   *Stedman's Medical Dictionary*. 28th ed. Philadelphia, PA: Lippincott Williams & Wilkins, 2006.

Considered by many to be the premier medical dictionary in the United States, *Dorland's Illustrated Medical Dictionary* has been in existence for over 100 years. The 30th edition offers definitions on over 122,000 terms, 1,100 illustrations, 18 appendices, and a very helpful section on medical etymology. *Dorland's* is thumb-indexed, a useful feature in a book that weighs nearly nine pounds. There is a very practical guide on using the source printed on the inside of the front cover.

Entries have pronunciations, etymologies, synonyms, and subentries. MeSH headings are provided for some terms. Terms that are considered subentries are grouped under their larger headword. Definitions of the subentries are included within the body of the main entry. In cases of synonyms, they are cross-referenced to the preferred terms. Thus, Alzheimer's Disease is cross-referenced under *dementia* as well as *disease*. A CD-ROM is included with purchase of the print edition.

Now in its 28th edition, *Stedman's Medical Dictionary* boasts over 107,000 entries. Its organization is not unlike *Dorland's*; alphabetization is letter by letter. Subentries are defined within the framework of the main entry. Synonyms are also cross-referenced with "see" references to preferred terms, printed in blue.

There are extensive illustrations and photographs. This edition features three large sections of color plates dispersed evenly throughout the dictionary. An effort was made in this edition to update the design in order to increase ease of use. *Stedman's* is thumb-indexed so that the reader can more quickly locate a term. Another feature of this edition is the addition of usage notes that, as stated in the Preface, are used extensively "to enhance the usefulness of the dictionary by alerting users to common errors of sense, spelling, and pronunciation, including confusion between words of similar form or meaning."

The expanded appendices provide information on units of measure, abbreviations and symbols, medical etymology, physical terminology, reference values, coding and classification systems, body mass and surface calculations, tests, botanicals, and infection control.

Dorland's Illustrated Medical Dictionary and *Stedman's Medical Dictionary* enjoy comparable coverage, authority, depth, and breadth. Their respective publishers issue new editions with regularity. There are, however, differences between the two. Some terms are present in one, but not the other. As there is no one current source with total comprehensiveness, it is recommended that all medical libraries make every effort to have both of these dictionaries.

7.3   *Blakiston's Gould Medical Dictionary.* 4th ed. New York: McGraw-Hill, 1979.

Blakiston's Gould Medical Dictionary has been out of print for some time; and there has been no new edition since 1979. The fourth edition contains 90,000 terms. Despite its age, it has some interesting features. Unlike the other unabridged medical dictionaries in this section, there are no subentries—all terms are arranged in alphabetical order for ease of use. The text is cross-referenced, and synonyms are defined by their preferred terms.

7.4   Venes D, ed. *Taber's Cyclopedic Medical Dictionary.* 20th ed. Philadelphia, PA: F.A. Davis Co., 2005.

7.5   Marcovitch H, ed. *Black's Medical Dictionary.* 41st ed., Lanham, MD: Scarecrow Press, 2006.

7.6   *The Bantam Medical Dictionary.* 5th ed. New York: Bantam Books, 2004.

7.7   Dox I, Melloni BJ, Melloni JL, Eisner G, eds. *Melloni's Illustrated Medical Dictionary.* 4th ed. Boca Raton, FL: CRC Press, 2001.

An abridged dictionary, *Taber's Cyclopedic Medical Dictionary* contains 56,000 definitions. It is suitable for clinicians, students, allied health professionals, and nurses. Written in encyclopedic format, many entries have subheadings on etiology, symptoms, treatment, prognosis, and patient care. Cross-references and patient care sections are highlighted in red. The majority of the 700 illustrations are in color.

The latest edition includes increased coverage of alternative and complementary medicine, bioethics, evidence-based care, informatics, nutrition, and patient safety. There are also a number of very useful appendices on topics such as medical emergencies, integrative therapies, laboratory values, nomenclature, phobias, immunization schedules, and health professions. One appendix of note is called "The Interpreter in Three Languages," which provides questions and answers that could be used during an examination. Access to the online edition is free with the purchase of the book.

Black's Medical Dictionary is meant not so much for the medical professional as it is for someone who wishes to have informed communication with the physician. Both the headings and language are broad, making the source more accessible to the layman. Over 5,000 terms and 100 diagrams and drawings are provided in this source. Entries are encyclopedic in nature; where appropriate, these contain cross-references. The format is clear and readable.

Providing definitions for over 11,000 medical terms, *The Bantam Medical Dictionary* is meant to be accessible to laymen as well as those in the health professions. In order to allow space for more current terminology, older and obsolete terms were removed from this edition. One particular feature worth noting is the inclusion of subentries—that is, definitions within definitions. The source is cross-referenced and has 150 illustrations. The layout is clear and readable, making this useful as a quick reference tool.

Melloni's Illustrated Medical Dictionary offers definitions for nearly 30,000 medical terms. The extensive illustrations, of which there are over 3,000, play an enormous part in the usefulness of this source. Entries and illustrations are color coded in order to make the information more comprehensible. Where applicable, entries contain phonetic pronunciations, synonyms, cross-references, and abbreviations. Using easily understood language, *Melloni's* is accessible to both the layman and the health sciences student.

Medical Etymology

Etymological sources are critical to anyone attempting to comprehend medical terminology. Medical terms generally have their basis in Latin and Greek prefixes, suffixes, and roots. By understanding how medical words and phrases are formed, one can arrive at a reasonable definition of a word. The sources listed below focus exclusively on etymology.

7.8 Skinner HA. *Origin of Medical Terms*. 2nd ed. Baltimore, MD: Williams & Wilkins, 1961.

7.9 Haubrich WS. *Medical Meanings: A Glossary of Word Origins*. 2nd ed. Philadelphia: PA: American College of Physicians, 2003.

7.10 Casselman B. *A Dictionary of Medical Derivations: The Real Meaning of Medical Terms*. New York: Parthenon Publishing Group, 1998.

7.11 Jaeger EC. *A Source-Book of Biological Names and Terms*. 3rd ed. Revised 2nd printing. Springfield, IL: Charles C Thomas, 1959.

Origin of Medical Terms covers both medicine and the basic sciences. The book is illustrated. Some eponyms are included, although others are cross-referenced to the official medical term. Biographical information is provided for the eponymous individual. Some sources are cited, and there is an extensive bibliography. Although the source has considerable breadth and scope, it is out of print.

According to its author, *Medical Meanings: A Glossary of Word Origins* was to fill the gap left since the last edition of *Origin of Medical Terms* was published. This source contains over 3,000 words and phrases. Since the first edition, almost one third have been revised and updated. Entries are cross-referenced. *Medical Meanings* is accessible to the layman. Both the format and the engaging narrative make for a very readable reference source.

A Dictionary of Medical Derivations: The Real Meaning of Medical Terms contains etymologies for 50,000 Latin and Greek words. It is meant to be accessible to anyone in the health sciences. The very readable section explaining how words are formed breaks down words into understandable parts. There is also a review listing of frequently used Latin and Greek roots used in medical words. Both terms and roots are indexed.

A Source-Book of Biological Names and Terms is somewhat different from the other books in this section. Although medical terms are included, the scope of the source is considerably larger; it encompasses biology as well as medicine. Over 13,000 words and phrases are listed, and there are some illustrations. In general, an entry includes the language of origin, the etymologic meaning, and an example of its use in scientific nomenclature. With a few exceptions, geographic and biographical names are limited and confined to an appendix. There is a section on the formation of words.

Medical Abbreviations

The use of abbreviations and acronyms is pervasive in every field of health care and the health sciences. Their popularity is unsurprising given the length and complexity of some medical terms and phrases, and the general need for a medical shorthand. However, as any given abbreviation can have multiple meanings, it becomes necessary for not only care, but also accurate reference tools. Given that some of these sources have listings that the others do not, more than one source is needed.

7.12 Jablonski S, ed. *Dictionary of Medical Acronyms and Abbreviations.* 5th ed. Philadelphia, PA: W.B. Saunders, 2005.

7.13 *Stedman's Abbreviations, Acronyms, and Symbols,* 3rd ed. Baltimore, MD: Lippincott Williams & Wilkins, 2003.

7.14 Davis NM. *Medical Abbreviations: 26,000 Conveniences at the Expense of Communication and Safety.* 12th ed. Warminster, PA: Neil B. Davis, 2005.

7.15 Melloni BJ, Melloni JL. *Melloni's Illustrated Dictionary of Medical Abbreviations.* Boca Raton, FL: CRC Press, 1998.

7.16   Tsur SA. *Elsevier's Dictionary of Abbreviations, Acronyms, Synonyms, and Symbols Used in Medicine.* 2nd enl. ed. Amsterdam: Elsevier, 2004.

7.17   Mitchell-Hatton SL. *The Davis Book of Medical Abbreviations: A Deciphering Guide.* Philadelphia, PA: F.A. Davis, 1991.

Jablonski's *Dictionary of Medical Acronyms & Abbreviations* is a simply organized source of a small, convenient size. Its latest edition features over 10,000 new entries. Acronyms and abbreviations are listed alphabetically in bold typeface, with possible expanded terms listed beneath them. There are no definitions, which might be considered a disadvantage. Some of the new terms reflect the advances of the latest virus nomenclature, computer technology, medical informatics, and molecular biology. The fifth edition is accompanied by a CD-ROM.

Stedman's Abbreviations, Acronyms, and Symbols has over 75,000 entries. As with Jablonski's *Dictionary*, there are no definitions. Slang terms are also included and are printed in red ink. All of these terms are alphabetized by letter. The book is cross-referenced. There are 11 useful appendices that cover: angles, triangles, and circles; arrows; genetic symbols; numbers; pluses, minuses, and equivalencies; primes, checks, dots, roots; statistical symbols; professions, titles, and degrees; professional associations and organizations; chemotherapy and other drug regimens; and clinical trials.

The easy-to-use *Medical Abbreviations: 26,000 Conveniences at the Expense of Communication and Safety* contains 17,000 abbreviations with 26,000 of their possible meanings and a list of nearly 3,500 cross-referenced commonly prescribed brand and generic drug names. Neil Davis makes a convincing case on the need for standardization in the form of a controlled vocabulary. There are several chapters including one on dangerous, contradictory, and ambiguous abbreviations. The book also comes with a 24-month single-user license for the Internet version of the book.

Melloni's Illustrated Dictionary of Medical Abbreviations contains 17,000 abbreviations and acronyms. Its over 150 illustrations are a unique characteristic of the book. Terms were compiled from the most current medical journals and textbooks. The format and layout are clear and concise.

Elsevier's Dictionary of Abbreviations, Acronyms, Synonyms and Symbols Used in Medicine contains over 30,000 abbreviations. The coverage extends to related medical fields such as anatomy, pathology, pharmacology, and bacteriology. It also includes biology, chemistry, and veterinary medicine.

Regardless of type, terms are organized alphabetically, making this a straight-forward source to use.

The Davis Book of Medical Abbreviations: A Deciphering Guide possesses certain unusual features that merit the book's inclusion. Some of the more than 30,000 abbreviations and acronyms include pronunciations. After the definition (i.e. the complete form of the abbreviation or acronym) is the specialty in parentheses. In addition, the source includes uncommon abbreviations and slang terms.

Word Finders and Concept Dictionaries

Conventional dictionaries are traditionally used when one knows a term, but not its meaning. If, however, one does not know the proper term, one can look up the concept or definition and locate the word. These are a selection of word finders or inverted concept dictionaries that can assist in filling this need.

7.18   Lorenzini JA, Lorenzini-Kley L. *Medical Phrase Index: A Comprehensive Reference to the Terminology of Medicine*. 3rd ed. Los Angeles, CA: Practice Management Corporation, 1994.

7.19   Stanaszek MJ, et al. *The Inverted Medical Dictionary*. 2nd ed. Lancaster, PA: Technomic, 1991.

7.20   Willeford G Jr., comp. *Webster's New World Medical Word Finder*. 4th ed. New York: Prentice-Hall, 1987.

Of the sources listed in this section, *Medical Phrase Index* is the most comprehensive. Compiled by two medical transcriptionists, it contains nearly 250,000 formal and informal medical phrases. In addition, common abbreviations and "sound alike" words and phrases are included. If the terms have multiple spellings, all are presented, with the most commonly used spelling indicated. All entries are cross-referenced. For ease of use, the book is thumb-indexed.

The Inverted Medical Dictionary consists of alphabetical lists of terms and of definitions or concepts. As described above, this is ideal when one is unsure of the proper word or phrase for a known concept. For example, if one were trying to find the word that describes a fear of open spaces, one would look up "fear of open spaces" and discover that the proper term was "agoraphobia." *The Inverted Medical Dictionary* also contains several useful sections on abbreviations, terms used for writing prescriptions, chemical abbreviations, as well as eponyms. This last segment presents the eponymic term, the proper medical term, and then a short description.

Webster's New World Medical Word Finder is meant to help health professionals, quickly spell, syllabicate, divide, and accentuate medical terms. The source is divided into ten sections. Of these, two focus on phonetic spellings and one offers a list of troublesome or difficult words. These should be of especial help to medical transcriptionists. Due to the age of the book, certain sections such as the drug names lists may be outdated.

Subject Dictionaries

Subject dictionaries are many in number and varied in topics. Although their breadth is limited, the depth of their coverage is not.

7.21 Zwemer TJ. *Mosby's Dental Dictionary*. St. Louis, MO: Mosby, 2003.

7.22 Jablonski S. *Jablonski's Dictionary of Dentistry*. Reprint edition of *Illustrated Dictionary of Dentistry*. Malabar, FL: Krieger, 1992.

7.23 Miller BF. *Miller-Keane Encyclopedia & Dictionary of Medicine, Nursing, and Allied Health*. 7th ed. Philadelphia, PA: Saunders, 2003.

7.24 Anderson DM. *Mosby's Medical, Nursing, & Allied Health Dictionary*. 6th ed. St. Louis, MO: Mosby, 2002.

7.25 King RC, Stansfield WD, Mulligan PK. *A Dictionary of Genetics*. 7th ed. New York: Oxford University Press, 2006.

7.26 Campbell RJ. *Campbell's Psychiatric Dictionary*. 8th ed. New York: Oxford University Press, 2004.

7.27 Blauvelt CT, Nelson FRT. *A Manual of Orthopaedic Terminology*. 6th ed. St. Louis, MO: Mosby, 1998.

Mosby's Dental Dictionary offers definitions for over 9,500 terms from all fields of dentistry. Its appendices cover such topics as symbols and abbreviations; American Dental Association Dental Codes; clinical oral structures; HIPPA; how dental terms are made and read; and pharmacology. Terms are listed alphabetically and are cross-referenced. It is accompanied by a CD-ROM with a searchable database and audio pronunciations.

Jablonski's Dictionary of Dentistry presents a compilation of dental terms from all dental and dental-related specialties. Older and more obscure terms are also included. The source is illustrated. Standard entries have the preferred name of the term, the pronunciation, the etymology, a definition, and if applicable, synonyms, trademarks, and cross-references.

Miller-Keane Encyclopedia and Dictionary of Medicine, Nursing, and Allied Health is exceptionally well organized. The book's "How to Use Miller-Keane" section is a model of clarity. In addition to the briefer, dictionary definitions, there are encyclopedic entries. These are lengthier and much more detailed. Many of the shorter entries are cross-referenced; *Miller-Keane* is illustrated. All entries are given phonetic respellings. The appendices are useful. They include: anatomical plates; assessment charts; nutrition; weights and measures; immunization schedules; symbols; reference intervals for laboratory tests; nursing vocabularies; and a great deal more.

Mosby's Medical, Nursing & Allied Health Dictionary is targeted at nurses and those in the allied health professions. Like *Miller-Keane*, some of the entries are encyclopedic in nature; all have sentence definitions. Abbreviations and cross references are actually alphabetized into the text. The book has over 2,200 color photos and illustrations. There is a color atlas of human anatomy. The 20 appendices cover such subjects as: symbols and abbreviations, anatomy, Spanish-English-French commonly used phrases, health promotion, nutrition, herbs, complementary and allied health, nursing diagnoses, infection control, nursing interventions classification, and nursing outcomes classification. The layout and the typeface are clear and readable.

A Dictionary of Genetics has nearly 7,000 definitions drawn from not only genetics, but from disciplines that are related to genetics such as molecular biology, cell biology, evolutionary studies, and so on. This edition was extensively revised. It is illustrated and cross-referenced. In addition to the dictionary portion, there are a number of useful appendices. Of note is a Chronology section in which there are over 1,000 entries for significant discoveries, events, and publications for genetics or genetics-related fields.

Campbell's Psychiatric Dictionary is targeted toward psychiatrists, but has the secondary goal of being accessible for those in the behavioral sciences and the health professions, and even a lay audience. In this it is successful. The entries are primarily encyclopedic. The book is cross-referenced.

Although *A Manual of Orthopaedic Terminology* is a dictionary, it is organized somewhat like a textbook. Instead of a traditional A to Z arrangement, there are chapters on broad topics which are broken down further into subtopics. There is an index for easy location of a particular term. There are several appendices, including one featuring orthopedic abbreviations and one on anatomic positions and directions.

7.28   Gray P. *The Dictionary of the Biological Sciences.* Reprint. Malabar, FL: Krieger, 1982.

7.29   Lawrence E. *Henderson's Dictionary of Biological Terms.* 11th ed. New York: John Wiley & Sons, 1995.

Although the coverage of biological dictionaries is broader than those of their medical counterparts, it is exactly for this reason that these sources are useful in a health sciences collection. *The Dictionary of the Biological Sciences* is somewhat complex to use. Descriptive terms are organized in the same fashion as a thesaurus. Wherever possible, vernacular terms are included, as are the anglicized terms of Greek and Latin words. The dictionary contains word roots, taxa of ordinal rank and above, synonyms where applicable, and some personal names. The vernacular, chemical, and biochemical terms are in alphabetical order.

Henderson's Dictionary of Biological Terms has over 23,000 terms. More current than *The Dictionary of the Biological Sciences*, it is also directed at a similar audience. Acronyms are presented at the beginning of each letter; otherwise it is organized alphabetically. It is illustrated. Its coverage includes Latin and Greek derivations, units, structural formulae, as well as plant and animal classification tables. The layout is easy to master.

Foreign-Language Dictionaries

Although there are plenty of generalized foreign-language dictionaries extant, the specialized nature of medicine and health care demands that there also be foreign-language medical dictionaries. For those treating the non-English speaker or looking for translation tools for other purposes, these are a selected sampling of some of the available sources.

7.30   McElroy OH, Grabb LL. *Spanish-English/English-Spanish Medical Dictionary/Diccionario Médico Español-Inglés, Inglés-Español.* 3rd ed. Philadelphia, PA: Lippincott Williams & Wilkins, 2005.

7.31   Rogers GT. *English-Spanish/Spanish-English Medical Dictionary.* 3rd ed. New York: McGraw-Hill, 2007.

7.32   Dorian AF, comp. *Elsevier's Encyclopaedic Dictionary of Medicine.* New York: Elsevier, 1988–1990, 4 parts.

7.33   Unseld DW. *The Medical Dictionary of the English and German Languages.* 10th ed. Revised and enlarged. Stuttgart: Wissenschaftliche Verlagsgesellschaft, 1991.

McElroy's *Spanish-English/English-Spanish Medical Dictionary* is an excellent example of what a foreign language medical dictionary should be. With over 20,000 terms, its layout is a model of clarity. Every section of the book is presented in both languages. Some entries are illustrated. In addition to the terms, general abbreviations as well as medical abbreviations are included. There are extensive appendices on patient communication, medical history, diagnosis, newborns, surgical procedures, anatomy, tests, and trauma and emergency problems. The deluxe edition also includes a CD-ROM and a PDA-compatible module.

The third edition of the *English-Spanish/Spanish-English Medical Dictionary* includes more than 5,000 new terms. These include medical and technical terms as well as slang and colloquialisms. If a word or phrase is specific to a particular Spanish-speaking nation, it is labeled as such. The book's small size makes this ideal for quick reference. There is also a section of sample conversations for interviews with patients on a number of topics.

Elsevier's Encyclopaedic Dictionary of Medicine has the advantage of presenting medical terms in five languages: English, French, German, Italian, and Spanish. There are four volumes that are available separately. These four parts consist of: general medicine; anatomy; biology; genetics and biochemistry; and therapeutic substances. The organization is the same throughout each volume. The first part is the designated "the basic table," which is a list of the alphabetized entries in English. Every entry is numbered, possesses an English definition, and then lists the term in French, German, Italian, and Spanish. In the second section, there are four indexes, one for each language. These indexes list the terms in that language; they are numbered as well. This number can be used to lead the user back to the entry in the basic table.

The Medical Dictionary of the English and German Languages is a simple foreign-language dictionary. It has two sections. The first lists English terms and their German equivalents. The second lists German terms and then their English equivalents. There is also an appendix with weights, measures, and temperatures in both tongues.

Syndromes, Eponyms, and Quotations

A syndrome is a collection of symptoms or conditions that typify a certain disease. These can be significant as the presence of a sign or symptom can indicate a particular disease. Syndromes are either eponymous, which means that they are named for the person who first reported the syndrome, or they are descriptive.

7.34 Magalini SI, Magalini SC. *Dictionary of Medical Syndromes*. 4th ed. Philadelphia, PA: Lippincott-Raven, 1997.

7.35 Durham RH. *Encyclopedia of Medical Syndromes*. New York: Hoeber, 1960.

7.36 Jablonski S. *Jablonski's Dictionary of Syndromes and Eponymic Diseases*. 2nd ed., Malabar, FL: Krieger 1991.

7.37 Kelly EC. *Encyclopedia of Medical Sources*. Baltimore: Williams & Wilkins, 1948.

Of the sources listed in this section, *Dictionary of Medical Syndromes* is the most current. The syndromes, of which there are nearly 3,000, are listed in alphabetical order. Each entry lists synonyms; symptoms and signs; etiology; pathology; diagnostic procedures; therapies; and prognosis. A bibliography is also given and the index is cross-referenced. The well-designed layout of the syndromes makes this book very useful as a quick reference source.

Encyclopedia of Medical Syndromes includes both eponymic and descriptive syndromes. Symptoms, treatment, etymologies, and medical references are included if known. This is a useful source because its coverage includes sources not listed in *Dictionary of Medical Syndromes*. Some syndromes are more detailed than others. The text is cross-referenced. The book also contains references to the literature that provide additional information on the syndromes. There is an index by classification, meaning that syndromes are organized by type or organ system.

Jablonski's Dictionary of Syndromes and Eponymic Diseases' self-expressed aim is to collect all eponymous diseases as well as all eponymous and non-eponymous syndromes. Biographical information such as name, nationality, specialty, and birth and death dates is provided for eponymic entries where possible. Many entries, although not all, include symptoms, etiology, pathology, diagnoses, prognosis, and synonyms. Most entries include the original report for the syndrome or disease. Selected entries are illustrated.

Despite its age, *Encyclopedia of Medical Sources* is still a relevant and authoritative work. Inspired by the discovery that certain historical and eponymic references were inaccurate, Kelly began compiling a more reliable list of the person for whom medical discoveries, eponymic diseases, signs, and syndromes were named. The result is *Encyclopedia of Medical Sources*.

In 95 percent of the entries, he has verified the reference in the original source. In some cases, biographic information is also provided. The book is organized by name and cross-referenced. The index lists the terms such as the diseases, procedures, and anatomical parts instead of the names themselves.

7.38 Huth EJ, Murray JT. *Medicine in Quotations: Views of Health and Disease through the Ages.* Philadelphia, PA: American College of Physicians, 2000.

7.39 Strauss MB. *Familiar Medical Quotations.* Boston, MA: Little, Brown, 1968.

7.40 Daintith J, Isaacs A. *Medical Quotes: A Thematic Dictionary.* New York: Facts on File, 1989.

Compilations of quotations not only serve to help those looking for suitable statements; they also present an historical perspective on the thoughts on medicine, health care, and disease. *Medicine in Quotations: Views of Health and Disease through the Ages* is an excellent source for finding applicable medical quotations. As it has been published more recently than the other books listed here, it has the advantage of currency. There is an extensive range of subjects. Quotations are arranged by topic and then alphabetically. Topic headings are broad and more standard so that the book can be accessible to a layman. The subject index is cross-referenced and should make up for any confusion.

One of the chief strengths of *Medicine in Quotations* is the author-citation index. Each quotation is numbered. Where possible the editors list the exact location of the quotation rather than just the name of the original source. This is an easy-to-use reference book that would be a helpful addition to most collections.

Familiar Medical Quotations contains over 7,000 entries in the fields of medicine and an array of health-related topics. Each quotation is organized by theme and then chronologically. The entries include the author's birth and death years. There is both an author index and a keyword index. The latter provides paraphrases of the quotations. Where the entries were not verified, secondary sources are listed, making *Familiar Medical Quotations* an authoritative source.

As might be surmised from the title, *Medical Quotes: A Thematic Dictionary,* is organized by theme. They are then arranged by alphabetical order of the author's surname. Quotations include some biographical information and a general citation where the original reference can be found. Terms are cross-referenced. There are two indexes: an author index and a keyword index, which leads one to the specific quote as well as the theme.

CHAPTER 8

Handbooks and Manuals

Katherine Schilling

Handbooks and manuals serve as useful reference guides to factual data in the basic sciences and for information for clinical diagnosis and treatment. Reviewed here are a variety of data books in the sciences and popular resources for laboratory methods and clinical decision-making. This chapter organizes handbooks and manuals into four broad categories: Scientific Data Books and Compendia, Disease Classification and Nomenclature, Laboratory Methods and Laboratory Diagnosis, and Clinical Diagnosis and Treatment. Format options are indicated for resources that are available online, on CD-ROM, or for PDAs or other format.

Scientific Data Books and Compendia

8.1   Lind DR, ed. *CRC Handbook of Chemistry and Physics*. 88th ed. Boca Raton, FL: CRC Press, 2007/2008.

Now in its 88th edition, the printed *CRC Handbook of Chemistry and Physics* includes a broad range of physical scientific data commonly required by chemists, physicists, and engineers. Included are properties of inorganic and organic compounds, chemical bonds, tables of isotopes, and scientific abbreviations and symbols. This edition also includes updated tables as well as new tables on Properties of Ionic Liquids, Solubilities of Hydrocarbons in Sea Water, Solubility of Organic Compounds in Superheated Water, and Nutritive Value of Foods.

The full 87th edition is available on the Web through CRC Press at http://hbcpnetbase.com. It features interactive tables that can be sorted, filtered, and combined in various ways. The following tables are regularly updated and expanded online: Physical Properties of Inorganic Compounds, Enthalpy of Fusion, Bond Dissociation Energies, Table of the Isotopes (updated through 2005), Inorganic Ion and Ligand Nomenclature, Chemical Carcinogens, and Global Temperature Trend. Within these tables, substances can be searched by name, formula, or CAS Registry Numbers. The *CRC Handbook of Chemistry and Physics* on CD-ROM contains the full, updated 87th edition in searchable PDF format.

8.2   *CHEMnetBASE*. Boca Raton, FL: CRC Press, 2006. Available: www.chemnetbase.com

CHEMnetBASE is an online collection of products from CRC Press. It includes several dictionaries: *Commonly Cited Compounds, Drugs, Inorganic and Organometallic Compounds, Natural Products* and *Organic Compounds*; and other products such as the Periodic Table Online, Properties of Organic Compounds, and Polymers: A Property Database. Also available is the 87th edition of the *CRC Handbook of Chemistry and Physics*. The Properties of Organic Compounds database contains thousands of organic compounds with physical and spectral data and structures. The system is designed for locating unknown compounds, and retrieving references for known compounds. Polymers: A Property Database provides scientific and commercial information on polymers. It is searchable by polymer, properties, trade name, application, and other fields. CHEMnetBASE is available via multiuser subscriptions only: no individual subscriptions. The search interface allows only for each product to be searched independently.

8.3   Detrick B, Hamilton R, Folds J, eds. *Manual of Molecular Clinical Laboratory Immunology*. 7th ed. Washington, DC: ASM Press, 2006.

8.4   Murray PR, Baron EJ, Jorgensen JH, et al, eds. *Manual of Clinical Microbiology*. 9th revised ed. Washington, DC: ASM Press, 2007.

8.5   Wild D, ed. *The Immunoassay Handbook*. 3rd ed. Boston: Elsevier Science, 2005.

The revised seventh edition of the *Manual of Molecular Clinical Laboratory Immunology* (formerly known as *Manual of Clinical Laboratory Immunology*) provides both standard and the latest immunological tests and procedures in clinical laboratory immunology. This immunology technique and diagnosis tool is organized into 17 primary sections, each with multiple chapters on various topics including general methodology, laboratory management, molecular testing, Clinical Chemistry, Hematopathology, Medical Microbiology, and others. Also included are more thorough sections on transplantation, allergic diseases, cancer, and others. Expanded treatment information has been added throughout.

The *Manual of Clinical Microbiology*, known primarily for its content in medical microbiology, diagnostic microbiology, and microbiological techniques, is now in its ninth edition. It was recently expanded into a two-volume set in its eighth edition. Volume 1, "General Issues in Clinical Microbiology," is organized into multiple broad sections including several chapters on laboratory management issues, microorganisms, specimen collection and handling, and storage procedures. Volume 2, "Virology," includes sections on virus taxonomy and classification, specimen handling procedures, algorithms for detecting and identifying viruses, and so on. The *Manual of Clinical Microbiology* is further organized into more than 140 chapters across its major sections.

The Immunoassay Handbook is a useful scientific text for clinical applications and practical information in the field of immunoassay technology. Designed for a broad audience of pathologists, chemists, biochemists, and students, *The Immunoassay Handbook* covers a wide range of popular immunoassay tests used for medical diagnosis and for commercial purposes. It is organized into 68 chapters, including the useful introduction "Immunoassay for Beginners." Chapters include brief guides to normal and disease states, with analytes described in depth. The revised third edition has four major parts: Part 1 describes the theory of immunoassay. Part 2 explains 32 representative commercial systems that are used in laboratories and physicians' offices. Part 3 addresses laboratory management; and Part 4 describes major applications of immunoassays.

8.6   Bronzino JD. *Biomedical Engineering Fundamentals.* Volume 1 of *The Biomedical Engineering Handbook.* Boca Raton, FL: CRC Press, 2006.

8.7   Bronzino JD. *Medical Devices and Systems.* Volume 2 of *The Biomedical Engineering Handbook.* Boca Raton, FL: CRC Press, 2006.

8.8   Bronzino JD. *Tissue Engineering and Artificial Organs.* Volume 3 of *The Biomedical Engineering Handbook.* Boca Raton, FL: CRC Press, 2006.

The Biomedical Engineering Handbook is a comprehensive manual on all aspects of biomedical engineering. It has been updated into three volumes in its third edition. Volume 1, *Biomedical Engineering Fundamentals*, covers foundational concepts, including coverage of physiologic systems, bioelectric phenomena, biomechanics, biomaterials, physiologic modeling, ethics, and neuroengineering.

In Volume 2, *Medical Devices and Systems*, topics include sensor and imaging technologies, signal analysis, medical instrumentation, and many others. Volume 3, *Tissue Engineering and Artificial Organs*, has 77 chapters covering topics such as molecular biology, transport phenomena, biomimetics systems, biotechnology, prostheses, artificial organs, ethical issues, and bionanotechnology.

Disease Classification and Nomenclature

The *ICD-10* and *DSM-IV* were reviewed in the fourth edition of *Introduction to Reference Sources in the Health Sciences*, with new online versions, modification, and compilations included here in the fifth edition [1].

8.9 *World Health Organization. International Classification of Diseases ICD-10: International Statistical Classification of Diseases and Related Health Problems*. 10th revised ed. Geneva, Switzerland: World Health Organization, 2005. CD-ROM.

8.10 *ICD-9-CM: International Classification of Diseases, 9th revision, Clinical Modification*, 6th ed. Los Angeles, CA: Practice Management Information, 2006.

8.11 *ICD-9-CM: International Classification of Diseases, 9th revision, Clinical Modification*. Volumes 1, 2, and 3 for Hospitals, Volumes 1 and 2 for Physicians. Los Angeles, CA: Practice Management Information, 2006. Available: www.statref.com/

The *International Classification of Diseases (ICD)* is the standard international coding tool for diseases, injuries, and related health problems. It is broadly designed for morbidity and mortality information for statistical purposes and for the indexing of hospital records by disease and operations for data storage and retrieval [2]. The National Center for Health Statistics has worked with the World Health Organization to develop the *ICD-10* for morbidity purposes, with the *ICD-10* used for coding and classifying mortality from death certificates in the United States. The *ICD-10* replaced the *ICD-9* for this purpose as of January 1999.

The printed *ICD-10* is presented in three volumes: (1) the tabular list, (2) related definitions, standards, rules and instructions, and (3) the alphabetical list. Other notable changes include "the addition of information relevant to ambulatory and managed care encounters, expanded injury codes, the creation of combination diagnosis/symptom codes to reduce the number of codes needed to fully describe a condition, the addition of a sixth character, incorporation of common fourth and fifth digit subclassifications, and greater specificity in code assignment" [3].

The *ICD-10-CM* is planned as the replacement for the *ICD-9-CM*, volumes one and two. The current version of *ICD-10-CM* contains a significant increase in codes over *ICD-10* and *ICD-9-CM*. In addition, *ICD-10-CM* chapters have been retitled, rearranged, and added in order to increase the level of clinical detail.

International Classification of Diseases ICD-10: International Statistical Classification of Diseases and Related Health Problems is packaged as a CD-ROM and in a network version for multiple users. The database includes the full contents of the print edition's three volumes, corrigenda to Volume 1, and World Health Organization committee updates from 1983 to 2003.

The full 2006 edition of the *International Classification of Diseases, 9th Revision, Clinical Modification (ICD-9-CM)* is available online through STAT!Ref (www.statref.com).

8.12 *Diagnostic and Statistical Manual of Mental Disorders, Text Revision, (DSM-IV-TR).* 4th ed. Washington, DC: The American Psychiatric Association, 2000. Available: www.statref.com/

The fourth edition of the American Psychiatric Association's *Diagnostic and Statistical Manual of Mental Disorders*, or *DSM-IV*, is also available online via STAT!Ref (www.statref.com). The online manual is organized into four primary sections beginning with detailed instructions about the manual's organization and usage, followed by the DSM-IV-TR Classification, a systematic list of codes and categories. The DSM-IV Multiaxial System for assessment is described. Finally, detailed diagnostic criteria for DSM-IV disorders are delineated, along with descriptive text.

8.13 Schulte-Markwort M, P Riedesser P, Marutt K, eds. *Cross-walks ICD-10/DSM-IV: A Synopsis of Classifications of Mental Disorders.* Cambridge, MA: Hogrefe & Huber, 2003.

Cross-walks ICD-10/DSM-IV is worth noting for its easy comparisons between the most current text revision (TR) editions of the *ICD-10* and *DSM-IV*. This manual is made up of tables comparing and contrasting the classifications, with "crosswalks" in both directions. The first half of the book provides tables from the *ICD-10* perspective: listing *ICD-10* mental disorders in the left column, the *DSM-IV-TR* diagnosis in the right column, with the cross-comparison in the center column. Included in these "crosswalks" are explanations of the correspondence between the codes, as well as differences or omissions in each of the coding systems. The second half of the book is organized similarly, but in reverse, with the *DSM-IV-TR* classification on the left and the *ICD-10* on the right. No indices are provided.

8.14   *Current Procedural Terminology: CPT 2008 Standard Edition.* Chicago, IL: American Medical Association, 2007.

Current Procedural Terminology (CPT) codes include hundreds of medical codes for identifying and describing all performed medical procedures that are used for reporting, and billing Medicare or private insurers. *CPT* codes are published by the American Medical Association (AMA) and are updated annually. Yearly editions include code additions, changes, and deletions. Electronic access is also available from the AMA (www.ama-assn.org).

8.15   *Enzyme Nomenclature.* Nomenclature Committee of the International Union of Biochemistry and Molecular Biology (NC-IUBMB) in consultation with the IUPAC-IUBMB Joint Commission on Biochemical Nomenclature (JCBN). Department of Chemistry, Queen Mary University of London, London, UK, 1992–1999. Available: www.chem. qmul.ac.uk/iubmb/enzyme/

The Enzyme Nomenclature database is a publicly available Web-based alternative to printed enzyme nomenclature tools. The database is based on the sixth edition (1992) of *Enzyme Nomenclature*, with multiple supplements through 1999. Data are presented in enzyme number-order giving a recommended name for each enzyme. EC numbers and details are provided. Users can click on EC categories to identify specific enzymes, then link to a detailed scope note for each enzyme.

Laboratory Methods and Laboratory Diagnosis

8.16   Walker JM, Rapley R. *Medical Biomethods Handbook.* Totowa, NJ: Humana Press, 2005.

The *Medical Biomethods Handbook* includes a large collection of molecular biology techniques that are used mostly by medical and clinical researchers, primarily in diagnostics. One of the strengths of this tool is that it can be effectively used by students, researchers, or clinicians who do not have advanced knowledge or expertise in laboratory methods. Arranged into 17 distinct chapters, the *Medical Biomethods Handbook* covers southern and western blotting techniques, electrophoresis, PCR, cDNA and protein microarrays, liquid chromatography, in situ hybridization, karyotyping, flow cytometry, bioinformatics, genomics, and ribotyping. The applications assays for mutation detection, mRNA analysis, chromosome translocations, inborn errors of metabolism, protein therapeutics, and gene therapy are included. Practical procedures and applications are described, as are their underlying theories.

8.17   *Current Protocols Series*. Indianapolis, IN: John Wiley & Sons, 2000– 2007. Available: www.currentprotocols.com/WileyCDA/

Current Protocols includes hundreds of research protocols and overviews for 13 primary areas: bioinformatics, cell biology, cytometry, human genetics, immunology, magnetic resonance imaging, microbiology, molecular biology, neuroscience, nucleic acid chemistry, pharmacology, and toxicology. Within each protocol is a materials list, with overviews that detail the purposes, applications, limitations, advantages and other issues associated with each method. Commentary and guidelines are provided, along with a variety of illustrations, tables, data charts and diagrams. *Current Protocols* is available in print, CD-ROM, or online via Wiley InterScience.

8.18   McPherson RA, Pincus MR, eds. *Henry's Clinical Diagnosis and Management by Laboratory Methods*. 21st ed. Philadelphia: Saunders Elsevier, 2007.

The revised 21st edition of *Henry's Clinical Diagnosis and Management of Laboratory Methods* gives comprehensive coverage of laboratory test selection and the interpretation of results. This edition includes a new organ-system organization scheme, a new section on cancer testing, and new chapters on laboratory regulations, nutrition, point-of-care testing, bioterrorism, proteomics, microarray analysis, and the human genome project. Also included are details about instrumentation and clinical laboratory automation, medicolegal aspects of environmental toxicology, occupational exposures, workplace and employment drug testing, molecular microbiology testing, bioterrorism nutritional status testing, point-of-care testing, and others.

8.19   Pagana KD, Pagana TJ. *Mosby's Diagnostic and Laboratory Test Reference.* 8th ed. St. Louis, MO: Mosby, 2007.

8.20   Chernicky CC, Berger BJ. *Laboratory Tests and Diagnostic Procedures.* 5th revised ed. Philadelphia, PA: Elsevier, 2007.

8.21   Van Leeuwen AM. *Davis's Comprehensive Handbook of Laboratory and Diagnostic Tests with Nursing Implications.* 2nd ed. Philadelphia, PA: F.A. Davis, 2006.

Mosby's Diagnostic and Laboratory Test Reference is a pocket-sized handbook that provides access to clinical laboratory and diagnostic tests. Tests are listed by their complete names with abbreviations and alternate names. Purposes of tests are identified, as are the source of the laboratory specimen or location of procedure. A description of each test is provided in a section on test explanations and related physiology. Normal findings are listed for infants, children, adults, and the elderly. Possible critical values are given. Where appropriate, values are separated into male or female. Contraindications, potential complications, procedure and patient care, and home care responsibilities are also included. *Mosby's Diagnostic and Laboratory Test Reference* includes a "User's Guide to Test Preparation and Procedures," a guide for clinicians that delineates their responsibilities for guaranteeing the safety of test procedures and accuracy of results. Four appendices list tests by body system, tests by type, disease and organ panels, and symbols and units of measurement.

The fifth edition of *Laboratory Tests and Diagnostic Procedures* (2007) is one of the more comprehensive laboratory test references. It includes over 900 tests and diagnostic procedures. Organized alphabetically, with A-to-Z thumb tabs for easy browsing, *Laboratory Tests and Diagnostic Procedures* is divided into two parts. Part 1 provides an alphabetical list of more than 600 diseases, conditions, and symptoms, and the most commonly used corresponding diagnostic tests and procedures. Part 2 presents key information on laboratory and diagnostic tests. Cross-referenced alternatives provide test names and acronyms. Tests for toxic substances are included, along with Panic Level Symptoms and Treatment for dangerously elevated levels. Age and gender-specific norms are provided, along with risks and contraindications. Minimum volumes for blood samples are provided for patients for whom blood preservation is important. Special consent form requirements are indicated as well.

Davis's Comprehensive Handbook of Laboratory and Diagnostic Tests with Nursing Implications is one of several laboratory handbooks designed specifically for nurses. *Davis's* includes concise explanations of each test, synonyms or acronyms for the test name, names of related tests, pre- and post-test considerations, type specimen needed, critical values, differences in age range and gender, rationale, indications, results, and factors affecting results. Content is arranged alphabetically by test, with critical considerations labeled with color-coded icons. Nursing implications are presented for each test, including explanations that the patient and family may need for pre- and post-test preparation.

8.22   Vandenpitte J, Engbaek K, Rohner P, eds. *Basic Laboratory Procedures in Clinical Bacteriology*. 2nd ed., Geneva: World Health Organization, 2003.

This updated second edition of *Basic Laboratory Procedures in Clinical Bacteriology* provides World Health Organization guidelines on the sampling of specimens for lab investigation, identification of bacteria and the testing of antibiotic resistance. Part 1 covers bacteriological investigations regarding blood, cerebrospinal fluid, urine, stools, upper and lower respiratory tract infections, sexually transmitted diseases, purulent exudates, wounds and abscesses, anaerobic bacteriology, antimicrobial susceptibility testing and serological tests. Part 2 covers key pathogens, media and diagnostic reagents. A list of media and reagents needed for the isolation and identification of the most common bacterial pathogens is included, together with an indication of their relative importance for the intermediary laboratory. Instead of focusing on basic techniques of microscopy and staining, the handbook focuses on procedural issues related to quality control and assessment. Particular attention is given to the need for quality control in laboratory procedures, with step-by-step instructions for obtaining specimens, isolating and identifying bacteria, and assessing their resistance to antibiotics. *Basic Laboratory Procedures in Clinical Bacteriology* is also available online through Netlibrary (http://netlibrary.com), a division of OCLC.

Clinical Diagnosis and Treatment

8.23   Rakel RE, Bope ET, eds. *Conn's Current Therapy*. Philadelphia: W.B. Saunders, 2007.

Updated annually since its inception in 1984, *Conn's Current Therapy* is a handbook of diagnostics, therapeutics, and patient care, with descriptions of current therapeutic techniques for managing nearly 300 common diseases and disorders. Disease conditions are referenced by body system. In the later editions, "diagnosis boxes" and "treatment boxes" highlight key points in diagnosis and treatment for easier scanning. *Conn's Current Therapy* also covers herbal products and recently approved and soon-to-be-approved drugs.

Web-based access to the complete 2006 and 2007 printed texts is available with the purchase of the 2007 printed handbook (www.connscurrent therapy. com). Features of *Conn's Current Therapy* online include a frequently-updated drug database, a variety of clinical algorithms and tables, and an option to download content onto a PDA.

8.24   Domino FJ. *The 5-Minute Clinical Consult 2008*. Philadelphia: Lippincott Williams & Wilkins, 2007. Available: www.statref.com

Lippincott Williams & Wilkins publishes multiple individual titles its *5-Minute* series, including *The 5-Minute Emergency Medicine Consult*, *The 5-Minute Pediatric Consult* (print, CD-ROM, www.statref.com), and titles on neurology, nurses' clinical consult, orthopaedics, pain management, pediatrics, veterinary medicine, and others. The titles listed here are the most current updates in the series since 2005; various format options are available:

- *AHA 5-Minute Clinical Cardiology Consult*, 2nd ed.
- *5-Minute Consult: Clinical Companion to Women's Health*
- *5-Minute Emergency Medicine Consult*, 3rd revised ed.
- *5-Minute Orthopaedic Consul*, 2nd revised ed.
- *5-Minute Pain Management Consult*

The revised 2007 edition of *The 5-Minute Clinical Consult 2008* provides information on the diagnosis, treatment, medications, follow-up, and associated conditions of 675 medical conditions. This edition is evidence-focused, with evidence-based references for most topics. Organized alphabetically, this reference presents concise, bulleted points on disease topics in a three-column format. Differential diagnosis algorithms are located in the front of the book; *ICD-9* codes are presented in blue. Full contents of the 2007 (15th) edition are currently available on CD-ROM and online via STAT!Ref (www.statref.com). *The 5-Minute Clinical Consult 2008* is also available for a PDA.

8.25   Beers MH, Jones TV, Porter RS, eds. *Merck Manual of Diagnosis and Therapy*. 18th revised ed. Hoboken, NJ: John Wiley & Sons, 2006.

8.26   Beers MH, Jones TV, Porter RS, eds. *Merck Manual of Diagnosis and Therapy*. 18th revised ed. Whitehouse Station, NJ: Merck Research Laboratories, 2006. Available: www.statref.com

8.27   Beers MH, ed. *Merck Manual of Medical Information, Second Home Edition*. Little Rock, AR: Handheldmed, 2005. Available: www.handheldmed.com

First published in 1899 as the *Merck's Manual of the Materia Medica*, the *Merck Manual of Diagnosis and Therapy* (usually called *The Merck Manual* or *Merck's*) is a widely used medical textbook that provides essential information on diagnosing and treating medical disorders [4]. Simon and Schuster published the popular *Merck Manual* series, which has grown to include the *Merck Manual—Home Edition*, a lay version of the *Merck Manual of Diagnosis and Therapy*, the *Merck Manual of Geriatrics*, the *Merck Index*, a chemical encyclopedia, and titles in children's health, women's and men's health, health and aging, and veterinary medicine. A variety of product formats—print, online, CD-ROM, PDA—are available. Included in this chapter are major *Merck* titles that have been updated since 2005.

The *Merck Manual of Diagnosis and Therapy* covers diagnosis and treatment in internal medicine. The small-format handbook is organized with thumb-tab access into 22 major sections by body system and medical specialty. In its 18th edition in 2006, the handbook has been updated with significant clinically focused content, including 34 new chapters and 69 new illustrations, and specific guidance on patient examinations. Appendixes include common drugs and key reference values. An extensive index is provided. The 18th edition (2006) is available online from *STAT Ref* (www.statref.com) and Merck (www.merck.com).

The 2006 *Merck Manual of Medical Information, Second Home Edition* is a comprehensive consumer health version of the *Merck Manual of Diagnosis and Therapy*, written in a lay-focused style and format. This title has been further adapted into the *Merck Manual of Women's and Men's Health* (2006), and the *Merck Manual of Children's Health* (2006). The *Merck Manual of Medical Information, Second Home Edition* is available online from *STAT!Ref* (www.statref.com), Merck (www.merck.com), and for use with PDAs through Handheldmed (www.handheldmed.com).

8.28   Oyelowo T. *Mosby's Guide to Women's Health: A Handbook for Health Professionals*. Geneva: Elsevier Health Sciences Division, 2007.

Mosby's Guide to Women's Health is a clinical guide to managing common issues arising in women's health. Concise and well organized, this guide includes protocols for the diagnosis and treatment of a range of conditions.

Traditional medical information is included, as is information on alternative treatments such as physical therapy, chiropractic, naturopathic therapies, nutrition, and herbs.

8.29   Bartlett JG, Auwaerter JG, Pham PA, eds. *The ABX Guide: Diagnosis and Treatment of Infectious Diseases.* Montvale, NJ: Thompson Healthcare, 2005.

The ABX Guide: Diagnosis and Treatment of Infectious Diseases is a pocket-sized handbook designed to be a point-of-care decision support tool for preventing, diagnosing, and treating most infectious diseases. *The ABX Guide* is organized into four sections: "Anti-infectives," which includes prescribing information for a variety of drug categories; "Vaccines," which provides agents used for immunization and prophylaxis and includes information on diagnostic criteria, indications, administration, and adverse reactions; "Diagnoses," which features common infectious diseases with diagnostic criteria, common pathogens, treatment regimens, and drug recommendations; and "Pathogens," which covers clinical information on bacteria, fungi, parasites, and viruses. Each entry includes clinical relevance, sites of infection, treatment regimens, and general comments and references. The handbook also provides a variety of tables in a rear section, and fold-out chart covering the spectrum of activity for key drugs. An online version, current to mid-2005, is available free of charge from the Division of Infectious Diseases at Johns Hopkins University (www.hopkins-abxguide.org).

8.30   Ackley BJ, Ladwig GB. *Nursing Diagnosis Handbook: An Evidence-Based Guide to Planning Care.* St. Louis, MO: Elsevier Health Sciences Division, 2007.

The *Nursing Diagnosis Handbook* is designed to be used to build customized care plans based on individual patient's needs. A step-by-step approach to the process assists nurses in identifying a diagnosis, then generating a care plan that includes the desired outcomes, interventions, and evidence-based rationales. The handbook is organized alphabetically, with evidence-based practice information incorporated throughout. It provides care plans for every 2007–2008 North American Nursing Diagnosis Association (NANDA-I) approved nursing diagnosis, including multiple new, revised, and replacement diagnoses. Also included are explanations of Nursing Interventions Classifications (NIC) and Nursing Outcomes Classifications (NOC) taxonomies and samples of NIC and NOC interventions, as well as outcomes for each care plan.

Additional features include information on teaching sections with wellness and health promotion information, and coverage on pediatric, geriatric, and multicultural considerations. A free-of-charge Care Plan Constructor Web site (www1.us.elsevierhealth.com/Evolve/Ackley/NDH6e/Constructor/) allows nurses to create customized plans of care.

8.31   *Professional Guide to Diseases*, 8th ed. Ambler, PA: Lippincott Williams & Wilkins, 2005.

The *Professional Guide to Diseases*, in its eighth edition in 2005, mirrors the *Merck Manual* in coverage and content. This handbook covers over 600 disorders, including emerging diseases, antibiotic-resistant infections, and terrorist agents. Each entry includes a descriptive overview, and information on causes, incidence, signs, symptoms, diagnosis, treatment, and special considerations such as nutrition information, support referrals, or congenital abnormalities. Charts, illustrations, and anatomic drawings supplement the text.

8.32   *Guide to Clinical Preventive Services*. Washington, DC: U.S. Department of Health and Human Services, Agency for Healthcare Research and Quality, 2006. Available: www.ahrq.gov/clinic/pocket gd/index.html.

The *Guide to Clinical Preventive Services* includes recommendations on screening, counseling, and preventive medication topics and clinical considerations from the U.S. Preventive Services Task Force (USPSTF), an independent panel of experts in primary care and prevention that provides systematic reviews of the evidence of effectiveness and develops recommendations for clinical preventive services. The 2006 pocket guide includes all recommendations from 2001 to 2005, and can be downloaded or used on the Web (www.ahrq.gov/clinic/pocketgd/index.html). More recent recommendations are listed alphabetically on the free-of-charge Web site (www.ahrq.gov/clinic/uspstf/uspstopics.htm). USPSTF recommendations are also available for PDAs and via the Web through the Electronic Preventive Services Selector (www.epss.ahrq.gov), which can be searched by age, gender, and selected behavioral risk factors.

References

1. Boorkman JA, Huber JT, Roper FW. *Introduction to reference sources in the health sciences*. 4th ed. New York: Neal-Schuman, 2004.

2. *ICD-9-CM: International Classification of Diseases, 9th revision, Clinical Modification.* 6th ed. Los Angeles, CA: Practice Management Information, 2006.

3. National Center for Health Statistics. Classifications of Diseases and Functioning & Disability. *About the International Classification of Diseases, Tenth Revision, Clinical Modification (ICD-10-CM)*, 2007. Available: www.cdc.gov/nchs/about/otheract/icd9/abticd10.htm.

4. Beers MH, Jones TV, Porter RS, eds. *Merck manual of diagnosis and therapy.* 18th revised ed. Hoboken, NJ: John Wiley & Sons, 2006.

CHAPTER 9

Drug Information Sources

Susan M. McGuinness and Nancy F. Stimson

Librarians, as experts in keeping current with new information resources and technologies, face challenges in the current environment of drug information. Drug information, and the resources and tools associated with it, have evolved rapidly in the past decade. Major factors driving changes in drug information include the emergence of pharmacogenomics, maturation of the Internet, and changing roles of health care practitioners. Drug information encompasses the fields of pharmacology (the study of the physiological actions of drugs), pharmacy (the compounding, manufacture, and dispensing of drugs), and toxicology (the study of hazardous effects of chemicals).

Pharmacogenomics, which accompanied the completion of the human genome project, involves the study of the genetic basis of drug and chemical actions in the body. Pharmacogenomics deals with genetic variations in individual responses to medications and promises a new era of personalized medicine, in which health care practitioners will have the ability to predict unique responses to drugs, either adverse or beneficial, in each patient. Pharmacogenomics impacts all areas of pharmacology and pharmacy, from drug design and development to education and practice. This adds complexity to drug information, not only by accelerating growth in the sheer volume of information, but by introducing new terminologies, new types of data, and new information resources. For example, the National Center for Biotechnology Information maintains a database of genetic sequence variations, or polymorphisms (SNP: Single nucleotide polymorphisms). SNP data may be used to investigate a myriad of questions, such as identifying new potential targets for drugs, variations in individuals' positive or negative responses to certain drugs, variations in how individuals metabolize drugs, and how these differences translate to dosing calculations. This example illustrates a broader scope of information needs in the post-genome era.

The Internet has transformed scientific investigation and communications and contributed to the increasingly multidisciplinary nature of drug information. Boundaries between disciplines are disappearing, and librarians may be called upon to access information not traditionally included in the category of drug information, such as DNA or protein sequences, chemical structures, and physical properties of drug molecules.

Clinical drug or therapy questions continue to proliferate with the changing roles of health care professionals. Today's pharmacists function as integral members of health care teams, partnering with physicians to customize drug regimens for individuals [1]. As high-level practitioners who are qualified to advise patients and physicians about drug therapies, they require drug information to support clinical decision-making. With their professional responsibility for patient care, therapeutic outcomes, and medical standards of care requiring evidence-based practice, pharmacists rely heavily on timely and accurate drug information. Librarians serving this population are challenged to efficiently and effectively access current, relevant drug information in a highly dynamic field. While it may not be necessary for every health sciences librarian to master the use of research tools such as genetics databases, it will be important to maintain awareness of new developments in drug information resources.

Drug information questions are directed to librarians from a number of sources. A physician may want to know all adverse effects associated with the administration of a particular drug, or if the drug interacts with other drugs under physiological conditions. An occupational health specialist may ask if there is a relationship between a clinical symptom and daily exposure to a chemical in a work environment. A pharmacist may need the U.S. equivalent of a drug prescribed in another country. A nurse may want information about a drug being administered to a patient to assist in monitoring the patient's response to the drug. Increasingly complex drug information questions are also directed to librarians from patients. The Internet provides many sources of consumer health information, some more authoritative than others, and patrons often need help evaluating Web sites. Another factor affecting the scope of information needs is direct-to-consumer drug advertising. Armed with information from the Internet and drug company advertising, consumers and their families are questioning the recommendations of their physicians. As a result, patients may use the library to investigate questions about drugs they are taking or about additives in the foods they eat. Physicians and pharmacists may need drug information written in lay language to optimize their communications with patients.

The number of drugs (both prescription and nonprescription) available on the market has increased substantially in recent years. The use of herbal products and other alternative therapies has also expanded, in large part due to the empowerment of consumers with increased access to health information. With the increase in the number of drugs in use, there exists a proportional increase in the potential for adverse effects, and an exponential increase in the number of possible interactions between these drugs. As a result, iatrogenic (practitioner-induced) pathology continues to play a significant role in medicine today, and the need for reliable drug information sources is vital to reducing the incidence of medication errors.

Government Regulation and the Drug Approval Process

Government regulation adds another layer of complexity to drug information. The Food and Drug Administration (FDA) regulates all drugs in interstate commerce and is responsible for overseeing the labeling of drugs and ensuring that they are both safe and effective. These regulations are published in the *Code of Federal Regulations, Title 21: Food and Drugs* (available electronically through the National Archives and Records Administration, Code of Federal Regulations Web site at www.gpoaccess.gov/cfr). The FDA requires pharmaceutical companies to notify prescribing physicians of contraindications, warnings, and adverse effects of drugs. In December 2000, the FDA proposed new requirements for drug packaging information, also known as "package inserts," to make them more user-friendly for physicians and patients (21 CFR part 201; 65 FR 81082, December 22, 2000). The agency gathered information through physician surveys, focus groups, and other communications to determine what information was most important, and developed a "Structured Product Labeling" format for the content of all drug labeling submitted to the FDA. The final rule, "Requirements on Content and Format of Labeling for Human Prescription Drug and Biological Products," appeared in the Federal Register (21 CFR parts 201, 314, and 601 FR 3922). Effective June 30, 2006, changes included the reorganization of information to include tables of contents and introductory sections entitled "Highlights of Prescribing Information," which list the most important facts about the drug. Without these highlights, it can be difficult to extract the most relevant information, because pharmaceutical companies are required to list all precautions and contraindications regardless of their probability. The National Library of

Medicine maintains a publicly available Web site, "Daily Med," which in-cludes current FDA-approved labeling of drugs (http://daily med.nlm.nih. gov/dailymed/about.cfm). This is a useful resource for health care practitioners to access essential information about the medications they prescribe and dispense (see 9.54).

In the industrial setting, the U.S. Department of Labor, Occupational Safety and Health Administration (OSHA) creates and enforces safety stan-dards in the workplace. OSHA works together with the U.S. Department of Health and Human Services, National Institute for Occupational Safety and Health (NIOSH), which is responsible for conducting research and providing education and training for occupational safety. Both organizations were formed as a result of the Occupational Safety and Health Act of 1970. This chapter contains a section on adverse effects, toxicology, and poisoning, which includes information on drugs and other chemical substances. Sources of government regulations, standards, and practices as well as drug packaging information are also covered (see 9.53 and 9.54).

There are many stages of development before a drug gets to market, with investigators at each stage creating and accessing different kinds of informa-tion [2]. Understanding the stage of development associated with a drug-related question can be helpful in finding relevant drug information. In the drug discovery stage, various chemical and pharmacogenomic research methods and molecular modeling techniques are used to identify potential drug targets and design new molecules optimizing the chemical interactions at those sites. Chemical literature from the Chemical Abstracts Service (see 9.50) is the best source of information about drugs in development. Next, in vitro and animal studies are conducted. In vitro tests usually involve the determination of drug concentrations that kill or inhibit the growth of various types of human cells in culture. Animal models are used to mimic human disease states for testing drug efficacy and determining appropriate therapeutic drug concentrations. In the next stage, routes of administration are chosen, prototype drugs are formulated, and formulations are evaluated for purity, stability and toxicity in animal models. Information about in vitro and animal drug studies can be found in the biological literature through *BIOSIS Previews* (see Chapter 4).

When a pharmaceutical company has a chemical entity that it believes has significant therapeutic value, it files an Investigational New Drug (IND) application with the FDA. The category of "new drugs" not only include new chemical entities, but any existing drug proposed to be used in a way other than previously approved. IND applications are required for new dosage forms, routes of administration, and uses for new indications ("off-label" uses). The IND application must be reviewed and approved before clinical trials in humans can begin. The IND application includes preliminary safety data based on laboratory testing in animals; manufacturing, formulation, and chemical information about the drug; and detailed protocols for the proposed clinical trials. The IND approval process involves review by medical, chemical, pharmacological, and statistical experts to validate the preliminary data and determine if there is sufficient evidence that it is safe to proceed with human testing. After the IND application is approved, the applicant must then conduct documented studies to demonstrate the therapeutic value and safety of the drug. Testing begins in very small groups (fewer than 100) of human volunteers (Phase 1 studies) to evaluate safety. Phase 1 studies may be conducted in patients, but usually are conducted in healthy volunteers and are designed to generate information on drug metabolism, pharmacology, and side effects associated with high doses; they sometimes provide evidence on effectiveness. Phase 2 studies evaluate safety and dose range, as well as efficacy in patients (up to several hundred) with the disease the drug is intended to treat. If these trials show evidence of drug efficacy, the study moves into Phase 3, where the drug is given to a larger (several thousand) and more diverse population. When sufficient data have been collected, the pharmaceutical company submits another application to the FDA, a New Drug Application (NDA), with its data on the safety and effectiveness of the drug. The IND Application becomes part of the NDA. Approval of the NDA means that the drug is approved for marketing and can be prescribed by licensed practitioners. Prior to this approval, the drug may be used only by certain physicians who have been approved to handle investigational drugs. As the drug is made available to potentially millions of patients, additional side effects may appear, since some effects are idiosyncratic, occurring in a very small percentage of the population, and are often missed in the preclinical phases. Phase 4 studies, or post-marketing surveillance, investigate differences between drugs of the same type, or intended to treat the same condition, to determine advantages and disadvantages of one drug over another. Information on drugs in Phase 3 or 4 clinical trials can be found in the clinical literature through MEDLINE (see Chapter 4)

Information on drugs in development, prior to clinical trials and in the early phases of clinical trials, especially before they are patented, may be difficult to obtain. Clinical trials can be found in MEDLINE, the Clinical Trials Web site (ClinicalTrials.gov), and other professional organizations' Web sites such as the World Health Organization and the National Cancer Institute.

Early studies on drug development appear in the chemical literature or the biological literature if the drug is a naturally derived substance. The biological literature is also a good place to search for early toxicity or carcinogenicity animal studies performed before the IND application is submitted. The post-clinical trial NDA, with its documented evidence, never becomes a part of the public domain; it is considered to be proprietary information available only to the pharmaceutical company and the FDA. However the FDA's printed review of NDA content is available for most drugs on their Center for Drug Evaluation and Research (CDER) Drugs@FDA Web site (see 9.53). Also, researchers often publish their experiences with the drug during clinical trials in the journal and report literature.

After a drug patent expires, other companies may wish to market a generic equivalent. These companies must submit an Abbreviated New Drug Application (ANDA) to show that the generic drug has the same indications for use, active ingredients, route of administration, dosage form, strength, bioavailability, and labeling. Information on therapeutic equivalence of generic drugs is listed in the FDA publication, "Approved Drug Products with Therapeutic Equivalence," available on the Web at www.fda.gov/cder/ob/default.htm and included in the *United States Pharmacopeia Dispensing Information*, Volume 3 (see 9.17).

This chapter describes many standard and new Web-based resources, reflecting the influence of the Internet on drug information organization and delivery, as well as essential print reference sources recommended for health sciences libraries; many of the classic print resources are now available online. Some of the information in this chapter articulates "universal truths" from earlier editions, and that information has not been changed, so we extend our appreciation to Julie Kuenzel Kwan, Diane L. Fishman, and Amy Butros for their work. Other areas and newer resources are the current authors' contributions.

Guides to the Literature

Librarians and information professionals new to the drug information field can consult guides to the literature to put drug information in perspective. Current drug information bibliographies and comprehensive guides to the literature are few; however, Bonnie Snow's *Drug Information* compilation is essential to any collection. A new book by Sharon Srodin, *Using the Pharma-ceutical Literature*, is an excellent addition to the field and a complement to

Snow's work. A more specialized list of resources is available from the American Association of Colleges of Pharmacy Web site.

9.1   Snow B. *Drug Information: A Guide to Current Resources.* 3rd ed. Latham, MD: Medical Library Association and Neal-Schuman, 2008 (anticipated).

9.2   Srodin S, ed. *Using the Pharmaceutical Literature.* New York: Taylor & Francis, 2006.

9.3   American Association of Colleges of Pharmacy. *Basic Resources for Pharmaceutical Education.* 2006 ed. Available: www.aacp.org/ Docs/ MainNavigation/Resources/7645_BasicResources2006.pdf

The second edition of Snow's *Drug Information* provides good background and descriptive information supported by many resources in several areas. It covers drug nomenclature and identification, laws and regulations, adverse drug reactions and interactions, industrial pharmacy, sources for statistical information, plus online and Internet resources. Practicum exercises, a glossary, and a detailed index add to this guide's value. A third edition is in preparation.

Using the Pharmaceutical Literature by Sharon Srodin is intended for those who provide informational support to the pharmaceutical industry. It includes chapters on the drug discovery and development process; chemistry; genomics, proteomics, and bioinformatics; toxicology; pharmacology; drug regulation; sales and marketing; competitive intelligence; pharmacoeconomics; intellectual property; and medical devices and combination products. The sections of the book correspond to the stages of the drug development process and cover the types of information required at each point. Chapter 6, "Drug Regulation," is written by Bonnie Snow. Each chapter includes an introduction to the topic and annotated lists of associations, abstracts and indexes, journals, books, Web sites, and other categories appropriate for the topic.

The American Association of Colleges of Pharmacy (AACP) Web site provides a detailed and lengthy list of resources for any collection involved with educating pharmacists. The AACP has an alphabetical and hierarchical listing of over 800 sources; most books include price and electronic resources include URLs.

Drug Nomenclature

One of the major problems in using the drug literature is recognizing the multiplicity of names for a given chemical compound and understanding how reference sources must be approached depending on the type of name. A thorough understanding of these names is essential (see Figure 9-1). When a pharmaceutical company is investigating a large number of chemicals for possible therapeutic activity, it frequently assigns alphanumeric designations or code names. Often, a code name is the first designation in the primary literature.

The Chemical Abstracts Service (CAS) provides a unique Registry Number for each chemical compound, including drugs. One thing to remember about the Registry Number is that European countries commonly name the drug for the parent compound. In the United States, it is more usual to use the salt form (the compound formulated as a salt so that it will dissolve more easily in water), which will generally have a different Registry Number. Because indexes vary on whether the parent or salt Registry Number is used, the experienced searcher should try to identify both Registry Numbers for full retrieval.

The chemical name describes the chemical structure of a drug. There are a number of conventions for these chemical names, which are often very lengthy. Consequently, there is a need for a shorter, "common" name to describe a chemical. "Aspirin" and "tetracycline" are examples of these common names. Common names are also called "generic" and "nonpropri-etary" names. Names used by a manufacturer to describe marketed products are called, "proprietary," "brand," or "trade," names. Proprietary names are registered trademarks, as are the color, shape, and markings of each pill or capsule. Two or more manufacturers may market the same generic drug, but each may also have its own trade name representing the specific product. These products may differ; although the active ingredients are the same, each manufacturer may use different ingredients in compounding the drug or in holding it together. The composition of a pill, other than amounts of active ingredients, is proprietary or a trade secret, but the inactive ingredients for many drugs are included with drug packaging information, which can be found in the *Physician's Desk Reference*. Inactive ingredients are also sometimes listed in resources such as POISINDEX in Micromedex's Healthcare Series of online databases (see 9.52).

Another source of confusion is the multiplicity of generic names. Two companies working with the same drug may call it by different generic names. In the past, this practice has led to such confusion that now "official" generic names are designated. The United States Adopted Names (USAN) Commission has the authority to declare a specific generic name as the offi-cially recognized common name, the "adopted name," in the United States.

If another company wants to market a preparation of that drug, it uses this "official" generic name.

The nomenclature problem is compounded on an international scale. Other countries also have authorized bodies to establish official names—for example, Japanese Adopted Names (JAN) and British Adopted Names (BAN). The World Health Organization's International Nonproprietary Names (INN) attempts to unify official names in all participating countries, but differences still exist. These variations in nomenclature cause a range of difficulties. For instance, a patient taking a French drug travels to the United States and needs a refill of an American equivalent. A British doctor, taking an American medical licensure exam, finds "meperidine" on the examination questions rather than "pethidine," the name to which British doctors are accustomed. American researchers looking for information on the antiviral agent "acyclovir" will miss sources that use the INN "aciclovir."

Librarians must understand the many types of names to use literature sources effectively. Some publications, particularly commercial sources, may be arranged by proprietary or trade name. Others, especially those from

Figure 9-1. Types of Drug Names

Research code designation:	U-18, 573
CAS Registry Number:	15687-27-1
Chemical names:	Benzeneacetic acid, α- methyl-4-2(methylpropyl) ($\pm$)- ($\pm$) p - Isobutylhydratropic acid ($\pm$) -2- (p-Isobutylphenyl) propionic acid
Generic Name:	Ibuprofen
USAN, INN, BAN, JAN:	Ibuprofen
Proprietary Names:	Advil (Whitehall-Robins) Midol 200 (Sterling Health U.S.A.). Motrin (Pharmacia and Upjohn) Nuprin Caplets and Tablets (Bristol-Meyers Products)
Molecular Formula:	$C_{13}H_{18}O_2$
Structural Formula:	

professional associations, are usually arranged by nonproprietary or generic name. Books published in other countries use their own official generic names, which are sometimes different from the American form. Some sources are limited to prescription drugs, while others include nonprescription (over-the-counter or OTC) medications. The librarian, presented with a drug name, may not immediately know what type of name it is. The first step is to determine the type of name and then go to appropriate reference sources. Descriptions of essential sources of drug identification follow.

Sources of Drug Names

Considering the many names that can be associated with a given drug, it is essential for libraries to have access to sources of proprietary and nonproprietary drug names. While there are increasing numbers of sources available in electronic drug information databases or on the Web (see 9.31, 9.51 and 9.52), the following key print sources are recommended for health sciences reference collections.

9.4   *American Drug Index*. St. Louis, MO: J.B. Lippincott, 1956–. Annual.

9.5   United States Pharmacopeial Convention and United States Adopted Names Council. *USP Dictionary of USAN and International Drug Names*. Rockville, MD: U.S. Pharmacopeial Convention, 1994–. Annual.

9.6   O'Neil MJ, ed. *The Merck Index: An Encyclopedia of Chemicals, Drugs, and Biologicals*. 14th ed. Whitehouse Station, NJ: Merck, 2006.

The *American Drug Index* is an ideal source to consult first when starting your search for drug information. This source has a comprehensive alphabetical listing of proprietary and non-proprietary names for both prescription and non-prescription. The entries for proprietary names include the manufacturer's name, the nonproprietary (generic or chemical) name, composition and strength, pharmaceutical forms available, dosage, and a brief indication of use. The generic names frequently include the pronunciation, a designation of USP, USAN, or NF (National Formulary), an indication of where the drug name is listed, and brief indication of use and a "see" reference to the proprietary name. Useful appendices at the back of this book include a list of medical abbreviations used in medical orders, tables of normal values for commonly requested laboratory tests, a medical terminology glossary, a list of addresses and Web sites for drug manufacturers and distributors, and unique information such as oral dosage forms that should not be crushed or chewed and drug names that look alike and sound alike.

The *USP Dictionary* is updated annually and provides a compilation of the United States Adopted Names (USAN) selected and released since June 15, 1961. This source is very useful because it is a compilation and provides entries for earlier drug names. Each USAN entry lists the year the drug name was adopted, a pronunciation guide, molecular formula, molecular weight, chemical name, Chemical Abstracts Service (CAS) Registry Number, pharmacological or therapeutic activity, brand names under which the drug is marketed, manufacturer or distributor, and the structural formula. A detailed introduction describes the purpose and history of the USAN Council and the procedures that establish a USAN. Several helpful appendices are included, such as a listing of brand and nonproprietary names for the USAN names, a listing of molecular formulas and CAS Registry Numbers, and a grouping of USAN names by category, such as Analgesic, Antibacterial, Food Additive, and Ultraviolet Screen. Since this source also includes International Nonproprietary Names (INN), it should be noted that inclusion in this book does not necessarily mean that the drug is marketed in the United States; it only means that an official name has been designated. Frequently U.S. drugs are named around the time that they are patented and go into clinical trials. Thus, many years may pass before the drug receives final approval for marketing.

Another brief dictionary-type source is the *Merck Index*. This publication began in 1889 as a brief listing of drugs marketed by the Merck Company. Now in its 14th edition, it has grown to be a comprehensive encyclopedia of drugs, chemicals, and biological substances. The *Merck Index* should be considered an essential part of a basic drug information collection. Although this source is arranged alphabetically by chemical name, it is easier to use the index as the entry point into the descriptive paragraphs. There are several helpful listings of tables and chemical reactions at the end of this book, in addition to the in-depth indexes. The indexes that lead to the entries include Registry Numbers, therapeutic categories, molecular formulas, and chemical names. The entries in the *Merck Index* include Registry Number, chemical name, common names in some cases, molecular formula, molecular weight, brief description of use, plus the added benefit of historical references, patent references, and preparation, synthesis or review journal article references.

Comprehensive Treatises and Textbooks

In the medical or pharmacy library, questions frequently arise concerning the physical and chemical properties of drugs and associated mechanisms of biological activity. The librarian may begin with the sources in the previous section to obtain the necessary proprietary and generic drug names and brief information on pharmacological action. For more in-depth discussions, the following comprehensive sources are essential.

9.7 Brunton LL, Lazo JS, Parker KL, eds. *Goodman and Gilman's The Pharmacological Basis of Therapeutics*. 11th ed. New York: McGraw-Hill Medical Publishing Division, 2006.

9.8 Remington JP, Beringer P. *Remington: The Science and Practice of Pharmacy*. 21st ed. Baltimore, MD: Lippincott Williams & Wilkins, 2005.

Goodman and Gilman's The Pharmacological Basis of Therapeutics, published since 1941, is still known as "the bible of pharmacology." A standard textbook on fundamental principles of drug action, it continues to be a valuable tool in medical and pharmacy schools. The book is divided into fifteen sections, beginning with general principles of pharmacology (including new chapters about drug transporters, drug metabolism, pharmacogenetics, and patient-centered therapeutics), and proceeding with sections organized by modes of action on physiological systems or actions related to disease states. For example, the twelve chapters of Section III describe drug actions on the central nervous system, and the nine chapters of Section VIII describe chemotherapy of microbial diseases. Each chapter provides in-depth discussions of pharmacologic mechanisms in terms of classes of drugs (e.g., hypnotics and sedatives), emphasizing the comparison between individual drugs of the same class and including many useful tables of drug names and properties. As in the previous edition, the appendices include "Principles of Prescription Order Writing and Patient Compliance" and "Design and Optimization of Dosage Regimens: Pharmacokinetic Data." The detailed index allows the user to access information by a variety of terms such as drug names, type of drug action, physiological systems, or symptoms.

Remington: The Science and Practice of Pharmacy is a standard text of pharmaceutical science used by many pharmacy schools. With an emphasis on basic science, it covers a broad range of topics including pharmaceutical chemistry; pharmaceutical testing, analysis and control; pharmaceutical manufacturing; pharmacokinetics and pharmacodynamics; and many topics related to pharmacy practice. Since the last edition, the pharmacy practice section has been expanded and updated to reflect current practices and trends and includes new topics such as ethics, statistics, technology, communication, medication errors, "re-engineering pharmacy practice," special risk medicines, specialization of pharmacy practice, disease state management, emergency patient care, and wound care. It also provides an extensive section on therapeutic agents organized by drug class and including brief monographs on specific drugs. Brief discussions of the indications, chemical properties and preparation are also included. The text concludes with a useful glossary of acronyms and a comprehensive subject index. This source, and most other sources, use the term "monographs" for the descriptive drug entries. These monographs generally include chemical names, formulas and molecular weights, as well as information on dosing, adverse effects, contraindications, and interactions with other drugs or food.

Commercial Sources of Drug Information

Numerous and varied sources exist that give information about specific drugs and pharmaceuticals. One mechanism by which the manufacturer informs physicians and the public about a specific product is the FDA-approved package insert, which includes the trade and chemical names; pharmacological action; indications and contraindications; warnings, precautions, and adverse reactions; dosage and overdosage; dosage forms; and, in most cases, references. The package insert is not necessarily complete or balanced. Although the FDA has agreed to the manufacturer's statements about the product and the manufacturer is legally responsible for the accuracy of the information included, the package insert remains a publicity and promotion mechanism for the manufacturer. A package insert does not compare or evaluate a given drug with other agents.

9.9 *Physicians' Desk Reference: PDR*. Montvale, NJ: Thomson PDR, 1947–. Annual. (Free for U.S. medical professionals).

9.10 *PDR for Ophthalmic Medicines*. 35th ed. Montvale, NJ: Thomson PDR, 2006.

9.11 *PDR for Nonprescription Drugs, Dietary Supplements, and Herbs*. 28th ed. Montvale, NJ: Thomson PDR, 2006.

The *Physicians' Desk Reference (PDR)* is an annual compilation of package inserts. (The introduction to this chapter discusses FDA requirements regarding package inserts.) However, the *PDR* does not just contain package inserts. In addition, according to the Introduction to Section 5, "for products that do not have official package circulars, *PDR* has asked manufacturers to provide comprehensive product information." In fact, it is difficult to tell which entries are official package inserts and which are not. The information in the *PDR* is arranged by company name. Most of the products marketed in the United States are listed in the *PDR*, making it a handy and frequently requested source. The *PDR* is very useful for drug dosage, composition, contraindications, warnings, use, and adverse effects. The indexes included in the front of the *PDR* are a manufacturers' index, with addresses and contact information for most companies, a brand and generic name index, a product category index, and a product identification guide with color photographs of over 1600 tablets, capsules and other dosage forms. Other sources to consider for visual drug identification are *Drug Facts and Comparisons*, *USP DI*, *Micromedex's IDENTIDEX*, and *Clinical Pharmacology*, all available online (see 9.12, 9.15, 9.51, and 9.52). Since the *PDR* is a source of manufacturer disclaimers, cautions, precautions, and side effects are enumerated in great detail, although there is sometimes no indication of the severity or frequency of the side effects.

The earliest editions of the *PDR* carried the subtitle "for the physician's desk only," and volumes are still often distributed free to physicians as a marketing tool. However, with the recent consumer movement in health care, this statement has been removed, and the *PDR* is now for sale throughout the country in bookstores. Librarians should be concerned about the public's reliance on the *PDR*. First, the information is not necessarily unbiased but represents only what the FDA has approved for the manufacturer. Second, the coverage is selective, as drug companies are charged for inclusion. Therefore, not all drug companies participate, and those that do typically only include their more profitable drugs. Third, librarians should understand that the information included about drug use is not necessarily complete. Physicians can legally prescribe drugs for therapeutic applications which have not yet been approved by the FDA, and these off-label uses will not generally be addressed in the *PDR*. Finally, the information in the *PDR* is written in technical language and may be difficult for the general public to understand. Because rare side effects are included, the work may prove unnecessarily frightening to the nonprofessional. An ongoing challenge for the health sciences librarian is to channel members of the public from the *PDR* to more appropriate sources.

The popularity and success of the *PDR* have caused a whole series of *PDR* books to appear. Some of these titles are worth listing here; others will be covered in the following sections. The *PDR for Herbal Medicines* will be discussed in more detail in the "Herbal Medicines and Natural Products" section of this chapter (see 9.41). Although the *PDR Guide to Drug Interactions, Side Effects and Indications* is described by the *PDR* publishers as one of the most useful drug references in current clinical practice, it really is a companion book that acts as an interactions index to the *PDR*, and thus will be discussed in more detail in the "Drug Interactions" section of this chapter. Two complementary *PDR* publications that librarians may consider are the *PDR for Nonprescription Drugs, Dietary Supplements and Herbs* and the *PDR for Ophthalmic Medicines*. There is some overlap between these sources and the *PDR*, but there is also a lot of unique information that may be necessary in some collections.

9.12   *Drug Facts and Comparisons.* 61st ed. St. Louis, MO: Wolters Kluwer Health, 2007. Available: http://onlinefactsandcomparisons.com/

9.13   *Red Book.* Montvale, NJ: Thomson PDR, 1896–. Annual.

Drug Facts and Comparisons is a comprehensive compendium of drug information. It is updated annually and is available as a bound volume, looseleaf format with monthly updates, and also online as Facts & Comparisons 4.0. This source is arranged by drug therapeutic category, for example nutritional agents, anticonvulsants, penicillins, immunologic agents, etc. are each grouped together in distinct sections. Each entry, or group of entries, in *Drug Facts and Comparisons* includes indications, dosage, actions, contraindications, warnings, interactions, adverse reactions, and patient information. Included are many useful tables that list comparisons between different brands, specific drug interactions, combinations, and supply methods. A thorough general index lists product brand names, generic names, synonyms, and therapeutic groups, for easy page reference to each entry. Additional indexes include a Canadian Trade Name index and a Manufacturers and Distributors index. Twelve useful appendices (FDA new drug classification, controlled substances, FDA pregnancy categories, etc.) are also included. This source is worth considering for any collection; it is quite current, comprehensive, and authoritative, with an Editorial Advisory Panel and a Contributing Review Panel of physicians and pharmacists and other health care professionals from academic, private, and government institutions across the United States.

The *Red Book* is well known and trusted in the pharmaceutical market-place. This source is in its 110th year of publication. Since it is so well known and used by pharmacists, it has become a highly requested source from any library. The *Red Book* is more of a catalog of drug products than a comprehensive drug information text. It is divided into distinct sections that can be easily accessed and browsed. Included is a brief herbal medicine guide listing descriptions of popular herbs, with a warning section in most cases, plus a short herb/drug interactions section. Other sections include lists of the "Top 200" brand-name, prescription drugs and generic prescription drugs. Pharmacists and other health care professionals frequently ask for these lists. There is also a clinical reference guide (e.g., generic availability, drugs that should not be crushed, sugar-free products, alcohol-free products, sulfite-containing products, drugs that may cause photosensitivity, lactose- and galactose-free drugs, etc.), a listing of pharmacy organizations (e.g., state boards of pharmacy, state Medicaid drug programs, DEA offices), manufacturer addresses and phone numbers, a product identification guide with color photos, and other useful information. The largest section, "Rx Products," is an alphabetical list of prescription drugs where each entry includes product names, supplier name, National Drug Code (NDC) numbers, route of administration, strength and quantity, Orange Book Code (OBC), and Average Wholesale Price and Direct Price. There are similar entries in an "Over the Counter/Non-Drug Products" section. This is a good standard source for drug prices and some hard-to-find addresses, although there are advertisements.

Professional Sources of Drug Information

The sources described in this section come from professional pharmacy organizations and provide authoritative information on drugs in terms of the disorders they treat and their specific activities and formulations.

9.14   American Society of Hospital Pharmacists. *AHFS Drug Information.* Washington, DC: American Society of Health-System Pharmacists, 1959–. Annual.

9.15   *USP DI: United States Pharmacopeia Dispensing Information.* 22nd ed. Greenwood Village, CO: Micromedex Thomson Healthcare, 1980–.

9.16   Berardi RR et al. *Handbook of Nonprescription Drugs: An Interactive Approach to Self-Care.* 15th ed. Washington, DC: American Pharmaceutical Association, 2006.

Formerly known as the *American Hospital Formulary Service Drug Information, AHFS Drug Information* is produced and updated annually by the American Society of Health-System Pharmacists. Recommended by the National Association of Boards of Pharmacy as part of the standard reference library, it is the only comprehensive drug information resource published by a nonprofit professional organization. It is an authoritative source of evaluative information on drugs available in the U.S. *AHFS* provides drug monographs arranged by therapeutic classification, such as anti-neoplastic agents, diagnostic agents, and gastrointestinal drugs. It also includes a section on vitamins. This organization by class enables the user to easily compare drugs from the same family. Each section begins with a listing of the generic names of drugs described in that section, with some sections divided into subcategories. Classification numbers are assigned to major sections and subsections. For example, "Anti-Infective Agents" (section 8:00) includes subsections of amebicides (8:04), antibiotics (8:12), and more. The antibiotics subsection is further divided into nine subcategories including cephalosporins (8:12.06). The list of drugs in the cephalosporin family refers the user to page numbers but individual drugs are not assigned classification numbers. These numeric classifications are important to pharmacists; the International Pharmaceutical Abstracts database, also published by the American Society of Health-System Pharmacists, enables searching by these numbers (see 9.49). Each section includes general statements on pharmacology and basic principles of drug action for that class of compounds. The descriptions of individual drugs (monographs) emphasize the critical evaluation of clinical drug data and include information on conventional, off-label, and investigational uses; preparations; dosages and administration; drug interactions and laboratory test interferences; mechanisms of action, pharmacokinetics, cautions, and contraindications. In cases where only the drug name is known, but not the drug classification, users may refer to the general index. The index contains both generic and proprietary names with useful cross references. *AHFS* is available in a variety of electronic formats including Web- and PDA-based based versions.

The *USP DI: United States Pharmacopeia Dispensing Information* was introduced by the U.S. Pharmacopeia to provide prescribing and dispensing information not included in the official compendia (see 9.17). In 1998 the *USP DI* was sold to Micromedex, a Thomson health care company, with the agreement that an advisory council of USP experts would continue to participate and develop authoritative information. However, as of May 2004, Thomson has sole editorial responsibility for Volumes 1 and 2, while the USP maintains Volume 3. Volume 1 is a set of monographs written for the health care provider. Information on specific dosage forms such as tablet, injection and ointment, is also provided. Each entry lists the drug category and describes indications, pharmacology, precautions, adverse effects, overdose, patient consultation information, dosing information, and dosage forms. To find a specific drug, the general index is the best entry point because some drugs are listed individually while others are included in large monographs of drug classes. For example, there is an entry for acetaminophen listed in alphabetical order before antihistamines, but the entry for ibuprofen is found under anti-inflammatory drugs. Monographs on drug classes include tables comparing drug characteristics as well as useful summaries of differences. Volume 1 of the *USP DI* has several useful appendices including a listing of poison control centers in the U.S and Canada, and drug names indexed by indication or off-label uses.

The *USP DI* Volume 2 is written in lay language for the patient. The first section is an alphabetical index of generic and proprietary names, followed by general information on the use of medications. The drug monographs include information on proper usage and storage of the medication, precautions, information on pregnancy and breast-feeding, and information for different age groups. The third volume, *Approved Drug Products and Legal Requirements*, is a compilation of a variety of sources including the FDA's "Orange Book," *Approved Drug Products with Therapeutic Equivalence Evaluations* (see 9.53). This is an excellent source of legal information related to drug prescribing and dispensing, as well as information on therapeutic equivalence (the extent to which drugs contain the same active ingredients in equal amounts, are administered by the same route, and produce the same clinical effect). Pharmacists refer to therapeutic equivalence values in determining which drugs may be substituted for others. This volume can be used to see if a prescription or nonprescription drug has been approved by the FDA and the date in which each of its forms (liquid, tablet, etc). was approved.

The *Handbook of Nonprescription Drugs: An Interactive Approach to Self-Care*, published by the American Pharmaceutical Association, deals with over-the-counter and nonprescription drugs, including herbal remedies and dietary supplements. This information is extremely important, especially to users who may not be aware of risks associated with the use of nonprescription drugs. It is also useful to pharmacy students in developing problem-solving skills and to practitioners who interact with patients. The handbook is presented in textbook format beginning with introductory chapters on non-prescription drug therapy and followed by chapters on various disorders (mental disorders, dermatologic disorders, etc.). The chapter on home medical equipment covers self-testing and monitoring devices. Other chapters describe signs and symptoms, treatment approaches, and products that can be used in treatment. Also included are useful case studies, as well as treatment algorithms with assessment questions and answers. Each chapter has a bibliography at the end. Appendices on drug use during pregnancy and lactation and general subject index are also provided.

Official Compendia

In the drug information field, an official book of legal pharmaceutical standards is known as a *pharmacopeia*. Pharmacopeias are published in different countries to define the accepted purity and standards of chemicals used in therapy. Many pharmacopeias also include information on chemical tests and assay preparation.

9.17   United States Pharmacopeial Convention and United States Pharmacopeial Convention Committee of Revision. *The United States Pharmacopeia/The National Formulary: USP-NF*. Rockville, MD: United States Pharmacopeial Convention, 1979–. Annual.

In the United States, the two official compendia are the *United States Pharmacopeia* and the *National Formulary*. These two publications have been producing official standards since 1820 and 1888, respectively, although under different sponsorship. Beginning in 1979 the *United States Pharmacopeia* and the *National Formulary* were published in one volume, since the *National Formulary* was acquired by the *United States Pharmacopeia* after the publication of its 14th edition. There is a note at the beginning of the *National Formulary* monographs stating that although both compendia, the *United States Pharmacopeia* and the *National Formulary*, currently are published under one cover, they remain separate compendia. The latest combined edition *(USP 30-NF 25)* is a three-volume set due to the increase in content. The first volume includes the mission statement and lists of people involved (e.g., board of trustees, Council of Experts, executive committees, collaborators, and members of the U.S. Pharmacopeial Convention); new drug admissions and revisions; tests and assays; reagents, indicators and solutions; reference tables; dietary supplement monographs; and *NF* monographs. The second volume includes *USP* monographs A–L, and the last volume contains *USP* monographs M–Z. All three volumes contain the full index. Although the *NF* monographs and *USP* monographs differ in terms of the entry elements, most contain information about packaging and storage, labeling, identification, properties (e.g., pH, viscosity, and solubility), and other standards information.

It should be noted that the need to collect pharmacopeias from other countries is often misinterpreted. Most drug questions relate to therapeutic use or to the general identification of a drug, rather than to official standards of purity as given in these compendia. Caution should always be exercised in evaluating any title with the word *pharmacopeia* in it, since most sources using that term may not be pharmacopeias in the true sense of the word since they are not listings of legal standards.

Adverse Effects, Toxicology, Poisoning

Some of the most commonly asked questions in the field of drug information deal with adverse effects of drugs and chemicals. What are the side effects of Prozac? Does tamoxifen cause hair loss? What is the lethal dose of aspirin? Many of the sources previously described provide information on adverse effects, drug interactions, toxicity and poisoning, and the following sources focus specifically on this area. Since it is not possible, or ethical, to randomize patients to receive potentially toxic doses of medications, the drug toxicology literature is based primarily on case studies. Sometimes, adverse effects are discovered during clinical trials, but more often these effects do not become apparent until a drug has been on the market and administered to large numbers of patients. Generally, the older the drug, the more information will be available on toxicity. The following sources are compilations of observed adverse effects of drugs.

9.18   Aronson JK. *Meyler's Side Effects of Drugs: The International Encyclopedia of Adverse Drug Reactions and Interactions*. 15th ed. Amsterdam: Elsevier, 2006.

9.19   Van Boxtel CJ, Aronson JK, eds. *Side Effects of Drugs Annual*. Amsterdam: Elsevier, 1977–. Annual.

9.20   Leikin JB, Paloucek FP. *Poisoning & Toxicology Compendium: With Symptoms Index*. 3rd ed. Hudson, Ohio: Lexi-Comp, 1998.

9.21   Shepard TH , Lemire RJ. *Catalog of Teratogenic Agents*. 12th ed. Baltimore, MD: Johns Hopkins University Press, 2007.

9.22 Briggs GG, Freeman RK and Yaffe SJ. *Drugs in Pregnancy and Lactation: A Reference Guide to Fetal and Neonatal Risk.* 7th ed. Philadelphia, PA: Lippincott Williams & Wilkins, 2005.

9.23 Goldfrank LR et al. *Goldfrank's Toxicologic Emergencies.* 7th ed. New York: McGraw-Hill Medical Publishing Division, 2002.

9.24 Lewis, RJ, Sr. *Sax's Dangerous Properties of Industrial Materials.* 11th ed. New York: John Wiley & Sons, 2007.

9.25 Lewis RJ, Sr. *Hazardous Chemicals Desk Reference.* 5th ed. New York: John Wiley-Interscience, 2002.

9.26 *TOXNET.* Bethesda, MD: U.S. National Library of Medicine. Available: http://TOXNET.nlm.nih.gov

Meyler's Side Effects of Drugs is an encyclopedia of comprehensive articles that summarize adverse drug reactions and interactions. Its presentation of data organized by drug classification enables the user to easily review a family of drugs as a whole. Each chapter describes a broad class of drugs, such as central nervous system stimulants, and is divided into monographs on drug families such as amphetamines. Each monograph provides an overview of the toxic effects and patterns of adverse reactions, specific effects on organs and systems, withdrawal effects, overdosage information, patient susceptibility factors, and brief reviews of individual drugs belonging to that family. With the 15th edition, *Meyler's Side Effects of Drugs* has gone from one volume to a six-volume set and is also available online. A complementary guide to *Meyler's* is the *Side Effects of Drugs Annual*, which provides a survey of the latest developments in this field. Chapter titles correspond to those in *Meyler's*, enabling the user to easily combine the general encyclopedic information with annual updates. Libraries should retain the full series because both sources refer to earlier editions.

The *Poisoning & Toxicology Compendium* includes six chapters on medicinal agents: non-medicinal agents, biological agents, herbal agents, diagnostic tests and procedures, and antidotes. Each chapter lists chemicals arranged alphabetically by the common chemical name or generic drug name. Entries include proprietary names, Chemical Abstracts Registry Numbers, and information on dosage forms and stability, drug interactions, test interactions, mechanisms of toxicity, and more. The entries consist of brief summaries with references at the end. A symptoms index, though not comprehensive, is unique and useful for looking up symptoms such as "amnesia," and obtaining lists of substances known to cause that symptom. Also included are a subject index, a pregnancy risk factor index and an index of Chemical Abstracts Registry Numbers. The subject index includes the generic and proprietary names, making it a good source for the user who does not know the generic name. Given the date of this source, many drugs will not be included, but it remains and excellent look-up guide for questions on adverse effects of drugs, and is especially useful for questions on what to do in case of poisoning.

Teratology, the study of the adverse effects of drugs on the fetus, is a widely recognized area of concern. Shepard's *Catalog of Teratogenic Agents* covers fetal exposure to over 2000 drugs and other agents. It also includes gene mutations known to cause congenital defects. Entries are organized alphabetically by the chemical name, and include synonyms, Chemical Abstracts Registry Numbers where available, descriptions of teratogenicity, and references. Author and subject indexes are also provided. This book is available in electronic format, through Micromedex (see 9.52).

As its name implies, *Drugs in Pregnancy and Lactation* includes information on possible harm to the fetus from drugs taken during pregnancy, or possible harm to breast-feeding infants from drugs present in breast milk. Summaries of drug toxicity, in encyclopedia format, are listed alphabetically by generic drug name. Risk factors, defined in the introduction to the book, are assigned to each drug, allowing the user to quickly assess toxicity. Each entry lists the generic name, drug class, risk factor, summaries of fetal risk and breast feeding risk, recommendations for pregnancy and lactation, and references. A useful appendix of drugs, organized by category, lists drug names and risk factors. This is helpful for identifying drugs of the same class with different risk factors. The subject index lists both generic and proprietary names.

Goldfrank's Toxicologic Emergencies is a comprehensive textbook of medical toxicology covering basic principles; biochemical, molecular, and pathophysiologic foundations; and chapters on specific agents such as prescription and nonprescription drugs, drugs of abuse, household toxins, heavy metals, pesticides, and other environmental and occupational toxins. Chapters on toxins describe classes of compounds, followed by specific information related to individual chemicals. Each chapter offers a case study, history and epidemiology, pharmacology, clinical manifestations, management and antidotes, summaries, and references. Answers to study questions and case studies are given at the end of the book. A subject index is also included.

An essential source of authoritative data on environmental health and safety, *Sax's Dangerous Properties of Industrial Materials (DPIM)* provides detailed toxicity information on over 26,000 chemicals found in the workplace, including drugs, food additives, pesticides, dyes, lubricants, soaps, plastics and more. Each item is encoded with a unique identifier, the DPIM entry code, consisting of three letters followed by three numbers. Chemicals are listed in alphanumeric order by code. For example, the entry for acethion amide (AAT000) precedes the entry for acetic acid (AAT250). The synonym cross index of 108,000 chemical names refers to DPIM codes, and is the best entry point for the user searching for substances by name. The online version, in which users can browse articles by the common name of the chemical, is more user-friendly. Each chemical listing provides the DPIM code, the chemical name, Chemical Abstracts Registry Number where available, and the U.S. Department of Transportation (DOT) Hazard Code. DOT codes are recognized internationally and are used in regulating shipping and labeling of hazardous materials. Also included are the molecular formula, molecular weight, and other physical properties such as solubility and flammability data. Numeric coded toxicity data are listed next, including skin and eye irritation, acute toxicity, mutagenic, teratogenic, carcinogenic, and other lethal or non-lethal effects. All toxicity data include citations to the scientific literature. These citations consist of a journal "CODEN" character code, followed by the number of the volume, the page number of the first page of the article, and a two-digit number referring to the year of publication. Each chemical entry also lists standards and recommendations from U.S government or expert groups including the Occupational Safety and Health Administration (OSHA). Safety profiles, which verbally summarize toxicity and hazard data, are also provided with each entry. Consensus reports are included where applicable. The *DPIM* is a three volume set, the first volume containing indexes needed to translate the chemical listings of toxicological information in the second and third volumes. Volume 1 provides instructions for using the *DPIM*, a key to abbreviations, a cross index of DOT hazard codes with DPIM codes, a cross index of Chemical Abstracts Registry Numbers with DPIM codes, the synonym cross index, detailed descriptions, and definitions of the toxicity data found in Volumes 2 and 3. Volume 1 also includes a bibliography of cited references listed in order of CODEN and including journal titles with publishing information. The *Hazardous Chemicals Desk Reference* is a condensed version of this work. This more manageable single volume lists only the most relevant substances, according to the U.S. Environmental Protection Agency Toxic Substances Control Act (TSCA) inventory.

The U.S. National Library of Medicine produces TOXNET, a set of databases with information on toxicology, hazardous chemicals, and environmental health. These databases are freely available worldwide. Four categories of information are available: toxicology databanks on toxicity and additional hazards of chemicals; toxic release information; chemical information, with nomenclature, identification, and structures; and toxicology literature, including scientific studies, reports, and other bibliographic material. The toxicology databanks include the Hazardous Substances Data Bank (HSDB), Integrated Risk Information System (IRIS), Chemical Carcinogenesis Research Information System (CCRIS), GENE-TOX, and LactMed. The HSDB contains emergency handling procedures, human health effects, detection methods, OSHA standards and other regulatory requirements for over 4,500 potentially harmful chemicals. Records are divided into categories including human health effects, emergency medical treatment, pharmacokinetics, and many others. This enables users to quickly navigate to specific topics. IRIS provides information from the EPA about the potential health effects of environmental pollutants, including carcinogenic and noncarcinogenic health risk information for over 500 chemicals. CCRIS contains scientifically evaluated data from the National Cancer Institute (NCI) on carcinogenicity, mutagenicity, tumor promotion and tumor inhibition tests for over 8,000 chemicals. GENE-TOX contains information from the EPA on over 3,000 potentially DNA-damaging chemicals. LactMed is a database of drugs and other chemicals, with information on levels in breast milk and infant blood, possible alternatives to drugs that are contraindicated in breast-feeding, recommendations from the American Academy of Pediatrics, and references to primary literature.

TOXNET's Toxics Release Inventory (TRI) database provides annual estimates of toxic chemicals released to the environment. The database is searchable by chemical name, company name or geographic region (including by ZIP code). ChemID*plus* contains over 350,000 chemical records, of which over 114,000 include chemical structures, and is searchable by subject, chemical generic or proprietary name, CAS Registry Number, molecular formula, and structure. The bibliographic sources in TOXNET are reviewed in the section on Bibliographic Databases. Users may search all TOXNET databases simultaneously or select individual sources.

Drug Interactions

With the popularity of herbal supplements, nutritional supplements, and other over-the-counter products and with the proliferation of advertising about drugs, health care providers are facing a complex and growing problem of drug interactions. There is overwhelming evidence that the pharmacological action of a drug can be affected by the administration of other drugs, foods, alcohol, and even environmental factors, such as excessive exposure to sun or chemicals. Depending on the interaction and the chemicals involved, a drug's intended action could be minimized or increased, absorption and metabolism rate changed, toxicity levels raised, and other untoward effects could occur. For example, a person taking a monoamine oxidase inhibitor antidepressant should avoid cheese, since eating tyramine rich foods could bring about life-threatening hypertension. Similarly, a person prescribed a tetracycline or quinoline antibiotic should be warned to avoid dairy products or antacids in certain circumstances, since these substances can reduce or negate the effectiveness of the antibiotic.

This is a very important and challenging area of drug information. Sources of information on drug interactions are proliferating, but the following trusted sources continue to rise to the top. There is some overlap but unique material in each, so librarians should collect a variety of well-balanced sources to meet their users' needs.

9.27   *PDR Guide to Drug Interactions, Side Effects and Indications* (formerly *Physicians' Desk Reference (PDR) Companion Guide*). Montvale, NJ: Thomson PDR. Annual.

9.28   *Drug Interaction Facts.* St. Louis, MO: Wolters Kluwer Health, 1998–. Annual.

9.29   *Hansten and Horn's Drug Interactions Analysis and Management.* St. Louis, MO: Wolters Kluwer Health, 2002–. Loose-leaf, updated quarterly.

9.30   Baxter K, ed. *Stockley's Drug Interactions: A Source Book of Interactions, Their Mechanisms, Clinical Importance and Management.* 7th ed. London: Pharmaceutical Press, 2006.

The main section in the *PDR Guide to Drug Interactions, Side Effects, and Indications* is an extensive interactions index. Over 1,500 pages are dedicated to interactions listed in the *PDR*, the *PDR for Ophthalmic Medicines*, and the *PDR for Nonprescription Drugs and Dietary Supplements and Herbs*. The interactions index is arranged alphabetically by brand name. Under each brand name there is a summary of the major pharmaceutical categories with which the product is said to interact. A list of the specific compounds in these categories follows. Each entry in this list includes an alphabetical listing of the brands of the compound found in the *PDR* and its companion volumes, along with page numbers where the compounds can be found in these volumes. An appropriate warning to people using this publication states, "This index lists only interactions cited in official prescribing information as published by *PDR*. Because product labeling varies in the scope of its interaction reporting, the most prudent course is to check each product in the patient's regimen." Following the interaction index is a very brief section on food interactions, and a lengthy, useful side effects index. The side effects index lists the physiological effect followed by a listing of drug brand names, for example under "Numbness, face" there is a listing for "Invirase." This brand name can then be looked up in the interactions index. In addition to indexes for indications, contraindications, and an international drug name index for equivalents of over 33,000 foreign pharmaceutical products, there is a generic availability guide and an imprint identification guide.

Drug Interaction Facts has been published since 1983 by Facts and Comparisons, then a division of J.B. Lippincott and now part of the Wolters Kluwer Health company. This source is in loose-leaf format due to frequent updates. The introduction states, *"Drug Interaction Facts* attempts to present all drug-drug and drug-food interactions that have been reasonably well documented to occur in humans. Recently we began including significant and well-documented interactions with herbal products as well. Simple additive or antagonistic effects that are anticipated to occur based on known pharmacological activity are not necessarily included." This is considered an authoritative source due to its reliance on current biomedical literature and a review board of physicians, pharmacologists and clinical pharmacists. The comprehensive index is essential as it lists entries by generic drug name and drug class name, with frequent cross-references for product trade names. The index also notes the significance of the interaction using a numeric code. Each entry is about one page long with the interaction significance number listed first (i.e., the onset, severity, and interaction documentation), then the effects, mechanism and management, with a brief discussion and references at the end. This source is relatively easy to use, and seems to be widely accepted and consulted in most health sciences libraries. A companion publication, *Drug Interaction Facts: Herbal Supplements and Food*, is provided gratis with subscriptions to *Drug Interaction Facts*. It is discussed in greater detail in the "Herbal Medicines and Natural Products" section of this chapter.

Hansten and Horn's Drug Interactions Analysis and Management is also published by Facts and Comparisons. This source has been in publication for over thirty years, and the authors, Philip D. Hansten and John R. Horn, have been recognized as experts in the field of drug interactions for years. *Hansten and Horn's* is updated quarterly and is available in loose-leaf binder format. Drugs are listed first alphabetically by generic name, and then by the interacting drug name. For this reason, the index is the key to using this source. Each combination of drug and interacting drug has a number listed beside it. This number indicates the "intervention needed to minimize the risk of the interaction," for example 1 = avoid combination, 2 = usually avoid combination, 3 = minimize risk, 4 = no action needed, and 5 = no interaction. Each entry includes a brief summary, risk factors, clinical evaluation, related drugs, and references. There is also a very useful and easy to spot "Management Options" boxed section in each entry that is very helpful for clinicians and pharmacists with headings such as "consider alternative," "circumvent/minimize" and "monitor." This source is very similar to *Drug Interaction Facts*. In some cases the clinical evaluation section (called discussion section in *Drug Interaction Facts*) lists the same clinical trial or evidence, with the same references. There are some differences in the index entries. Often *Drug Interaction Facts* lists more drug interactions for a particular drug than *Hansten and Horn's*. For example, there are over 100 drug entries listed under "Aspirin" in *Drug Interaction Facts*, while there are only about 50 listed in the same index category in *Hansten and Horn's*. One reason that *Drug Interaction Facts* sometimes has more index entries for a particular drug appears to be that it includes more therapeutic drug categories. However, it should be noted that there are some interactions that are unique to each of these sources that are listed in one and not in the other.

Stockley's Drug Interactions is an excellent secondary source for the circulating collection of a pharmacy school or large health sciences library. According to the Preface, its purpose is to "inform busy doctors, pharmacists, surgeons, nurses and other health care professionals, of the facts about interactions." It contains over 2,800 monographs that briefly describe the clinical evidence, mechanism, importance, and management of proven drug interactions. All of the monographs include references, and many of them have lengthy reference lists. After an informative introduction, 34 chapters address drugs in broad therapeutic categories (e.g., analgesics and NSAIDS, anticoagulants, beta-blockers, calcium channel blockers, immunosuppressants, etc.) with the drugs that cause reactions in each category. The final chapter deals with "Miscellaneous Drugs." This is a valuable resource, but maybe not for every collection.

Of course, drug interactions can also be checked in online resources such as Clinical Pharmacology, Thomson Micromedex, and Facts and Comparisons 4.0 (formerly eFacts); see 9.12, 9.51, and 9.52. It is important to check more than one source, since these sources do not provide identical information in terms of the drugs included and the severity of the interactions.

International Drugs

Questions about foreign drugs are particularly challenging. For example, spelling may vary in different languages. Users often have insufficient information, and the librarian begins a search looking for the proverbial needle in a haystack. Whenever possible, the requestor should be queried for further information: Do you have the generic or chemical name and the exact spelling? For what purpose is the drug used? Do you know the manufacturer? Several sources described earlier are very useful for foreign drug names. The *USP dictionary of USAN and international drug names, with INN, JAN and BAN* is a good place to start if the patron knows the generic or USAN name. The *Merck Index* is useful because of its broad international coverage and its inclusion of many chemical, generic, and even trade names. Maintaining a collection to include every country would be impractical for most libraries, and key sources will depend on geographic location and ethnicity. In the U.S., Canadian and Mexican sources are often particularly useful. These four sources are helpful for international drug information.

9.31 Sweetman SC., ed. *Martindale: The Complete Drug Reference*. 35th ed. London and Chicago: Pharmaceutical Press, 2007.

9.32 Swiss Pharmaceutical Society. *Index Nominum: International Drug Directory*. 18th ed. Stuttgart, Germany: Medpharm Scientific, 2004.

9.33 *Compendium of Pharmaceuticals and Specialties: The Canadian Drug Reference for Health Professionals*. Toronto, Canada: Canadian Pharmaceutical Association, 1974–. Annual.

9.34 *Diccionario de Especialidades Farmaceuticas*. Mexico: Ediciones PLM, 1944–. Annual.

Martindale: The Complete Drug Reference is extremely valuable for its wide coverage of European drugs and extensive indexing under trade names. It provides comprehensive information similar to *Goodman and Gilman's*, but with international coverage, less emphasis on basic pharmacology, and more specific information on individual drugs. This work is divided into five parts, the first and major part being the "Monographs on Drugs and Ancillary Substances." Each chapter gives a general description of a class of drugs, with particularly useful discussions of the drugs' indications. For example, the chapter on analgesics defines analgesia and pain, and describes the drugs of choice for various categories of pain such as headache, low back pain, labor pain, and more. The chapters include detailed descriptions of drugs belonging to that class, including adverse effects, drug interactions, preparations, and countries of origin for each drug. Because regulations regarding new drugs are not as stringent in other countries as in the United States, *Martindale* includes many drugs not available in the United States and provides international equivalents of drugs marketed in this country. Drug monographs list British Adopted Names (BANs) first, followed by International Non-Proprietary Names (INNs) and United States Adopted Name (USANs) where available. Also listed are chemical formulas, molecular weights, and Chemical Abstracts Service (CAS) Registry Numbers. References are provided at the end of each monograph. Part 2, "Supplementary Drugs and Other Substances," contains shorter monographs of similar format on herbal and other preparations. Part 3 is an index of proprietary preparations from a number of countries. Records generally include proprietary names, manufacturers or sources, and ingredients, as well as page references to the complete monographs. At the end of the book a directory of manufacturers is included, in addition to the general index. The directory lists manufacturers in alphabetical order using abbreviations from Part 3. The general index includes both generic and proprietary drug names, as well as synonyms and chemical names. Diseases and associated terms are also listed. The Micromedex Healthcare Series of databases includes the contents of *Martindale*, and is therefore an excellent source of international drug information, providing proprietary names used worldwide, for both FDA-approved and investigational drugs (see 9.31 and 9.52).

The *Index Nominum* is published in English with introductory information also provided in German and French. This resource describes over 5000 drugs and drug derivatives, arranged in alphabetical order by International Nonproprietary Name (INN) in English. Each entry lists German, French, Spanish and Latin names, as well as the World Health Organization's ATC (Anatomical Therapeutic Chemical) code. Also included are therapeutic classifications (e.g., "calcium antagonist"), Chemical Abstracts Registry Numbers, chemical names, molecular formulas, chemical structure diagrams, and lists of proprietary names used in different countries. At the end of each entry is an alphabetical list of drug derivatives, salts for example. The book starts with an alphabetical listing of therapeutic categories, a list of ATC classification codes, a list of abbreviations and symbols, and a list of country codes. Following the drug monographs is an extensive index of proprietary names and synonyms. This index is the primary access point for patrons seeking drug information with only a proprietary foreign name to go on.

The Canadian *Compendium of Pharmaceuticals and Specialties*, a guide to drugs available on the Canadian market, is divided into seven sections. The first section is a list of new and discontinued products, including brand names, generic names, manufacturers, drug classifications, and comments. Unlike many of the resources described in this chapter, this book lists drugs in alphabetical order by proprietary name. The second section provides a useful brand and generic name index. Next comes a therapeutic guide listing drugs by therapeutic classification, for example antidepressants and diuretics. The fourth section is a product identification table with color photographs of drug products. The fifth section is a directory of Canadian poison control centers, health organizations, and pharmaceutical manufacturers. The "Clin-Info" section contains information for clinicians on selected topics including dosing and monitoring tools, drug use guides and summaries of therapeutic interventions, and drug interactions. This is followed by information for patients on the safe and effective use of drugs written in lay language. The major part of the book is devoted to product monographs, listed in alphabetical order by brand name. This information is voluntarily submitted by manufacturers and may include either the complete or abridged versions of the drug package inserts. Each entry describes pharmacology, indications for use, contraindications and other precautions, drug interactions, adverse effects and dosing information. Appendices contain supplemental information such as medical and pharmaceutical abbreviations, nomenclature for microorganisms, and new reports of adverse drug events. The sections of this book are color coded for convenient access.

Written entirely in Spanish, the *Diccionario de Especialidades Farmaceuticas* is similar in organization to the Canadian *Compendium* and the *Physician's Desk Reference*. It contains four color-coded indexes, starting with a list of drugs having known contraindications, followed by a therapeutic index of drugs organized by classification. The third section is an index of active ingredients, which provides product names of medicines containing the ingredient either alone or in combination with other active ingredients. The fourth section is an index of drugs available in Mexico, listed by brand name with therapeutic classes, generic names, and manufacturers. This is followed by a directory of manufactures with contact information and product listings. This resource also includes a product identification table, which can be very useful in border states where patients may use medications made in Mexico.

Drug Information for Patients and the Public

In spite of the proliferation of Web sites claiming to offer consumers the best in health care information and attempting to sell them health care products and drugs, it is hoped that some consumers may wish to consult authoritative sources for reliable information on medications and products they are taking. To this end, librarians need to have a basic collection of easy-to-understand, authoritative, print drug information sources, and also be able to point consumers to trustworthy online resources. Any information given to patients should be accompanied by encouragement to consult with health care professionals for help in interpreting and evaluating the information obtained.

9.35   Rybacki JJ. *The Essential Guide to Prescription Drugs*. New York: Collins, 2006.

9.36   Griffith WH, Moore S and Boesen K. *Complete Guide to Prescription and Nonprescription Drugs*. New York: Penguin Group. Annual.

9.37   Hochadel M, ed. *The AARP Guide to Pills*. New York: Sterling, 2006.

9.38   *Drugs, Supplements and Herbal Information*, part of *MedlinePlus*. Bethesda, MD: U.S. National Library of Medicine. Available: www. nlm.nih.gov/MEDLINEplus/druginformation.html

9.39   *PDRhealth Drug Information*. Montvale, NJ: Thomson Healthcare. Available: www.pdrhealth.com/drug_info

9.40   *Consumer Reports Best Buy Drugs*. Yonkers, NY: Consumers Union. Available: www.crbestbuydrugs.org/

The Essential Guide to Prescription Drugs was authored by James W. Long from 1977 to 1993, by James W. Long and James J. Rybacki from 1996 to 2000, and most recently by James J. Rybacki for the 2002–2006 editions. This book has been a well known and trusted source for drug information for patients for almost thirty years. The 2006 edition begins with "Points for Patients and Their Families." This introductory section provides helpful advice on the importance of medication regimens, steps to follow when getting the prescription from the physician and then when picking up the prescription from the pharmacist, and suggestions for containing the costs of drug therapy. An extensive "How to Use this Book" section is followed by guidelines for safe and effective drug use and a brief section on "True Breakthroughs in Medicines." The main section of the book consists of the drug profiles, with usually four to six pages of information for each drug entry. About 400 generic drugs and over 2,000 brand name drugs are listed in the drug profiles section. New in this edition are "First Look Drug Nooks," which highlight new medications and "tell you a little about new medicines." Drug entries are listed alphabetically by generic name and in some instances by broad category. The detailed index in the back provides another mode of access. Many drug entries have *over 40* categories of information, including pronunciation, year introduced, drug class, brand names, whether or not a prescription is required, whether or not a generic form is available, benefits versus risks, principal uses, dosage ranges, usual duration of use, reasons to inform physicians before taking the drug, possible side effects, possible adverse effects, cautions, suggested periodic examinations, and "while taking this drug, observe the following." This source is revised and updated annually and is worth adding to any consumer collection due to its thoroughness and patient-friendly approach.

Winter H. Griffith's *Complete Guide to Prescription and Nonprescription Drugs* provides information on more than 5,000 brand name drugs and over 800 generic name drugs. Griffith is the author of 25 medical books for consumers. His name is well known and respected enough that he is listed as the primary author on the book even though he died in 1993. The last few editions of this book, which is updated annually, have been "revised" by Stephen W. Moore. Each entry in the book includes up to 33 elements including some information not included in similar works such as whether or not the drug is habit-forming, time lapse before the drug works, frequency of symptoms in people who take the drug, considerations for people over age 60, and warnings about premature discontinuation of the drug. Drugs are listed alphabetically by generic name, and there are also some entries for categories of drugs such as "anticoagulants" and "antihistamines." In the front of the book, there is a listing of "medical conditions and their commonly used drugs" and at the back there is a brand name directory, listing of "additional drug interactions," glossary, and extensive index that includes both generic and brand names.

While the *AARP Guide to Pills* covers fewer drugs than other print guides, it is exceptionally user friendly for consumers, and photos of the drugs, when available, are included within the drug entries instead of in a separate section. Drugs are listed alphabetically by generic name. Each entry includes patient-focused information about what the drug is, what the health care professional should know before the patient takes the drug, how the drug should be taken, what to do if a dose is missed, drug interactions, what to watch for while taking the drug, side effects, and where to keep the medication. The entries are in a bulleted format that makes them easy to read and understand. Color tabs on the edges of the pages indicate the section of the alphabet. There are two indexes: diseases and disorders, and generic and brand names.

The U.S. National Library of Medicine MedlinePlus Web site (medline plus.gov) is one of the best, if not the best Web site, for consumer health information, as it is comprehensive, comprehensible, and authoritative. The "Drugs, Supplements and Herbal Information" section of the site includes drug information from MedMaster from the American Society of Health-System Pharmacists, and herb and supplement information from Natural Standard. Drugs, herbs, and supplements are listed alphabetically and can also be accessed from "drug therapy" and "complementary and alternative therapy" pages. Each drug entry includes information about brand and other names, why the drug is prescribed, how it should be used, special precautions, what to do if a dose is missed, side effects, storage, and what to do in case of overdose.

Another good resource, *PDRhealth Drug Information*, is written in lay terms and is based on the FDA-approved drug information found in the *PDR*. There are links to information about prescription drugs, over-the-counter drugs, herbal medicines, and nutritional supplements, all organized alphabetically. The drug entries contain most of the same types of information as MedlinePlus. Interestingly, there is also a "search drugs" search box that you can set to "search all drugs" and use to search for any term in a drug entry, for instance, "sweating" as a side effect.

The Consumers Union, creator of *Consumer Reports* magazine and renowned for its expertise, independence and lack of bias, has created a series of *Consumer Reports Best Buy Drugs* reports. These reports compare prescription drugs by category and combine an expert review of the scientific evidence with pricing information. Current topics include antidepressants, beta-blockers for heart disease and high blood pressure, statins for high cholesterol and heart disease, nonsteroidal anti-inflammatory drugs (NSAIDSs) for osteoarthritis, sleeping pills for insomnia, and several other drug categories. The reviews of the scientific evidence are conducted by teams of physicians and researchers at several medical schools under the auspices of the Drug Effectiveness Review Project (DERP). Reports can be located by report title, drug name, or disease. Each report, written in lay language, includes a recommendations page, table of generic and brand names, discussion of what the drugs do and who needs them, "Best Buy Picks," and a discussion of the evidence. Drug cost information is also included. The full text of the reports (about 15 to 20 pages long), in English, and two-page summaries, in English and Spanish, are available in PDF format.

In addition to the above sources, the second volume of the *USP DI* that is entitled *Advice for the Patient Drug Information in Lay Language* is an accepted authoritative source for consumer information (see 9.15). In addition to information about the use of drugs written in lay terms, it includes a drug information photographic section, an extensive index, a glossary of terms, a listing of Poison Control Centers, and pregnancy and breast-feeding precaution listings.

Herbal Medicines and Natural Products

In these days of increased interest and usage of herbal and natural preparations, a few authoritative sources are a must for any collection. These resources may be located in the pharmacy and pharmacology sections or in the complementary medicine area. These sources are especially important because consumers often do not realize that herbal medicines and natural products can have harmful effects and interactions with prescription drugs. The following selections are representative of increasing numbers of excellent reference works in this field.

9.41   *PDR for Herbal Medicines.* 3rd ed. Montvale, New Jersey: Thomson PDR, 2004.

9.42   *Herbal Companion to AHFS DI.* Bethesda, MD: American Society of Health System Pharmacists, 2000.

9.43   Duke JA. *Handbook of Medicinal Herbs.* 2nd ed., Boca Raton, FL: CRC Press, 2002.

9.44   Duke JA. *A Guide to Popular Natural Products.* 2nd ed. St. Louis, MO: Facts and Comparisons, 2001.

9.45   Tatro DS. *Drug Interaction Facts: Herbal Supplements and Food.* St. Louis, MO: Facts and Comparisons, 2002–. Quarterly.

9.46   *Natural Medicines Comprehensive Database.* 7th ed. Stockton, CA: Therapeutic Research Faculty, 2005. Available: www.naturaldatabase. com

9.47   *Natural Standard.* Cambridge, MA: Nature Medicine Quality Standards. Available: www.naturalstandard.com

As with other *PDR* publications, the *PDR for Herbal Medicines* has several helpful indexes in the front of the book. After the informative foreward, there is an in-depth alphabetical index of all the scientific, common, and brand names included in this source. There are also indexes by therapeutic categories, indications, homeopathic indications, an Asian Indications Index, side effects index, drug/herb interactions guide, safety guide, and a manufacturers index. There is also an extensive herb identification guide with color photographs of over 300 common medicinal plants, followed by the herbal monographs arranged in alphabetical order. The monographs include common name, genus species, description, actions and pharmacology, indications and usage, precautions and adverse reactions, dosage and references.

The *Herbal Companion to AHFS DI*, though not comprehensive, is a trustworthy source published by the American Society of Health-System Pharmacists. Several herbal medicine sources state in their introductions that they base their information on the *Complete German Commission E Monographs*, which were developed in 1998 by the German Federal Institute for Drugs and Medicinal Devices, Germany's equivalent to the US Food and Drug Administration. The introduction to the *Herbal Companion to AHFS DI* describes the German Commission and states that the "accuracy of the information available within the Commission E Monographs creates a benchmark for the safety and efficacy of phytomedicine, and the monographs are regarded as *the* authoritative compendium on therapeutic medicinal herbs for health care professionals, representing today's highest standard in phytomedical evaluation." The *Herbal Companion to AHFS DI* is getting its information indirectly from the *German Commission E Monographs*, since this publication is derived from the Integrative Medicine Communications' database, which is based on an English translation of the *German Commission E Monographs*. The *Herbal Companion to AHFS DI* strives to offer unbiased, scientific reference information for clinicians to assist them in integrating complementary medicine into their patients' care. A disclaimer at the beginning of this book notes that the content was not developed by the American Society of Health-Systems Pharmacists, but rather the Integrative Medicine Commission (IMC) is responsible for the content, and that all inquires should be directed to the IMC. An Advisory Board consisting of physicians, naturopaths, pharmacists, ayurvedics, herbalists, and osteopaths was consulted. This is not a very large source, under 200 pages, but the entries are well written and organized. Each entry contains the English, botanical, and family names of the product, an overview section, usage and pharmaceutical designations, medicinal uses/indications, recommended dosage, cautions, interactions, regulatory status, and references. There are no illustrations or photographs, and a brief index at the end is the only other information in this source.

The *Handbook of Medicinal Herbs* describes over 1,000 herbs used for medicinal purposes. In the introduction the author states that he has tried to cover most of the important and widely-used medicinal plants. He also states, "Unlike Commission E and the Herbal PDR, which seem to stress European and American traditions, I include proportionately more herbs from the older African, Ayurvedic, and Chinese traditions as well, not wanting to slight any major medicinal plant from any major tradition." The herbs are listed in alphabetical order with a scientific name index and a common name index at the end of the book. Each herb entry lists the scientific name in parentheses after the common name, then a safety rating system (the safety score is explained in the introduction). Many entries include an illustration of the plant, and there are some color plates in the center of the book. The entry descriptions include many abbreviations, some of which are listed in the Abbreviations section in the beginning and others in the introduction. The entries include synonyms, activities, indications, dosages, contraindications, interactions, and side effects. This source is very comprehensive and extensive, but not that easy to interpret due to the abundance of abbreviations in the descriptions.

James A. Duke, the author of *A Guide to Popular Natural Products*, is a professor of pharmacognosy and medicinal chemistry. In his editorial work he is assisted by an Advisory Panel and the Facts and Comparisons Editorial Advisory Panel, both of which comprise a considerable number of notable physicians, chemists, and pharmacists. This authoritative source is well written and organized for easy access to patient information and references to the literature. There are several color photographs of the herbs in the center of the book and many helpful appendices including a lengthy table of herb-drug interactions and herbal diuretics. There is a therapeutic index and primary index listing common names and scientific names. Each entry includes scientific names, common names, and a highlighted box with patient information.

Following that are descriptive sections on botany, history, pharmacology, toxicology, and references. The key information is in the patient information box, which lists uses, side effects, and drug interactions when applicable. The references at the end of each entry are mainly from standard authoritative books and peer reviewed journal articles.

Drug Interaction Facts: Herbal Supplements and Food is a companion to *Drug Interaction Facts* (see 9.28). It is similar in format to *Drug Interaction Facts*, but the monographs are listed by the herbal or food product, rather than the drug. This makes it easy for users to look up all drug interactions associated with a particular herbal or food product. Another difference is that *Drug Interaction Facts: Herbal Supplements and Food* does not include drug class monographs. Because documentation is often sparse, the type of documentation (e.g., controlled trial, case report) is noted so the reader knows the quality of the evidence. Significance ratings are indicated by icons rather than numbers, and include "avoid," "use with caution," and "minimal risk." An index in the front lists generic drug names, herbal topics, and interacting foods. Appendices include "Potential Drug Interactions with St. John's Wort," "Selected Dietary Sources of Vitamin K," "Standard Abbreviations," and "Tyramine-Containing Foods."

The *Natural Medicines Comprehensive Database* is an important resource because it is based on scientific evidence gathered and evaluated by a team of medical and pharmacy professionals. In many cases the uses of herbal products is based on tradition, rather than science. The *Natural Medicines Comprehensive Database* describes the available evidence; in cases where scientific data is lacking, this is clearly stated. There are over 1,000 herbal and non-herbal natural products listed in this source. The print version arranges products alphabetically by their most common name, with an index at the end to help provide cross-references from other names. Each entry starts with a section labeled "Also Known As" to include other names and synonyms for the herbs, plus scientific names, usage, safety, effectiveness, mechanism of action, adverse reactions; interactions with herbs, dietary supplements, drugs, foods, and lab tests; dosage and comments. All references cited in various paragraphs appear at the end of the entries, arranged in numerical order by citation number. Included is a section on brand name natural products and the ingredients they contain. There are notes in several sections of the book stating that the online database contains more current and extensive information. This is a source worth considering if the online version's cost is prohibitive.

The online version of *Natural Medicines Comprehensive Database* is more current, interactive, and comprehensive than the print product. Updated daily, it is easily browseable by product name or disease/condition name. The product records include ingredients, effectiveness, adverse effects, and interactions with drugs. When searching a disease or condition, the results include the products known to have been used to treat or improve that condition. For example, a search of "leukemia" retrieves a record on vitamin C, describing how it has been suggested to be useful, and the record is clearly labeled, "Insufficient Evidence." The online version of *Natural Medicines Comprehensive Database* also includes an interactions checker where interaction between natural products or drugs and natural products can be found. This resource is worth considering due to comprehensiveness and relative low cost.

Natural Standard is edited and compiled by an international, multidisciplinary group of experts who use a systematic grading system to evaluate the evidence underlying uses of complementary and alternative therapies. The Web site includes a thorough description of how the scientific evidence is evaluated. *Natural Standard* covers not only herbs and supplements, but other "alternative" treatments such as accupuncture, and health and wellness activities such as yoga. It also has an interactions checker. *Natural Standard* is a good complement to the *Natural Medicines Comprehensive Database*; it is worth considering subscribing to multiple sources of complementary and alternative medicine because of the quickly changing applications of these therapies and the constantly mounting evidence supporting or opposing their uses.

Bibliographic Databases

This section focuses on bibliographic databases that are specific to drug information, or that contain considerable drug information. For more general indexing services and sources, and in-depth descriptions, please refer to Chapter 4.

MEDLINE, and its most popular interface, PubMed, is a key bibliographic database for drug information (see Chapter 4), and it is important for librarians to be aware of effective strategies in using the U.S. National Library of Medicine's Medical Subject Headings (MeSH) to find drug information. MeSH terms for drugs are generic names; entry terms include many, but not all brand names, and CAS Registry Numbers. Therefore, MeSH users may often need tools such as the *American Drug Index* (see 9.4) or *USAN and the*

USP Dictionary of Drug Names (see 9.5) to convert trade names to generic names. A number of MeSH subheadings are especially useful in searching for drug information. MeSH terms for diseases and conditions always include the subheadings "drug therapy" and "chemically induced." MeSH terms for drugs include the subheadings, administration and dosage, adverse effects, chemical synthesis, metabolism, pharmacokinetics, poisoning, and toxicity.

MeSH has shown a dramatic increase in its inclusion of drug names since its inception. Originally, drug entries in MeSH were grouped under the "Chemicals and Drugs" branch of the MeSH tree structure and organized by chemical classification. For example, aspirin, introduced in 1965, falls under salicylic acids. Since 1996, the NLM assigns pharmacologic actions to the MeSH records. The MeSH heading for aspirin includes four pharmacologic actions, including "anti-inflammatory agents, non-steroidal." The pharmacologic action field [pa] is a powerful tool because users often need to find lists of drugs belonging to a particular class. For example, health care professionals or consumers may seek alternatives to a prescribed drug because of an adverse affect, allergy, cost, or other reasons. In the MeSH database, a search for a pharmacologic action (e.g., anti-hypertensive agents [pa]) will yield a list of drugs indexed with that same pharmacologic action.

With increasing numbers of drug names needing to be indexed, the NLM added "substance names" as supplementary concepts, which map to MeSH headings. Concept mapping is transparent to the user searching PubMed; for instance, a search for the older term, aspirin, maps to aspirin [MeSH], and a search for the newer term, celecoxib, maps to celecoxib [substance name]. Generally, new drug name entries are added to MeSH as substance names, unless there is a significant amount of literature on analogs and derivatives, which fit well in the chemically oriented MeSH hierarchy. Substance name records include pharmacologic actions, but they do not include subheadings. If a subheading is needed for a substance name, the searcher may use a floating subheading. Also, because substance names map to the MeSH heading, the searcher can select "Heading Mapped to" from a substance name record, or from any citation indexed with a substance name, and add that concept, with the desired subheading to their search. For example, a search for adverse effects of atorvastatin could include the terms "atorvastatin"[Substance Name], "adverse effects" [Subheading], and Heptanoic Acids/adverse effects" [MeSH]. Librarians should be familiar with drug-related MeSH subheadings, and the best methods for working with MeSH terms and supplementary concepts for drugs.

NLM is also developing a new drug vocabulary, called RxNorm. RxNorm is a more granular vocabulary than MeSH; the concepts it describes are "clinical drugs," which are the actual drug products used in patients. A clinical drug concept includes the active ingredient, strength, and dosage form of the drug. Part of the Unified Medical Language System (UMLS) Metathesaurus, RxNorm provides a link between the various names used for drugs in many different vocabularies. It is intended to assist in interoperability of different drug information systems which use different drug nomenclatures. Librarians should be aware of RxNorm, because it will have impact on hospital information systems used in patient care.

All of the databases mentioned below are available online. As with all resources, licensing costs vary, and different vendors' search interfaces can also vary considerably, so librarians should be careful in selecting the most appropriate, cost effective resource possible. Almost all vendors allow trial access to their products, which makes it easier to decide which vendor and interface to choose. Most libraries have noticed a significant decrease in the number of patrons coming through their doors, and have shifted their collections to mainly electronic resources that can be accessed remotely. Since users are so self-reliant, it is important to select user-friendly search interfaces whenever possible.

9.48   *TOXNET.* Bethesda, MD: U.S. National Library of Medicine. Available: http://TOXNET.nlm.nih.gov

9.49   *International Pharmaceutical Abstracts.* Bethesda, MD: American Society of Health-System Pharmacists. Available electronically from Cambridge Scientific Abstracts, DataStar, Dialog, DIMDI, EBSCO, Optionline div.PTI, OVID, Silverplatter, and STN.

9.50   *Chemical Abstracts.* Columbus, OH: American Chemical Society, Chemical Abstracts Service. Available: http://www.cas.org/

TOXNET (see 9.27) includes two literature databases: TOXLINE and the Developmental and Reproductive Toxicology/ Environmental Teratology Information Center (DART/ETIC). TOXLINE is a collection of more than 3 million bibliographic citations on drugs and other chemicals, and is included in MEDLINE/PubMed as the subset, "Toxicology." DART/ETIC covers teratology and other aspects of developmental and reproductive toxicology. It contains over 100,000 references to literature published since 1965. DART/ETIC covers teratology and other aspects of developmental and reproductive toxicology.

International Pharmaceutical Abstracts (IPA) has been produced in print and electronic versions by the American Society of Health-System Pharmacists since 1964; in 2005 it was purchased by Thomson Corporation. *IPA* covers a substantial volume of worldwide pharmacy practice literature not indexed in MEDLINE (note that the print version of *IPA* does not contain as many abstracts as the online version). *IPA* covers drug use and development literature from 1971 to the present and includes meeting abstracts of the American Society of Health-System Pharmacists (ASHP), International Pharmaceutical Federation (FIP), and American Association of Colleges of Pharmacy (AACP). Journals unique to *IPA* include state journals of health system pharmacy (e.g., *New York State Journal of Health-System Pharmacy*), and other journals such as *Journal of Herbs, Spices and Medicinal Plants* and *World Health Organization Drug Information*. In addition to the typical searchable fields found in electronic bibliographic databases, *IPA* can be searched by Chemical Abstracts Registry Number or AHFS therapeutic drug classification. The latter is especially useful for accessing information on entire families of drugs. For example, a search of "4.00" in the therapeutic class field retrieves articles on antihistamines. *IPA* is a useful supplement to MEDLINE for any library supporting pharmacy education or practice.

Chemical Abstracts is also a useful source of drug information. When searching for chemical or physical properties of drugs, such as solubility; or information on chemical synthesis and product formulations, searching *Chemical Abstracts* is often more efficient and effective than searching the biomedical literature. *Chemical Abstracts* also includes abstracts from patents, dissertations, technical reports, and other document types, in addition to journal articles. Because it indexes over 9,500 journals and patents from over 50 patent-issuing agencies worldwide, it offers a broader scope than MEDLINE/PubMed. Because of its great breadth, *Chemical Abstracts* is often used to locate citations not indexed elsewhere. Patents describing the manufacture of a specific drug fall into this category. Although the emphasis is not primarily on clinical medicine, extensive research material is included and there is substantial coverage of drugs in research. It is therefore very important to remember this source in order to be comprehensive in searching for drug information outside of purely clinical topics. *Chemical Abstracts* is available in print as a weekly serial, which includes indexes to authors, subjects, patents, chemical substances, and formulas. It also includes an Index Guide for finding the correct index terms. When using *Chemical Abstracts* as an electronic database, the CAS Registry Number for the compound may provide one of the most efficient ways of searching a drug with multiple names. SciFinder Scholar is an easy-to-search interface for *Chemical Abstracts* and is licensed by many large institutions for users to do their own chemical, structure, and patent searching.

Other Online Resources

Today, electronic versions of standard print sources are proliferating; many of the sources described in this chapter are available online. For example, Facts and Comparisons provides a suite of 11 reference books in a cross-searchable online format, many of which are described in this chapter. There are also some excellent electronic drug information resources that are not just electronic versions of books, but online full-text databases or freely available Web sites. This section describes online resources, either Web sites or drug information databases that have not already been covered in this chapter. Since these sources abound, a comprehensive list would soon be out of date. This section lists a few of the major, more reputable electronic resources and stable Web sites available at this writing.

Full-Text Databases

9.51   *Clinical Pharmacology.* Tampa FL: Gold Standard. Available: www. clinicalpharmacology.com

9.52   *Micromedex.* Denver, CO: Thomson. Available: www.Micromedex. com

Clinical Pharmacology is an excellent source of authoritative, full text drug information. Information on prescription, over-the-counter, herbal, new, and investigational drugs can be found using either generic or proprietary names. Upon entering a drug name, the system retrieves an alphabetical list of drug names and formulations, from which the user can select specific products. For a given product, the user can access a broad range of information through links to a variety of sources. The Drug Information section includes monographs similar to the print sources described in this chapter, with lists of alternative names and discussions of indications, dosages, adverse effects, drug interactions, product photographs, manufacturing information, and costs. Drug monographs present highlighted keywords in context. Clinical Pharmacology also contains several useful tools for identifying and comparing drugs. The Product Comparison tool allows the searcher to enter any number of ingredients to build comparison tables of available drugs containing the ingredients. For example, a user could find a list of all drugs containing acetaminophen and pseudoephedrine, but no alcohol. The product ID tool allows the user to enter characteristics such as color, shape, and imprint to identify drug products. This is very useful in the clinical setting where patients often keep their medications in containers other than the original labeled package, and the health care practitioner needs to identify the medications. The Clinical Reports tool generates summaries of known interactions, adverse effects, or IV compatibility for combinations of drugs. Patient information is available in English and Spanish. Convenient links provide navigation between these tools from all sections of the database.

The Micromedex suite of databases offers a variety of environmental health, toxicology, and drug information through its Corporate Solutions series and Healthcare series. It includes full text electronic books such as *Martindale*, the *USP DI*, and the *PDR*, as well as sets of drug monographs, product lists, dosing calculators, drug interactions, alternative medicine, and information for patients. The drug interactions tool is particularly useful, allowing the user to build a profile, add drugs to the profile, and display drug interactions. Micromedex resources can be purchased in various combinations or as a complete set. Examples of available databases include:

- DrugDex—evaluative and comparative drug information for the health care professional including investigational, non-prescription, and international drugs
- AltMedDex—peer reviewed information on herbal and other dietary supplements
- DiseaseDex—evidence-based disease information for general and emergency medicine
- POISINDEX—product identification and toxicological information on over one million drugs and chemicals
- REPRORISK—reproductive risk information for males, females and unborn children including the full text of Shepard's *Catalog of Teratogenic Agents* (see 9.21)

The system has the capability to search across all databases or by a specific database. Search results are grouped into sets retrieved from each database. Each link leads to a more specific, narrower category while indicating the hierarchical path. Links are provided to return to search results, a new search, or the main menu. Links to product information are also provided if there are products associated with the search term. Considering the depth of information contained in this system, navigation is relatively simple due to the hierarchical organization.

Web Sites

9.53   *U.S. Food and Drug Administration Center for Drug Evaluation and Research.* Available: www.fda.gov/cder

9.54   *Daily Med.* Bethesda, MD: U.S. National Library of Medicine. Available: http://dailymed.nlm.nih.gov

9.55   *National Center for Complementary and Alternative Medicine (NCCAM).* Bethesda, MD: National Institutes of Health. Available: http://nccam.nih.gov

9.56   *SafeMedication.com.* Bethesda, MD: American Society of Health-System Pharmacists. Available: www.safemedication.com

9.57   *RxList: the Internet Drug Index.* New York, NY: WebMD. Available: www.rxlist.com

The FDA Center for Drug Evaluation and Research is an excellent site with essential information such as public health alerts and warnings, drug information pages, patient information, and clinical trials. Unique to this site are drug approval histories and reports and therapeutic equivalents to drugs. The site includes the *Approved Drug Products with Therapeutic Equivalence Evaluations/Orange Book* (see 9.15), which provides information on therapeutic equivalence for generic drugs. The drug information pages list therapeutic equivalents where appropriate.

Daily Med, maintained by the NLM, is a database of all approved labeling of drug products. Free to the public, it provides easy access to a collection of over 2,800 package inserts for medications. It is updated daily and includes RSS feeds of updates.

The NCCAM is an authoritative Web site published by the National Institutes of Health. It includes informative pages defining and describing complementary and alternative medicine. It is searchable by disease or condition, and treatment or therapy. Very consumer-friendly, the entries on treatments or therapies include sections on "what it is used for," "how it is used," "what the science says," and "side effects and cautions." The records also include references to primary literature.

SafeMedication.com is an authoritative source geared to consumers, developed by the American Society of Health-System Pharmacists (ASHP). It includes drug news, patient information, and a searchable database (Medmaster), based on *ASHP's Medication Teaching Manual: The Guide to Patient Drug Information*, a publication developed for use in patient education on side effects, precautions, and more.

The RxList Web site is part of the WebMD network, with content written by pharmacists and physicians. It contains an alphabetical listing of drug monographs, which include information on pharmacology, adverse effects, and many of the same categories of information provided through other drug resources. It also includes herbal and natural products. Because it is free, this is a good site to recommend to users who do not have access to the drug information reference books and licensed resources described in this chapter.

Drug Information Services

Over 100 pharmacist-run drug information services are operating today in the United States, although the numbers have been steadily declining since 1986 [3]. These services are usually affiliated with hospitals, medical centers, and schools of medicine and pharmacy. They provide specialized consultation on a variety of questions related to patient care. Topics may include drug identification, prescribing, prevention and management of adverse effects, and drug interactions. Drug information services have access to specialized resources often found only in medical libraries, and pharmacists will often analyze literature and provide expert advice where conflicting information exists. However, it is difficult to make general observations because services vary from place to place. Some may offer services only to medical and nursing staffs, while others may extend their services to the community. Fees for service also vary. The International Drug Information Center at the Arnold and Marie Schwartz College of Pharmacy and Health Sciences, Long Island University, has published directories of drug information centers since 1974. These authors periodically conduct surveys to obtain names and addresses of centers, hours of operation, and contact information. Directories are organized alphabetically by state. Recent articles cite previous articles so that updates can be found through a citation search. Librarians should be aware of nearby drug information centers and make efforts to build relationships with staff and collaborate on delivering the best possible services to users.

References

1. Keely JL. Pharmacist scope of practice. *Ann Intern Med* 2002; 136(1):79–85.
2. FDA Center for Drug Evaluation and Research. New Drug Development and Review Process, In: *The CDER handbook*. Available: www.fda.gov/cder/handbook
3. Rosenberg JM, Koumis T, Nathan JP, Cicero LA, McGuire H. Current status of pharmacist-operated drug information centers in the United States. *Am J Health Syst Pharm* 2004; 61(19):2023–32.

CHAPTER 10

Consumer Health Sources

Mary L. Gillaspy

An Overview of the Consumer Health Phenomenon

Individuals have always sought information about their health. From ancient times, shamans and other healers within cultures have provided treatments of varying efficacy to relieve disease and suffering, and the recipients of this traditional (or folk) medicine have welcomed their interventions, or at least accepted them in the absence of any better alternative. Patients in every age have also talked with others who have shared the same or a similar experience and sought their counsel and support. When Web browsers began providing easy access to the World Wide Web in the 1990s, early adopters—both searchers and content managers—recognized the power of the new medium for posting information about health and wellness. With the launch of the MedlinePlus Web site in October 1998, Donald A.B. Lindberg, M.D., director of the National Library of Medicine, commented, "carefully used, the Internet offers the public a wonderful opportunity for accessing timely and critical health information" [1]. Nearing the end of the first decade of the twenty-first century, consumer access to health information is more critical than ever because of new technology and the potential for change in the delivery of health care, in part to rein in soaring costs and to accommodate the largest and longest-lived population of seniors in history. Yet, partly because of the growth of the Web, the amount of information of all kinds, including health information, threatens to overwhelm even sophisticated users.

Despite the complexity of the subjects, millions of people every day search for topics ranging from tests and procedures, to drug information, to information about a new diagnosis. Profound scientific advances and an emphasis on translational applications—moving research more quickly from the bench to the bedside—mean that people have even more pressing decisions to make about their health. Consider just these factors: genomics and personalized medicine, along with varying degrees of literacy, and one begins to see how "consumer health information" and facilitating access to it has grown far beyond the 44 basic topics covered by MedlinePlus by the end of 1998. A brief examination of these factors lends greater understanding of the vital role that authoritative information aimed at consumers plays in today's health care arena.

Genomics and the Era of Personalized Medicine

By 2003, the sequencing of the human genome, accomplished ahead of schedule, was changing the face of medicine and its clinical practice. At the end of 2004, federal government agencies, corporations, venture capital firms, patient advocacy organizations, research and educational institutions, and various other groups combined to launch the Personalized Medicine Coalition. Personalized, or predictive, medicine combines genomic science, information technology, and empowered patients [2] to transform the practice of clinical medicine and the physician-patient relationship. It is an approach that "uses molecular analysis to achieve optimum medical outcomes in the management of . . . disease" [3] or a predisposition to disease and holds great promise for the future of patient care and the ability to reduce risk and sometimes prevent disease in the first place. Pharmacogenomics represents perhaps the most intense area of research, since the goal of the discipline is to identify which genes are responsible for the "wide variability in people's responses to many common drugs" [4]. The earliest research focused on tests to determine how an individual would respond to common chemotherapy drugs as well as antidepressants, anticoagulants, and other medications that can either build up to toxic levels in some individuals or be flushed from the body too quickly in others, preventing a therapeutic effect [5]. The emerging science promises that eventually physicians will test patients during their office visit; on the basis of the information obtained, the doctor will know whether a given medication is safe for that person and the dose that will be most effective. Designer drugs will have left the street and become part of the practice of medicine.

Scientific Literacy in the United States

Besides the many legal, ethical, and societal questions that personalized medicine raises, however, the remarkable scientific advances are unfortunately colliding with a crisis in literacy, including scientific literacy, among some segments of the U.S. population. The National Center for Education Statistics (NCES) measured health literacy among adults in the United States in a 2003 assessment. Literacy levels were described as below basic, basic, intermediate, or proficient. The study found that 53 percent of adults had intermediate literacy, while only 12 percent measured proficient. An alarming 14 percent had below basic literacy, while 22 percent measured at the basic level [6]. In a report issued in 2004, the Institute of Medicine (IOM) put the number of Americans who have difficulty both comprehending and using health information provided to them by physicians, nurses, and pharmacists at 90 million, or nearly half the adult population [7]. The majority of people with limited health literacy are Caucasian and born in the United States; however, a disproportionate number live in rural areas, are socioeconomically disadvantaged, are part of ethnic or racial minorities, or are elderly [8]. By any standard, literacy rates generally, and health literacy rates specifically, must improve for people to understand the kinds of information and make the kinds of choices regarding their care that are on the near horizon.

Genomics and personalized medicine, scientific literacy among consumers—what does all this have to do with medical librarians? Medical librarians who work with the public are uniquely positioned to make a positive impact on patients' understanding of and compliance with medical instructions, their health decision making, and their navigating not only a complicated, multitiered health care system but also a bewildering array of new technologies. The Medical Library Association (MLA) translated their concern about health literacy among consumers into action more than a decade ago when they developed a brochure entitled *Deciphering Medspeak*. In 2002, they added links to the "top ten most useful Web sites" to MLANet. In 2006, three additional brochures became available to help lay people understand terms associated with breast cancer, diabetes, and heart disease. In September 2006, the U.S. National Library of Medicine awarded a two-year, $250,000 contract to MLA to determine the degree to which hospital providers and administrators are aware of health literacy issues and their value to patient care. One of the outcomes of the study will be a health information literacy curriculum, designed to be taught by librarians and used internationally to raise awareness among providers of the difference that literacy makes in health outcomes.

The very first objective of the MLA Health Information Literacy Research Project is the following: "To demonstrate whether or not hospital administrators favor funding consumer health information resource centers over hospital libraries targeted for health care providers" [9]. Hospitals that have been in the forefront of offering "learning centers" to their patients and families, and sometimes to the public, include such institutions as the Beth Israel Deaconess and Brigham and Women's hospitals in Boston, the Mayo Clinic in Minnesota, Northwestern Memorial Hospital in Chicago, cancer centers throughout the United States, and Planetree clinics; many other institutions have set aside an area of traditional medical libraries for consumers. (MedlinePlus devotes a section of its Web site to libraries that provide services to health consumers; as complete a list as is available can be found there [10].) With the growing use of electronic resources for health care professionals, and the need for educating patients and families, hospital libraries may continue a trend toward providing more physical space for lay people and increased programming for consumers, a possibility obviously observed by the writers of the MLA's research project.

Undoubtedly one of the issues addressed by the MLA Health Information Literacy Research Project will be the preponderance of health care information available on the Internet. The Pew Internet & American Life Project has been tracking Internet use among U.S. adults since 2000. The *Online Health Search 2006* reported several interesting findings. First, the number of Internet users searching for health information has remained constant over four years—63 percent in 2002, 66 percent in 2004, and 64 percent in 2006—despite the increase in Internet connectivity and the ubiquity of broadband access. Two thirds of health information seekers begin their search at a search engine rather than at a trusted source, such as MedlinePlus, and three fourths of the users do not routinely note the authority of the source or the date of the information they find online. One fourth reported feeling "overwhelmed" by the quantity of what they found, and 18 percent reported feeling "confused" by the information they accessed. Only one third of users discussed their findings with their physician, and more than half (56 percent) reported feeling "relieved or comforted" by their findings [11]. A role for librarian services exists in this realm. Increasingly, hospitals, organizations, and even large clinics offer some professional information service for patients, though the practice is far from universal. When visionary leaders establish such services, librarians in these consumer-health settings play a vital role connecting the information consumers receive and their interactions with the rest of the health care system.

Consumer health libraries are no longer the "new kid on the block" of medical libraries. They are rapidly maturing into sophisticated entities, with their reach expanded across communities through innovative partnerships of all kinds. Indeed, consumer health librarianship is now recognized as its own specialty, and MLA offers a credential in the provision of such information [12].

The role of the information professional in the provision of health information to the public includes all of the following factors: emphasizing the importance of and defining trusted sources of health information; knowing when to consult a physician; understanding the nuances of communicating with physicians, nurses, and pharmacists; and using authoritative information to make decisions about testing, treatment, and risk reduction. Medical librarians can guide laypeople in all of these directions. Their role is a critical one as the information becomes not only easier to locate but also more complex in its content and presentation. The references discussed in the remainder of this chapter represent the best resources available to guide health care consumers through the complicated maze of information they face in the medical environment.

What Makes Consumer Health Information Different from Traditional Medical Reference?

Providing health information to lay people differs considerably from traditional medical reference. First, though the information may be delivered in a hospital or academic health science library setting, the venue may also be a storefront, public library, or community-based organization. Personnel providing the information may also be different from those in traditional settings. Most important of all, the information needs and information-seeking behaviors of a health consumer are usually quite different from those of a physician, researcher, nurse, or allied health professional. Consumers vary widely in their level of literacy, for example, and they often seek narratives that describe the experience of others who have faced the same issues.

Venues for Dissemination of Consumer Health Information

Consumer health information (CHI) is provided in both formal and informal settings. Informal settings include person-to-person contact, support groups, online moderated discussion lists, chat rooms, and similar venues. Discussion in this chapter will be limited to formal situations, particularly those that occur in a hospital, a public library, a health organization library that serves the public, or an academic health science library that provides a special area and collection for members of the public. Libraries in community-based organizations, clinics, or storefronts may also find the resources that follow are useful when building reference collections for their users.

Obviously, the venue affects the resources that are required to respond appropriately to the information needs of health care consumers. For example, some settings may offer a computer terminal, or special software, with or without personal assistance. Others may set aside a room or a corner dedicated to serving patients, families, and the general public. Still other settings may dedicate an entire facility to serving only or primarily health care consumers. The resources that are selected will vary by venue. Whether they include only print, only computer access, or a combination of the two, the information included in this chapter will help library and education professionals have references on hand that will meet many of the health information needs of consumers.

Personnel in Consumer Health Library Settings

Given the unique information needs of the lay public, information professionals play a very different role in CHI settings from the typical ones found in libraries that serve only health professionals. Their role is at least as much that of educator as of health information professional, and sometimes it is mainly educator. Health care consumers often want to discuss the information they are receiving and may require considerable assistance in locating and then understanding what they have found.

No matter the location of the CHI service, multiple medical librarians may not be available. Many of these services are operated without any information professional at all; rather, health educators, nurse educators, or other groups establish, operate, and maintain the center. In such situations, a medical librarian or staff of a nearby medical library may provide consultation services. Ideally, consumer health information services are staffed by a multidisciplinary team, the members of which may be full time, part time, or a combination. A medical librarian, health educator, social worker, registered nurse, and volunteers from varied professional backgrounds can make for a powerful team.

Volunteers are ubiquitous in these settings and generally perform useful, even essential work for the center. From answering the telephone, to assisting with technical service tasks, to sorting mail and creating information packets, to independent projects, to helping customers directly, volunteers enhance the services that consumer health information services provide. Their training should be developed and overseen by a coordinator of volunteers, who can also act as the primary contact and screener for the program.

Information Needs of Health Care Consumers

While clinicians and researchers exhibit somewhat predictable information needs, the same cannot be said for the health care consumer. Arguably, their needs are often more difficult to meet, since they frequently are unsure of how to frame their questions and may be distraught from the gravity of a diagnosis, sudden financial stress, grief, or other stressors associated with negotiating the health care system. The responsibility lies with the information professional to (1) select and make available the best resources; (2) assess the consumer's level of need and willingness to learn; and (3) stage the information correctly so that the person can learn incrementally and move as far along a continuum of health information need as s/he wishes, using resources appropriate to the individual's learning style. Literacy level must also be determined and taken into account when providing health information to consumers. A study conducted among English-speaking parents in the Bronx, New York, found that 77 percent of the subjects made errors in dosing medication prescribed for their children [13]. Additionally, when consumers use search engines to find information on the Internet, Berland found that they find documents that are typically written at a tenth-grade level or higher [14].

Successful librarians possess finely honed interpersonal skills, and in no field are these skills more important than in consumer health. Providing health information to the public has in the past been the purview of physicians and nurses. This situation has begun to change, but the first and most important thing that any librarian working in consumer health in a hospital, clinic, or academic medical center must do is gain the trust of the providers in the institution. Once that hurdle has been overcome, providers are grateful for the support of a well run consumer health information center, because they simply do not have the time to meet the increasing health information needs of their patients. Trust and respect for the librarian, other staff, and volunteers must be earned and carefully nurtured with all providers for the consumer health library program to prosper.

General Reference Sources for Consumer Health Information

Consumer health information encompasses a broad spectrum of resources, from easy-to-read to medical textbooks and journal articles. The most important principle regarding reference sources for consumers is to provide an array of resources, at an array of levels, in multiple formats to match individual learning styles. Literally thousands of books and Web sites are available today for consumer health information. What is listed here is not meant to be comprehensive. The references that are discussed are ones that have been found in our setting to be the most authoritative and useful to laypeople and the librarians and educators who help them satisfy their health information needs.

In some cases, core medical textbooks are included as key consumer health references. The use of such resources may be controversial. Though the number of their subjects was very small, Baker and Gollop devised a study that indicated some of "the problems involved in reading medical materials," even among well educated users, and they identified some of the factors of which librarians and educators should be aware as they "help lay people in their quest to read and understand medical terminology." They concluded that "library and information science professionals should test the reading comprehension of medical textbooks so that they can tailor medical and health material to the specific needs of their communities" [15].

Guides to the Literature

10.1   Baker LA, Manbeck V. *Consumer Health Information for Public Librarians*. Lanham, MD: Scarecrow Press, 2002.

10.2   Barclay DA, Halsted DD. *Consumer Health Reference Service Handbook*. New York: Neal-Schuman, 2001.

10.3   Rees AM. *Consumer Health Information Source Book*. Westport, CT: Greenwood Publishing Group, 2003.

10.4   *Consumer and Patient Health Information Section (CAPHIS) of the Medical Library Association*. Chicago, IL: CAPHIS. Available: caphis.mlanet.org

10.5   *Healthnet: Connecticut Consumer Health Information Network*. Lyman MaynardStowe Library: University of Connecticut. Recommended Books for a Consumer Health Reference Collection. Farmington, CT: University of Connecticut. Available: library.uchc.edu/departm/hnet/corelist.html

Consumer Health Information for Public Librarians focuses on meeting the information needs of health care consumers through partnerships with community entities. Though aimed specifically at public librarians, this work is useful for any information professional working with laypeople.

Consumer Health Reference Service Handbook provides information about how to start a reference service for consumers, as well as including a section on common health concerns of consumers, recommended consumer health Web sites, and key print resources for collections.

The *Consumer Health Information Source Book*, now in its seventh edition, has long been the most important work available for assessing and reporting the best materials available for consumer health. Recent editions have added electronic resources and Spanish-language materials; the seventh edition continues this tradition and has added a chapter about consumer health libraries in North America that are models for excellence.

Consumer and Patient Health Information Section (CAPHIS) of the Medical Library Association includes several key documents for consumer health, as well as an article describing how to establish and manage a consumer health library.

Healthnet: Connecticut Consumer Health Information Network is an excellent resource that includes a core bibliography for consumer health reference from the Lyman Maynard Stowe Library at the University of Connecticut Health Center. Items with new editions since December 2005 are noted with a checkmark. Also included is a list of recommended serials.

Directories

Many of the directories that were once essential are now marginal purchases, since so much of this type of information is available on the Web. However, some directory information, such as that in the database from the American Board of Medical Specialties, is available only for an annual subscription fee; however, when available, it is frequently used by consumers.

10.6   *AHA Guide to the Health Care Field.* Chicago, IL: American Hospital Association, 1997–. Annual. *Formerly American Hospital Association Guide to the Health Care Field, 1974–1996.* Annual.

10.7   *The Official ABMS Directory of Board Certified Medical Specialists.* St. Louis, MO: W.B. Saunders, 1992–. Annual.

10.8   *Medical and Health Information Directory.* Detroit, MI: Thomson Gale, 1977–. Triennial.

10.9   *Directory of Self-Help and Mutual Aid Groups.* Chicago, IL: Mental Health Association of Illinois, 1990/91–. Biannual.

10.10 *AMA Physician Select (DoctorFinder).* Chicago, IL: American Medical Association. Available: www.ama-assn.org/aps/amahg.htm

AHA Guide to the Health Care Field, an annual publication, lists all hospitals in the United States alphabetically by state. Helpful information such as address, telephone number, types of service, number of beds, and more is provided.

Published annually, *The Official ABMS Directory of Board Certified Medical Specialists* is an excellent resource for consumers who want to know as much as they can about their physicians, particularly specialists to whom they have been referred or whom they might see only rarely.

Medical and Health Information Directory, a three-volume work, includes 1) organizations, agencies, and institutions; 2) publications, libraries, and other information resources; and 3) health services, which includes such items as sleep disorder clinics, sports medicine clinics, transplant centers, and more.

Self-help directories are published annually or biannually in most states. In Illinois, the biannual *Directory of Self-Help and Mutual Aid Groups* includes a definition of self-help, questions to ask when looking for the "right" self-help group, and the directory itself, organized by large areas such as addiction, disability, or family issues. An alphabetical index and a concern index make the volume easy to use.

More than 690,000 licensed medical doctors and osteopaths are included in the AMA Physician Select (DoctorFinder) database, which can be searched by name and city or state or by medical specialty and city or state. This Internet database and several other similar ones of health professionals are also available from MedlinePlus, at: Available: www.nlm.nih.gov/Med linePlus/directories.html.

Dictionaries

Even with good online medical dictionaries available, print editions continue to be valuable and necessary in a consumer health setting. Following are the most important titles.

General Medical Dictionaries

10.11 *Dorland's Illustrated Medical Dictionary*. Philadelphia, PA: W.B. Saunders, 2007.

10.12 *Stedman's Medical Dictionary*. Philadelphia, PA: Lippincott Williams & Wilkins, 2005.

10.13 *Miller-Keane Encyclopedia & Dictionary of Medicine, Nursing & Allied Health*. Philadelphia, PA: W.B. Saunders, 2003.

10.14 Venes D, ed. *Taber's Cyclopedic Medical Dictionary*. Philadelphia, PA: F.A. Davis, 2005.

Often considered the most venerable resource in its field, *Dorland's* is an optional selection for a consumer health collection. The definitions are written using sophisticated medical vocabulary, and users are directed from common names (e.g., Bell's palsy) to the name of the nerve and to the entry for *palsy*. Best for sophisticated users and staff.

Excellent illustrations, many in color, make *Stedman's Medical Dictionary* very useful for consumers. Helpful appendices, including common medical abbreviations and symbols; arteries, muscles, and nerves of the human body; and laboratory values and reference ranges enhance the value of this standard work.

Miller-Keane Encyclopedia & Dictionary of Medicine provides very approachable content for consumers, with copious color illustrations.

Clearly written entries make *Taber's Cyclopedic Medical Dictionary* an exceptional resource for consumer use. Its many illustrations (some in color), and extensive appendices are also helpful.

Specialty Dictionaries

10.15 Sarg M, Gross AD, Altman R. *The Cancer Dictionary*. New York: Facts on File, 2006.

10.16 Jablonski S. *Dictionary of Medical Acronyms and Abbreviations*. Philadelphia, PA: Elsevier Saunders, 2005.

10.17 *Stedman's Abbreviations, Acronyms, and Symbols*. Philadelphia, PA: Lippincott, Williams & Wilkins, 2005.

10.18 Tsur SA. *Elsevier's Dictionary of Abbreviations, Acronyms, Synonyms and Symbols used in Medicine*. Philadelphia, PA: Elsevier Science, 2004.

10.19 Sternberg MLA. *American Sign Language: Unabridged Edition*. New York: HarperCollins, 2005.

10.20 Valli C, ed. *Gallaudet Dictionary of American Sign Language*. Washington, DC: Gallaudet University Press, 2006.

The Cancer Dictionary is written especially for the cancer patient and the general public who seek to know more about the constellation of diseases we call *cancer*. A well-written index and attractive format make this resource easy to use.

The updated edition of *Dictionary of Medical Acronyms and Abbreviations* includes explanations of molecular biology terms in an approachable format.

In addition to *Stedman's Abbreviations, Acronyms, and Symbols*, Stedman's also produces an entire series of "wordbooks," including such titles as *Stedman's Radiology Words*, *Stedman's Alternative and Complementary Medicine Words*, and *Stedman's Surgery Words*, which also includes anesthesia and pain management. A complete listing of these resources can be found at www.lww.com.

Elsevier's Dictionary of Abbreviations, Acronyms, Synonyms, and Symbols Used in Medicine is most useful for allowing the investigation of a large class of abbreviations, such as "hormone" or "vitamins," and for having all the information listed under that heading as well as separately in the alphabetic list. Variations in terminology are included and explained.

American Sign Language: Unabridged Edition is an excellent resource for consumers who are learning American Sign Language (ASL), for school-children who are writing reports about it, and for hearing-impaired individuals and their families as well.

Gallaudet Dictionary of American Sign Language includes a DVD showing how to form each of the more than 3,000 signs included in the book. The work also features examples of idioms in American Sign Language (ASL) and an article about the place of ASL in the deaf community.

Encyclopedias

Thomson Gale's products, available electronically as well as in print, are the best general consumer health encyclopedias on the market. They are plainly written, well illustrated, updated in a timely manner, and provide introductions to most common diseases and conditions as well as some rare ones. Information is easy to find because of multiple access points within each set, and biographical and historical sidebars in all the volumes enrich understanding. A resource list is included at the end of every entry. Entries in all volumes are arranged alphabetically, with an index in the final volume. The list of titles continues to grow.

10.21 Longe JL, ed. *The Gale Encyclopedia of Medicine*. Detroit, MI: Thomson Gale, 2006.

This set was first published in 1999. Cross-references have improved in successive editions. The content is excellent. There are entries for diseases and disorders as well as tests and treatments. In the first category, the entries typically include definitions, descriptions, causes and symptoms, diagnosis, treatments, alternative treatments (if any), prognosis, and prevention. Entries for tests and treatments include definitions, purposes, precautions, descriptions, preparation, aftercare, risks, and normal and abnormal results.

10.22 Narins B, ed. *The Gale Encyclopedia of Genetic Disorders*. Detroit, MI: Thomson Gale, 2005.

This resource brings much of the work of the Human Genome Project to the medical consumer at the place they care about, the disorders themselves. Relatively common disorders (epilepsy, cystic fibrosis) are included, as well as much rarer ones (Fahr disease, Li-Fraumeni syndrome). Articles include definitions, descriptions, genetic profile, demographics, signs and symptoms, diagnosis, treatment and management, and prognosis.

10.23 Krapp KM, Wilson J, eds. *Gale Encyclopedia of Children's Health: Infancy through Adolescence*. Detroit, MI: Thomson Gale, 2005.

This resource follows the format of other resources in the series. A part of most of the articles is "Parental Concerns," a very helpful guide for both parents and librarians assisting them.

10.24 Krapp K, Longe JL, eds. *The Gale Encyclopedia of Alternative Medicine*. Detroit, MI: Thomson Gale, 2005.

Entries in the general categories of diseases and conditions, herbs and remedies, and therapies are included. Training requirements for practitioners and lists of organizations comprise a portion of the relevant entries. The most important feature of this encyclopedia is its balance. The content is straight-forward and makes no unwarranted claims.

10.25 Longe JL, ed. *The Gale Encyclopedia of Cancer: A Guide to Cancer and Its Treatments*. Detroit, MI: Thomson Gale, 2005.

Included in this set are entries on 120 different cancers, common cancer drugs, traditional and alternative treatments, and diagnostic procedures. The drug section entries are quite helpful. They appear in the encyclopedia under generic name but are indexed under both brand and generic name, with a cross-reference from the brand name to the generic. Most helpful of all, treat-ment acronyms like MOPP and EVA are explained, and the names of all the drugs included in the combination therapies and the types of cancer for which they are administered are also included in the entry. These articles, generally about one and one half pages long, are an approachable adjunct to *The Chemotherapy Sourcebook* (4th ed. Baltimore, MD: Lippincott Williams & Wilkins, 2007) an excellent but technical reference. Articles on specific therapies are lengthy; for example, the "Chemotherapy" article is nine pages long, while "Radiation Therapy" is four pages in length. Terms commonly used in cancer and cancer treatment—such as adjuvant chemotherapy—are explained clearly, and when several terms are used for the same procedure, like internal radiation therapy, all of them are named and described.

10.26 Thackery E, Harris M, eds. *The Gale Encyclopedia of Mental Disorders.* Detroit, MI: Thomson Gale, 2007.

Entries for all 150 disorders classified in the *Diagnostic and Statistical Manual of Mental Disorders, Fourth Edition, Text Revision (DSM-IV-TR)* (see 10.87) are included in this very approachable and useful work. Medications—prescription, alternative, and over-the-counter—are discussed in detail. The large classes of drugs, like selective serotonin reuptake inhibitors (SSRIs), do not have their own entry but are treated in the entry for each individual agent and are grouped in the index by general class. Therapies beyond pharmaceutical agents, like electroconvulsive therapy, are also included, as are diagnostic tools like electroencephalography.

10.27 Brickland BR, ed. *The Gale Encyclopedia of Psychology.* Detroit, MI: Thomson Gale, 2001. (E-book released in 2003.)

First published in 1996, the nearly 700 articles of this resource provide access to important individuals, theories, and vocabulary; ground-breaking studies and experiments; applied psychology in the world around us; and psychology as a career.

10.28 Senagore AJ, ed. *The Gale Encyclopedia of Surgery.* Detroit, MI: Thomson Gale, 2004.

Excellent supplement to online resources like MedlinePlus tutorials (see 10.48). A feature that consumers especially appreciate is an appendix listing the preeminent centers for specific surgical procedures.

10.29 Chamberlin SL, Narins B, eds. *The Gale Encyclopedia of Neurological Disorders.* Detroit, MI: Thomson Gale, 2005.

Because of the serious nature and unfortunately common occurrence of neurological disorders, a separate title for this class of diseases and conditions is warranted. It follows the same format as other titles by this publisher. Nervous system aspects of diseases and syndromes that may have neurological components, such as HIV disease, are discussed in detail. Pharmaceuticals that are commonly prescribed for neurological disorders are also included.

10.30 Schmidt R, Willis W, eds. *The Encyclopedia of Pain*. Detroit, MI: Thomson Gale, 2007.

Provides detailed overview of various aspects of pain. For example, searching on the term *headache* yields 70 articles, and *back pain* yields 48 results. Pharmaceuticals commonly prescribed for pain, as well as specific procedures such as various types of epidural injections, are also included. The articles are more technical than those in *The Gale Encyclopedia of Medicine*, and some of the references are dated. Even so, for people suffering from intractable pain, this resource is an important one for a consumer-health librarian to have on hand.

10.31 Schmidt R, Willis W, eds. *The Gale Encyclopedia of Diets*. Detroit, MI: Thomson Gale, 2007.

Nutrition and diet therapy comprise one of the most frequent areas of inquiry in consumer health settings. This encyclopedia helps users understand the basics of the Zone, Atkins, Pritikin, and other diets which have received so much attention in the media.

10.32 Albrecht GL, ed. *Encyclopedia of Disability*. Thousand Oaks, CA: Sage. 2006.

No other source matches this five-volume compendium of information. Black-and-white illustrations depict disability as it has appeared in art and film. The final volume makes available important primary source documents on disability, which are arranged chronologically. Noted disabled individuals, such as the cellist Jacqueline du Pré; events having to do with disability, such as Paralympics; and special situations, such as children of disabled parents and sexuality, are all covered in well-written articles.

Handbooks and Manuals

10.33 Beers MH et al, eds. *Merck Manual of Medical Information, Second Edition. The World's Most Widely-Used Medical Reference: Now in Everyday Language*. 2nd ed. Whitehouse, NJ: Merck, 2004–2007. Available: www.merck.com/mmhe/index.html

10.34 Beers MH et al, eds. *Merck Manual of Health and Aging*. White-house Station, NJ: Merck, 2005. Available: www.merck.com/pubs/ mmanual_ha/contents.html

10.35 Rakel RE, Bope ET, eds. *Conn's Current Therapy*. Philadelphia, PA: W.B. Saunders, 1984–. Annual.

10.36 Tierney LM, ed. *Current Medical Diagnosis & Treatment*. New York: Lange Medical Books/McGraw-Hill. 1974–. Annual.

The first and most important resources in the area of handbooks and manuals are the two Merck manuals, which should be used in their online versions because the Web sites contain corrections and changes from the original or current print editions. The date of the "last full review/revision" is posted at the bottom of each topic page. The online versions also provide multimedia enhancements that can be very helpful to consumers' understanding of a topic, especially if literacy is a barrier to learning. For example, technical terms are pronounced correctly with a single click, and mouse-overs provide common trade names for drugs, such as Zovirax for acyclovir.

The Lange and Conn series of handbooks have long been used by consumers and by reference librarians helping consumers answer questions. Before there were many quality consumer health resources available, except for pamphlets from organizations, these two series offered a gateway to medical knowledge that helped patients understand what was happening to their bodies and what to expect from treatment.

Today they are the middle ground between materials written specifically for consumers and medical textbooks. For the literate consumer who wants to go beyond the basic information offered by an encyclopedia article or printouts from a Web site, these handbooks are a good choice. They delve more deeply into actual disease processes than the consumer material and allow a deeper understanding of the actual medical problem. The reading level of both resources, however, is very high. Baker and Gollop found that the reading ease (Flesch reading ease score) for Conn was 13.56, while that for Lange was 13.80, where the score range is from zero (very difficult to read) to one hundred (easy to read). (See note 15.) As in all cases, librarians must know their users and make appropriate resources available. Where education and literacy rates are high, Conn and Lange may be helpful.

(Also available in the Lange series are titles for cardiology, critical care, emergency medicine, family medicine, geriatrics, neurology, obstetrics and gynecology, orthopaedics, otolaryngology–head and neck surgery, pain, pediatrics, psychiatry, pulmonary medicine, and rheumatology. These specialized volumes are less helpful in the consumer health realm than the more general one. All are available electronically.)

Key Medical Series Written for the Consumer

Certain institutions and publishers have developed consumer health information series that, like the Thomson Gale encyclopedias, follow a similar format and exhibit a recognizable "look and feel." In alphabetical order by producer or sponsoring institution, the best of the best include the following. The Web site, if available, follows the name of the organization, publisher, or series.

10.37 *American Medical Association. AMA Consumer Publications.* Chicago, IL: AMA Press. Available: catalog.ama-assn.org/Catalog/ home.jsp

Click on "Health Books" to find publications written for consumers. The cookbooks and "essential guides" are especially fine.

10.38 American Academy of Pediatrics. AAP Online Bookstore. Elk Grove Village, IL: American Academy of Pediatrics. Available: www.aap. org/bst/index.cfm?DID=15

Click on a topic under "Parent Resources" to find authoritative publications. One of the best features of these resources is that they are frequently updated; moreover, many publications are available in both English and Spanish.

10.39 *Harvard Medical School Guides.* Available: www.health.harvard. edu/books/

Nearly two dozen titles are available in this outstanding series.

10.40 Johns Hopkins University Press. Available: www.press.jhu.edu/ books/health_med.html

Click on "Consumer Health" to find more than one hundred titles. Some of the most important consumer health resources, such as *The 36-Hour Day*, are published by this press.

10.41 Mayo Clinic books for consumers. Available: bookstore.mayoclinic. com/home.cfm.

Excellent references on common diseases and conditions, from arthritis to vision and eye health. Some or all of them should be available for reference in consumer health libraries.

10.42 Omnigraphics Health Reference Series. Available: www.omni
graphics.com/category_view.php?ID=3

Nearly 150 volumes are available in this series. The series directed toward
adolescents, the Teen Health Series, is well worth including in a consumer
health collection that serves teenagers, as the format is engaging and the titles
address important concerns of this age group: diet, drugs, mental health,
sexual health, skin health, and sports injuries. All volumes are frequently
updated.

Category-Specific Reference Resources for Consumer Health Information

Category 1: General Health and Medical References

Librarians that serve the public may find that in order to answer the
questions asked of them, they need access to a core set of medical textbooks,
even though the material will not necessarily be understood in depth without
medical training. On a continuum of resources (an array of levels) running
from materials written at a fourth- to sixth-grade reading level on up the
scale, these works are the upper end of the collection. Today they may be
obtained either in print or in an electronic database or both.

10.43 Braunwald EG et al, eds. *Harrison's Principles of Internal Medicine.*
New York: McGraw-Hill, 2001.

The most authoritative reference available on the diagnosis and treatment of
diseases and conditions, Harrison's is one of the two "bibles" of internal medicine. It is, however, very technical, and only the most highly educated consumer
will find it useful. If only one such advanced reference is included in a consumer
health collection, make it *Cecil's Textbook of Medicine*, which follows.

10.44 Goldman L, Bennett JC, eds. *Cecil's Textbook of Medicine.* 22nd
ed. Philadelphia, PA: W.B. Saunders, 2004.

With *Harrison's Principles of Internal Medicine*, this work is the other
"bible" of internal medicine. Its engaging approach to its subjects makes it a
good choice for highly literate readers. For example, the two paragraphs at
the beginning of the chapter on cystic fibrosis may lead a user to explore
other, more simply written resources about medicine in history or folklore
and genetics:

The first known reference to cystic fibrosis is an adage from northern European folklore: "Woe to that child which when kissed on the forehead tastes salty. He is bewitched and soon must die." That saying describes the salty sweat that is the basis of an important diagnostic test and the early mortality. The first pathologic and clinical description came in 1938, when the disease was called cystic fibrosis of the pancreas. The severity and frequency of lung disease was soon appreciated. Since then, marked improvements have occurred in diagnosis, clinical management, understanding, and treatment of the disease. As a result, the current median survival is approximately 30 years.

In addition to its importance as a clinical disease, the study of cystic fibrosis is important because it provides an instructive example of the pathway of discovery in the investigation of a genetic disease. Because it was one of the earliest diseases identified by positional cloning, a review of the advances, problems, and opportunities that physicians and scientists have encountered since discovery of the CFTR gene may presage events that will be repeated and varied as an increasing number of disease-associated genes are discovered [16].

10.45 Goldmann DR, ed. *American College of Physicians Complete Home Medical Guide*. New York: DK Publishing, 2003.

This is an excellent example of its type of reference. Home medical guides, by their nature, provide only cursory information about health topics. This one is beautifully produced, with well-written text, colorful illustrations, and excellent graphics. Other good choices for works of this type are listed below:

10.46 American Medical Association. *American Medical Association Family Medical Guide*. 4th ed. New York: John Wiley & Sons, 2004.

10.47 Komaroff AL, ed. *Harvard Medical School Family Health Guide*. New York: Free Press, 2004.

Many excellent portals to consumer health information are available today on the Internet. The National Institute of Diabetes, Digestive, and Kidney Disorders (NIDDK), at www.digestive.niddk.nih.gov/, and the National Heart, Lung, and Blood Institute (NHLBI), at www.Nhlbi.nih.gov/, besides the two sites mentioned below, produce excellent information for consumers, as do most other entities within the National Institutes of Health. Some of the information is available in more than one language, and easy reading pamphlets are sometimes present. Many private organizations (like the American Heart

Association, the American Diabetes Association, and the American Cancer Society) have excellent information as well. The first consumer health portal from the federal government, healthfinder.gov is continually enhanced and is—because of its clean, bright format—particularly easy to use for seniors or persons with poor vision. Medem (medem.com/), KidsHealth (kidshealth.com/), MayoClinic.com, and many other sites provide particular inducements. However, by going to one of the two sites described below, consumers are directed to an enormous array of resources, including everything available through the federal government as well as the independent sites listed above. They truly offer one-stop shopping for consumer health reference information.

10.48 *MedlinePlus.* Bethesda, MD: U.S. National Library of Medicine. Available: medlineplus.gov/

MedlinePlus is the premier free portal to consumer health information on the Web. Beginning with pages devoted to fewer than 50 health topics in 1998, the site has grown to include more than 700. It also includes the A.D.A.M. medical encyclopedia, drug information, and more than 150 interactive health tutorials covering common diseases and conditions, diagnostic tests and procedures, surgeries and surgical procedures, and prevention and wellness information.

10.49 *Cancer.gov: Cancer Information.* Bethesda, MD: National Cancer Institute. Available: cancer.gov.

Cancer.gov contains comprehensive cancer treatment information from the National Cancer Institute. The site covers all aspects of cancer and should be a first stop for information about this disease. It also links out to other sources of information. Treatment documents are updated whenever new information is available.

Category 2: Procedures, Therapies, Symptoms, and Manifestations

Drug Information

10.50 *The United States Pharmacopoeia: USP DI.* Rockville, MD: United States Pharmacopoeial Convention, Inc. Annual. Volume 1, *Drug Information for the Health Care Provider*; Volume 2, *Advice for the Patient.* Volume 2 available: www.nlm.nih.gov/MedlinePlus/drug information.html

Consumers expect to see a current *Physician's Desk Reference* in a health library, though online resources are more authoritative (because of frequent updates) and generally much easier to use. Volume 2 of the *USP DI, Advice for the Patient* is available online for free from *MedlinePlus*. In most consumer health information settings, a print edition of this resource is not required, though the online version will be used extensively.

10.51 *Micromedex CareNotes*. Thomson Micromedex. Available: www. micromedex.com/products/carenotes

CareNotes, the patient information tool from Micromedex, provides 2,500 information sheets on medications and diseases and conditions; all are available in either English or Spanish.

10.52 *Clinical Pharmacology*. Tampa, FL: Gold Standard Multimedia. Available: goldstandard.com.

Clinical Pharmacology, produced by Gold Standard Multimedia, is a very attractive product that provides technical monographs as well as patient education handouts, available in Spanish as well as English. The database includes all Food and Drug Administration-approved prescription and over-the-counter pharmaceuticals, investigational drugs that are being investigated at Phase 3 or 4, and dietary supplements for which evidence of benefit or harm exists.

Diagnostic Tests

10.53 Fischbach FT, et al. *Manual of Laboratory & Diagnostic Tests*. Philadelphia, PA: Lippincott Williams & Wilkins, 2006.

The Fischbach book is a core title that will provide background for material written specifically for the consumer.

10.54 American Association for Clinical Chemistry. *Lab Tests Online*. Available: labtestsonline.org/index.html

Lab Tests Online is the primary source that MedlinePlus uses for their laboratory tests page and is by far the most authoritative free online site for reading about diagnostic or screening tests. Users can employ pull-down menus to search by the name of the test, condition for which the test is being performed, or screening guidelines by age. A general search box is also available. A special section entitled "Understanding Your Tests" provides information about reference ranges, genetic testing, pharmacogenomics, and more. Another section called "Inside the Lab" affords users a glimpse of different types of laboratories, who works in them, who provides oversight, and many more details. Absent institutionally approved patient education for specific tests, Lab Tests Online is the place to start to provide this sort of information to consumers. An e-mail function for asking detailed questions is also available, with a "certified clinical laboratory scientist" available to respond.

Genetics

10.55 *Genetics Home Reference.* Bethesda, MD: U.S. National Library of Medicine. Available: ghr.nlm.nih.gov/

Outstanding resource for consumers that continues to grow as scientists uncover more and more of the secrets of the human genome. Users may search under genetic conditions, genes, or chromosomes for specific information regarding diseases or conditions. A handbook, glossary, and links to additional information about genetics is also included.

10.56 *MedlinePlus: Genetics/Birth Defects.* Bethesda, MD: U.S. National Library of Medicine. Available: nlm.nih.gov/medlineplus/genetics birthdefects.html

Links to specific diseases and conditions as well as to entire pages devoted to genetic testing, genetic counseling, and gene therapy.

10.57 *A Science Primer.* Bethesda, MD: National Center for Biotechnology Information. Available: ncbi.nlm.nih.gov/About/primer/

For the consumer who would like to explore genetic topics in more depth, this primer offers an excellent quick course in the most important technologies currently being explored.

Symptoms and Manifestations

10.58 Margolis S. *Johns Hopkins Complete Home Guide to Symptoms and Remedies.* New York: Black Dog and Leventhal, 2004.

Many health care consumers use a library service to "check out" symptoms prior to seeing a physician. This book is an authoritative answer to such an information need. The first half of the book lists symptoms, such as "swallowing difficulty," with three columns of information: associated symptoms, possible diagnosis, and distinguishing features. The possible diagnoses are listed in alphabetical order. The second half of the book is an alphabetical arrangement of disorders, with each article explaining the condition and the cause, prevention, diagnosis, treatment options, and when to call a doctor. A textbox with each article provides cross-references to symptoms.

MedlinePlus also offers a way to investigate symptoms such as abdominal pain or fever, but the Margolis book is more comprehensive.

Nutrition and Diet Therapy

10.59 Duyff RL. *American Dietetic Association Complete Food and Nutrition Guide*. New York: John Wiley & Sons, 2006.

An outstanding, well-written resource that provides important nutrition information for individual health issues like fibromyalgia and hypertension, use and abuse of supplements, food-drug interactions, and much more. The chapter on fiber is especially useful.

10.60 Mahan LK, Escott-Stump S, eds. *Krause's Food, Nutrition, and Diet Therapy*. Philadelphia, PA: Elsevier/Saunders, 2004.

Krause's is the most authoritative resource available on diet therapy. The reference offers tables and illustrations for individual diseases and conditions and how they can be managed through diet.

10.61 Pennington JAT. *Bowes and Church's Food Values of Portions Commonly Used*. Philadelphia, PA: Lippincott Williams & Wilkins, 2005.

This resource answers many typical consumer questions regarding the specific nutrient content of certain foods and even indexes items by brand name.

Alternative, Complementary, and Integrative Medicine

As in so many other instances, current, authoritative information for alternative, complementary and integrative medicine is better found online than in print. Two proprietary databases offer evidence-based information, while additional information is available at various government and institutional Web sites. The listing below begins with the two products that require purchase, followed by authoritative free resources on the Web.

10.62 *Natural Medicines Comprehensive Database*. Stockton, CA: Therapeutic Research Faculty. Available: www.naturaldatabase.com

Produced and maintained by the same company that publishes *Pharmacist's Letter* and *Prescriber's Letter*, Natural Medicines Comprehensive Database offers access to evidence-based information about more "natural" products than any other single source. A natural product/drug interaction checker enables users to determine very quickly if any known ingredients in specific products may interact harmfully with a pharmaceutical. Safety and effectiveness ratings, based on available evidence, are noted along a continuum that ranges from unsafe, possibly unsafe, likely unsafe, possibly safe, likely safe, and safe, with the same scale for efficacy. Information regarding potential interactions with laboratory or diagnostic tests is also included. Searches may also be performed by disease or medical condition. Both professional and consumer monographs are available for hundreds of products, and the company has recently introduced a special consumer version of the database.

10.63 *Natural Standard Integrative Medicine Database*. Cambridge, MA: Natural Standard. Available: www.naturalstandard.com

Natural Standard Integrative Medicine Database features a very attractive interface and uses grades of A, B, C, D, or F to rate safety and effectiveness for the substances evaluated and the disease or condition for which its use is touted. The grades, which are easy for laypeople to understand, reflect the level of evidence available to support each claim. The interface also features "bottom line" monographs in both English and Spanish and a "flash card" that serves as a patient handout. Color photographs of varying quality picture the herbals in natural habitats. The Natural Standard Integrative Medicine Database represents an international research collaboration composed of more than one hundred institutions; consequently, many of these partners use the consumer information that the company produces on their Web sites. MedlinePlus, for example, uses the flash cards to provide information on a limited number of common herbals.

10.64 *MedlinePlus: Complementary and Alternative Therapies*. Available: www.nlm.nih.gov/medlineplus/complementaryandalternativetherapies.html

This site contains a number of pages with links to authoritative sources. Lacking access to one of the sources listed above, this is the best place to begin for information about integrative medicine.

Other authoritative sites providing information on alternative, complementary and integrative medicine include the following:

10.65 National Center for Complementary and Alternative Medicine (NIH). Available: nccam.nih.gov/

10.66 *Office of Cancer Complementary and Alternative Medicine (NIH).* Available: cancer.gov/cam/

10.67 *Complementary/Integrative Medicine Education Resources (CIMER).* University of Texas, M.D. Anderson Cancer Center. Available: www.mdanderson.org/departments/CIMER/

10.68 *About Herbs, Botanicals, and Other Products.* Memorial Sloan-Kettering Cancer Center. Available: www.mskcc.org/mskcc/html/11570.cfm

Surgery

Gale Encyclopedia of Surgery (see 10.28).

10.69 *MedlinePlus: Surgery and Rehabilitation.* Available: www.nlm.nih.gov/medlineplus/surgeryandrehabilitation.html

This portal offers easy access to a number of organizations' patient Web sites, such as the American Academy of Orthopaedic Surgeons. Videos of some surgeries are also available here.

10.70 Brunicardi FC, ed. *Schwartz's Principles of Surgery.* New York: McGraw-Hill, 2005.

10.71 Hagege JC. *The Power of Seduction: Concepts of Beauty and Cosmetic Surgery.* New York: Other Press, 2006.

Reconstructive surgery and aesthetic surgery represent two very different aspects of plastic surgery. For people who are considering aesthetic surgery, this book, written by an experienced plastic surgeon, offers several ways to weigh the decision.

Category 3: Anatomy and Physiology

10.72 Page M, ed. *The Human Body: An Illustrated Guide to Every Part of the Human Body and How It Works.* New York: Dorling Kindersley, 2001.

Beautiful illustrations, coupled with detailed yet lucid text, make this book an outstanding reference for laypersons. A section on the human life cycle describes changes occurring in the body from conception to old age.

Very general medical conditions, such as infections and cancer, are also described, with the emphasis on exactly what goes wrong inside the body when one of these conditions is present.

10.73 Netter FH. *Atlas of Human Anatomy*. 4th ed. New York: W.B. Saunders, 2006.

The magnificent illustrations in this volume make it an essential purchase for any library that has a biomedical collection.

10.74 Thibodeau GA, Patton KT. *The Human Body in Health and Disease*. St. Louis, MO: Mosby, 2006.

A text written for students in health professions programs, this volume is a good choice for a midlevel resource in anatomy and physiology.

Category 4: Selected Disorders and Conditions

Bones, Joints, and Muscles

10.75 Klippel JH et al, eds. *Primer on the Rheumatic Diseases*. New York: Springer, 2007.

This is an excellent midlevel resource that discusses individual rheumatic diseases, what is known about the role of genetics in these diseases, rehabilitation, self-management, the economic consequences of rheumatic disease, and much more. Illustrations and tables enhance the text. Appendices include criteria for the classification and diagnosis of specific rheumatic diseases, guidelines for management, drugs, and supplements.

Brain and Nervous System

Gale Encyclopedia of Neurological Disorders (see 10.29)

10.76 Ropper AH, Brown RH. *Adams and Victor's Principles of Neurology*. New York: McGraw-Hill, 2006.

Straightforwardly written, this text can answer many involved neurology questions posed by consumers.

Cancers

Gale Encyclopedia of Cancer (see 10.25).

10.77 Morra M, Potts E. *Choices: The Most Complete Sourcebook for Cancer Information*. New York: Collins, 2003.

This fourth edition of one of the most respected and important cancer references for laypeople ever published is accessible and authoritative.

10.78 Dollinger MA et al. *Everyone's Guide to Cancer Therapy: How Cancer is Diagnosed, Treated, and Managed Day to Day*. Kansas City, MO: Andrews McMeel, 2002.

This resource covers all aspects of the disease, from what cancer is, to what to expect during treatments, to psychosocial factors affecting cancer patients and families, to survivorship. The two references that follow are written by one of the coauthors; the three extensive works comprise an excellent set of references for anyone affected by cancer.

10.79 Rosenbaum EH, Rosenbaum I. *Everyone's Guide to Cancer Supportive Care: A Comprehensive Handbook for Patients and Their Families*. Kansas City, MO: Andrews McMeel, 2005.

10.80 Rosenbaum EH et al. *Everyone's Guide to Cancer Survivorship: A Road Map to Better Health*. Kansas City, MO: Andrews McMeel, 2007.

10.81 Buckman R. *Cancer Is a Word, Not a Sentence: A Practical Guide To Help You Through the First Few Weeks*. New York: Firefly Books, 2006.

Buckman's *What You Really Need to Know about Cancer* (1997) broke new ground with respect to plain yet authoritative information for consumers about malignancies. This new work is also an excellent one for newly diagnosed patients and their families to read.

10.82 Eyre H, Lange DP, Morris LB. *Informed Decisions: The Complete Book of Cancer Diagnosis, Treatment, and Recovery*. 2nd ed. New York: Viking, 2001.

In this American Cancer Society resource, much of the same ground is covered as in the Dollinger book, but the arrangement is different, with a great deal of emphasis being placed on the actual decision-making process encountered by cancer patients.

10.83 DeVita VT, Hellman S, Rosenberg SA, eds. *Cancer: Principles and Practice of Oncology*. Philadelphia, PA: Lippincott Williams & Wilkins, 2004.

The core medical textbook in its field, this is an essential reference for researching cancer questions.

Many other excellent books have been written regarding specific types of cancer, especially common ones like lung, breast, and prostate cancer. Included here are only the primary references which cover the general field very broadly.

Diabetes

10.84 American Diabetes Association. *American Diabetes Association Complete Guide to Diabetes.* New York: Bantam, 2006.

Clearly written and well organized, this book is an essential reference because of the prevalence of Type II diabetes. Type I diabetes is covered as well. Visit the association's Web site (diabetes.org/home.jsp) or an online bookstore to view the many other resources available. Cookbooks, sources for carbohydrate counting, and many other materials are available.

10.85 Levin ME, Pfeifer MA, eds. *Uncomplicated Guide to Diabetes Complications.* New York: McGraw-Hill/Contemporary Books, 2002.

This resource is also available from the American Diabetes Association, under whose auspices it is published. It is an essential reference that will answer many consumer questions about peripheral neuropathy, hypoglycemia, and much more that can affect the health and quality of life of diabetic patients.

10.86 Metzger BE. *American Medical Association Guide to Living with Diabetes: Preventing and Treating Type 2 Diabetes—Essential Information You and Your Family Need To Know.* New York: John Wiley & Sons, 2006.

This is an excellent reference that is limited to discussion of Type 2 diabetes.

Mental Health and Behavior

Gale Encyclopedia of Mental Disorders (see 10.26).

10.87 *Diagnostic and Statistical Manual of Mental Disorders: DSM-IV-TR. Fourth Edition, Text Revision.* Washington, DC: American Psychiatric Association, 2000.

This is an essential reference for any biomedical collection. Family members, friends, and caregivers of individuals diagnosed with a mental illness will find this resource very helpful, since it lists the diagnostic criteria for all recognized mental disorders.

Look also for current works on specific disorders, especially depression, bipolar disorder, schizophrenia, eating disorders, and self-mutilation.

Skin, Hair, and Nails

10.88 Wolff K, et al. *Fitzpatrick's Color Atlas & Synopsis of Clinical Dermatology: Common & Serious Diseases.* New York: McGraw-Hill, 2005.

The table of contents and excellent index make this reference easy to use. Brief articles include an illustration of the disorder, with textual content organized by description, epidemiology, pathogenesis, history, physical examination, differential diagnosis, laboratory tests, diagnosis, prognosis, and management.

10.89 Bouillon C, Wilkinson J. *The Science of Hair Care.* New York: Informa/Taylor & Francis. 2006.

While written for dermatologists, this book is a good one to have for patients with disorders affecting their hair or for anyone who simply wants to know whether one shampoo is as good as any other.

Wellness

10.90 *MedlinePlus: Health and Wellness.* Available: www.nlm.nih.gov/medlineplus/healthtopics.html

10.91 *Familydoctor.org: Health Information for the Whole Family: Healthy Living and Smart Patient Guide.* Available: familydoctor.org/online/famdocen/home/healthy.html and familydoctor.org/online/famdocen/home/pat-advocacy.html

The American Academy of Family Physicians (AAFP) has compiled a lengthy list of their Web publications for individuals to maintain the healthiest life possible and to use the health system effectively.

10.92 Roizen MF, Oz M. *You, the Owner's Manual: An Insider's Guide to the Body that Will Make You Healthier and Younger.* New York: HarperCollins, 2005.

10.93 Roizen MF, Oz M. *You, the Smart Patient: An Insider's Guide for Getting the Best Treatment.* New York: Free Press, 2006.

Roizen and Oz have written a series of books since 1999 based on a concept they call "real age." The information they provide represents sound research and common sense.

Category 5: Demographic Groups

Child and Teen Health

American Academy of Pediatrics (some Spanish) (see 10.38) and Omnigraphics *Teen Health Series* (see 10.42). Available: omnigraphics.com/category_view.php?ID=46.

10.94 *MedlinePlus: Child and Teen Health.* Available: www.nlm.nih.gov/medlineplus/childandteenhealth.html

10.95 *Familydoctor.org: Health Information for the Whole Family: Parents and Kids.* Available: familydoctor.org/online/famdocen/home/children.html

The American Academy of Family Physicians (AAFP) has compiled a lengthy list of their Web publications for parents and children on this page. Separate sections for parents, teens, and children are available here.

10.96 Pruitt DB, ed. *Your Adolescent: Emotional, Behavioral, and Cognitive Development from Preadolescence Through the Teen Years.* New York: HarperCollins, 2000.

This essential resource from the American Academy of Child and Adolescent Psychiatry covers normal development, problem behaviors, serious problems and abnormalities, and how and when to seek help.

10.97 Pruitt DB, ed. *Your Child: Emotional, Behavioral, and Cognitive Development from Birth Through Preadolescence.* New York: HarperCollins, 2000.

Another essential resource from the American Academy of Child and Adolescent Psychiatry that covers normal development, problem behaviors, serious problems and abnormalities, and how and when to seek help.

Senior Health

Merck Manual of Health and Aging (see 10.34).

10.98 *MedlinePlus: Seniors' Health.* Available: www.nlm.nih.gov/medlineplus/seniorshealth.html

10.99 *Familydoctor.org. Health Information for the Whole Family: Seniors.* Available: familydoctor.org/online/famdocen/home/seniors.html

The American Academy of Family Physicians (AAFP) has compiled a lengthy list of their Web publications for seniors on this page. Items as diverse as urinary incontinence, memory loss, driving skills, as well as much more, are covered here.

Men's Health

10.100 *MedlinePlus: Men's Health.* Available: www.nlm.nih.gov/medline plus/menshealth.html

10.101 *Familydoctor.org. Health Information for the Whole Family: Men.* American Academy of Family Physicians (AAFP). Available: family doctor.org/online/famdocen/home/men.html

The American Academy of Family Physicians (AAFP) has compiled a lengthy list of their Web publications for men on this page. Items as diverse as blood pressure monitoring at home, gout, Viagra, as well as much more, are covered here.

Women's Health

10.102 *MedlinePlus: Women's Health.* Available: www.nlm.nih.gov/ medlineplus/womenshealth.html

10.103 *Familydoctor.org. Health Information for the Whole Family: Women.* American Academy of Family Physicians (AAFP). Available: familydoctor.org/online/famdocen/home/women.html

10.104 Boston Women's Health Book Collective. *Our Bodies, Ourselves: Menopause.* New York: Simon & Schuster, 2006.

In 1973, *Our Bodies, Ourselves: A Book by and for Women* first appeared. Women had never before seen such a work, which was devoted just to them and their health. In the ensuing decades, the work has been updated several times. This volume on menopause is accompanied by the following one, the latest in this remarkable publishing venture.

10.105 Boston Women's Health Book Collective. *Our Bodies, Ourselves: A New Edition for a New Era.* New York: Simon & Schuster, 2005.

10.106 Brody JE. *New York Times Book of Women's Health: Living Longer and Better in the New Millennium.* New York: Lebhar-Friedman Books, 2000.

This is an outstanding reference that includes 13 sections, from nutrition to domestic violence to menopause, and much more. Attractive layout, helpful graphics and illustrations, and a special section on raising healthy daughters make this a good reference resource for consumers.

Individuals with Disabilities

Encyclopedia of Disability (see 10.32).

10.107 *MedlinePlus: Disabilities.* Available: www.nlm.nih.gov/medline plus/disabilities.html

References

1. National Library of Medicine. *Public library initiative/new consumer health site.* [Web document]. Bethesda, MD: The Library, 2004. Available: www. nlm.nih.gov/archive/20040831/news/press_releases/medplus.html. Accessed: 2 May 2007.
2. Millenson ML. *Personalized medicine: finding the patient's "doctor within."* [Web document]. New York: Medscape General Medicine, 2006. Available: www.medscape.com/viewarticle/530922. Accessed: 2 May 2007.
3. Personalized Medicine Coalition. *New report cites emerging impact of personalized medicine on healthcare.* [Web document]. Washington, DC: Personalized Medicine Coalition, 2006. Available: www.personalizedmedicine coalition.org/communications/pr_2006-11-13_case_of_pm.php. Accessed: 2 May 2007.
4. Collins FS. *Personalized medicine: a new approach to staying well.* [Web document]. Boston, MA: Boston Globe, 17 July 2005. Available: www.boston. com/news/globe/editorial_opinion/oped/articles/2005/07/17/personalized_ medicine/. Accessed: 2 May 2007.
5. Mayo Clinic staff. *Personalized medicine: tailoring treatment to your genetic profile.* [Web document]. Rochester, MN: Mayo Clinic Foundation for Education and Research, 2006. Available: www.mayoclinic.com/health/ personalized-medicine/CA00078. Accessed: 2 May 2007.
6. Kutner M, Greenberg E, Jin Y, Paulsen C. *The health literacy of America's adults: results from the 2003 national assessment of adult literacy (NCES 2006–483).* [Web document]. Washington, DC: U.S. Department of Education, National Center for Education Statistics, 2006. Available: nces.ed.gov/ pubsearch/pubsinfo.asp?pubid=2006483. Accessed: 2 May 2007.
7. Nielsen-Bohlman L, Panzer AM, Kindig DA, eds. *Health literacy: a prescription to end confusion.* [Web document]. Washington, DC: Institute of Medicine, 2004. Available: www.iom.edu/?id=19750. Accessed: 2 May 2007.
8. Kutner M et al. op cit.
9. Shipman JP, Funk C. *MLA health information literacy project: overview.* [Web document]. Chicago, IL: Medical Library Association, 2006. Available: www.mlanet.org/resources/healthlit/hil_project_overview.html. Accessed: 2 May 2007.

10. National Library of Medicine. *MedlinePlus: find a library*. [Web document]. Bethesda, MD: The Library, 2007. Available: www.nlm.nih.gov/medlineplus/libraries.html. Accessed: 2 May 2007.

11. Fox S. *Online health search 2006*. [Web document]. Washington, DC: Pew Internet & American Life Project, 2006. Available: www.pewinternet.org/PPF/r/190/report_display.asp. Accessed: 2 May 2007.

12. Medical Library Association. *Consumer health information specialization program*. [Web document]. Chicago, IL: The Association, 2007. Available: www.mlanet.org/education/chc/index.html. Accessed: 2 May 2007.

13. Lo S, Sharif I, Ozuah PO. Health literacy among English-speaking parents in a poor urban setting. *J Health Care Poor Underserved* 2006; 17(3):507.

14. Berland GK et al. Health information on the Internet: accessibility, quality, and readability in English and Spanish. *JAMA* 2001; 285(20):2612–21.

15. Baker LM, Gollop CJ. Medical textbooks: Can lay people read and understand them? *Libr Trends* 2004; 53(2):346. [All quotes from this page]

16. Goldman L, Bennett JC, eds. *Cecil Textbook of Medicine*. New York: Saunders, 2004:515.

Readings

Besides the items in the Reference List, the articles below provide useful insights and some historical perspective on consumer health reference services.

1. Anonymous. The librarian's role in the provision of consumer health information and patient education. *Bull Med Libr Assoc* 1996; 84(2):238–9.

2. Baker LM, Pettigrew KE. Theories for practitioners: two frameworks for studying consumer health information-seeking behavior. *Bull Med Libr Assoc* 1999; 87(4):444–50.

3. Calabretta N. The hospital library as provider of consumer health information. *Med Ref Serv Q* 1996; 15(3):13–22.

4. Calabretta N, Cavanaugh SK. Education for inpatients: working with nurses through the clinical information system. *Med Ref Serv Q* 2004; 23(2):73–9.

5. Calvano M, Needham G. Public empowerment through accessible health information. *Bull Med Libr Assoc* 1996; 84(2):253–6.

6. Cosgrove TL. Planetree health information services: public access to the health information people want. *Bull Med Libr Assoc* 1994; 82(1):57–63.

7. Fox N, Ward K. Health identities: from expert patient to resisting consumer. *Health: An Interdisciplinary Journal for the Social Study of Health, Illness & Medicine* 2006; 10(4):461–79.

8. Goodchild EY, Furman JA, Addison BL, Umbarger HN. The CHIPS Project: a health information network to serve the consumer. *Bull Med Libr Assoc* 1978; 66(4):432–6.

9. Lindner KL, Sabbagh L. In a new element: medical librarians making patient education rounds. *J Med Libr Assoc* 2004; 92(1):94–7.

10. Marill JL, Miller N, Kitendaugh P. The MedlinePlus public user interface: studies of design challenges and opportunities. *J Med Libr Assoc* 2006; 94(1):30–40.

11. Perryman C. Medicus deus: a review of factors affecting hospital library services to patients between 1790–1950. *J Med Libr Assoc* 2006; 94(3):263–70.

12. Pifalo V et al. The impact of consumer health information provided by libraries: the Delaware experience. *Bull Med Libr Assoc* 1997; 85(1):16–22.

13. Spatz MA. Providing consumer health information in the rural setting: Planetree Health Resource Center's approach. *Bull Med Libr Assoc* 2000; 88(4): 382–8.

14. Tattersall RL. The expert patient: a new approach to chronic disease management for the twenty-first century. *Clin Med* 2002; 2(3):227–9.

15. Wood FB et al. Public library consumer health information pilot project: results of a National Library of Medicine evaluation. *Bull Med Libr Assoc* 2000; 88(4):314–22.

16. Zipperer L, Sykes J. The role of librarians in patient safety: gaps and strengths in the current culture. *J Med Libr Assoc* 2004; 92(4):498–500.

CHAPTER 11

Medical and Health Statistics

Jocelyn A. Rankin and Mary L. Burgess

Reference staff in health sciences libraries encounter health care statistics questions on a regular basis. However, finding the precise statistic that answers a reference question is usually a challenge, even for the most experienced reference librarian. More health care statistics are being published than ever before, both on the Internet and in print, yet it is often difficult to locate the perfect match to the reference inquiry. The successful reference librarian must not only be able to track down the requisite statistic, but also must be able to understand it and evaluate its credibility. It is also important to recognize that in spite of the ever-increasing quantities of statistical data being produced, sometimes the statistical factors being requested by a library patron are either not collected at all or possibly not analyzed in a way that serves the patron's inquiry.

So, what to do when faced with:

- How many HMOs are there in the United States, and how many enrollees?
- What is the extent of alcohol consumption in the United States?
- What is the number of physicians in Iraq?
  (See end of chapter for answers to these questions.)

Challenges clearly abound with medical and health statistics. However, there is a logical strategy to locating answers to questions about statistics [1].

1. Determine what type and category of statistic is being requested. For example, is the question about disease occurrence, vital statistics, or demographics?

2. Understand what variables are being asked for. Is the library patron asking for data about a specific population group, a certain time period, a certain geographic location?
3. Consider which Web sites or print resources will provide credible, timely data in the subject area. Which government and/or private organizations collect these data?
4. If there is no logical primary resource, search secondary or related resources, such as journal literature, agency reports, and so forth.
5. After a reasonable search, confer with the patron, recognizing that not all statistics are collected or analyzed in a way that satisfies every inquiry.

Why Are Health Statistics So Important?

Despite the fact that statistics may frustrate, confound and challenge the health sciences reference librarian, they are a fact of life in today's health care environment. At the national level, efforts are under way to monitor systematically the health status of our country in order to promote healthy people and healthy lifestyles. *Healthy People 2010*, the ten-year road map for America's public health system, identified two overarching public health goals: to increase the quality and years of healthy life and to eliminate health disparities. Ten "Leading Health Indicators" addressing mental health, behavioral, lifestyle, and health access issues support these goals and also correlate with many specific health objectives for national, state, and local communities [2]. Health statistics provide the tools to measure our progress as a nation in meeting these goals and objectives and also to identify the priorities for the coming decades.

Health statistics can describe health conditions and also the factors that affect health, including economic, environmental, behavioral, and lifestyle characteristics of populations. These statistics guide health care planning, health care delivery, and health care evaluation. They influence decisions and priorities about health policy, health care services, workforce training, and resource and funding allocations. As the health care industry refines its business models related to accountability, managed care, and cost containment, statistics may also inform health care and financial decisions at many levels, including in government, in health care organizations and facilities, and in health sciences universities, affecting the full range of health care, from policy to day-to-day operations.

Improving health outcomes is a goal for public health and also for individual case management. Concerns about patient safety and the emphasis on evidence-based medicine (EBM) have given health sciences librarians the opportunity to serve as valuable members of educational and clinical care teams. EBM, "the conscientious, explicit and judicious use of current best evidence in making decisions about the care of individual patients," [3] formalizes the process of incorporating the best relevant research evidence with clinical expertise in the practice of medicine. While statistical data do not alone provide complete information about disease etiologies, diagnoses, therapies, and outcomes, the use of data from clinical trials and reports of best practices can advise health care providers on the efficacy and safety of proposed approaches to patient care. There is often great difficulty in conducting EBM searches and identifying the best evidence. Roles for librarians include assisting in formulating the clinical questions, teaching students and clinicians effective search skills, and searching for and identifying the best resources. The critical appraisal skills of librarians help in recognizing clinical studies with strong methodologies, appropriate statistical analyses, and valid conclusions.

The EBM perspective has also given impetus to other health professions to move toward greater scientific rigor in their own disciplines, including nursing, public health, and social work. In our own field of health sciences librarianship, the evidence-based library and information practice (EBLIP) initiative has its roots in EBM. Today it is not only important for librarians to understand statistics in their work with library patrons, but they must apply these same analytical skills in contributing to information best practices within their institution and also in developing the profession's knowledge base. With the increasingly complex and costly information landscape, decisions in health libraries that are informed by evidence ensure that the best quality and scope of information services are provided for the institution.

New Approaches in Health Statistics

New approaches to discovering, tracking, and understanding health data are introducing additional resources for health statistics. An important method for understanding health data is Geographic Information Systems (GIS). GIS technologies have provided an added dimension to medicine and public health by enabling the graphical display of datasets. For example, GIS can support epidemiological research by allowing for visualization of patterns of disease incidence, chemical spills, or other health-related incidents. More complex geospatial analyses through layering of datasets can illustrate additional factors, such as associated health and social impacts.

Another new strategy is use of powerful new data mining tools that are being developed to maximize the benefits of recent technological advances in large-scale data collection, data access, and data warehousing. These tools, which are essentially a new generation of statistics, can be applied to massive databases in order to search for previously unrecognized patterns, data clusters, and data models. Data mining may also yield predictive information relating to future trends and behaviors. In the health care sector, data mining and knowledge discovery tools are being applied to support clinical care, health research and improved business management.

11.1   *Nationwide Health Information Network (NHIN)*. Washington, DC: U.S. Department of Health and Human Services. Available: www.hhs.gov/healthit/healthnetwork

11.2   *Public Health Information Network (PHIN)*. Atlanta, GA: U.S. Department of Health and Human Services, Centers for Disease Control and Prevention. Available: www.cdc.gov/phin

While compiling health data continues to be a complex process and fraught with variability, the tracking and collection of health data is moving toward greater standardization. A strategic vision for a coordinated national approach to health statistics has been developed along with recommendations that will result in better informed health policy and programs [4]. This vision, together with the emerging Nationwide Health Information Network (NHIN), will enable health information sharing at national, state, and local levels. The NHIN aims to create an overarching framework for a network of networks that is supported by interoperable technologies, data standards, and systems [5]. Benefits to this national planning extend from improving individual patient care to building a more informed public health system. For example, disease outbreaks could be detected more rapidly and there will be improved capacity to monitor the nation's health care system on issues of national importance, such as health disparities, health costs, and incidence of chronic diseases. As part of the NHIN, the Centers for Disease Control and Prevention is coordinating a national approach to disease surveillance through the Public Health Information Network (PHIN). Surveillance, which is the ongoing, systematic collection and analysis of health data, is fundamental to detecting epidemics, emerging or reemerging infectious diseases, and bioterrorist events.

Biostatistics Basics

Introductory classes in statistics at a local college or continuing education courses at a conference are both good approaches to gaining an overview of statistical measures and values. A basic knowledge of statistics is useful when answering reference questions and also in managing the library reference department or conducting information science research. The following are helpful resources:

11.3 Glantz SA. *Primer of Biostatistics*. 6th ed. New York: McGraw-Hill, 2005.

11.4 Hebel JR, McCarter RJ. *A Study Guide to Epidemiology and Biostatistics*. 6th ed. Sudbury, MA: Jones and Bartlett, 2006.

These two books are good examples of readily understandable introductions to biostatistics. Both resources are useful for health sciences library patrons as well as for reference staff members wanting to acquire a basic knowledge of statistical principles and methods. They are easy to read and, by placing statistics in the context of reports seen in the medical literature, the explanations and examples are particularly relevant to the health sciences.

Primer of Biostatistics is an enjoyable introductory handbook that emphasizes the concepts behind data analyses and statistical tests. For example, the primer covers power, sample size, how to summarize data, basic comparisons between groups, and approaches to nominal data. Practice exercises are provided. The *Study Guide to Epidemiology and Biostatistics* discusses statistics from an epidemiological viewpoint, a discipline perspective needed in effective reference work in the health sciences. Chapters are succinct and include investigation of an epidemic, measures of mortality, and incidence and prevalence of diseases, along with more classic statistics topics. The final chapter describes how to do a critical review of epidemiological research. Suggestions for further reading are provided.

11.5 Straus SE, Richardson WS, Glasziou P, Haynes RB. *Evidence-Based Medicine: How to Practice and Teach EBM*. 3rd ed. Edinburgh and New York: Churchill Livingstone, 2005.

11.6 Greenhalgh T. *How To Read A Paper: The Basics of Evidence-Based Medicine*. 3rd ed. Malden, MA: BMJ Books/Blackwell, 2006.

Straus' handbook, the classic resource for evidence-based medicine, is written for the busy physician and all others interested in applying the principles of EBM to the practice of clinical medicine. The chapter on searching for the best current evidence is a must-read for reference librarians. Separate chapters are devoted to each of the following: diagnosis, prognosis, therapy, and harm, the latter addressing studies related to causative interventions or agents. Each chapter describes the types of published reports in that area and then gives guidance on how to understand and evaluate the merits of these reports. The handbook includes a CD-ROM that provides clinical examples and extended descriptions.

Greenhalgh's text, which is popular with both health care professionals and library school students, is a very readable compilation of EBM articles based on papers originally published by the author in *BMJ*, the *British Medical Journal*. The latest edition includes chapters on literature searching, assessing methodology and basic statistics, as well as discussions of article types such as systematic reviews and meta-analyses, guidelines, and economic analyses. There is also a new chapter on qualitative research ("Beyond the Numbers").

Many medical schools have developed Web sites about EBM. The University Health Centre Network provides a variety of EBM tools as well as support for this handbook at www.cebm.utoronto.ca.

11.7 Delwiche LD, Slaughter SJ. *The Little SAS Book: A Primer.* 3rd ed. Cary, NC: BBU Press, 2003.

11.8 Einspruch EL. *An Introductory Guide to SPSS for Windows.* 2nd ed. Thousand Oaks, CA: Sage, 2005.

SAS and SPSS are the two major commercially available software programs used for data analysis and statistics in the health sciences sector. SAS also offers JMP which has an interface that guides users to the appropriate analyses. These software packages have manuals; however, an independently produced introductory guide keyed to the most current version of the software is very useful for both the scientific researcher and the librarian. These two examples provide information on basic statistical concepts; how to input, modify, and manage datasets using the selected software; and how to run basic statistical tests. Both are easy to follow and include examples and screen shots to assist the software user.

11.9 *Epi Info.* Atlanta, GA: U.S. Department of Health and Human Services, Centers for Disease Control and Prevention. Available: www.cdc.gov/epiinfo

Epi Info is a public domain statistics software available from the Centers for Disease Control and Prevention Web site. Regularly updated to maintain compatibility with the desktop environment, Epi Info is designed to assist with basic public health data collection and analysis. However, many of its functions have broader applicability. In addition to performing basic statistical tests, Epi Info includes tools for developing a questionnaire or form as well as for entering and analyzing data. Epidemiologic statistics, tables, graphs, and maps are produced with simple commands. The Epi Map feature displays geographic maps and supports data mapping.

The Epi Info Web site includes the software, instructions for downloading, and user manuals in several languages. There are also tutorials for new users that can be downloaded as well.

11.10 *Supercourse: Epidemiology, the Internet, and Global Health.* Pittsburgh, PA: University of Pittsburgh, and others. Available: www.pitt.edu/~super1

Supported by funding from NASA and now from the National Library of Medicine, the Supercourse Web site contains free lectures and learning opportunities on a wide range of public health topics. Of particular interest in the area of statistics are the mini-courses on research, various methodologies, and evidence-based medicine. Supercourse is hosted by 45 mirrored sites around the world.

What Is a Good Statistic?

The statistics seeker expects statistics to be drawn from consistent reporting and reliable comparisons on a specific topic or combination of topics. This can be a difficult expectation to meet. Some difficulties stem from fragmented and uncoordinated data collection efforts as well as varying data collection and statistical analysis methods. Differences in terminology, data definitions, and coverage, such as geographical areas or time periods, can influence the validity of the statistical data that the librarian may retrieve to answer a specific question.

All credible statistical tables should be accompanied by technical documentation that provides detailed information on what kind of data were collected, how they were collected, the population sample used for analysis, the methods used to construct the statistical result being evaluated, and other important information. Examine these technical notes carefully, matching the patron's parameters to the documentation.

Terminology

An understanding of the terminology used in health statistics is critical to formulating a successful search. Although the jargon used in the area of health statistics is not as extensive as in many other health-related disciplines, there are some terms that searchers should keep in mind when looking for statistical health data. Appendix 11-1 is a list of key health statistics terms that have been drawn from a variety of sources [6–9].

Among these definitions, *rate* is a very important term in health statistics. Rate is used with terms such as natality, mortality, incidence, and prevalence. As noted in the definition, rate expresses the frequency with which an event occurs in a defined population in a specified period of time. The use of rate rather than raw numbers is essential for comparison of experience between populations at different times, different places, or among different classes of persons. For example, it is meaningless to say there were over 65,000 deaths from pneumonia and influenza in the United States without knowing the time period during which they occurred and the population in which they occurred. A rate will express this concept. Stating that the incidence rate of death from pneumonia and influenza in all races, both sexes, ages 10 to 14 years in the United States was 0.2 per 100,000 population in the year 2000, gives an indication of the real magnitude of the problem.

The components of a rate are the numerator (the number of events in a specified period), a denominator (average population during the specified period), and a multiplier (a power of 10 to convert fractions and decimals to whole numbers).

Getting Started on the Search for Health Statistics

11.11 *National Center for Health Statistics.* Hyattsville, MD: U.S. Department of Health and Human Services, Centers for Disease Control and Prevention, National Center for Health Statistics. Available: www.cdc.gov/nchs

The Internet provides a burgeoning resource of health statistics and data sets. A good place to begin is the Centers for Disease Control and Prevention's National Center for Health Statistics (NCHS) home page. As the nation's principal health statistics organization, NCHS provides national leadership in health statistics and epidemiology, and in collecting, analyzing, and disseminating national health statistics on vital events and health activities. Changes in the health status of people and environmental, social, and other health hazards are noted and statistically documented. Data are also collected, analyzed, and disseminated about illness, injury, and impairment; the physical, mental, and physiological characteristics of the U.S. population; the supply and utilization of health facilities and manpower; health costs and expenditures; and the operation of the health services system. The NCHS also administers the Cooperative Health Statistics System, stimulating and conducting basic and applied research in health data systems and statistical methodology.

The NCHS has two major types of data systems: systems based on populations, containing data collected through personal interviews or examinations; and systems based on records, containing data collected from vital and medical records. Some are ongoing annual systems whereas others are periodically conducted. The current data systems and surveys are:

- *National Vital Statistics System (NVSS)*: Responsible for the Nation's official vital statistics. These vital statistics are provided through State-operated registration systems recording births, deaths, marriages, divorces, and fetal deaths.
- *National Health Interview Survey (NHIS)*: The principal source of information on the health of the civilian noninstitutionalized population of the United States.
- *National Health and Nutrition Examination Survey (NHANES)*: Based on laboratory and examination centers that move around the United States to obtain standardized medical information from direct physical exams, diagnostic procedures, and lab tests, this survey monitors trends in the prevalence, awareness, treatment, and control of selected diseases, trends in risk behaviors and environmental exposure, and studies the relationship between diet, nutrition, and health.
- *National Health Care Survey (NHCS)*: Covers a family of health care provider surveys to obtain information about the facilities that supply health care, the services rendered, and the characteristics of the patients served. Each survey is based on a multistage sampling design that includes health care facilities or providers and patient records. Data are collected directly from the establishments and/or their records rather than from the patients. These data identify health care events such as hospitalizations, surgeries, and long-term stays and offer the most

accurate and detailed information on diagnosis and treatment as well as on the characteristics of the institutions. To mention a few applications of this survey information, these data are used by policymakers, planners, researchers, and others in the health community to monitor changes in the use of health care resources, to monitor specific diseases, and to examine the impact of new medical technologies.

The NCHS Web site provides a robust source of information about America's health. Some features of the Web site follow:

11.12 *FASTSTATS A to Z.* Hyattsville, MD: U.S. Department of Health and Human Services, Centers for Disease Control and Prevention, National Center for Health Statistics. Available: www.cdc.gov/nchs/fastats/default.htm

FASTSTATS is a rich source of quick statistics organized topically. Each topic page contains commonly requested statistics and links to other sites (including those outside NCHS) that contain similar statistical information on that specific topic.

11.13 *Health Data for All Ages.* Hyattsville, MD: U.S. Department of Health and Human Services, Centers for Disease Control and Prevention, National Center for Health Statistics. Available: www.cdc.gov/nchs/health_data_for_all_ages.htm

This page gives tables of health statistics of health conditions for infants, children, adolescents, adults, and older adults. Tables can be customized by age, gender, race/ethnicity, and geographic location. Charts and graphs can also be generated and exported for use offline or in another format.

11.14 *Vital Stats.* Hyattsville, MD: U.S. Department of Health and Human Services, Centers for Disease Control and Prevention, National Center for Health Statistics. Available: www.cdc.gov/nchs/Vital Stats.htm

Vital Stats is a collection of vital statistics products including tables, data files, and reports that allow users to access and examine vital statistics and population data. There are prebuilt tables and reports for quick access to statistics. Or, the data files can be used to create your own tables, choosing from over 100 variables. Using the data files takes a little more time but gives you access to more data. Tables can be customized to meet specific needs. Charts, graphs, and maps can also be generated and exported for use offline or in another format.

11.15 *Data 2010.* Hyattsville, MD: U.S. Department of Health and Human Services, Centers for Disease Control and Prevention, National Center for Health Statistics. Available: wonder.cdc.gov/DATA2010

Data 2010 is an interactive database to track state progress toward achieving *Healthy People 2010* objectives.

11.16 *Office of Women's Health Quick Health Data Online.* Hyattsville, MD: U.S. Department of Health and Human Services, Centers for Disease Control and Prevention, National Center for Health Statistics, Office of Women's Health. Available: www.healthstatus 010.com/owh

This tool provides access to many sources of data in women's health, including NCHS birth and death data.

11.17 *Trends in Health and Aging.* Hyattsville, MD: U.S. Department of Health and Human Services, Centers for Disease Control and Prevention, National Center for Health Statistics. Available: www. cdc.gov/nchs/agingact.htm

Trends in Health and Aging provides access to a collection of data tables with information on trends in health and health care used by older Americans. Tables on trends in the health of older Americans shows data by age, sex, race and Hispanic origin are included. The tables are easy to customize for specific needs and graphs can also be made and downloaded.

11.18 *National Center for Health Statistics—Other Sites.* Hyattsville, MD: U.S. Department of Health and Human Services, Centers for Disease Control and Prevention. Available: www.cdc.gov/nchs/ sites.htm

This site provides access to a list of statistical sites (federal, nonfederal, and international) which provide alternative sources of health-related information.

After fully exploring the NCHS Web site, take a look at these resources as well:

11.19 *Statistical Resources on the Web.* University of Michigan Documents Center, Ann Arbor, MI. Available: www.lib.umich.edu/gov docs/stats.html

11.20 *Inter-university Consortium for Political and Social Research (ICPSR).* Ann Arbor, MI: University of Michigan. Available: www. icpsr.umich.edu/index.html

Statistical Resources provides access to a listing of statistical resources on the Web. This mature site includes a page of health statistics links to government and private Web sites. The links are well annotated with highlights about each site's content and coverage as well as useful tips on locating and using data from these sources. Additional pages of interest at the University of Michigan Web site cover other statistical topics related to health, including demographics, economics and finances, environment, education, and sociology.

The ICPSR, located within the Institute for Social Research at the University of Michigan, is a membership-based not-for-profit organization serving member colleges and universities in the United States and abroad. This site provides searchable access to a variety of data sets.

11.21 *DataFinder*. Washington, DC: U.S. Department of Health and Human Services. Available: www.hhs-stat.net/scripts/datafinder.cfm

11.22 *Gateway to Data and Statistics*. Washington, DC: U.S. Department of Health and Human Services Data Council. Available: www.hhs-stat.net

DataFinder and the Gateway provide access to health and human services-related data and statistics resources supported by the Department of Health and Human Services, other federal agencies, states, and local governments.

Other helpful tools for the health sciences reference librarian are:

11.23 Melnick D. *Finding and Using Health Statistics: A Self-Study Course*. Bethesda, MD: National Library of Medicine, 2007. Available: www.nlm.nih.gov

This Web-based self-study program introduces health statistics sources to librarians and other researchers. The course covers the major health statistical resources with an emphasis on Internet availability. The resources are given context through explanations about the goals of various data collection efforts of organizations and government entities. The course also describes how statistics are commonly used. There is introductory material on assessing the benefits and limitations of statistics search results. Practice exercises are integrated into the tutorial. This independent study program is easy to use and organized to allow the student to navigate through the presentation according to interests and knowledge level.

11.24 *Public Health Information and Data Tutorial*. Washington, DC: Partners in Information Access for the Public Health Workforce, 2005. Available: phpartners.org/tutorial/index.html

This online tutorial, intended for the public health workforce but also useful for the beginner reference librarian, includes modules on health statistics and evidence-based public health, as well as on news and health education resources. The health statistics module provides a general introduction to statistics resources and datasets. Case studies are used to illustrate search strategies. A free training manual, offered in both PDF and Word formats, accompanies the tutorial.

General and Health Statistics

11.25 *U.S. Census Bureau.* Washington, DC: U.S. Department of Commerce, Census Bureau. Available: www.census.gov

The U.S. Census Bureau is the gold standard for U.S. demographic data. The U.S. Census is conducted every ten years; work is already under way for the 2010 census. The Census serves as the nation's official demographic record, guiding decisions in local, state, and federal governments related to changing population trends such as for funding and other federal assistance, for legislative reapportionment, and for construction projects. The Census covers major population data, demographic profiles, and usually each decennial survey includes several special topics of interest.

The Census Web site provides a wide range of data, from national and international up-to-the-minute population totals ("Population Clock") to extensive state and county level data. The site is updated very frequently with newly released reports, some of which are filed monthly while others are more topical, such as reports on the effects of Hurricane Katrina on the Gulf Coast and the extent of health insurance coverage in the United States. Many of the U.S. Census Bureau's classic publications, including *Statistical Abstract of the United States*, are available at the Web site, along with older editions. An A–Z subject index link off the Census Bureau home page provides visitors with assistance in navigating the site. The Gateway to Census 2000 page provides access to the most current population data and analytical reports. Among the searchable functions at the Web site are the Census 2000 Demographic Profiles where a specific city or county can be entered to obtain a detailed report of demographic and social characteristics, such as age, race, income, major industries, and so forth. Also noteworthy for health sciences librarians is the disability statistics information at: census.gov/hhes/ www/disability/disability.html.

11.26 *FedStats.* Washington DC: Interagency Council of Statistical Policy. Available: www.fedstats.gov

FedStats, which has been available to the public since 1997, provides access to the full range of official statistical information produced by the federal government without the searcher having to know in advance which agency produces which particular statistic. This interagency Web site, which is maintained by the U.S. Census Bureau, thus serves as a portal to federal statistics that are published by more than 100 U.S. federal agencies. The statistical coverage is broad, with data and trend information on such topics as economic and population trends, crime, education, health care, aviation safety, foreign trade, energy use, farm production and more. However, considerable health statistics data can be reached through this site. Quick subject access to FedStats' Web site links is available through a Topics A–Z index. The site is also directly searchable by program or subject area, agency, and geographical area.

11.27 *Statistical Abstract of the United States.* Washington, DC: Department of Commerce, Census Bureau, 2007. Annual. Available: purl.access.gpo.gov/GPO/LPS2878

First published in 1878, *Statistical Abstract* is the leading, authoritative reference source for U.S. statistical information. The breadth and scope of information makes this reference tool the first place to look for many statistical questions. It is also readily available or accessible from every type of library. While primarily a compilation of federal statistics, *Statistical Abstract* does also include information from the private sector. The focus is on national data although some state and local information is provided.

The *Statistical Abstract* contains both primary and secondary statistical information. All tables have explanatory footnotes and source information, so further detail can usually be found. The statistics may be several years old but should be considered the most current available at the time of publication.

Statistical data are presented under broad subject categories, and subject access is further augmented by a good subject index. Statistics of particular interest to health sciences librarians include population data, vital statistics, national health costs by type of expenditure, health resource utilization data, and selected national nutrition information. Also related to health care are national statistics on education, income levels and environmental quality measures.

The *Statistical Abstract* is available in print, on CD-ROM, and online at the U.S. Census Bureau Web site. Not all data tables from private sources are published on the Web site.

11.28 *Health: United States.* Washington, DC: U.S. Department of Health and Human Services, Centers for Disease Control and Prevention, National Center for Health Statistics, 2007. Annual. Available: www.cdc.gov/nchs/hus.htm

An annual first published in 1975–1976, *Health, United States* is one of the few sources providing trend data on the nation's health status and other health care topics. It presents national trends in health statistics on such topics as Population; Fertility and Natality; Mortality Determinants and Measures of Health; Ambulatory Care; Inpatient Care, Personnel and Facilities; National Health Expenditures; Health Care Coverage and Major Federal Programs; and State Health Expenditures and Health Insurance. Each annual volume includes a chartbook that examines a current topic of interest. For example the 2002 volume includes a chartbook on "Trends in the Health of Americans." All volumes are available in PDF format on the NCHS Web site and on CD-ROM. Links to updated Trend Tables and errata are posted with the each PDF version.

11.29 *CDC WONDER.* Atlanta, GA: U.S. Department of Health and Human Services, Centers for Disease Control and Prevention. Available: wonder.cdc.gov

CDC WONDER serves as a gateway to a wide variety of reports and numeric public health data from CDC. Arranged topically, subjects cover CDC research areas including chronic disease, communicable disease, injury, environmental health, occupational health, behavior and health, immunizations, and mortality data. Specialized reports can be generated by following menu prompts. Notes and data source aid in interpretation of results.

11.30 *Historical Statistics of the United States: Colonial Times to 1970.* 2 volumes. Washington, DC: U.S. Census Bureau, 1975. Available: www.census.gov/compendia/statab/past_years.html

Published as part of the bicentennial celebration, this edition of *Historical Statistics* serves as a supplement to the annual *Statistical Abstract of the United States. Historical Statistics* has a wealth of information and its references are a rich resource for locating primary historical data. As in *Statistical Abstract*, the statistical data are drawn primarily from U.S. government sources but also come from private organizations and individuals. In general, only annual or census period data are included. Statistics are national with only occasional data shown for regions, states, and local areas.

The challenges in compiling statistical summaries are compounded when dealing with historical data. The variations over time and by resource in data availability, data collection methods, sampling approaches, concepts and/or levels of coverage, and definitions of geographic regions and categories are just a few of the changes over the years. To aid in understanding the data, each major section in *Historical Statistics* has an introductory narrative and discussion of the data sources. This information is essential to interpreting the statistical data presented in the tables. It is also a rich resource for locating primary historical data sources. Each statistical table includes the source(s) of the data along with explanatory footnotes, so further analysis and research is possible.

Historical Statistics includes sections on vital statistics, life expectancy and death rates, health and medical care statistics including birth and fertility rates, national health expenditures, health care providers and their educational facilities, disease rates, hospital data, and some general public health trends such as nutrition and water fluoridation. The final chapter on colonial and pre-federal statistics is a fascinating review of then contemporary issues, focusing primarily on population, trade, and commerce data.

Databases

PubMed, a bibliographic database, connects the searcher to citations of articles that contain a wealth of statistical information that has been published in the medical and research literature. Full-text databases, such as Statistical Universe and the Cochrane Library, provide access to primary and secondary resources.

11.31 *PubMed*. Bethesda, MD: U.S. Department of Health and Human Services, National Institutes of Health, National Library of Medicine. Available: www.pubmed.gov

PubMed is the leading search tool for the U.S. National Library of Medicine's (NLM) MEDLINE database. Citations of articles published in the major health sciences statistics journals can be obtained though a PubMed search. In addition, references to research reports published in the medical literature and containing statistical data can be retrieved through PubMed.

Major medical subject headings (MeSH) such as Infant Mortality or Life Expectancy retrieve general articles on these statistical topics. For more precise search results related to particular topics or diseases, the searcher should use PubMed's statistics subheadings attached to major MeSH term(s). These sub-headings include: economics; epidemiology; ethnology; manpower; mortality; statistics and numerical data; supply and distribution; trends; and utilization.

PubMed also provides Clinical Queries and Systematic Reviews filters to assist in retrieving statistical data from clinical trial reports and the EBM literature. These filters can be applied during a search of a broader subject heading, such as Breast Neoplasms, using one or more of the four major disease-related subheadings: etiology, diagnosis, therapy, and prognosis. The searcher can optimize these search filters for sensitivity (recall) or specificity (precision) and retrieve references to systematic reviews, meta-analysis studies, randomized controlled trials, cohort studies, and other case-controlled studies related to the topic and subheading(s) selected.

11.32 *Health Services and Sciences Research Resources.* Bethesda, MD: U.S. Department of Health and Human Services, National Institutes of Health, National Library of Medicine. Available: www.nlm.nih. gov/nichsr/hsrr_search

A newer database at NLM is Health Services and Sciences Research Resources (HSRR). HSRR contains information about research datasets, instruments, and data analysis software employed in health services research as well as in public health and the behavioral and social sciences. Examples of content are clinical records, discharge summaries, claims records, epidemiological and other health-related surveys, birth and disease registries, and data about practitioners, programs, and facilities.

11.33 *The Cochrane Library (Cochrane Database of Systematic Reviews).* Oxford, UK: The Cochrane Collaboration. Available: www.inter science.wiley.com/cgi-bin/mrwhome/106568753/HOME

While the Cochrane Library is a literature search tool and not a source for statistics per se, it is included in this chapter on statistics because it serves as a primary database for finding evidence based medicine (EBM) literature reports of clinical trials, systematic reviews, and meta-analyses of clinical data. It is also the place to learn about the Cochrane Collaboration's approach to evaluating clinical outcomes and data published in the literature and their approach to performing systematic reviews.

The Cochrane Collaboration (cochrane.org) is an international not-for-profit organization whose purpose is to identify and make available the evidence-based literature. The primary product is a database of systematic reviews and controlled clinical trials register, the Cochrane Database of Systematic Reviews, which is published electronically and available by subscription to the Cochrane Library. The collection of articles is relatively small; these resources can be searched using the same MeSH headings as suggested in the PubMed section, although subheadings cannot be applied.

The highly regarded Cochrane Collaboration prepares and maintains its database through a group of volunteer health care professionals worldwide who work in one of the more than 50 Collaborative Review Groups. The review groups prepare and maintain the Cochrane reviews, working in various specialty areas and collectively covering the major areas of health care. The groups compile systematic reviews of randomized controlled trials (RCTs) that have been published in the current literature. The goal is to make the evidence-based literature more widely known by highlighting the up-to-date evidence relevant to the prevention, treatment, and rehabilitation of health problems.

11.34 *Lexis-Nexis Statistical Universe.* New York, NY: Lexis-Nexis Group. Available: www.lexisnexis.com/academic/1univ/stat/features.asp

While the availability of this commercial database is usually limited to larger libraries, it is nonetheless useful for health sciences librarians to be aware that Statistical Universe offers the most comprehensive online searching of statistics. Statistical reports and abstracts from federal, state, and private sources are indexed and accessible through Statistical Universe. The service provides for a single search of three Congressional Information Services statistical indexes including *American Statistics Index*, which covers all federal statistical publications from 1973 forward; *Statistical Reference Index*, which indexes state and private statistical resources from 1980 to date; and the *Index to International Statistics*, whose coverage begins in 1983. Searching options include by simple keyword, by Boolean operators, and by comparative data. Retrievals include tables, content within tables, and full-text material.

Health Care Facilities

11.35 American Hospital Association. *Hospital Statistics.* Chicago: Health Forum, 2007. Available: www.AHAData.com

Under slightly varying titles for more than 50 years, the American Hospital Association (AHA) has published an annual compilation of hospital statistics. The statistics are derived from AHA's annual survey of its accredited hospitals and are presented at the aggregate level. *Hospital Statistics* is the leading source for data on trends, current marketplace issues, and comparative hospital services. The statistical tables are presented to allow comparisons at local, state, and national levels as well as by hospital bed size. Information is provided on such categories as hospital utilization rates, staffing, physician and hospital organization structures, and hospital finances. The availability of various specialized hospital services, such as hemodialysis, emergency departments, and so forth, is reported in regional and state groupings. In some categories, historical trend data are given.

Hospital Statistics is published in print and on CD-ROM, which can be purchased with Excel tables. The AHAData Web site is also available for online searching and provides for fee-based queries and reports. An AHAData search accesses the most recent set of AHA Hospital Statistics data as well as information from AHA's Healthcare Systems & Networks, the periodic AHA Complementary and Alternative Medicine (CAM) survey, and the U.S. Centers for Medicare and Medicaid Services (CMS) Healthcare Cost Report Information System dataset.

11.36 *HCUPnet*. Rockville, MD: U.S. Department of Health and Human Services, Agency for Healthcare Research and Quality. Available: hcupnet.ahrq.gov

The Agency for Healthcare Research and Quality (AHRQ) is the federal agency that supports and engages in research on health care quality, costs, outcomes, and patient safety. Using data from their Healthcare Cost and Utilization Project (HCUP), AHRQ provides a Web-based query system that gives information on hospital stays at the national, regional, and state level. HCUP data comes from the agencies in each state that are listed on the site. A query of the dataset can retrieve hospital stays by diagnosis or procedure. These can be further refined by specific outcome measures such as number of discharges or costs, then by patient and hospital characteristics such as patient type, hospital type or location. There are several options for display of the results. Data on child hospitalizations is available as well.

The Web site, which includes clear instructions for use and a tutorial, is well designed and easy to use. A menu-driven query system leads the user through the steps to formulate a data query. A bar on the right side of the screen provides definitions of parameters while a bar at the top of the screen tracks steps as the query progresses. For more complex queries that cannot be placed through the web-based system, HCUP databases are available for purchase.

Health Education Statistics

11.37 *AAMC Data Book: Medical Schools and Teaching Hospitals by the Numbers.* Washington, DC: AAMC, 2006. Annual. Available: www. aamc.org

The Association of American Medical Colleges (AAMC) publishes an annual compilation of statistics about medical education programs at accredited medical schools and teaching hospitals. The *AAMC Data Book* draws its information from member schools and also from other government and educational sources, all of which are noted on each table. In addition to the print version, a web subscription is available which provides access to up-to-date information as it becomes available during the year. The AAMC Surveys and Data Web site at www.aamc.org/data also contains considerable statistical information that is freely available.

The *AAMC Data Book* covers 12 topics: accredited medical schools, medical school applicants and students, faculty, medical school revenues, tuition, graduate medical education, teaching hospitals, national health care financing data, biomedical research, physicians, faculty compensation, and general statistical information. Examples of statistics about medical students are mean admission test scores, enrollment demographics, and specialty and geographic location choices of graduating seniors. Faculty characteristics and distribution by academic department are tabulated, including for full-time, part-time, and volunteer faculty members. Medical school and student financial data is included. Teaching hospitals are profiled by size, staffing characteristics, utilization rates, and finances. There is a small amount of information about graduate medical education, biomedical research, and national health care financing relevant to medical education.

11.38 Medical Education Issue. *JAMA: Journal of the American Medical Association.* Chicago, IL: American Medical Association. Published annually, usually in September. Available: www.jama.com

Since the early 1900s, this annual *JAMA* issue has contained extensive statistical data on undergraduate and graduate medical education. Much of the undergraduate data is drawn from surveys by the joint American Medical Association-Association of American Medical Colleges medical school accrediting committee, called the Liaison Committee on Medical Education. Statistics describe characteristics of the medical school applicant pool, medical school students and faculty. Each year, several topics of special interest are also included in the survey. A recent issue, for example, included data on the frequency of use of standardized clinical examinations of patients to assess clinical skills. The graduate medical education report is a more recent addition and includes survey data from accredited graduate medical education programs. Specialty and subspecialty programs are reported, along with information about residents by ethnicity, gender, and geographic location. This issue of *JAMA* also typically includes other articles about medical education topics.

11.39 *Bureau of Health Professions.* Rockville, MD: U.S. Department of Health and Human Services, Health Resources and Services Administration, Bureau of Health Professions. Available: bhpr. hrsa.gov

While medical education statistics have been well-covered historically by several sources, this is not the case for other health professionals. Statistics about educational programs in the nursing, dental, and allied health education programs have been produced irregularly over time by their professional societies. Currently, the most consistent resources for these data can be found in the annual volume of *Health, United States* under Health Care Resources in the Table of Contents (see 11.28). Each annual volume is featured on the National Center for Health Statistics Web site (www.cdc.gov/nchs/hus.htm).

11.40 *Nursing Data Review, Academic Year 2004–2005: Baccalaureate, Associate Degree, and Diploma Programs.* New York: National League for Nursing, 2006.

11.41 Kovner C, Fairchild S, Jacobson L. *Nurse Educators 2006: A Report of the Faculty Census Survey of RN Programs and Graduate Programs.* New York: National League for Nursing, 2006.

The National League for Nursing currently tracks statistics on all educational programs preparing students for registered nurses' licensure including both NLN accredited and non-accredited programs. The *Nursing Data Review* (published irregularly) includes statistics and graphs showing program types, admissions data, enrollments, tuition, and student information such as ethnicity, gender, age and geographic location. The new *Nursing Educators* report is based on a faculty survey of 1,374 nursing schools. Information covers number of faculty and full-time positions by program type; racial, ethnic, geographic, and gender profiles of faculty; faculty degrees and academic ranks; salaries; and recruitment and turnover data. Some trend data are shown based on the prior 1996 and 2002 surveys.

The NLN Web site at nln.org posts some excerpts from the *Nursing Data Review* and the *Nurse Educators* reports that are freely available. The National League for Nursing also publishes a variety of one-time reports on the nursing profession and nursing education. An example of a recent report is "Trends in Registered Nurse Education Programs: A Comparison across Three Points in Time—1994, 1999, 2004," which is available at nln.org/about nln/nursetrends.htm.

Health Care Workforce

As part of its mission to achieve equitable access to health care professionals across the nation, the Bureau of Health Professions (BHP) in the U.S. Health Resources and Services Administration maintains a wide range of data on the health care workforce at its Web site at bhpr.hrsa.gov. The Bureau of Health Professions conducts its own research studies, data collections, and analyses to assess supply and demand in the health care professions and to analyze the effects on the workforce of changes in the health care system.

The Bureau of Health Professions is responsible for designating geographic areas with health professional shortages (HPSAs), Medical Underserved Areas (MUAs), and Medically Underserved Populations (MUPs). These designations provide widely recognized evidence of need and eligibility for specialized federal programs. The BHP Web site offers a Web-based query for the current HPSA status of states and geographic regions. The MUA/MUP database is also online and provides county-level data. In addition, the HRSA Geospatial Data Warehouse at datawarehouse.hrsa.gov provides this information along with other county data.

The following resources are also useful for health workforce data.

11.42 *United States Health Workforce Personnel Factbook.* Washington, DC: U.S. Department of Health and Human Services, Health Resources and Services Administration, Bureau of Health Profession, 1998–. Available: bhpr.hrsa.gov/healthworkforce/reports/factbook.htm

The *Health Workforce Personnel Factbook* maintains fairly current information in its publication and on its Web site. Through 67 detailed tables, information is provided about the health care workforce including physicians, nurses, dentists, and selected allied health professionals. Historical and current health workforce trends are reported as well as future projections. Data on current enrollments in health educational institutions, graduates, and the currently employed are provided. Physician-to-population ratios are given by geographic area and specialty group. Data on the public health workforce are also included, along with some health economic data. This factbook is available in print and also in PDF format.

11.43 *Physician Characteristics and Distribution in the U.S.* Chicago, IL: American Medical Association, 1963-. Annual.

11.44 *Access Physician Statistics Now.* Chicago, IL: American Medical Association. Available: www.ama-assn.org/ama/pub/category/ 2676.htm

The American Medical Association publishes extensive summary data on physician characteristics for annual comparisons and analyses of the physician population. The statistics are drawn from the AMA's Physician Masterfile, which is derived primarily from survey data but also includes information from other organizational and institutional sources. Each of the five chapters in *Physician Characteristics and Distribution in the U.S.* has a short introductory text with summary findings. Among the physician characteristics that are profiled are age, specialty and board certification, gender, ethnicity, geographic region, and year and school of graduation. Trends in manpower and supply are presented, along with physician-to-population ratios. If physician information cannot be found in the print version, the AMA can be contacted for specialized data requests.

Access Physician Statistics Now at the AMA Web site contains a limited amount of physician statistical information. The site offers high-level specialty data and selected demographic characteristics about physicians, but has the advantage of being current.

11.45 *The Registered Nurse Population: Findings from the 2004 National Sample Survey of Registered Nurses.* Rockville, MD: U.S. Department of Health and Human Services, Health Resources and Services Administration, Bureau of Health Professions, 2006. Available: bhpr.hrsa.gov/healthworkforce/rnsurvey04

Since 1977, the HRSA Bureau of Health Professions has conducted eight *National Sample Surveys of Registered Nurses.* These surveys provide the most comprehensive data about registered nurses in the United States. Information collected is extensive; examples are numbers of RNs, their educational preparations, current employment status, employment setting, income, gender, race, age, and family status. The full report is available online; print copies may also be ordered. The report is supplemented by Public Use Files that can be downloaded or ordered on CD-ROM. These files present the survey data in a format that can be used for research purposes.

11.46 *State Health Workforce Profiles.* Rockville, MD: U.S. Department of Health and Human Services, Health Resources and Services Administration, Bureau of Health Professions, various dates. Available: bhpr.hrsa.gov/healthworkforce/reports/profiles

State Health Workforce Profiles are available for all the states at the Bureau of Health Professions (BHP) Web site. These reports provide current overview information on each state's health status followed by more detailed data describing the health care workforce. Tables, graphs, charts and narrative provide extensive information on more than 25 different categories of health care professionals. Data are presented on supply, demand, distribution, education and use of health personnel. The size of the state's health workforce and per capita ratios facilitate comparisons with other states and the nation. Highlights of each state's *Workforce Profile* are available on the Web. Requests for complete reports in PDF format can be placed at the BHP Web site.

Health Utilization and Costs

Health care utilization rates and costs are covered in many of the general statistical resources. *Health, United States* (see 11.28 above) is particularly useful for this kind of information. Other sources include the following:

11.47 *Vital and Health Statistics.* Hyattsville, MD: U.S. Department of Health and Human Services, Centers for Disease Control and Prevention, National Center for Health Statistics, 1963–. Available: www.cdc.gov/nchs/products/pubs/pubd/series/sr13/ser13.htm

Series 13 of the *Vital and Health Statistics* presents statistics on the utilization of the health workforce and facilities providing long-term care, ambulatory care, and family planning services. Reports with the highest numbers are most recent publications. All volumes of Series 13 are also available in PDF format on the NCHS Web site (www.cdc.gov/nchs).

11.48 *Research, Statistics, Data & Systems*. Washington, DC: U.S. Department of Health and Human Services, Centers for Medicare and Medicaid Services. Available: www.cms.hhs.gov/home/rsds.asp

The Centers for Medicare and Medicaid Services (CMS) Web site includes a Research, Statistics, Data & Systems portal to a variety of reports and datasets, including links to CMS data as well as to other relevant government sites. In addition to Medicare and Medicaid reports, there is other information such as trends and projections in national and state health care expenditures.

11.49 *U.S. Census Bureau Health Insurance*. Washington, DC: U.S. Department of Commerce, Census Bureau. Available: www.census. gov/hhes/www/hlthins/hlthins.html

The U.S. Census Bureau maintains a Web site on health insurance. The site includes reports, briefs and working papers. Examples of reports are: Income, Poverty, and Health Insurance Coverage; Child Health Insurance; and Employment-Based Insurance. Reports include extensive tables and data. A Data Access feature enables the visitor to generate customized tables and/or download datasets.

11.50 *Health Care Financing Review*. Washington, DC: U.S. Department of Health and Human Services, Centers for Medicare and Medicaid Services, Volume 1–, 1979–. Available: www.cms.hhs.gov/Health CareFinancingReview

Health Care Financing Review is the CMS subscription journal. The *Review* intends to improve understanding of the Medicare and Medicaid programs and the U.S health care system by publishing information and analyses on a broad range of health care financing and delivery issues. The journal highlights the results of policy-relevant research and provides a forum for different viewpoints. The target audience includes policymakers, planners, administrators, insurers, researchers, and health care providers. The *Review* appears quarterly, with an occasional article made available at the Web site. It is indexed by PubMed. A statistical supplement every year provides a comprehensive picture of U.S. health care financing.

11.51 *statehealthfacts.org*. Menlo Park, CA: Kaiser Family Foundation. Available: statehealthfacts.kff.org

The Kaiser Family Foundation provides this Web site, which includes some general information but focuses primarily on health care costs. Individual state profiles, and also U.S. national data, are presented on a variety of health cost issues. Data shown include comparisons among states and with national averages. Examples of types of information are health coverage, private and public insurance spending, and health expenditures such as hospital in-patient cost and health spending as a percent of Gross State Product. Specialized topics include minority health, women's health status and insurance coverage; HIV/AIDS data and funding issues; and state's use of Tobacco Settlement Funds. Data sources are noted.

11.52 Medical Group Management Association. *Physician Compensation and Production Survey: 2006.* Denver, CO: Medical Group Management Association, 2006.

Based on survey data from medical group practices and organizations involved in practice management, this annual report gives physician compensation and benefits by specialty and geographic region. Productivity measures are derived by relating physician compensation to various measures of health care costs. Tables are included giving hours worked per week by different specialty groups. Some data are provided for nurse practitioners, physician assistants, and selected allied health professionals. Retrospective physician compensation data can be located in similar publications from the American Medical Association (AMA).

Vital Statistics

Vital statistics are records of life's major milestones. They are systematically tabulated information concerning births, marriages, divorces, separations, and deaths based on registration of these events by various local and national governments. In the United States, the National Center for Health Statistics tracks these events across the U.S. population through a series of publications, many of which are available and searchable at the NCHS Web site (see 11.11 above). Access to these reports is also possible through PubMed (see 11.31 above) and Statistical Universe (see 11.34 above).

11.53 *Vital Statistics of the United States.* Hyattsville, MD: U.S. Department of Health and Human Services, Centers for Disease Control and Prevention, National Center for Health Statistics, 1937–. Available: www.cdc.gov/nchs/products/pubs/pubd/vsus/vsus.htm

First published in 1937, *Vital Statistics* is the official record of numbers of U.S. births, deaths, fetal deaths, marriages, and divorces. Consequently, the most current data available are always several years old. The Web site provides historical marriage and divorce data through 1988 and annual compilations of mortality and natality data. Beginning with 1997, mortality and natality data, users can access extensive demographic and geographic detailed tables through the NCHS Web site (see 11.11 above).

11.54. *National Vital Statistics Reports.* Hyattsville, MD: U.S. Department of Health and Human Services, Centers for Disease Control and Prevention, National Center for Health Statistics, 1952–. Available: www.cdc.gov/nchs/products/pubs/pubd/nvsr/nvsr.htm

Formerly *Monthly Vital Statistics Report*, this series provides monthly and cumulative data on vital events (birth, death, marriage, and divorce) with brief analyses. Because each issue carries the same type of information from month to month, the current issue should be a useful tool at any reference desk where vital statistics are in demand.

11.55 *Advance Data from Vital and Health Statistics.* Hyattsville, MD: U.S. Department of Health and Human Services, Centers for Disease Control and Prevention, National Center for Health Statistics, 1976–. Available: www.cdc.gov/nchs/products/pubs/pubd/ad/ad.htm

These are summary reports that provide the first release of data from NCHS health and demographic surveys. Topics include hospital discharge, ambulatory medical care, adoption, injury statistics, and office visits to physicians.

11.56 *Vital and Health Statistics Series.* Hyattsville, MD: U.S. Department of Health and Human Services, Centers for Disease Control and Prevention, National Center for Health Statistics, 1963–. Available: www.cdc.gov/nchs/products/pubs/pubd/nvsr/nvsr.htm

Also known as the "'Rainbow Series," these publications include background information, methodology, and analytical studies and presentations of findings from NCHS data collection programs. The various active subseries and areas they cover are listed in Appendix 11-2. Series information can be located on the NCHS Web site.

11.57 *Morbidity and Mortality Report (MMWR).* Atlanta, GA: U.S. Department of Health and Human Services, Centers for Disease Control and Prevention, 1952–. Available: www.cdc.gov/mmwr

Morbidity and Mortality Weekly Report is the leading national publication of up-to-date statistical information on vital statistics, disease outbreaks, and other health incidents occurring both nationally and internationally. It is important to remember that the data in the weekly *MMWR* are provisional, based on weekly reports to CDC by state health departments. The reporting week concludes at close of business on Friday and compiled data on a national basis are officially released to the public during the succeeding week. The *MMWR* also publishes some Early Release reports on the web outside of the routine weekly publication schedule. The full text of *MMWR* is available electronically at the *MMWR* Web site beginning with volume 31, 1982. An e-mail table of contents alert service is also offered.

In addition to the weekly publication, *MMWR* releases quarterly and annual *Surveillance Summaries* as well as *Recommendations and Reports*. The *Surveillance Summaries*, available at the *MMWR* Web site beginning with volume 32 in 1983, give detailed interpretation of trends and patterns based on surveillance data collected by the CDC. The *Recommendations and Reports*, also available at the Web site from 1990, provide updated and in-depth guidelines on prevention and treatment in all health areas related to CDC's scope of responsibility.

Recent additions to the Web site include podcasts on timely topics and an *MMWR* RSS service that provides the latest report feeds, including links to the full text of reports. The Web site now also offers the ability to search mortality tables by geographic region.

State and Local Statistics

Measures of the public's health are first and foremost local and state data. However, the resources yielding state and local health statistics vary widely. Nearly all states have some level of health statistics on their official state Web site. In addition, the state public health departments, which can be linked to from the Association of State and Territorial Health Officials Web site (astho.org), often provide statistics. Medical school libraries within a state are also an excellent resource for these statistics because many specialize in collecting health data related to their own states. The U.S. National Center for Health Statistics Web site (see 11.11) maintains state data on vital statistics and other major health issues.

Additional resources include:

11.58 *State and Metropolitan Area Data Book: 2006.* 6th ed. Washington, DC: U.S. Department of Commerce, Census Bureau, 2006. Available: www.census.gov/prod/www/abs/smadb.htm

11.59 *County and City Data Book*. 13th ed. Washington, DC: U.S. Department of Commerce, Census Bureau, 2000. Available: www.census.gov/statab/www/ccdb.html

Published as supplements to the *Statistical Abstract of the United States*, these two references provide detailed state and local information. Both include statistics drawn from the latest national census as well as other government and private sources. Therefore, the source material is variable but documentation is provided.

First published in 1979, the *State and Metropolitan Area Data Book* contains tables of demographic data for individual states and metropolitan areas. These data come from a variety of sources including the U.S. Census Bureau, other federal government entities, and also private sector research groups, associations, and companies. Information of particular interest is births and deaths, other population demographics including poverty and race, and health information such as hospitals, health insurance coverage, public health and chronic disease information. Metropolitan area information is not as comprehensive as state-level data. When comparing with retrospective data, be aware that the U.S. definition of a metropolitan area has changed over time.

The *County and City Data Book*, although currently somewhat out of date, has been published irregularly since 1944. It provides official population and housing data as well as other social and economic statistics. Statistics are reported for all U.S. counties, cities with populations of 25,000 or more, and incorporated places with 2,500 or more inhabitants. Health science librarians will find this a useful resource for local demographics, vital and health statistics, birth and death rates, health care practitioner statistics and rates, Medicare enrollment, education, and income and poverty levels.

More current demographic information is available at the Census Bureau's USA Counties Web site: censtats.census.gov/usa/usa.shtml. Also the State and County QuickFacts at quickfacts.census.gov provides regularly updated demographic information on states, counties and cities with population of 25,000 or more. The Census Bureau's American FactFinder Web site at: factfinder.census.gov is another good source for quick simple factsheets about cities including data about population, race and ethnic origin, income, disability.

11.60 *Community Health Status Indicators*. Washington, DC: CHSI Workgroup. Available on the Web, Fall 2007.

The Community Health Status Indicators (CHSI) project is undergoing substantial updating and expansion due to the work of a partnership of federal agencies, universities, and other organizations. In the past, CHSI provided county data (1993–98), but this older information is now available only by purchase of a CD-ROM. The current initiative is updating and refining the earlier health status indicators and making them broadly available on the Web. The Web-based database will produce county reports on various health status indicators, such as incidence of lung cancer, along with comparative data from "peer" counties as defined by population size and density, poverty levels, and age composition. The project makes a unique contribution in bringing these data together in a way that provides a context for areas needing health improvements.

11.61 *Health Care State Rankings*. 15th ed. Lawrence, KS: Morgan Quitno Press, 2007. Annual.

This annual publication compiles health data from all the states and displays them in rank order. Over 500 tables of state health comparisons are provided which cover the following major categories: birth and reproductive health, deaths, health care facilities, health insurance and finance, disease incidence, health care providers, and physical fitness measures. The tables are easy to understand; however, the content is wide-ranging under each of the major categories, requiring familiarity with the resource to anticipate its applicability in a reference inquiry. For example, tables address teen birth rates, births by Caesarian delivery, percentage of mothers not receiving prenatal care, death rate from drugs, in-patient days in community hospitals, persons not covered by insurance, average health care employee pay, and participation in selected sports. The data are drawn from both private and government sources. Based on their annual data compilations, the publishers announce a "Healthiest State" award each year. A CD-ROM version includes a searchable database.

11.62 *Community Sourcebook of County Demographics*. 18th ed. Redlands, CA: ESRI Business Information Solutions, 2006.

This sourcebook presents demographic, marketing, and income data by state and then by county. While primarily a market research tool, county-level data are given for population, households, families, income, race, age, and consumer spending. Health finance information is provided for health insurance spending, HMOs, and Medicare payments. The *Community Sourcebook* also includes forecasts.

International Statistics

Numerous Internet sites provide international health data. As with all statistical data, but particularly with international statistics, it must be emphasized to the library patron that the data sources vary widely, with the result that statistical reports may be inconsistent and incompatible for valid comparative analyses. A selection of the major Web sites and print resources is described below.

11.63 *WHO Statistical Information System (WHOSIS)*. Geneva: World Health Organization. Available: www.who.int/whosis/en

The World Health Organization Web site is a key source for international health information and statistical data. WHOSIS serves as the gateway for international statistical and epidemiological information. Many WHO technical programs generate statistical information and these data are available here. Datasets relate to mortality, burden of disease, disease incidence, health personnel, immunizations, health systems, child health and selected topical health issues such as AIDS and current disease outbreaks. WHOSIS provides several searchable databases including core health indicators by country, chronic diseases, causes of death, reproductive health indicators, and a global diseases map. The *WHOSIS Country Profiles* are quick fact sheets of demographics, health information, and include data on communications/technology infrastructure. The page of Links to National Health-Related Web sites leads to health information of many countries, including at their national ministries of health and health statistics offices, when available.

11.64 *Weekly Epidemiology Record; Releve epidemiologique hebdomadaire*. Geneva: World Health Organization, 1926–. Available: www.who.int/wer

This newsletter is the international reporting mechanism for epidemiological information about disease outbreaks subject to International Health Regulations and other major communicable diseases. Published weekly in a bilingual English and French format, the *Weekly Epidemiology Record (WER)* provides a method for rapid communication of newly emerging or reemerging infections and other diseases of public health importance. In addition to outbreak news, *WER* publishes international health regulations, position statements and recommendations, and other information essential to global surveillance.

Volume 71, 1996 forward can be accessed at the Web site. Additionally, an electronic archive of *WER* issues from 1926 to 1995 is available. An e-mail service provides tables of contents and summary information.

11.65 *United Nations Statistics Division*. New York: United Nations. Available: unstats.un.org/unsd

11.66 *Population Information Network*. New York: United Nations. Available: www.un.org/popin

The U.N. Statistics Division maintains a Web site with a wide range of statistical information about U.N. countries. Information is provided on demographics, population and vital statistics, housing, social indicators and measurements including age distributions of populations, education levels, and employment status. The Statistics Division compiles statistics from many international sources and also works to facilitate data comparability by developing specifications for compiling statistical data. A statistical databases page offers several datasets on social indicators, demographics and population counts. The Distat disability statistics database gives incidence of disability by country, although methods of calculating these data vary widely. The database page includes links to other national and international data sources. The Population Information Network also provides population and some demographic data for countries of the world including information on special groups such as refugees.

11.67 Pan American Health Organization. *Health in the Americas*. 2nd ed. Washington, DC: PAHO, 2007 (anticipated). 2 volumes.

This publication is considered the authoritative resource for health trends and health data for Central and South America. *Health in the Americas* offers an overview of the health status of the Pan American region, often emphasizing health disparities. Volume 1 includes chapters describing regional health issues, demographics, and mortality trends as well as current sociological factors affecting health, including health reform efforts and environmental and political conditions. Volume 2 provides health data and information by country including an overview, demographics and mortality data, disease incidence, national health plans, policies and organizations, and expenditure information.

The main PAHO Web site (www.paho.org) is itself an excellent resource, providing information on diseases endemic to the region as well as health indicators of the various Pan American countries. The Health Data page provides reports such as the annual Health Situation in the Americas: Basic Indicators, the Country Health Profiles, and other reference documents. Statistical data are drawn from various timeframes.

11.68 *World Factbook*. Washington, DC: U.S. Central Intelligence Agency (CIA), 2007. Available: www.cia.gov/cia/publications/factbook/index.html

Published since 1981, the *World Factbook* is now available in both printed and Internet versions. The online publication, which also has a search feature, is updated periodically throughout the year. For each country, there is introductory information, followed by an outline format of geographic, governmental, economic and population data. Of particular interest for the health sciences are the demographics, birth and death rates, infant mortality, and HIV/AIDS prevalence.

11.69 *NationMaster*. Sydney, Australia: Rapid Technology. Available: www.nationmaster.com

Launched in 2003, NationMaster is an independently owned and operated Web site that intends to be a popular central resource for data and information on countries around the world. The Statistics page includes a full range of statistical categories including Health Statistics. Examples of health statistics are immunizations, bird flu human deaths, cancer, and so forth. Links to specific datasets are further subdivided by country with graphs and/or interactive map features for many datasets. Statistics, which are updated regularly, are compiled from familiar sources such as the CIA, United Nations and the World Health Organization. A source link at the bottom of graphs and datasets provides reference information. A sister site, StateMaster (available at: statemaster.com) provides similar information for U.S. states.

11.70 *U.S. Department of State*. Washington, DC: U.S. Department of State, Bureau of Public Affairs. Available: www.state.gov

11.71 *Organization for Economic Cooperation and Development (OECD)*. Paris: Organization for Economic Cooperation and Development. Available: www.oecd.org

11.72 *World Agricultural Information Centre*. Rome: Food and Agricultural Organization of the United Nations. Available: www.fao.org/waicent/portal/statistics_en.asp

11.73 *UNICEF*. New York: UNICEF. Available: www.unicef.org/statis/

The category of the international statistics being sought may suggest searches of specialized Web sites. For example, the U.S. State Department Web site provides basic population, health, and mortality data for many countries. The Organization for Economic Cooperation and Development (OECD) offers a statistics portal linked from its home page for demographic, economic, and environmental data of its member nations. The Food and Agriculture Organization (FAO) of the United Nations has a statistics gateway page that retrieves reports on topics such as nutrition and pesticide use. UNICEF also has a searchable statistics Web site that provides access to country-specific child health indicators.

Specialized Topics

The search for statistics that relate to a clearly defined subject domain, such as a specific disease entity, causative agent or population group, will often include visits to credible, non-partisan Web sites related to the subject domain. Several examples follow.

11.74 *Profiles of America*. U.S. Department of Agriculture. Economic Research Service. Available: www.ers.usda.gov/Data/ProfilesOf America

Concerns about diet and food safety cross over several U.S. government agencies. This Web site, developed by USDA's research unit, allows for mapping, charting, and downloading various socioeconomic data related to the topic of interest. For example, the Diet, Health and Safety page includes interactive tools to calculate costs related to food consumption and food borne illnesses, as well as links to numerous reports and datasets.

11.75 Federal Interagency Forum on Child and Family Statistics. *America's Children in Brief: Key National Indicators of Well-Being, 2006*. Rockville, MD: Health Resources and Services Administration, 1997–. Available: childstats.gov/pubs.asp

The Federal Interagency Forum on Child and Family Statistics (Forum) is a group of 20 agencies that come together to publish an annual status report of U.S. children and their families. The publication alternates yearly from a brief report of highlights to a more extensive report in the odd years. Chapters include health but also child and family demographics, economics, education, and behavioral and social aspects. The health chapter provides a general health status overview, mortality data, and also information on timely topics such as obesity. Some trend analyses are provided showing both national progress and remaining challenges.

11:76 *PeriStats.* Washington, DC: March of Dimes Birth Defects Foundation. Available: www.marchofdimes.com/peristats

The March of Dimes Perinatal Data Center Web site, PeriStats, provides free access to maternal and infant health data. Data are presented in several formats including maps, graphs, "quickfacts" and state summaries. There is a wide range of information such as birth rates, preterm births, delivery methods, incidence of smoking, substance abuse, and sexually transmitted diseases. Newborn screening requirements can be reviewed by state. The emphasis is on state data. Data sources are footnoted.

11.77 *Data Resource Center for Child and Adolescent Health.* Rockville, MD: U.S. Department of Health and Human Services, Health Resources and Services Administration, Maternal and Child Health Bureau, Child and Adolescent Health Measurement Initiative. Available: www.childhealthdata.org/content

The Data Resource Center for Child and Adolescent Health provides access to national, state and regional survey data. Measures of overall child health status are reported based on factors such as incidence of asthma, injury, and missing school days. Aggregate data is also presented on child health insurance coverage, preventive health care, schooling, family and neighborhood.

11.78 *Safety Net Monitoring Initiative.* Rockville, MD: U.S. Department of Health and Human Services, Agency for Healthcare Research and Quality, and Rockville, MD: Health Resources and Services Administration.
  - *Book 1. Data for Metropolitan Areas.* Available: www.ahrq. gov/data/safetynet/profile.htm
  - *Book 2. Monitoring the Healthcare Safety Net.* Available: www.ahrq.gov/data/safetynet/profile.htm
  - *Book 3. Tools for Monitoring the Health Care Safety Net.* Available: www.ahrq.gov/data/safetynet/tools.htm

AHRQ, along with the Health Resources and Services Administration (HRSA) has developed the Safety Net project to monitor the health care status of low-income and other vulnerable populations. While the statistical data are somewhat dated, the project is useful in that it brings together in one place measures related to the health of at risk populations included the uninsured, disabled, rural poor, and immigrants. The volumes are available in PDF format. The chapters in Book 1 and 2 on Access-Related Outcome Measures, for example, provide data tables on preventable hospitalizations. Book 3, intended as a toolkit for policymakers, has a good background discussion on issues related to finding and using administrative data, with information that will add to a reference librarian's expertise in the health statistics field. The AHRQ site also provides a Safety Net Profile Tool that can be queried to generate reports with multiple measures for specified geographic areas.

11.79 *SAMHSA Office of Applied Studies.* Rockville, MD: U.S. Department of Health and Human Services, Substance Abuse and Mental Health Services Administration. SAMSA Office of Applied Studies. Available: www.samhsa.gov

The SAMHSA Web site includes data on drug and alcohol abuse and mental health. These data can be viewed nationally and by state. The A–Z list of topics shows the wide range of available information. Data can be retrieved by specific drug, population group, and other topics such as binge drinking. Public use files are available for researchers to use in developing specialized data analyses. The site also contains reports on special topics such as, for example, nonmedical use of prescription pain relievers.

11.80 *Surveillance, Epidemiology, and End Results Program.* Bethesda, MD: U.S. Department of Health and Human Services, National Institutes of Health, National Cancer Institute. Available: seer.cancer.gov

The long established Surveillance, Epidemiology, and End Results (SEER) program of the National Cancer Institute collects and publishes cancer incidence and survival data of the U.S. population. Since 1973, SEER has gathered cancer statistics, drawing its data from cancer registries that currently cover about 23 percent of the population. The SEER Web site includes quick statistics (fast stats), state profiles, as well as links to numerous statistical reports and monographs. Public use data sets are available for researchers.

11.81 *Web-based Injury Statistics Query and Reporting System (WISQARS).* Atlanta, GA: U.S. Department of Health and Human Services, Centers for Disease Control and Prevention, National Center for Injury Prevention and Control. Available: www.cdc.gov/ncipc/wisqars

The WISQARS site provides searchable online access to U.S. data related to fatal and non-fatal injuries. Data can be retrieved for the nation and also by state and region, sex, race and ethnic origin, and age group. Charts are available for Years of Potential Life Lost (YPLL) by specific injury. A topical index leads to fact sheets and data on the leading causes of injuries and injury deaths. Online help and a tutorial are provided at the Web site.

Health Sciences Library Statistics

Today's academic, hospital, and specialty health sciences libraries operate in a health care environment that emphasizes performance measures and business strategies. To effectively secure programmatic support and funding within the organization, the library's contribution to the institution should be measured routinely through both quantitative and qualitative methods. Comparative library data are effective benchmarking indicators for demonstrating a library's successes and its needs. These data can suggest best practices and can also be used to demonstrate one library's performance relative to selected libraries at peer institutions. In addition to sources for comparative data resources for libraries, this section includes guides to library data analysis and library service evaluation.

11.82 *Annual Statistics of Medical School Libraries in the United States and Canada.* Seattle, WA: Association of Academic Health Sciences Libraries, 2006. Available: www.aahsl.org

Since 1978, the Association of Academic Health Science Libraries has published an annual compilation of medical school library statistics. Data on library collections, staffing, service utilization, and annual expenditures are reported by library. Descriptive information, such as library space allocations and reporting channels, are included every five years. Performance measures, ratios and statistical trends have been included in some years. Because many medical school administrators evaluate their programs by comparing themselves to other schools with comparable missions and characteristics, it is a valuable benchmarking tool. An initiative is underway to reframe these statistics in a broader context to derive outcomes measures. This publication is available in print and, for members only, in a Web-based format.

11.83 *The Composite Hospital Library: Benchmarking Aggregate Data Tables.* Chicago, IL: Medical Library Association, 2004. Available: www.mlanet.org/resources/benchmark/index.html

The Medical Library Association hospital librarians have responded to increased interest and requirements for institutional assessment, benchmarking and outcome measures by building a network to collect descriptive and performance statistics about hospital and specialty libraries. The 2004 edition, based on information from 281 study participants, presents composite hospital library profiles in the areas of finance; staffing; public services; special services; technical services; and Web access. The earlier 2002 edition can be purchased in print and PDF formats; the current edition is available electronically for members only.

11.84 Dudden, RF. *Using Benchmarking, Needs Assessment, Quality Improvement, Outcome Measurement, and Library Standards: A How-To-Do-It Manual.* New York: Neal-Schuman, 2007.

This manual is a straightforward guide to the use of evaluation and benchmarking tools in libraries. The book provides a strong argument for evaluation and benchmarking to inform library service improvements and also to demonstrate the library's value to the organization. The specific processes and steps needed to implement library evaluation are clearly outlined. Illustrative examples, checklists, forms and worksheets are provided. The extensive bibliography tempts the lifelong learner.

11.85 Burroughs CM. *Measuring the Difference: Guide to Planning and Evaluating Health Information Outreach.* Seattle, WA: National Network of Libraries of Medicine, Pacific Northwest Region; Bethesda, MD: U.S. National Library of Medicine, 2000. Available: nnlm.gov/evaluation/guides.html#A1

This manual is not a source of statistical information itself but rather is a step-by-step approach to generating credible library program performance measurements. Although focused on methods to assess the effectiveness of library outreach programs, this introduction to program evaluation provides a useful framework for all library services. Topics covered include conducting a community assessment, developing goals and measurable objectives, planning the program activities and strategies, planning the evaluation approach, gathering and analyzing data, and utilizing and reporting the results. Although somewhat dated, the manual continues to provide an important overarching framework for library evaluation projects. Supplemental booklets at the Web site give additional step-by-step planning and evaluation methods.

By now you know where to find the answers to the three questions at the beginning of this chapter.

1. *How many HMOs are there in the United States and how many enrollees?*

   Just go to Health Maintenance Organizations in the index of *Statistical Abstract of the United States* and you will be referred to a table on HMOs. Or, go to the 2007 Statistical Abstract Web site (www. census. gov/compendia/statab), click Health & Nutrition, then Health Insurance, then select the HMO Excel table.

2. *What is the extent of alcohol consumption in the United States?*

   Check out the FASTSTATS A–Z at the U.S. National Center for Health Statistics, at wwwcdc.gov/nchs/fastats/alcohol.htm.

3. *What is the number of physicians in Iraq?*

   Under the headings of Health System Statistics, then Health Workforce, WHOSIS, at www.who.int/whosis, gives numbers of physicians, nurses, dentists, and other health care workers by country.

References

1. Weise F., Johnson J. Medical and health statistics. In: Roper FW, Boorkman JA, eds. *Introduction to reference sources in the health sciences*. 3rd ed. Metuchen, NJ: Scarecrow Press, 1994.

2. *Healthy people 2010*. Washington, DC: U.S. Department of Health and Human Services, Office of Disease Prevention and Health Promotion, 2000. Available: www.health.gov/healthypeople.

3. Sackett DL, Rosenberg WM, Gray JA, Haynes RB, Richardson WS. Evidence-based medicine: what it is and what it isn't. *British Medical Journal* 1996; 312(7023):71–2.

4. U.S. National Center on Vital and Health Statistics. *Shaping a health statistics vision for the 21st century*. Washington, DC, 2002. Available: www.ncvhs.hhs.gov/hsvision/21st%20final%20report.pdf.

5. U.S. National Committee on Vital and Health Statistics. *Information for health: A strategy for building the national health information infrastructure: report and recommendations*. Washington, DC: 2001. Available: aspe.hhs.gov/sp/nhii/Documents/NHIIReport2001/default.htm.

6. Upton G, Cook I. *A dictionary of statistics*. New York: Oxford University Press, 2002.

7. Last JM, ed. *A dictionary of epidemiology*. 4th ed. New York: Oxford University Press, 2001.

8. Everitt B. *Cambridge dictionary of statistics in the medical sciences.* Cambridge: Cambridge University Press, 1995.

9. *International statistical classification of disease and related health problems: ICD-10.* Geneva: World Health Organization, 1992- (revised annually).

10. Ibid.

11. Ibid.

12. *Healthy People 2010*, op. cit.

Appendix 11-1

Frequently Occurring Health Statistics Terms	
Acute Condition	An acute condition is a type of illness or injury that ordinarily lasts less than 3 months, was first noticed less than 3 months before the reference data of the interview, and was serious enough to have had an impact on behavior. (Pregnancy is also considered to be an acute condition despite lasting longer than 3 months).
Age Adjusted Death Rates	Age-adjusted death rates are calculated using age-specific death rates per 100,000 population rounded to one decimal place. Adjustment is based on 11 age groups: under 1 year, 1–4 years, 5–14 years, 15–24 years, 25–34 years, 35–44 years, 45–54 years, 55–64 years, 65–74 years, 75–84 years, and 85 years and over. The exceptions to these groupings are: 1) the age-adjusted death rates for black males and black females in 1950 are based on nine age groups, with "under 1 year" and 1-4 years of age combined as one group, and 75–84 years and "85 years of age and over" combined as one group; 2) the age-adjusted death rates by educational attainment for the age group 25–64 years are based on four 10-year age groups (25–34 years, 35–44 years, 45–54 years, and 55–64 years); and 3) the age- adjusted rates for "years of potential life lost" (YPLL) before age 75 years also use the years 2000 standard population and are based on eight age groups: under 1 year, 1–14 years, 15–24 years, and 10-year age groups through 65–74 years.
Biometry	Biometry is statistics applied to the living world. Statistical methods are applied to the study of numerical data based on biological observations and phenomena. It includes demography, epidemiology, and clinical trials.
Birth Cohort	A birth cohort consists of all persons born within a given period of time, such as a calendar year.
Birth Rate	Birth rate is the number of births occurring in a stated population during a stated period of time, usually a year. The rate may be restricted to births to women of specific age, race, marital status, or geographic location (specific rate) or it may be related to the entire population (crude rate). It is calculated by dividing the number of live births in a population in a year by the mid-year resident population.

Frequently Occurring Health Statistics Terms (Continued)	
Birthweight	Birthweight is the first weight of the newborn obtained after birth. • Low birthweight is defined as less than 2,500 grams or 5 pounds 8 ounces. • Very low birthweight is defined as less than 1,500 grams or 3 pounds 4 ounces.* _____ * Before 1979, low birthweight was defined as 2,500 grams or less and very low birthweight 1,500 grams or less.
Cause-of-Death	Cause-of-death is also known as multiple cause-of-death. For the purpose of national mortality statistics, every death is attributed to one underlying condition, based on information reported on the death certificate and using the international rules for selecting the underlying cause-of-death from the conditions stated on the death certificate. The World Health Organization defines underlying cause-of-death as the disease or injury that initiated the train of events leading directly to death or the circumstances of the accident or violence that produced the fatal injury. Generally, more medical information is reported on death certificates than is directly reflected in the underlying cause of death. The conditions that are not selected as underlying cause of death constitute the non-underlying cause-of-death.
Cause-of-Death Ranking	Cause-of-death ranking is when selected causes-of death, which are determined to be of public health and medical importance, are tabulated and ranked according to the number of deaths assigned to these causes. The top-ranking causes determine the leading causes of death.
Chronic Condition	A chronic condition refers to any condition lasting 3 months or more or to a condition classified as chronic regardless of its time of onset (for example, diabetes, heart conditions, emphysema, and arthritis).
Chronic Disease	A chronic disease is a disease that has one or more of the following characteristics: • is permanent; • leaves residual disability; • is caused by nonreversible pathological alteration; • requires special training of the patient for rehabilitation; or • may be expected to require a long period of supervision, observation, or care.

Frequently Occurring Health Statistics Terms *(Continued)*	
Civilian Non-institutionalized Population	Civilian non-institutionalized population is the civilian population not residing in institutions. Institutions include correctional institutions, detention homes, and training schools for juvenile delinquents; homes for the aged and dependent (e.g., nursing homes and convalescent homes); homes for dependent and neglected children; homes and schools for the mentally or physically handicapped; homes for unwed mothers; psychiatric, tuberculosis, and chronic disease hospitals; and residential treatment centers.
Clinical Trial	A clinical trial is a research activity that involves the administration of a test regimen to humans to evaluate its efficacy and safety. The term is subject to wide variation in usage, from the first use in humans without any control treatment to a rigorously designed and executed experiment involving test and control treatments and randomization. Several phases of clinical trials are distinguished: **Phase I trial**—The first introduction of a candidate vaccine or a drug into a human population to determine its safety and mode of action. **Phase II trial**–Initial trial to examine efficacy usually in 200 to 500 volunteers. Usually, but not always, subjects are randomly allocated to study and control groups. **Phase III trial**—Complete assessment of safety and efficacy. It involves larger numbers, perhaps thousands of volunteers, usually with random allocation to study and control groups, and may be a multicenter trial. **Phase IV trial**—Includes research to explore a specific pharmacologic effect, to establish the incidence of adverse reactions, or to determine the effects of long-term use. Ethical review is required for Phase IV clinical trials.
Cohort Study	A cohort study is a longitudinal study of the same group of people over time. Usually the members of a cohort are of approximately the same age.
Communicable Disease	Communicable disease is a disease that can be communicated by an infectious agent or its products from an infected person, animal, or reservoir to a susceptible host.

Frequently Occurring Health Statistics Terms *(Continued)*	
Comparability Ratios	Comparability ratios measure the effect of changes in classification and coding rules. About every 10–20 years the International Classification of Diseases (WHO, 1992) is revised to stay abreast with advances in medical science and changes in medical terminology. Each of these revisions produces breaks in the continuity of cause-of-death statistics. Discontinuities across revisions are due to changes in classification and rules for selecting underlying cause of death. Classification and rule changes impact cause-of-death trend data by shifting deaths away from some cause-of-death categories and into others.
Death Rate	A death rate is calculated by dividing the number of deaths in a population in a year by the mid-year resident population. For census years, rates are based on unrounded census counts of the resident population, as of April 1. For the noncensus years of 1981–1989 and 1991, rates are based on national estimates of the resident population, as of July 1, rounded to 1,000s. Population estimates for 10-year age groups are generated by summing unrounded population estimates before rounding to 1,000s. Starting in 1992, rates are based on unrounded national population estimates. Rates for the Hispanic and non-Hispanic white populations in each year are based on unrounded state population estimates for states in the Hispanic reporting area. Death rates are expressed as the number of deaths per 100,000 population. The rate may be restricted to deaths in specific age, race, sex, or geographic groups or from specific causes of death (specific rate) or it may be related to the entire population (crude rate).
Demography	Demography is the study of human populations, particularly with respect to births, marriages, deaths, employment, migration, and health.
Disability	Disability is a general term that refers to any long- or short-term reduction of a person's activity as a result of an acute or chronic condition.
Disease Classification	The International Classification of Diseases (ICD) (WHO, 1992) provides the ground rules for disease classification. The ICD is developed collaboratively through the World Health Organization and 10 international centers, one of which is housed at the U.S. National Center for Health Statistics located *(Column continues)*

Frequently Occurring Health Statistics Terms *(Continued)*	
Disease Classification *(Continued)*	international comparability in the collection, classification, processing, and presentation of health statistics. Since the in Hyattsville, Maryland. The purpose of the ICD is to promote beginning of the century, the ICD has been modified about once every 10 years, except for the 20-year interval between ICD-9 and ICD-10.
Epidemic	An epidemic is the occurrence of an illness, specific health-related behavior, or other health-related event(s) that is prevalent and rapidly spreading among many individuals in a community or region at the same time and clearly in excess of normal expectancy.
Epidemiology	Epidemiology is the branch of medicine that investigates all the elements contributing to the occurrence or nonoccurrence of a disease, specific health-related behavior, or other health-related events in a population, and the application of this study to the control of health problems.
Ethnic Group	An ethnic group is a designation of a population subgroup having a common cultural heritage, as distinguished by customs, characteristics, language, and common history. Members of the group have distinctive features in their way of life, shared experiences, and often a common genetic heritage.
Ethnicity/Race	In 1977, the Office of Management and Budget issued standards for ethnicity/race for federal government statistics and administrative reporting in order to promote comparability of data among federal data systems. The 1977 standards called for the federal government's data systems to classify individuals into the following four racial groups: American Indian or Alaska Native, Asian or Pacific Islander, Black, and White. Depending on the data source, the classification by race was based on self-classification or on observation by an interviewer or other person filling out the questionnaire. In 1997, new standards were announced for classification of individuals by race within the federal government's data systems. The 1997 standards have five racial groups: American Indian or Alaska Native, Asian, Black or African American, Native Hawaiian or other Pacific Islander, and White. These five categories are the minimum set for data on race for federal statistics. The 1997 standards also offer an opportunity for respondents to select *(Column continues)*

Frequently Occurring Health Statistics Terms *(Continued)*	
Ethnicity/Race *(Continued)*	more than one of the five groups, leading to many possible multiple race categories. As with the single race groups, data for the multiple race groups are to be reported when estimates meet agency requirements for reliability and confidentiality. The 1997 standards allow for observer or proxy identification of race but clearly state a preference for self-classification. The federal government considers race and Hispanic origin to be two separate and distinct concepts. Thus, Hispanics may be of any race. Federal data systems were required to comply with the 1997 standards by 2003.
Fertility Rate	Fertility rate is the total number of live births, regardless of age of mother, per 1,000 women of reproductive age, 15–44 years.
Geographic Regions	The 50 states and the District of Columbia are grouped for statistical purposes by the U.S. Census Bureau into four geographic regions and nine divisions. The groupings are as follows: **Northeast** *New England:* Maine, New Hampshire, Vermont, Massachusetts, Rhode Island, and Connecticut. *Middle Atlantic:* New York, New Jersey, and Pennsylvania. **Midwest** *East North Central:* Ohio, Indiana, Illinois, Michigan, and Wisconsin. *West North Central:* Minnesota, Iowa, Missouri, North Dakota, South Dakota, Nebraska, and Kansas. **South** *South Atlantic:* Delaware, Maryland, District of Columbia, Virginia, West Virginia, North Carolina, South Carolina, Georgia, and Florida. *East South Central:* Kentucky, Tennessee, Alabama, and Mississippi. *West South Central:* Arkansas, Louisiana, Oklahoma, and Texas. **West** *Mountain:* Montana, Idaho, Wyoming, Colorado, New Mexico, Arizona, Utah, and Nevada. *Pacific:* Washington, Oregon, California, Alaska, and Hawaii.

Frequently Occurring Health Statistics Terms *(Continued)*	
Health Facilities	Collectively, all buildings and facilities used in the provision of health services.
Health Resources	Health resources are the resources (human, monetary, or material) used in producing health care and services.
Health Statistics	Health statistics are the aggregated data describing and enumerating attributes, events, behaviors, services, resources, outcomes, or costs related to health, disease, and health services. The data may be derived from survey instruments, medical records, and administrative documents. Vital statistics are a subset of health statistics.
Health Status	Health status is a measure of the nature and extent of disease, disability, discomfort, attitudes, and knowledge concerning health and of the perceived need for health care. Health status measures identify groups in need of, or at risk of needing, services.
Health Workforce	Health workforce (also called health manpower) is the collective of all men and women working in the provision of health services whether as an individual practitioner or as employees of health institutions and programs, whether or not professionally trained, and whether or not subject to public regulation. Facilities and manpower are the principal health resources used in producing health services.
Hispanic Origin	Hispanic origin includes persons of Mexican, Puerto Rican, Cuban, Central and South American, and other or unknown Latin American or Spanish origins. Persons of Hispanic origin may be of any race.
Hospice Care	Hospice care as defined by the National Home and Hospice Care Survey is a program of palliative and supportive care services providing physical, psychological, social, and spiritual care for dying persons, their families, and other loved ones. Hospice services are available at home and in-patient settings.
Incidence	Incidence is the number of cases of disease having their onset during a prescribed period of time. It is often expressed as a rate (e.g., the incidence of measles per 1,000 children 5–15 years of age during a specified year). Incidence is a measure of morbidity or other events that occur within a specified period of time.

Frequently Occurring Health Statistics Terms *(Continued)*	
Incidence Rate	Incidence rate is a rate expressing the number of new events or new cases of a disease in a defined population at risk, within a specified period of time. It is usually expressed as cases per 1,000 or 100,000 per annum.
Incubation Period	The incubation period is the time interval between invasion by an infectious agent and appearance of the first sign or symptom of the disease in question.
Instrumental Activities of Daily Living	Instrumental activities of daily living (IADL) are activities related to independent living and include preparing meals, managing money, shopping for groceries or personal items, performing light or heavy housework, and using a telephone.
Leading Health Indicators	The Leading Health Indicators are used to measure the health of the nation over the next 10 years. Each of the 10 Leading Health Indicators has one or more objectives from Healthy People 2010 (HHS, 2000) associated with it. As a group, the Leading Health Indicators reflect the major health concerns in the United States at the beginning of the twenty-first century. The Leading Health Indicators were selected on the basis of their ability to motivate action, the availability of data to measure progress, and their importance as public health issues. The Leading Health Indicators are physical activity, overweight and obesity, tobacco use, substance abuse, responsible sexual behavior, mental health, injury and violence, environmental quality, immunization, and access to health care.
Life Expectancy	Life expectancy is the average number of years of life remaining to a person at a particular age and is based on a given set of age-specific death rates, generally the mortality conditions existing in the period mentioned. Life expectancy may be determined by race, sex, or other characteristics using age-specific death rates for the population with that characteristic.
Life Table	A life table provides a comprehensive measure of the effect of mortality on life expectancy. It is composed of sets of values showing the mortality experience of a hypothetical group of infants born at the same time and subject throughout their lifetime to the age-specific mortality rates of a particular time period, usually a given year.

Frequently Occurring Health Statistics Terms *(Continued)*	
Meta-analysis	Meta-analysis refers to the analysis of analyses, that is, the statistical analysis of a large collection of analysis results from individual studies for the purpose of integrating the findings.
Metropolitan Statistical Areas	The U.S. Office of Management and Budget defines metropolitan areas according to published standards that are applied to U.S. Census Bureau data. The collective term "metropolitan area" includes metropolitan statistical areas (MSAs), consolidated metropolitan statistical areas (CMSAs), and primary metropolitan statistical areas (PMSAs). An MSA is a county or group of contiguous counties that contains at least one city with a population of 50,000 or more or a Census Bureau-defined urbanized area of at least 50,000 with a metropolitan population of at least 100,000. In addition to the county or counties that contain all or part of the main city or urbanized area, an MSA may contain other counties that are metropolitan in character and are economically and socially integrated with the main city. If an MSA has a population of 1 million or more and meets requirements specified in the standards, it is termed a CMSA, consisting of two or more major components, each of which is recognized as a PMSA. In New England, cities and towns, rather than counties, are used to define MSAs. Counties that are not within an MSA are considered to be nonmetropolitan.
Morbidity	Morbidity is any departure, subjective or objective, from a state of physiological or psychological well-being. In this sense, sickness, illness, and morbid condition are similarly defined and synonymous. Morbidity is usually stated in terms of incidence rate and prevalence rate.
Mortality Rate	Mortality rate is the number of deaths occurring in a population during a given period of time, usually a year, as a proportion of the number in the population. Usually the mortality rate includes deaths from all causes and is expressed as deaths per 1,000. Also referred to as death rate.
Natality Rate	The natality rate is calculated by dividing the number of live births in a population in a year by the mid-year resident population. For census years, rates are based on unrounded census counts of the resident population, as of April 1. For the noncensus years of 1981-1989 and 1991, rates are based on *(Column continues)*

Frequently Occurring Health Statistics Terms *(Continued)*	
Natality Rate *(Continued)*	national estimates of the resident population, as of July 1, rounded to 1,000s. Population estimates for 5-year age groups are generated by summing unrounded population estimates before rounding to 1,000s. Starting in 1992, rates are based on unrounded national population estimates. Birth rates are expressed as the number of live births per 1,000 population. The rate may be restricted to births to women of specific age, race, marital status, or geographic location (specific rate), or it may be related to the entire population (crude rate).
National Health Expenditures	National health expenditures estimate the amount spent for all health services and supplies and health-related research and construction activities consumed in the United States during the calendar year. Detailed estimates are available by source of expenditures (e.g., out-of-pocket payments, private health insurance, and government programs), type of expenditures (e.g., hospital care, physician services, and drugs), and are in current dollars for the year of report. Data are compiled from a variety of sources.
Notifiable Disease	A notifiable disease is one that, when diagnosed, health providers are required, usually by law, to report to state or local public health officials. Notifiable diseases are those of public interest by reason of their contagiousness, severity, or frequency.
Occupancy Rate	The American Hospital Association defines hospital occupancy rate as the average daily census divided by the average number of hospital beds during a reporting period. Average daily census is defined by the American Hospital Association as the average number of in-patients, excluding newborns, receiving care each day during a reporting period. The occupancy rate for facilities other than hospitals is calculated as the number of residents reported at the time of the interview divided by the number of beds reported. In the CMS administrative Medicare and Medicaid Online Survey Certification and Reporting database, occupancy is the total number of residents on the day of certification inspection divided by the total number of beds on the day of certification.
Over Sample	An over sample procedure is designed to give a demographic or geographic population a larger proportion of representation in the sample than the population's proportion of representation in the overall population.

Frequently Occurring Health Statistics Terms *(Continued)*	
Parity	Parity is defined as the total number of live births ever had by a woman.
Population	Population is the number of inhabitants of a given country or area but also, in sampling, the whole collection of units from which a sample may be drawn. A population is not necessarily composed of persons and its units may be institutions, records, or events. The sample is intended to give results that are representative of the whole population. The U.S. Census Bureau of the Census collects and publishes data on populations in the United States according to several different definitions. Various statistical systems then use the appropriate population for calculating rates.
Prevalence/ Prevalence Rate	Prevalence/prevalence rate is the number of cases of a disease, infected persons, or persons with some other attribute present during a particular interval of time divided by the population at risk of having the attribute or disease at this point in time or midway through the period.
Randomized Control Trial	A randomized control trial is an epidemiologic experiment in which subjects in a population are randomly allocated into groups, usually called study and control groups, to receive or not to receive an experimental preventive or therapeutic procedure, maneuver, or intervention.
Rate	Rate is a measure of the frequency of occurrence of a phenomenon in a defined population in a specified period of time. All rates are ratios, calculated by dividing a numerator (the number of events in specified time) by the denominator (the average population during the period), and multiplied by 10 to remove decimals.

Appendix 11-2

	Vital and Health Statistics Series
Series 1	*Programs and Collection Procedures.* Reports describing the general programs of the U.S. National Center for Health Statistics, its offices and divisions, and the data collection methods used. Series 1 reports also include definitions and other material necessary for understanding the data.
Series 2	*Data Evaluation and Methods Research.* Studies of new statistical methodology including experimental tests of new survey methods, studies of vital statistics collection methods, new analytical techniques, objective evaluations of reliability of collected data, and contributions to statistical theory. Studies also include comparison of U.S. methodology with those of other countries.
Series 3	*Analytical and Epidemiological Studies.* Analytical or interpretive studies based on vital and health statistics. These reports carry the analyses further than the expository types of reports in the other series.
Series 4	*Documents and Committee Reports.* Final reports of major committees concerned with vital and health statistics and documents such as recommended model vital registration laws and revised birth and death certificates.
Series 5	*Comparative International Vital and Health Statistics Reports.* Analytical and descriptive reports comparing U.S. vital and health statistics with those of other countries.
Series 6	*Cognition and Survey Measurement.* Reports from the National Laboratory for Collaborative Research in Cognition and Survey Measurement using methods of cognitive science to design, evaluate, and test survey instruments.
Series 10	*Data from the National Health Interview Survey.* Statistics on illness, accidental injuries, disability, use of hospital, medical, dental, and other services, and other health-related topics, all based on data collection in the continuing national household survey.
Series 11	*Data from the National Health Examination Survey and the National Health and Nutrition Examination Survey.* Data from direct examination, testing, and measurement of national samples of the civilian noninstitutionalized population provide the basis for estimates of the medically defined prevalence of specific diseases in
	(Column continues)

Vital and Health Statistics Series *(Continued)*	
Series 11 *(Continued)*	examination, testing, and measurement of national samples of the civilian noninstitutionalized population provide the basis for estimates of the medically defined prevalence of specific diseases in the United States and the distribution of the population with respect to physical, physiological, and psychological characteristics and analysis of relationships among the various measurements without reference to an explicit finite universe of persons.
Series 12	*Data from the Institutionalized Population Survey.* Discontinued after No. 24: Reports from the Health Records Survey now appear in Series 13.
Series 13	*Data on Health Resources Utilization.* Statistics on the utilization of health manpower and facilities providing long-term care, ambulatory care, and family planning services.
Series 14	*Data on Health Resources: Manpower and Facilities.* Professional and facilities statistics on the number, geographic distribution, and characteristics of health professionals and facilities.
Series 15	*Data from Special Surveys.* Statistics on health and health-related topics collected in special surveys that are not a part of the continuing data systems of the National Center for Health Statistics.
Series 16	*Compilations of Data from Vital and Health Statistics.* Although no longer being compiled, these reports provided early release of data from the health and demographic surveys of the National Center for Health Statistics. Many of these releases were followed by detailed reports in the Vital and Health Statistics series.
Series 20	*Data on Mortality.* Various statistics on mortality other than those included in regular annual or monthly reports. Special analyses by cause of death, age, and other demographic variables; geographic and time series analyses; and statistics on characteristics of death not available from the vital records based on sample surveys of those records.
Series 21	*Data on Natality, Marriage, and Divorce.* Reports of special in-depth analysis of birth, marriage, and divorce data by numerous variables.
Series 22	*Data from the National Mortality and Natality Surveys.* Discontinued after No. 15. Reports based on sample surveys of death records now appear in Series 20, and those based on sample surveys of birth records now appear in Series 21.

Vital and Health Statistics Series *(Continued)*	
Series 23	*Data from the National Survey of Family Growth.* These reports are based on data collected from periodic surveys of a nationwide probability sample of women 15-44 years of age.
Series 24	*Compilations of Data on Natality, Mortality, Divorce, and Induced Terminations of Pregnancy.* Although no longer being compiled, these advance reports of births, deaths, marriages, and divorces were based on final data from the National Vital Statistics System that were published as special reports to the National Vital Statistics Reports (NVSR). These reports provided highlights and summaries of detailed data subsequently published in annual volumes of Vital Statistics of the United States. Other special reports provided selected findings based on data from the National Vital Statistics System and may have been followed by detailed reports in Series 20 or 21.

CHAPTER 12

Directories and Biographical Sources

Cheryl Dee

Directories and biographical sources are often used for a quick answer to questions about people and organizations. Directories are available in print and electronic format or a combination of formats. Many libraries provide both the printed source and electronic access. Open-access Internet sites are easily accessible but care must be given to select an appropriate, authoritative site. For directory questions, the decision between printed references and electronic sources is often based on the librarian's perception of a quick, accurate, current, and easy to use resource.

Currency is a major factor to consider in the selection of a reference tool since the accuracy of the information will be related to the degree that the directory contains up-to-date material. In addition, Jo Anne Boorkman pointed out in the preface to the fourth edition of *Introduction to Reference Sources in the Health Sciences* that a printed directory with an easy to use index that is located close to the reference desk might be the quickest route to an answer for some librarians, while another librarian will choose the electronic version of the same directory believing it to be the most available [1]. Perceived ease of use and availability of the resource will also often determine its usage [2–3].

Biographical Sources and Directories of Scientists

Some of the most frequent reference requests are for biographical information. The selection of a source for biographical information is often driven by exactly what information is needed. Different biographical sources on the same person often include very different information. The Web has produced

303

a wealth of information about people but much of the information is biased at best. Print or electronic biographical sources must be based on accurate material to be authoritative. Biographical sources may rely on questionnaires supplied by the people in the directory, subsequently compiled and written by editors; or an expert in the health care field may write them; or, unfortunately, unknown and unqualified authors may write them. Librarians can verify a source by using publishers of reliable biographies such as Thompson Gale and Web sites from recognized health care organizations or institutions.

The biographical sources and directories discussed in this chapter are examples of major sources that are located in many libraries according to OCLC WorldCat or respected sites acknowledged by academic health science center libraries. In addition, useful sources include local, state, and regional directories as well as directories of professional associations and the telephone directory, sometimes said to be the most frequently used but overlooked reference book. An increasing number of resources are now available on the Web, and representative examples are included in this chapter.

The sources in this chapter are primarily for physicians, other health care professionals, scientists, and consumers seeking biographical or directory information in the United States with a few examples of directories in Great Britain and other countries.

United States

12.1   *American Men and Women of Science.* Farmington Hills, MI: Gale, 17th ed., 1989–. Irregular. Multiple vols. Also available electronically as an eBook Continues: *American Men and Women of Science. Physical and Biological Sciences.* New York: R.R. Bowker, 1972–1986. Continues: *American Men of Science; A Biographical Directory.* New York: R.R. Bowker, 1906–1968.

American Men & Women of Science, is a compendium of biographical profiles focusing on living scientists in the United States and Canada. This resource records the educational, personal, and career data of scientists from the physical and biological sciences, including the health sciences. Each edition profiles more than 130,000 active North American scientists, with cross-references to earlier editions for persons deceased. It also includes scientists from outside the United States and Canada if the majority of his/her work was performed within North America. Biographical profiles typically include birth/death dates and places, citizenship, spouse's/children's names, field of specialty, educational background/honorary degrees, professional experience, honors and awards, memberships, research/publication information, and contact information (address, fax and e-mail).

The following physicians' directories provide different approaches to biographical information.

12.2   *The Official ABMS Directory of Board Certified Medical Specialists.* New Providence, NJ: Marquis Who's Who, 1993–. Annual. Multiple vols. Published in cooperation with the American Board of Medical Specialists. Also available on CD-ROM. Formed by the union of: *Directory of Medical Specialists* and *The Official American Board of Medical Specialties (ABMS) Directory of Board Certified Medical Specialists*, continuing the edition numbering of the former. *BoardCertifiedDocs.* Available: www.boardcertifieddocs.com/default.asp

12.3   Bynum WF, Bynum H, eds. *Dictionary of Medical Biography.* Westport, CT: Greenwood Press, 2007.

12.4   *Directory of Physicians in the United States.* Chicago, IL: Division of Survey and Data Resources, American Medical Association. 33rd ed., 1992–. Biennial. 4 volumess. Continues *American Medical Directory, 1906–1990. Directory of Physicians in the United States (CD-ROM)* single user. *AMA DoctorFinder.* Available: webapps. ama-assn.org/doctorfinder/home.html

12.5   *Who's Who in Medicine and Healthcare.* New Providence, NJ: Marquis Who's Who. 1st ed., 1997–1998–. Biennial. *Marquis Who's Who on the Web.* Available: search.marquiswhoswho.com/executable/Search.aspx?db=E and Gale: Biography Resource Center.

The Official ABMS (American Board of Medical Specialists) *Directory of Board Certified Medical Specialists* is published annually in multiple volumes by Marquis Who's Who in cooperation with the American Board of Medical Specialists. The 2007 edition includes more than 695,000 board certified physician profiles, 25,000 more physicians than the previous edition, in the United States in addition to nearly 20,000 additional physicians in foreign countries who are certified by American specialty boards. The *Directory* is authorized by the 24 medical specialty boards of the American Board of Medical Specialists. Biographies include medical school and year of degree, place and date of internship and residency, fellowship, academic and hospital appointments, professional associations, type of medical practice (with addresses and telephone/fax numbers), specialty and certification by the twenty-four Member Boards of the ABMS. The *Directory* also includes an alphabetical index of the specialists, a geographical distribution of diplomats by state and by specialty, a medical association resource list with addresses and telephone numbers for national and international medical associations, names and addresses for U.S. and Canadian medical schools, state licensing boards, and a necrology of all deceased specialists identified since the last edition. Certification data are obtained from the certifying boards with additional data obtained from questionnaires mailed to the specialists. The electronic version of the *ABMS Directory of Board Certified Medical Specialists* is available by subscription from the American Board of Medical Specialists under the name BoardCertifiedDocs. The electronic version is updated daily using the data from the database used to compose the *ABMS Directory*. In addition, all of the information found in the 4-volume set of The *ABMS Directory* is available on a single user CD-ROM that is updated twice a year.

The *Dictionary of Medical Biography* began in 2007 and provides authoritative biographical coverage of major medical practitioners in all times and cultures. While its emphasis is on practitioners within the Western medical tradition, it also covers practitioners of alternative medicines as well as major figures within traditional Chinese, Indian, and Islamic medicine. In addition, special essays describe these medical traditions which are more difficult to appreciate within a biographical framework. At nearly 1.25 million words, the *Dictionary of Medical Biography* provides a comprehensive biographical dictionary of medicine with some 1,100 entries on almost every important figure in medicine. Entries are written by the leading scholars in the field, including some 400 scholars, researchers, and physicians. The text also has over 300 images that depict medical practitioners and medical practices from around the world.

The *Directory of Physicians in the United States*, compiled and published by the American Medical Association (AMA) from information contributed by the physicians themselves plus other professional organizations, includes both members and non-members of the American Medical Association. The 2007 four-volume 40th edition includes demographic and professional information on over 875,000 practicing physicians, residents, administrators, teachers, researchers and retired physicians located in the United States, Puerto Rico, Virgin Islands, and certain Pacific Islands. Volume one includes the alphabetical index and volumes two, three, and four are the geographical register, arranged alphabetically within each state and city. The AMA electronic DoctorFinder includes basic professional information about more than 690,000 AMA licensed physicians in the United States and each entry includes information such as phone number, specialization, education, a map to the office, and certifications. AMA member physicians are offered an expanded listing with additional information such as office hours, accepted insurance providers, educational history and other helpful information.

Who's Who in Medicine and Healthcare provides biographical background on over 25,000 successful medical professionals, administrators, educators, researchers, clinicians, and industry leaders from across the diverse fields of medicine and health care. The primary selection criteria for Marquis Who's Who publications are position of leadership held at significant organization; education, achievements, publishing or public speaking experience; or contributions to the community. With the publication *Who's Who in Medicine and Healthcare*, the subscriber gets access to Marquis Who's Who on the Web, searchable by name, gender, occupation, geography, hobbies and interests, religion, etc and including the following data elements: birth information, family, education and degree, career history, creative works, awards, military history, achievements, current memberships, interests/hobbies, and contact information. The online version has daily updates, the ability to print and download information, and a Web-based search engine with remote access (no software installation is necessary). *Who's Who in Medicine and Healthcare* is also available from Gale's Biography Resource Center.

The following references represent biographical directories of professional societies. Each organization has criteria for membership and lists only those individuals who have applied for or been sponsored for membership and meet the qualifications for inclusion.

12.6 *Membership Database.* Chicago, IL: American College of Surgeons. Available: web2.facs.org/acsdir/default_public.cfm Continues: *Yearbook American College of Surgeons.* Chicago, IL: Lakeside Press, 1974–1998. Continues: *American College of Surgeons. Directory.* Chicago, IL: American College of Surgeons, 1953–1971. Continues: *Yearbook American College of Surgeons.* Chicago, IL: American College of Surgeons, 1915–1950.

12.7 *American Veterinary Medical Association. AVMA Directory and Resource Manual.* Schaumburg, IL: Division of Membership and Field Services, American Veterinary Medical Association, 1997–.

Annual. *AVMA Membership Directory on the Web.* Available: www.avma.org/noah/members/memlog.asp Continues: *American Veterinary Medical Association. Division of Membershp and Field Services AVMA Directory.* Schaumburg, IL: Division of Membership and Field Services, American Veterminary Medical Associaiton, 1984–1996. Continues: *American Veterinary Medical Association. Directory.* Chicago, IL: American Veterinary Medical Association, 1924–1983.

12.8   *Who's Who in Managed Health Care Directory.* Laguna Hills, CA: HealthQuest Publishers, 1994–.

12.9   *ADA Find a Dentist.* Chicago, IL: American Dental Association. Available: www.ada.org/public/directory Continues: *American Dental Directory.* Chicago, IL: American Dental Association, 1947–2001.

12.10 *Find an AGD Dentist.* Chicago, IL: Academy of General Dentistry. Available: www.agd.org/findadentist/default.asp

The Membership Database continues the *Yearbook of the American College of Surgeons.* The American College of Surgeons Fellowship Database lists surgeons who are members of the College. Board certification and society membership information are provided by the Fellows. Self-reported data are not continuously verified by the College. Areas of special interest and expertise are self-reported.

The *AVMA* (American Veterinary Medical Association) *Directory and Resource Manual 2007* is a comprehensive directory containing alphabetic and geographic listings of American Veterinary Medical Association members and rosters of AVMA leadership volunteers. AVMA members may search the online directory, My AVMA, through a wide variety of search criteria as of March 2007.

The *Who's Who in Managed Health Care* 2006 edition identifies over 1,100 of contacts for business development, proposals, recruitment, collaborative arrangements, and company research. The *Who's Who Directory* is arranged in the following three sections: the Leadership Profiles arranged in alphabetical order, Health Plan CEO Listing organized by state by company, and Leadership Indexes sorted alphabetically by company, state and parent company. A CD-ROM version provides searchable features.

The print *American Dental Directory* ceased publication in 2001. The older editions may be of use for retrospective searching since the Directory listed all dentists, not just American Dental Association members. The online

American Dental Directory Find A Dentist: ADA Member Directory site gives the dentist's name, address and email address. When available, a dentist's name is hyperlinked to a map of the dentist's office location. In addition, the Find an AGD (Academy of General Dentistry) Dentist site provides similar information plus the Academy of General Dentistry hosts member Web sites as a benefit of membership.

Other Countries

12.11 *The Medical Register*. London: General Medical Council, 1859–. Print issues ceased publication with 2004. Volumes for 2005– available on CD-ROM. Currently updated by the *List of Registered Medical Practitioners*. Available: webcache.gmc-ukorg/ods/ home.do

12.12 *Canadian Medical Directory*. Don Mills, Ontario: Southam Business Information & Communications Group etc., 1955–. Volume 1–. Annual. Available on CD-ROM as *MD Select*. *MD Select* on the Web: mdselect.com/HTMLpages/mdselectonline.asp

The General Medical Council's *Medical Register* was published under the direction of the General Council of Medical Education and Registration of the United Kingdom and lists doctors who were registered to practice in the UK before the last printed edition in 2004. Volumes for 2005 forward are published on CD-ROM. The General Medical Council's *List of Registered Medical Practitioners* currently provides an online check of the GMC registration status of doctors that are currently registered or who have been on the Register at any time since 20 October 2005. The *List* provides the GMC registry number and registry status, physicians' name, gender, primary medical qualification and medical specialization with the date the physician began the specialization. The *List* is authoritative since doctors must be registered with the General Medical Council to practice medicine in the UK.

The *Canadian Medical Directory* offers three formats, print, online and CD-ROM. The print version provides 57,000 physicians with their e-mail addresses. Sections of this *Directory* include a Canadian physicians' directory, hospital directory, index of languages spoken by physicians, general practitioners and certificates of the College of Family Physicians of Canada, certified specialists listed geographically according to specialty, Canadian health care associations, information on medical faculties, and expert medical witnesses and their areas of expertise. The online version MD Select allows a search for doctors by keyword, export of data, and summaries of listings. MD

Select, the *Canadian Medical Directory* on CD-ROM, offers a search of the profiles of over 60,000 Canadian physicians with all the functionality of the online version plus it allows the addition of personal notes, printing call sheets, and mailing labels.

The following directories are international in scope:

12.13 *Who's Who in Science and Engineering.* Wilmette, IL: Marquis Who's Who, 1992–. *Marquis Who's Who on the Web.* Available: marquiswhoswho.com/products/ontheweb.asp and Gale: Biographical Resource Center.

The *Who's Who in Science and Engineering* 2006–2007 edition provides key biographical facts on the more than 50,000 men and women in the scientific and technological field and includes personal data, achievements, discoveries, research findings, patents, and career histories of today's leaders from all areas of pure and applied science and engineering including medicine and life sciences. The online Marquis Who's Who on the Web offers electronic access to the information that is available in *Who's Who in Science and Engineering.*

Internet Directories

12.14 *MedlinePlus: Directories.* Bethesda, MD: U.S. National Library of Medicine. Available: www.nlm.nih.gov/medlineplus/directories.html

12.15 *World Biographical Information System Online (WBIS Online).* Munich: K. G. Saur. Available: www.saur-wbi.de

12.16 *DocFinder.* Administrators in Medicine. Available: www.docboard. org/docfinder.html

12.17 *Participating Physician Directory.* Baltimore, MD: Centers for Medicare and Medicaid Services. Available: www.medicare.gov/ Physician/Search/PhysicianSearch.asp?CookiesEnabledStatus=True

The National Library of Medicine's MedlinePlus provides biographical directories to help the consumer find doctors, dentists, and other health care providers'. The site also offers a long locator list of doctors and dentists listed by specialty using the MedlinePlus "Directories" tab and scrolling to "Doctors and Dentists—Specialists."

The World Biographical Information System Online (WBIS Online) presents a comprehensive biographical online library to provide access to approximately 10 million entries from over 8,600 reference works: works written since the 16th century in 40 languages and comprising more than 15,000 volumes. WBIS Online is based on the digitization of the microfiche editions of K. G. Saur's Biographical Archives, which will be completed by 2009. Twenty-four digitized Biographical Archives are currently available in digitized form. WBIS Online will be enlarged each year by about 1 million original biographical entries.

The Association of State Medical Board Executive Directors DocFinder is searchable by a combination of the physician's name, state, and/or license number in states that are participating (17states) in the database. For these states, the site provides the physician's name, profession description, license number, office address, city, state, and year licensed. The site also includes links for non-participating states to the states' licensure Web site. Information on the individual states' site varies according to each state.

Medicare's Participating Physician Directory contains physicians listed by specialty and geographic area. The site presents detailed physician profiles, maps and driving directions. Site is searchable by geography, proximity and the name participating physicians who have agreed to accept assignment on all Medicare claims and covered services.

Directories of Organizations

Information requests about medical organizations, particularly hospitals, are popular. Addresses and telephone numbers are most often needed, although information about an organization's structure, purpose, meetings, and membership are often requested.

12.18 *Encyclopedia of Associations*. Detroit, MI: Gale Research Co., 1961–. Annual 1975–; Irregular 1961–73. *Gale's Ready Reference Shelf*. Available: www.galegroup.com

12.19 *Research Centers Directory*. Detroit, MI: Gale Research Co., 1965–. Irregular. Supplemented between editions by: *New Research Centers*. *Gale's Ready Reference Shelf*. Available: www.galegroup. com

12.20 *International Research Centers Directory*. Detroit, MI: Gale Research Co., 1981–. Annual (with 2 supplements), 1986–1987–.

12.21 *Medical and Health Information Directory*. Detroit, MI: Gale Research Co., 1977–. Irregular. *Health & Wellness Resource Center*. Available: www.galegroup.com

12.22 *Encyclopedia of Medical Organizations and Agencies*. Detroit, MI: Gale Research Co., 1983–.

12.23 *Directory of Special Libraries and Information Centers*. Detroit, MI: Gale Research Co, 1963–. Irregular. *Gale's Ready Reference Shelf.* Available: www.galegroup.com

The *Encyclopedia of Associations (EA)* is a general directory of organizations in the United States. Entries are arranged into 18 subject sections (Section 8: Health and Medical Organizations) and within each section organizations are arranged in alphabetical order according to the subject keyword. Within each subject keyword section, entries are listed alphabetically by the organizations' name. Also see volumes of *Encyclopedia of Associations: Regional, State and Local Organizations* and *Encyclopedia of Associations: International Associations*. The Gale Research Company publishes electronic formats of *Encyclopedia of Associations: National Associations, Encyclopedia of Associations: International Associations*, and *Encyclopedia of Associations: Regional, State and Local Associations* in *Gale's Ready Reference Shelf.* The complete *Encyclopedia of Associations* including international and regional, state and local editions is available electronically through the Gale Group.

Research Centers Directory covers about 13,600 entries about university, government, and other nonprofit research organizations established on a permanent basis to carry out research programs. Organizations are grouped into general categories including the medical and health sciences. Entries are classified by broad subjects, then alphabetical by unit name and indexed alphabetically by subject, geography, and personal name. Entries include the unit name, name of parent institution, address, phone, fax, name of director, e-mail addresses, URLs, year founded, governance, staff, educational activities, public services, sources of support, annual volume of research, principal fields of research, publications, special library facilities, and special research facilities. *New Research Centers* provides periodic supplements to the *Directory. RCD* is also available online through *Gale's Ready Reference Shelf.* The companion printed resource, *International Research Centers Directory*, covers over 9,700 non-U.S. research organizations in approximately 145 countries. The international directory includes detailed information on over 27,500 organizations conducting research worldwide.

The *Medical and Health Information Directory* is extremely useful since the directory brings together a wide range of medical and health information into a single source. Volume one provides contact and descriptive information on 33,200 medical and health organizations, agencies, and institutions. This volume consists of descriptive listings, and an alphabetical name and keyword index. Volume 2 covers over 14,300 publications, libraries and other information resources. Volume 3 lists 39, 800 health services, including clinics, treatment centers, care programs, counseling/diagnostic services. The *Medical and Health Information Directory* is included in Gale's *Health & Wellness Resource Center*.

The *Encyclopedia of Medical Organizations and Agencies* is a subject guide to medical and health-related organizations and institutions, including national, international, state and regional organizations; foundations and other funding organizations; U.S. federal and state government agencies; research centers and medical and allied health schools.

The *Directory of Special Libraries and Information Centers* provides contact and descriptive information on about 34,800 subject-specific resource collections from government agencies, businesses, publishers, educational and nonprofit organizations, and associations around the world. Volume 1 provides contact and descriptive information on subject-specific resource collections maintained by various government agencies, businesses, publishers, educational and nonprofit organizations, and associations around the world. In addition, volume 1 features seven appendixes and a comprehensive subject index. Volume 2, *Geographic and Personnel Indexes*, provides access to profiled libraries by geographic region, as well as by the professional staff that are cited in each listing. The *Directory* is accessible in electronic format from *Gale's Ready Reference Shelf.*

12.24 *World Guide to Scientific Associations and Learned Societies.* 10th ed. Munich, Germany: K.G. Saur, 2006.

12.25 *Yearbook of International Organizations.* Brussels: Union of International Associations, 1967–. Continues: *Annuaire des Organisations Internationales.* Geneva, Switzerland: Societe de l'Annuaire des Organisations Internationales, 1948–1964–65. *Yearbook of International Organizations Online.* Available: www.diversitas.org/db/x.php

The *World Guide to Scientific Associations and Learned Societies* is an international directory of associations and societies representing all fields of science, culture and technology. The work is arranged alphabetically by name of country and includes about 17,500 entries from 170 countries.

The *Yearbook of International Organizations*, available in book, CD-ROM and online formats contain entries on about 30,000 international non-governmental and intergovernmental organizations active in about 300 countries and territories including formal structures, informal networks, professional bodies, recreational clubs but not for-profit enterprises. Organization descriptions listed in Volume 1 are numbered in alphabetical sequence with reference to the main sections from Volumes 2 and 3 indexed by region or subject. Volume 4 cites publications and information resources. The Union of International Associations offers UIA Online Databases, including the Yearbook of International Organizations Online divided into files for international organizations, biographical profiles, bibliography, and statistics. The general entry point to all UIA databases may be visited at no charge; however, the files for the Yearbook of International Organizations Online can only be used by subscription. The online version contains descriptions of as many as 62,945 organizations with information including details of organization names, including multilingual variants, addresses of main offices with telephone, telex and fax numbers, e-mail addresses and Web site URLs, names and biography (career information, personal information, educational background, addresses) of presidents, general secretaries, executive directors, chairmen and other officers active in every field organizations' activities (related to printed *Who's Who in International Organizations*), memberships by country, publications by title, and statistical information on international organization activity and civil society networks. The organizations database is hyperlinked between organization profiles to organizations. The online version is updated continually and therefore may contain newer information. The online version contains more information than the print or CD-ROM formats.

The *Yearbook of International Organizations* provides considerably more information about each organization it lists, as well as more indexes, than the *World Guide*. However, both directories are useful in locating information about organizations outside the United States.

Internet Directories

Electronic sources for organizational information are popular because these sources are easily accessible. The sites can be updated as frequently as information changes a particular organization. As with any Web site, the quality varies and the reliability of the site is directly in proportion to the quality of the organization producing the Web site. Some examples follow.

12.26 *DIRLINE*. Bethesda, MD: U.S. National Library of Medicine. Available: dirline.nlm.nih.gov

12.27 *Health Hotlines: Toll-free Numbers from the U.S. National Library of Medicine*. Bethesda, MD: U.S. National Library of Medicine. Available: healthhotlines.nlm.nih.gov/

12.28 *MedlinePlus: Organizations*. Bethesda, MD: U.S. National Library of Medicine. Available: www.nlm.nih.gov/medlineplus/otherresources.html

12.29 *USA.gov*. Washington, DC: Federal Citizen Information Center, Office of Citizen Services and Communications, U.S. General Services Administration. Available: www.usa.gov

12.30 *SAMHSA's National Mental Health Information Center: The Center for Mental Health Services*. Washington, DC: Substance Abuse and Mental Health Services Administration, National Mental Health Information Center. Available: www.samhsa.gov/index.aspx

12.31 *The Internet Public Library. Associations on the Net*. Ann Arbor, MI: The Regents of the University of Michigan. Available: www.ipl.org/div/aon

12.32 *Scholarly Societies*. Waterloo, Ontario: University of Waterloo Library. Available: www.lib.uwaterloo.ca/society/overview.html

12.33 *World Health Organization*. Geneva: World Health Organization. Available: www.who.int/en

Sponsored by NLM, the high quality DIRLINE online database contains location and descriptive information about a wide variety of information resources including organizations, research resources, projects, and databases concerned with health and biomedicine. Each record may contain information on the publications, holdings, and services provided. DIRLINE contains over 8,000 records with information resources in a variety of categories including federal, state, and local government agencies; information and referral centers; professional societies; self-help groups and voluntary associations; academic and research institutions and their programs; information systems and research facilities.

Health Hotlines is derived from DIRLINE and provides information on health-related organizations operating toll-free telephone services with descriptions of over 14,000 biomedical information resources, including organizations, databases, research resources, etc. The database is searchable by keyword and browsing the subject list. The toll-free telephone numbers in Health Hotlines were provided by the organizations and verified; however, NLM does not review or evaluate the services of the organizations listed.

MedlinePlus Organizations is located on the NLM MedlinePlus site under "Other Resources." The database includes extensive information from the NIH from trusted sources aimed toward the consumer. Organizations are listed in alphabetical order and grouped by health topic. The entries link to the organizations' Web site.

USA.gov (formerly FirstGov.gov) is the U.S. government's official portal and provides extensive online services for citizens, business and governments including a category on "Health and Nutrition." Information can be located by using the site's search box, from a list of topics. The "Reference Center" includes information such as data and statistics, maps, historical documents, photographs, and publications from the U.S. government. The site has won many awards for its information and services since it launched in 2000.

SAMHSA is a specialized directory sponsored by the U.S. Department of Health and Human Services, Substance Abuse and Mental Health Services Administration for mental health statistics, resources, and services. This site includes a "Browse by Topic" selection that offers directory information for organizations related to mental health.

Associations on the Net is available from The Internet Public Library (IPL) and includes a guide to Web sites of prominent organizations and associations. The Health and Medical Sciences section covers all aspects of human and animal health and medicine. The site is searchable by a search box using an advanced search, by a "cluster retrieval" option, and by subject.

Scholarly Societies, sponsored by the University of Waterloo, facilitates access to information from about 4,117 scholarly societies and 3,787 Web sites throughout the world since 1994. The "Health and Medicine" category is further broken down by subject areas. The site includes a URL stability rank for the links to the organizations.

World Health Organization (WHO) provides topics by country, health topic, publications, research tools, and WHO sites. The "Health Topics" link to WHO projects, initiatives, activities, information products, and contacts, is organized by health and development topics.

Education Directories

Information about schools and universities is a popular request. General education reference books with health care facilities and the professional health associations formed by these schools and their administrators provide timely and accurate information about their programs, admission requirements, and curricula. Some examples follow.

12.34 *Graduate Medical Education Directory*. Chicago, IL: American Medical Association, 1993–. Annual. Continues: *Directory of Graduate Medical Education Programs*. Chicago, IL: American Medical Association, 1987–1992. Continues: *Directory of Residency Training Programs/ Accredited by the Liaison Committee on Graduate Medical Education*. Chicago, IL: American Medical Association, 1978–1986/87. *FREIDA Online*. Available: www.ama-assn.org/ama/pub/category/2997.html

12.35 *Health Professions Career and Education Directory*. Chicago, IL: American Medical Association. 2000–. Annual. Continues: *Health Professionals Education Directory*. Chicago, IL: American Medical Association, 1997–1999. Continues: *Allied Health and Rehabilitation Professions Education Directory*. Chicago, IL: American Medical Association, 1996–1997. Continues: *Allied Health Education Directory*. Chicago, IL: American Medical Association, 1978–1996. Continues: *Allied Medical Education Directory*. Chicago, IL: Council on Medical Education, American Medical Association, 1972–1976. Continues: *Directory of Approved Allied Health Medical Education Programs*. Chicago, IL: Council of Medical Education, American Medical Association, 1964–1971.

12.36 *Directory of American Medical Education*. Washington, DC: Association of American Medical Colleges, 1995–. Annual. Continues: *AAMC Directory of American Medical Education*. Washington, DC: Association of American Medical Colleges, 1967–1994.

12.37 *Medical School Admission Requirements, United States and Canada*. Washington, DC: Association of American Medical Colleges, 1964/65–. Annual. Continues: *Admission Requirements of American Medical Colleges, Including Canada*. Evanston, IL: Association of American Medical Colleges, 1951–1963/64. *Medical School Admission Requirements*. Available: www.aamc.org/ students/applying/msar.htm

The American Medical Association (AMA) has a series of publications related to medical education. Two publications in a variety of formats are described below.

The *Graduate Medical Education Directory* is available in three formats. This directory lists U.S. medical schools and Canadian graduate medical education (GME) programs with descriptions and data for 8,400 ACGME-accredited and combined specialty programs and 1,700 GME teaching institutions. Additional information includes ABMS medical specialty board certification requirements, medical licensure information, a GME glossary, and contact information for major GME organizations. The companion *Graduate Medical Education Library on CD-ROM, 2007–2008* offers advanced search functions to find programs or institutions using a Web browser interface with 30,000 clickable hyperlinks to archived copies of the Directory since the 1996/1997 edition. The FREIDA (Fellowship and Residency Interactive Databases) Online database has over 8,200 graduate medical education programs accredited by the Accreditation Council for Graduate Medical Education, as well as over 200 combined specialty programs.

The *Health Professions Career and Education Directory 2007–2008*, also produced by the American Medical Association, lists 6,800 educational programs and 2,500 educational institutions in 71 different allied health professions. This directory includes occupational descriptions, employment characteristics, and information on educational programs, such as length, curriculum, and prerequisites. A chart includes comparisons between programs; data include class capacity; month(s) classes begin; program length; yearly tuition; award granted; and availability of evening/weekend classes.

The Association of American Medical Colleges (AAMC) also provides a series of medical education directories. Two AAMC publications are listed below.

The *Directory of American Medical Education* from the Association of American Medical Colleges lists administrators, department and division chairs for all the accredited medical schools in the United States, Canada, and Puerto Rico. In addition to the faculty listings, each school entry also contains enrollment, type of support, clinical facilities and a brief historical statement. The beginning of the directory describes AAMC activities and efforts in research, communications, education and service to its members. Officers and members of the various AAMC organizations are also listed, including member academic societies and teaching hospitals.

Medical School Admission Requirements published by Association of American Medical Colleges, includes comprehensive admissions information on every United States and Canadian AAME-accredited medical school. The directory includes application procedures and deadlines, selection factors such as MCAT and GPA data, medical school class profiles, costs and financial aid packages, curriculum features, and MD/PhD and other combined degrees. In addition, the AAMC Medical School Admission Requirements Web page provides a topical list of Web sites to assist with the application process.

Specialized Education Directories

12.38 *Nursing Programs.* Lawrenceville, NJ: Thomson/Peterson's, 2002–. Biennial. Continues: *Peterson's Guide to Nursing Programs.* Princeton, NJ: Peterson's Guides, 1994–2001.

12.39 *ADEA Official Guide to Dental Schools.* Washington, DC: American Dental Education Association, 2001–. Annual. Continues: *Admission Requirements of U.S. and Canadian Dental Schools.* Washington, DC: American Association of Dental Schools, 1974/75–2001. Continues: *Admission Requirements of American Dental Schools.* Chicago, IL: American Association of Dental Schools, 1964/65– 1973/74.

Nursing Programs is published by Peterson's, a publisher of college guides, in collaboration with the American Association of Colleges of Nursing (AACN) and is a comprehensive guide to accredited baccalaureate, master's, doctoral, postdoctoral, and joint-degree nursing education programs. The guide profiles more than 2,000 nursing programs offered by nearly 700 colleges and universities and includes entrance qualifications, degree requirements, costs, RN and LPN fast-track opportunities, accelerated programs for non-nursing graduates, part-time opportunities, continuing education, and distance learning options. Other sections provide advice on how to select a program, tips for nurses returning to school, guidance on financial aid and scholarships, and information for international nursing students.

ADEA Official Guide to Dental Schools, published by American Dental Education Association, is an authoritative guide to information about applying to and attending dental school in the U.S. and Canada. The intended audience includes advisors, students, and parents.

12.40 *World Directory of Medical Schools.* Geneve: World Health Organization, 1953–2000. Irregular.

The *World Directory*, published by the World Health Organization, provided a printed directory for almost a half century. The World Health Organization's (WHO) Web site announces that the WHO Department of Human Resources for Health (HRH) has undertaken a preliminary agreement with the University of Copenhagen, Denmark, to establish a Global database of health professions educational institutions that will replace the *World Directory of Medical Schools*. The directory will include schools of dentistry, nursing, midwifery, pharmacy, public health, and rehabilitation specialist. The University of Copenhagen, will start (2007) with information related to schools' accreditation, number of admissions, students, graduates, Faculty, educational resources, address, national official recognition.

Internet Sources

The following internet sources also provide educational directory information.

12.41 *List of ACGME Accredited Programs and Sponsoring Institutions.* Chicago, IL: Accreditation Council for Graduate Medical Education. Available: Available: www.acgme.org

12.42 *FAIMER International Medical Education Directory*. Philadelphia, PA: Foundation for Advancement of International Medical Education and Research. Available: imed.ecfmg.org/search.asp

12.43 *MedicalStudent.com.* University of Iowa Hardin Library for the Health Sciences. Available: www.medicalstudent.com

12.44 *NLM Library Catalogs Home Page*. Bethesda, MD: National Library of Medicine. Available: nnlm.gov/members

The Accreditation Council for Graduate Medical Education is a private professional organization responsible for the accreditation of nearly 7,800 residency education programs. This application allows medical students, residents, program directors, the medical community, and the general public to view basic information about all ACGME accredited programs and sponsoring institutions. A search may be initiated by selecting "Accredited Programs" or "Sponsoring Institutions" or select "Reports" for a set of predetermined views. All results reflect accredited programs for the current academic year and include those newly accredited programs with future effective dates.

The International Medical Education Directory (IMED) is available online from the Educational Commission for Foreign Medical Graduates Web site and provides information on medical schools worldwide. Searches for medical schools can be performed by region, country, city, and/or medical school name. In addition to the usual directory information for name, address, phone/fax numbers, Web and email addresses, each listing includes: former official name(s) of the school; degree awarded; graduation years; year instruction began; language of instruction; duration of curriculum; entrance examination requirement; eligibility of foreign (non-national) students; and total enrollment. IMED search results are displayed in alphabetical order by the name of the medical school.

MedicalStudent.com provides a digital library of authoritative medical information for all students of medicine. The site was created and maintained by the University of Iowa Hardin Library for the Health Sciences with funding from the Centers for Disease Control and Prevention and the National Library of Medicine.

The U.S. National Library of Medicine, Library Catalogs Home Page provides a directory of medical research libraries by state in the United States that are resource libraries under NLM's National Network of Libraries of Medicine (NN/LM). Information provided includes to whom services are offered. The site also provides consumer health libraries searchable by state.

In the United States regions, states, counties, and cities often issue directories of physicians, other health personnel, services, and organizations and will answer questions about local people and places. Telephone directories can be an invaluable resource for questions regarding the immediate and surrounding communities.

Hospital and Clinic Directories

12.45 *AHA Guide to the Health Care Field*. Chicago, IL: Healthcare Infosource, 1997–. Annual. Continues: *American Hospital Association Guide to the Health Care Field*. Chicago, IL: American Hospital Association, 1974–1996/97. Continues: *AHA Guide to the Health Care Field*. Chicago, IL: American Hosptial Association, 1972–1973. Continues: *Hospitals, Guide Issue*. Chicago, IL: American Hospital Association, 1956–1971. Continues: *Hospitals; Administrators Guide Issue*. Chicago, IL: American Hospital Association, 1951–1955.

12.46 *Guide to Canadian Health Care Facilities. Guide des e'tablissements de soins de sante' du Canada*. Ottawa, ON: Canadian Healthcare Association, 1993–. Annual.

The *AHA Guide* is a comprehensive reference book of U.S. hospitals. This directory includes hospital services offered and detailed profile information such as facility ownership, admissions, beds, outpatient visits, and births. The publication primarily focuses on hospitals but also serves as a guide to the health care field in three major sections: Section A: Hospitals; Section B: Health care systems, networks, and alliances; and Section C: Health care organizations, agencies, and other health care providers with an index of hospitals arranged alphabetically by hospital, and health care professionals. The lists provide information about each hospital, including the address, telephone number, and chief administrator. Additional coded information indicates the hospital's facilities, service, governing structure, size of staff, accreditation by the Joint Commission on Accreditation of Healthcare Organizations (JCAHO), and utilization data (beds, admissions, census, outpatient visits, births), expenses (total, payroll) and personnel. The Health Care Systems, Networks and Alliances section is an alphabetical listing of health care systems and their hospitals, a list of the names and addresses of networks and their hospitals, and multi-state alliances and their members. The Health Organizations, Agencies and Other Health Care Providers section includes national, international and regional organizations; U.S. government agencies; state and local organizations and government agencies; and other health care providers. Data for this publication is compiled using AHA membership and the AHA Annual Survey of Hospitals. This directory is the leading hospital directory and represents both AHA Member and non-member hospitals.

The *Guide to Canadian Health Care Facilities* provides information for Canadian health care facilities, CEOs, directors of medicine, hospitals, closed or merged hospitals and health facilities, nursing homes and long-term care facilities, health associations, and hospital equipment and medical suppliers.

Internet Sources

12.47 *AHD.com* Louisville, KY: American Hospital Directory, Inc. Available: www.ahd.com

12.48 *Best Hospitals Finder. U.S. News & World Report.* Washington, DC: U.S. News & World Report. Available: www.usnews.com/usnews/ health/best- hospitals/tophosp.htm

12.49 *MedlinePlus. Find a Hospital.* Bethesda, MD: U.S. National Library of Medicine. Available: apps.nlm.nih.gov/medlineplus/directories/ index.cfm

12.50 *MedlinePlus. Directories. Hospitals and Clinics—Specialized.* Bethesda, MD: U.S. National Library of Medicine. Available: www.nlm.nih.gov/medlineplus/directories.html

12.51 *Quality Check.* Oakbrook Terrace, IL: The Joint Commission. Available: www.qualitycheck.org/consumer/searchQCR.aspx

AHD.com published by the American Hospital Directory provides online data for over 6,000 hospitals. The database about hospitals is built from both public and private sources including Medicare claims data (MedPAR and OPPS), hospital cost reports, and other files obtained from the federal Centers for Medicare and Medicaid Services (CMS). AHD is not affiliated with the American Hospital Association (AHA) and is not a source for AHA Data. Summary hospital data are provided as a public service. More detailed information about hospitals is available to subscribers and reports are downloadable in Excel.

Best Hospitals Finder from *U.S. News & World Report* ranks medical centers in different specialties. Centers are searchable by subject. The site provides the methodology used to identify the "best". The site is searchable by an A–Z or by state/region, metro area, or distance from home.

Using American Hospital Association data, Find a Hospital includes information on over 6,000 hospitals in the United States, including driving directions. The site is searchable by hospital name, zip code, and city. The information from *Find a Hospital* is derived from the annual American Hospital Association (AHA) survey of hospitals and licensed by the National Library of Medicine.

MedlinePlus: Hospitals and Clinics—Specialized from NLM and the National Institutes of Health and other trusted sources provides 23 links to Internet sites to locate general and specialized hospitals and clinics.

Quality Check from the Joint Commission on Accreditation of Healthcare Organizations provides information on nearly 18,000 health care organizations. The site is searchable by organization name, zip code, and state. Each entry includes an online quality report with information on accreditation, accredited programs, plus hospital sites and services.

Meta-Directories, Including Biography and Directories

Many Internet sites compile extensive lists of directories of health-related Web sites. Many of these are from trusted sources such as medical schools, hospital libraries, associations, and governmental agencies. A search of the National Network of Libraries of Medicine Members Directory (http://nnlm.

gov/members/) directs the searcher to medical school libraries, many of which are good sources for meta-directories with a list of references that include links to useful online directories. Examples of meta-directories are:

12.52 *Hardin-MD*. Iowa City, IA: University of Iowa Hardin Library for the Health Sciences. Available: www.lib.uiowa.edu/hardin/md

12.53 *HealthWeb*. Chicago, IL: National Network of Libraries of Medicine Greater Midwest Region. Available: healthweb.org

12.54 *MedWeb*. Atlanta, GA: Emory University. Available: 170.140.250. 52/MedWeb/

12.55 *Reference Resources*. New Haven, CT: Harvey Cushing/John Hay Whitney Medical Library at Yale University School of Medicine. Available: www.med.yale.edu/library

12.56 *InteliHealth*. Blue Bell, PA: Aetna InteliHealth Inc. Available: www. intelihealth.com/IH/ihtIH/WSIHW000/408/408.html

12.57 *Information Resources*. Denver, CO: Tucker Medical Library, National Jewish Medical and Research Center. Available: www.njc. org/research/med-library/index.aspx

12.58 *Medical Directories*. Los Angeles, CA: Louise M. Darling Biomedical Library. Available: www.library.ucla.edu/biomed/refresources/ medicine. html

12.59 *Internet Catalog*. Coral Gables, FL: Louis Calder Memorial Library, University of Miami School of Medicine. Available: calder.med. miami.edu/catalog/

The following meta-directories are examples from the United Kingdom. Each provides extensive categorized lists of sites.

12.60 *Patient UK*. United Kingdom: National Health Service. Available: www.patient.co.uk/

12.61 *Intute: Health and Life Sciences*. Nottingham, UK: University of Nottingham, Greenfield Medical Library. Available: www.intute. ac.uk/healthandlifesciences/medicine/

Images, Photographs and Portraits

The following Web sites present two directories of medical images that include photographs and portraits of important health care professionals.

12.62 *Public Health Image Library.* Atlanta, GA: Department of Health and Human Services. Centers for Disease Control and Prevention. Available: phil.cdc.gov/Phil/home.asp

12.63 *Images from the History of Medicine.* Bethesda, MD: U.S. National Library of Medicine. Available: wwwihm.nlm.nih.gov/cgi-bin/gw_44_3/chameleon?skin=nlm&lng=en

Public Health Image Library from the Centers for Disease Control and Prevention provides an extensive directory of still images, image sets, and multimedia files. The site contains a limited number of photographs of physicians and researchers, particularly those affiliated with the CDC. Photographs include detailed metadata.

Images from the History of Medicine allows access to nearly 60,000 images in the print and photograph collections of NLM's History of Medicine Division. The collection includes portraits, pictures of institutions, caricatures, genre scenes, and graphic art in a variety of media, illustrating the social and historical aspects of medicine. The site is searchable by keywords that includes terms from all fields in the record (author, title, subject, notes, order number, etc.); or specifically selected fields (subject, author, title); or with the browse function that displays specific lists of terms in the database in alphabetical order.

References

1. Boorkman, Jo Anne. "Preface." In *Introduction to reference sources in the health sciences,* compiled and edited by Jo Anne Boorkman, Jeffrey Huber, and Fred Roper. New York: Neal-Schuman, 2004.
2. Dee, Cheryl R., and Ron Blazek. "The information needs of rural physicians: a descriptive study." *Bull Med Lib Assoc* 1993; 81(3):259–264.
3. Dee, Cheryl R, and Ellen E. Stanley. "Information-seeking behavior of nursing students and clinical nurses: implications for health sciences librarians." *J Med Lib Assoc* 2005; 93(2):213–222.

CHAPTER 13

History Sources

Lucretia W. McClure

"The library is the historian's laboratory," and in health sciences libraries, the historian may be a resident, a student, a physician, or an individual interested in a particular topic or person in the fields of medicine or science. Gnudi goes on to say the historian must have the scholarly reference works that form the "working apparatus" of this laboratory [1].

The purpose of this chapter is to provide a sampling of the resources that hold the information necessary to the users seeking historical facts and knowledge. The earlier editions of this book included chapters on history sources by Judith A. Overmier [2]. They continue to be relevant and useful. This chapter will focus on new resources as well as those that may be found in a general collection. Many libraries in the health sciences do not have formal history of medicine departments or collections; yet users come with history-related questions. There are a surprising number of books, journals, materials in electronic format, and so forth, that may be useful in answering questions of a historical nature. Librarians must develop a creative mode of thinking when searching for answers in general works.

The Nature of Questions

Many of the questions fall into these categories: biographical, bibliographical, dates and facts, and illustrations. These are the "Who was it?" "What did he do?" "When did it happen?" "Do you have a picture of it?" questions. The development of the Internet brings a new dimension to the librarian's ability to find historical information. Once it was necessary to have the volumes at hand in order to search. Today, the library can supplement its print resources with an array of digital locations. Because the Internet changes rapidly, only a sample of Web sites will be provided because new URLs appear and disappear daily.

The librarian in a small medical, hospital, or special library now has more opportunity than ever to search for the answers to historical questions. When the search of print resources proves unfruitful, the Web opens doors to the home pages of libraries with spectacular history of medicine collections. These libraries often have librarians with extensive knowledge of the history of medicine who may provide assistance. The history of medicine organizations have Web sites as well as electronic discussion lists and all may be tapped for guidance and help.

Biographical Sources

One of the most frequently asked questions is about the individual physician or scientist. Often the person asking has sketchy information at best. Knowing the dates of birth or death, an institution from which the individual was graduated or taught, or a medical specialty can give the librarian a lead to an obituary or an announcement of an honor. The following are examples of resources of biographical information.

13.1   Bynum WF, Bynum H, eds. *Dictionary of Medical Biography.* Westport, CT: Greenwood Press, 2006. 5 vol.

13.2   Hafner AW, ed. *Directory of Deceased American Physicians, 1804–1929; A Genealogical Guide to over 149,000 Medical Practitioners Providing Brief Biographical Sketches Drawn from the American Medical Association's Deceased Physician Masterfile.* Chicago, IL: American Medical Association, 1993. 2 vol.

13.3   *The New York Times Obituaries Index.* New York: New York Times, 1970–1980. v.1, 1858–1968; v.2, 1969–1978.

13.4   Magill FN, ed. *The Nobel Prize Winners: Physiology or Medicine.* Pasadena, CA: Salem Press, 1991–. v.1, 1901–1944; v.2, 1944–1969; v.3, 1969–1990.

13.5   *JAMA: The Journal of the American Medical Association.* Chicago, IL: American Medical Association, 1919–. v.1–.

13.6   Sammons VO. *Blacks in Science and Medicine.* New York: Hemisphere, 1990.

13.7   Bullough VL, Church OM, Stein AP. *American Nursing; A Biographical Dictionary.* New York: Garland, 1988–1992. 2 vol.

13.8   Scrivener L, et al. *A Biographical Dictionary of Women Healers: Midwives, Nurses, and Physicians*. Westport, CT: Oryx Press, 2002.

13.9   Thacher J. *American Medical Biography*. Boston, MA: Richardson & Lord, 1828. 2 vols. in 1. Reprint: New York: DaCapo, 1967.

13.10 Atkinson WB. *The Physicians and Surgeons of the United States*. Philadelphia, PA: Robson, 1878.

13.11 Kelly HA. *Cyclopedia of American Medical Biography: Comprising the Lives of Eminent Deceased Physicians and Surgeons from 1610–1910*. Philadelphia, PA: W.B. Saunders, 1912. 2 vol.

13.12 Kelly HA, Burrage WL. *American Medical Biographies*. Baltimore, MD: Norman, Remington, 1920.

13.13 Kelly HA, Burrage WL. *Dictionary of American Medical Biography*. New York: Appleton, 1928.

13.14 Kaufman M, Stuart G, Savitt T, eds. *Dictionary of American Medical Biography*. Westport, CT: Greenwood Press, 1984. 2 vols.

13.15 Holloway LM. *Medical Obituaries: American Physicians' Biographical Notices in Selected Medical Journals before 1907*. New York: Garland, 1981.

13.16 Morton LT, Moore RJ. *A Bibliography of Medical and Biomedical Biography*. 3rd ed. Aldershot, Hants, England and Burlington, VT: Ashgate, 2005.

Each of these tools provides information for those seeking biographical material. The *Dictionary of Medical Biography* provides 1,100 biographies of major medical practitioners in all times and cultures. Practitioners of alternative medicine as well as major figures from traditional Chinese, Indian, and Islamic medicine are included. Some 3,000 images as well as bibliographies for further reading on these individuals and their work are also provided. The AMA *Directory of Deceased American Physicians* includes indexes of African-American practitioners, female practitioners, and self-designated eclectic, homeopathic, and osteopathic practitioners. *The New York Times Obituaries Index* provides the date of death and location of an obituary. Finding the death date of an individual is often the key to locating further information (i.e., an obituary, and so forth). Comprehensive information on a laureate's life and career is presented along with description of the speeches and commentary that accompany the awarding of the Nobel Prize in the series on the Nobel Prize winners in physiology or medicine.

One of the most useful sources for information is *The Journal of the American Medical Association (JAMA)*. The journal indexes list names of physicians under the terms Deaths or Obituaries, leading to brief obituaries that provide basic information. Specialty journals often have extensive obituaries of their noted members, and the transactions of many societies write elaborate memoirs of cherished members.

More than 1,500 African-American physicians, scientists, and other professionals are listed in *Blacks in Science and Medicine*. The first biographical dictionary to be published since Kelly and Burrage published the DAMB in 1928 was the work of the same name published in 1984. The work covers the seventeenth through twentieth centuries and in addition to physicians and surgeons, included representative blacks and women, biochemists, medical educators, and hospital administrators. The coverage is through 1976. Bullough's *American Nursing* directory includes biographies of 175 women and two men in nursing who were deceased or born before 1890. The *Dictionary of Women Healers* is another source for information on women in a variety of health professions.

The biographical tools for American physicians of an earlier age begin with Thacher. His work was followed by Atkinson, Kelly, and others. All are of value when searching for biographies and/or portraits of important practitioners. Holloway's work includes brief biographical information as well as sources of obituaries for some 17,350 physicians deceased before 1907. *A Bibliography of Medical and Biomedical Biography* is limited to works published in book form in the English language during the nineteenth and twentieth centuries. It includes those who have made significant contributions to the related biomedical sciences, making it broader than Thornton's *Select Bibliography of Medical Biography*.

13.17   Rosen G, Caspari-Rosen B, collected and arranged. *400 Years of a Doctor's Life*. New York: Schuman, 1947.

13.18   Comroe JH, Jr. *Retrospectroscope: Insights Into Medical Discovery*. Menlo Park, CA: Von Gehr Press, 1977.

Popular biographies or sources such as Rosen's *400 Years* portray physicians through short sketches or personal experiences. Other titles such as Comroe's *Retrospectroscope* offer background information concerning various discoveries, thus shining light on the scientist or physician seeking answers.

Good biographical information may be found in alumni directories, local newspapers, and historical society publications. Major textbooks often have biographical information concerning those who developed a treatment or device or who made significant breakthroughs in medicine or science. The standard medical, nursing, and dental directories are also useful in finding basic information about individuals. Databases such as MEDLINE as well as the print *Index Medicus* for earlier years are good sources for obituaries of well-known individuals in science and medicine. The *Journal of Medical Biography*, started in 1993 by the Royal Society of Medicine in London, has biographies of both patients and physicians.

Biographical Web Sites

With the advent of the Internet, a whole realm of resources has been developed. Never before has so much information been available at the touch of a keyboard. The caveat is, of course, to be certain of the creator of the information and to view all sites with a healthy skepticism. Among the useful sites are the following:

13.19 *Biography and Genealogy Master Index.* Farmington Hills, MI: Gale Group. Available: http://galenet.gale.com/a/acp/db/bgmi

13.20 *Whonamedit.com.* Oslo: Whonamedit.com. Available: www. Whonamedit.com

13.21 *Profiles in Science.* Bethesda, MD: U.S. National Library of Medicine. Available: www.profiles.nlm.nih.gov

13.22 *The Social Security Death Index.* Provo, UT: MyFamily.com, Inc. Available: http://ssdi.genealogy.rootsweb.com

13.23 *American National Biography Online.* New York: Oxford University Press, 2000. Available: www.anb.org

13.24 Bois Danuta. *Distinguished Women of Past and Present.* Available: www.distinguishedwomen.com/

13.25 *Women Physicians' Autobiographies.* Available: http://research. med.umkc.edu/teams/cml/WomenDrs.html

The Web tools listed above offer a great variety of coverage. The Gale resource lists persons from all time periods, geographical locations, and fields of endeavor. The Whonamedit source lists eponyms from A to Z, includes biographies by country, lists female entries, traces the eponym to the article by the named author, and identifies the source of an obituary.

The National Library of Medicine is producing the Profiles in Science database, listing prominent twentieth-century biomedical scientists. The listing may be reviewed chronologically or alphabetically and many have pictures and papers. The Death Index lists more than 70 million names, including dates of birth and death, social security number, last known residence, and date of last benefit. The American National Biography includes some 18,000 men and women who have influenced and shaped American history and culture.

Two Web sites that provide biographies of women in science and medicine are the Distinguished Women of Past and Present that includes women from fourth through the twentieth centuries and Women Physicians' Autobiographies that grew out of a project begun by Dr. Marjorie S. Sirridge including medical school graduates 1849–1920.

There are many such sources on the Internet today, and it is likely that many more will become available. A search may start with putting an individual's name on a search engine to bring forth an array of sites. Comparing the information with one of the standard biographical tools is one way to ensure that the information is accurate.

Portraits and Illustrations

While many of the biographical sources include portraits of the individuals, there is need for resources that point to the printed source or institutional location of portraits of widely known scientists, physicians, nurses, or others in the health field. Several works that include anatomical illustrations are also listed.

13.26 *Portrait Catalog of the Library of the New York Academy of Medicine.* Boston: G. K. Hall, 1960. 5 vol. Suppl. 1, 1959–1965; Suppl. 2, 1966–1970; Suppl. 3, 1971–1975.

13.27 Berkowitz JS. *The College of Physicians of Philadelphia Portrait Catalogue.* Philadelphia, PA: The College, 1984.

13.28 Burgess R. *Portraits of Doctors and Scientists in the Wellcome Institute of the History of Medicine. A Catalogue.* London: Wellcome Institute for the History of Medicine, 1973.

13.29 Roberts KB, Tomlinson JDW. *The Fabric of the Body: European Traditions of Anatomical Illustrations.* Oxford, UK and New York: Clarendon Press, 1992.

13.30 Porter R. *The Cambridge Illustrated History of Medicine*. Cambridge, UK: Cambridge University Press, 1996.

13.31 Netter FH. *The Ciba Collection of Medical Illustrations, A Compilation of Pathological and Anatomical Paintings*. Summit, NJ: Ciba Pharmaceutical Products, 1959–1993.

13.32 Sournia JC. *The Illustrated History of Medicine*. London: Harold Starke, 1992.

13.33 Naythons, M. *The Face of Mercy. Photographic History of Medicine at War*. New York: Random House, 1993.

The New York Academy of Medicine Library's catalog is the most comprehensive source for portraits. Included are the library's holdings of more than 14,000 original portraits, paintings, woodcuts, engravings, and photographs. In addition, it provides nearly 300,000 citations to portraits in journals and books, both primary and secondary sources. The College of Physicians and the Wellcome catalogs are examples of sources for portraits or paintings from these institutions.

Illustrations of a medical nature are often requested by historians, scholars, writers, and students. *The Fabric of the Body* is an anthology of anatomical illustrations from the medieval period to the present day. It includes text about the anatomists, their collaborators, and their books. It is also about the context in which anatomical illustrations were prepared and distributed. The work features some of the most beautiful and renowned anatomical illustrations. Porter's work uses illustrations to further describe the sections on disease, hospitals and surgery, medical science, and so forth. The *Ciba Collection* includes eight volumes, some with many parts, illustrating various parts of the body such as nervous system, respiratory system, reproductive system, and so forth. The English translation of Sournia's *Illustrated History of Medicine* as well as the French original have excellent illustrations. *The Face of Mercy* depicts medicine at war images on the Web. The Internet offers a wide range of sites with images and portraits. One has only to enter the words "medical illustrations" in a search engine to find dozens of possibilities. The National Library of Medicine has two important offerings.

13.34 *Images from the History of Medicine (IHM)*. Bethesda, MD: U.S. National Library of Medicine. Available: www.nlm.nih.gov/hmd/36

13.35 *The Visible Human Project*. Bethesda, MD: U.S. National Library of Medicine. Available: www.nlm.nih.gov/research/visible/visible_human.html

13.36 *Online Portrait Gallery of the Moody Medical Library, University of Texas Medical Branch at Galveston*. Galveston, TX: University of Texas. Available: www.utmb.edu

13.37 Wellcome Trust. *History of Medicine*. London: Wellcome Trust. Available: www.wellcome.ac.uk

13.38 *The Whole Brain Atlas*. Cambridge, MA: Harvard School of Medicine. Available: www.med.harvard.edu:80/AANLIB/home.htm

13.39 *Index of Medieval Medical Images With Illustrations (IMMI)*. Available: www.library.ucla.edu/biomed/his/immi/index.html

13.40 *Anatomia 1522–1867*. Available: http://link.library.utoronto.ca/anatomia/application/index.cfm

13.41 *Historical Anatomies on the Web*. Available: www.nlm.nih.gov/exhibition/historicalanatomies/browse.html

13.42 Wellcome Trust. *Medical Photographic Library*. Available: http://medphoto.wellcome.ac.uk/ixbin/hixclient.exe?_IXDB_=wellcome&_IXSE

13.43 *Images.MD*. Available: www.images.md/users/index.asp?flag

13.44 *Public Health Image Library (PHIL)*. Available: http://phil.cdc.gov/phil/

The National Library of Medicine's database has nearly 60,000 images from the Library's historical and photographs collection. It includes portraits, photographs, fine prints, caricatures, genre scenes, posters, and other graphic art illustrating the social and historical aspects of medicine from the Middle Ages to the present. The Visible Human Project is the creation of complete, anatomically detailed, three-dimensional representations of the normal male and female bodies.

Many libraries have mounted portraits and images from their collections on the Web. Two examples are the thirty-nine portraits from the 6,000 images relating to the history of the biomedical sciences in the Moody Medical Library and the Wellcome Trust's site that includes a medical photographic library with exquisite images from the library's collections.

The Whole Brain Atlas produced by Keith A. Johnson and J. Alex Becker is a source providing central nervous system imaging that integrates clinical information with magnetic resonance, computed tomography, and nuclear medicine images.

Many libraries are digitizing interesting and rare images from their collections. A variety of examples include the following. The *IMMI* comprises 509 images from thirteen medieval manuscripts up to the year 1500 owned by six institutions in this country. The 4500 full-page plates in the *Anatomia* were taken from the Thomas Fisher Rare Book Library at the University of Toronto. The illustrations, taken from 95 titles, are fully cataloged. The National Library of Medicine's Historical Anatomies on the Web includes images from some 35 anatomical atlases in NLM's collections. The Wellcome Trust's Medical Photographic Library has more than 160,000 historical and contemporary images. More than 50,000 images from ninety collections and 2,000 contributors are offered through Images.MD. The Centers for Disease Control and Prevention provides a wide range of photographs, illustrations, and multimedia files on topics of interest in all areas of public health.

Medical Instruments

Libraries receive many requests to identify medical instruments as well as to provide illustrations of scalpels, obstetric tools such as forceps, artificial hearts, and so forth.

13.45 Edmonson JM. *American Surgical Instruments: The History of Their Manufacture and a Directory of Instrument Makers to 1900.* San Francisco, CA: Norman Publishing, 1997.

13.46 Shultz SM. *Sources for Identification of Antique Medical Instruments in Print and on the Internet.* York, PA: WellSpan Health. Available: www.priory.com/homol/ant.htm

13.47 Truax CH. *The Mechanics of Surgery: Comprising Detailed Descriptions, Illustrations, and Lists of the Instruments, Appliances, and Furniture Necessary in Modern Surgical Art.* Chicago: Hammond Press, 1899.

13.48 Kirkup J. *The Evolution of Surgical Instruments; An Illustrated History from Ancient Times to the Twentieth Century.* Novato, CA: Historyofscience.com, 2006.

Edmondson's work is a comprehensive directory of surgical instrument makers in the United States prior to 1900 with some 280 illustrations. The Web site includes a bibliography of books and articles on antique instruments, Internet sites, catalogs, and dealers. Truax provides a wealth of descriptions of instruments prior to the twentieth century. The Kirkup book begins with ancient times and includes the nineteenth century.

Readers should be cautioned to note the copyright restrictions for use of images from both print and Web sources.

Discoveries/Chronologies

Questions concerning medical discoveries and happenings are among the most frequent. These questions take the form of who made a scientific discovery, when did an event take place, and were there controversies. The following tools provide answers.

13.49 Morton LT, Moore RJ. *A Chronology of Medicine and Related Sciences.* Aldershot, Hants, England: Scolar Press, 1997.

13.50 Friedman M, Friedland GW. *Medicine's 10 Greatest Discoveries.* New Haven, CT: Yale University Press, 1998.

13.51 Schmidt JE. *Medical Discoveries: Who and When; A Dictionary Listing Thousands of Medical and Related Scientific Discoveries in Alphabetical Order.* Springfield, IL: Charles C Thomas, 1959.

13.52 Simmons JG. *Doctors and Discoveries.* Boston: Houghton Mifflin, 2002.

Morton's work begins with 3000 BC and runs through 1996. Only 236 pages brings one to 1850; from 1851 to 1996 requires 430 pages. The Friedman work is a more detailed review of major discoveries whereas Schmidt's work is an easy to use dictionary with brief statements. The Simmons book provides brief biographies that focus on the discoveries of the individuals that have helped to shape medicine as we know it today.

There are dozens of Internet sites devoted to medical discoveries, both general and by specialty. The following example is from the National Institutes of Health:

13.53 *NIH Chronology of Events.* Bethesda, MD: National Institutes of Health. Available: www.nih.gov/about/almanac/historical/chronology_of_ events.htm

Bibliographies/Library Catalogs

The advent of the Internet and the ease and speed of citation retrieval has changed the way individuals search for information. While the MEDLINE database is a boon to searchers for literature from 1957 onward, historians and scholars as well as students need resources that cover the literature of earlier centuries. Medicine has an array of resources that serve users well.

13.54 *Index-Catalogue of the Library of the Surgeon-General's Office.* Washington, DC: Government Printing Office, 1880. 61 volumes in 5 series: 1880–1895; 1896–1916; 1913–1932; 1936–1955; 1959–1961. *IndexCat.* Available: http://indexcat.nlm.nih.gov

13.55 *Current Work in the History of Medicine.* London: Wellcome Institute for the History of Medicine, 1954–1999. Available: http://library.wellcome.ac.uk

13.56 Norman J, ed. *Morton's Medical Bibliography: An Annotated Check-List of Texts Illustrating the History of Medicine (Garrison and Morton).* 5th ed. Aldershot, Hants, England: Gower, 1991.

13.57 Hoolihan C, compiled and annotated. *An Annotated Catalogue of the Edward C. Atwater Collection of American Popular Medicine and Health Reform.* Rochester, NY: University of Rochester Press, 2001–.

13.58 Washington University (Saint Louis, MO) School of Medicine Library. *Catalog of the Bernard Becker, M.D. Collection in Ophthalmology.* 2nd ed. St. Louis, MO: Washington University School of Medicine Library, 1983.

13.59 Wygant LJ, compiled. *The Truman G. Blocker, Jr., History of Medicine Collections: Books and Manuscripts.* Galveston, TX: University of Texas Medical Branch, 1986.

13.60 *A Catalogue of Printed Books in the Wellcome Historical Medical Library.* New York: Martino Publishers, 1995–.

The publications of the National Library of Medicine, the largest medical library in the world, are the most comprehensive for users working in the history of medicine. The *Index-Catalogue* is the monumental work established by John Shaw Billings in 1880 that includes the holdings of the Surgeon-General's Library, now the National Library of Medicine. The dates of the volumes do not reflect the dates of the items; the first three series cover the books, articles, pamphlets, and dissertations from 1500 through the 1926. The project to digitize the *Index-Catalogue* was completed in 2004. Researchers will rejoice to have access to *IndexCat*, a catalog of more than 4.5 million references from 3.7 million bibliographic items. Included are journal articles, books, pamphlets, reports, dissertations, and portraits, dating from antiquity through 1950.

The *Index Medicus*, the index to the most important and most used journals in medicine, is also useful in the search for articles of an earlier time. Published under various titles, this print source includes obituaries. A complete description of *Index Medicus* will be found in Chapter 4. It should be noted here that MEDLINE does include the citations formerly in the Histline database. The print version of Histline, the *Bibliography of the History of Medicine*, was published by NLM from 1964 to 1993.

Current Work in the History of Medicine is an index to periodical articles on the history of medicine and includes a list of books received in the Wellcome Library. The Wellcome Library now publishes *Current Work in the History of Medicine* as the Wellcome Bibliography for the History of Medicine on its Web site.

In addition to the bibliographies cited above, there is a definitive bibliography now in its fifth edition. *Morton's Medical Bibliography* is a heavily used resource listing nearly 9,000 publications, classed by subject, that were of significance in the development of Western medicine. Translations and reprint editions are noted. The first four editions were produced by Leslie T. Morton, beginning in 1943. He based the work on a list of milestones in the development of medicine compiled by Fielding H. Garrison in the *Index-Catalogue*, volume 17:89–178, 1912. Morton undertook the task of expanding and updating the list after Garrison's death, hence the designation Garrison and Morton.

Many libraries have published catalogs of collections on special topics that can be of great help to historians and others searching for works on one subject. The Atwater collection on popular medicine and the Becker collection on ophthalmology are good examples of topical bibliographies. The Wellcome and the Blocker catalogs reflect the holdings of the libraries.

Histories

Histories of medicine provide a wide range of information. Some are general, covering the entire realm, others focus on an aspect or specific time period. Following are examples of a variety of histories.

13.61 Kiple KF, ed. *The Cambridge World History of Human Disease.* Cambridge, UK and New York: Cambridge University Press, 1993.

13.62 Bynum WF, Porter R, eds. *Companion Encyclopedia of the History of Medicine.* New York: Routledge, 1993. 2 vol.

13.63 Kohn GC. *Encyclopedia of Plague and Pestilence.* New York: Facts on File, 1995.

13.64 Major RH. *History of Medicine.* Springfield, IL: Charles C Thomas, 1954. 2 vol.

13.65 Sigerist HE. *A History of Medicine.* New York: Oxford University Press, 1951–61. 2 vol.

13.66 Castiflioni A, Krumbhaar EB, trans. *A History of Medicine.* 2nd ed., rev. and enl. New York: Alfred A. Knopf, 1958.

13.67 Garrison FH, ed. *An Introduction to the History of Medicine, With Medical Chronology, Suggestions for Study, and Bibliographic Data.* 4th ed., reprinted. Philadelphia, PA: W.B. Saunders, 1966.

13.68 Duffin J. *History of Medicine; A Scandalously Short Introduction.* Toronto: University of Toronto Press, 1999.

Histories abound in the fields of medicine and science. The Cambridge volume includes essays on distribution of diseases, medical traditions, various organs, and organ systems as well as a section on "Major Human Diseases Past and Present" arranged alphabetically by disease. The *Companion Encyclopedia* is a two-volume work arranged by topics whereas the *Encyclopedia of Plague and Pestilence* outlines and provides a timeline for specific epidemics.

Many older volumes of history continue to be of use. While they vary in style and organization, all serve as a starting point for those interested to learn from and about the past. The titles by Major, Sigerist, and Castiglioni have served generations of readers. The Garrison history includes a medical chronology and suggestions for study; a great book for anyone who wishes to use such a resource as a study guide with answers. Duffin's history was written in response to her medical students' request for an introductory text in the history of medicine. Her purpose is to raise awareness of history in order to understand the present and to instill a sense of skepticism with regard to the "dogma" of the medical curriculum.

History of Medicine Journals

Many journals contain historical articles along with their general topics. There are also journals devoted to the history of medicine. A number of the titles are now online.

13.69 *Bulletin of the History of Medicine.* Baltimore, MD: Johns Hopkins University Press; American Association for the History of Medicine, 1939–. 7–. Available: www.press.jhu.edu/journals/bulletin_of_the_history_of_medicine/

13.70 *Gesnerus.* Basel: Schwabe; Swiss Society of the History of Medicine, 1943–. 1–. Not online.

13.71 *Isis.* Chicago, IL: University of Chicago Press for the History of Science Society, 1913–. 1–. Available: www.journals.uchicago.edu/Isis/home.html

13.72 *Journal of the History of Medicine and Allied Sciences.* London: Oxford University Press, 1946–. 1–. Available:http://jhmas.oxford journals.org/

13.73 *Medical History.* London: Wellcome Trust Centre for the History of Medicine, 1957–. 1–. Available: http://pubmedcentral.gov/

13.74 *Canadian Bulletin of Medical History.* Wilfrid Laurier University Press, 1984–. 1–. Available: www.cbmh.ca

13.75 *Social History of Medicine.* London: Oxford University Press, 1970–. 1–. Available: http://shm.oxfordjournals.org/

History of medicine journals provide the works of today's medical and scientific historians. All of the journals cited contain articles and book reviews. The *Journal of the History of Medicine and Allied Sciences* also carries a list of recent dissertations in the history of medicine. The titles cover the social, cultural, and scientific aspects of medical history as well as the other disciplines that impinge on it. Readers should note that many of the titles are available online through various vendors. Dates of availability vary widely.

Tools for the Librarian

With libraries and Google digitizing books, journals, and other resources, a new range of full-text titles is available on the Internet. The Google scanning project with a number of university libraries, including Harvard, Oxford, Stanford, Princeton, and the universities of California, Michigan, Wisconsin, and the New York Public, will provide millions of titles in the public domain.

This rich resource will be a boon to historians, scholars, and students around the world. As libraries plan digitizing projects, the following will be of great use to those involved in the planning and digitizing.

13.76 Mugridge R. *Managing Digitization Activities.* Washington, DC: Association of Research Libraries, 2006.

13.77 Koelling JM. *Digital Imaging: A Practical Approach.* Walnut Creek, CA: AltaMira Press, 2004.

13.78 *Building and Sustaining Digital Collections: Models for Libraries and Museums.* Washington, DC: Council on Library and Information Resources, 2001.

13.79 Sitts MK, ed. *Handbook for Digital Projects: A Management Tool for Preservation and Access.* Andover, MA: Northeast Document Conservation Center, 2000.

Librarians must deal with questions concerning the book as a physical object as well as the content it contains. Many questions arise about the cost of books and other publications as well as how to care for books, determination of quality over time, and how to become a collector. Librarians must know and understand the structure of bibliography and be prepared to answer questions concerning collations, watermarks, signatures, and so forth. Medical publishing and medical literature are topics of great interest to historians and scholars, and the library will find the following array of sources to be a good basis for collecting in this area.

13.80 *American Book Prices Current.* Washington, CT: Bancroft-Parkman, 1894/95–. Vol. 1–. 110. CD-ROM 1975–2005.

13.81 *Bookman's Price Index.* Detroit, MI: Gale, 1964–. Vol. 1–.

13.82 Carter J. *ABC for Book Collectors.* 8th ed. New Castle, DE and Oak Knoll Press, London: British Library, 2004.

13.83 McKerrow RB. *An Introduction to Bibliography for Literary Students.* Winchester, St. Paul's Bibliographies and New Castle, DE: Oak Knoll Press, 1994.

13.84 Thornton JL. *Thornton's Medical Books, Libraries, and Collectors; A Study of Bibliography and the Book Trade in Relation to the Medical Sciences.* 3rd rev. ed. Aldershot, Hants, UK: Gower, 1990.

13.85 Blake JB, Roos C. *Medical Reference Works, 1679–1966, A Selected Bibliography.* Chicago, IL: Medical Library Association, 1967. Three supplements: 1970–1975.

Library users as well as librarians are interested in the prices of book they wish either to purchase or donate. The *American Book Prices Current* and

Bookman's Price Index are useful for this purpose as are recent catalogs from rare-book dealers. The world of the "book," its production, description, format, and terminology are identified in Carter's *ABC for Book Collectors* and in McKerrow's classic work on bibliography. The development of medical literature and the book trade are examined in Besson's revision of Thornton's *Medical Books*. Blake and Roos provide the standard list of medical reference works dating from 1679 through 1975.

13.86 Brooks C, Darling PW. *Disaster Preparedness.* Washington, DC: Association of Research Libraries, 1993.

13.87 Kahn, M. *First Steps for Handling & Drying Water-Damaged Materials.* Columbus, OH: MBK Consulting, 1994.

13.88 Waters P. *Procedures for Salvage of Water-Damaged Library Materials.* 2nd ed. Washington, DC: Library of Congress, 1979.

13.89 Harvey DR. *Preservation in Libraries: Principles, Strategies, and Practices for Librarians.* London and New York: Bowker-Saur, 1993.

13.90 Horton C. *Cleaning and Preserving Bindings and Related Materials.* 2nd ed., rev. Chicago, IL: Library Technology Program, American Library Association, 1969.

13.91 Harvey, DR. *Preserving Digital Materials.* Munich, Germany: Saur, 2005.

13.92 Schweidler, M. *The Restoration of Engravings, Drawings, Books, and Other Works on Paper.* Translated, edited, and with an appendix by Roy Perkinson. Los Angeles: Getty Conservation Institute, 2006.

13.93 Adcock, EP., compiled and ed. *IFLA Principles for the Care and Handling of Library Materials.* Washington, DC: International Federation of Library Associations and Institutions, Core Programme on Preservation and Conservation, 1998.

13.94 *Field Guide to Emergency Response.* Washington, DC: Heritage Preservation, 2006.

13.95 Halsted DD, Jasper RP, Little FM. *Disaster Planning: A How-To-Do-It Manual for Librarians with Planning Templates on CD-ROM.* New York: Neal-Schuman, 2005.

13.96 *Preservation of Library & Archival Materials: A Manual.* 3rd ed., rev. and expanded. Andover, MA: Northeast Document Conservation Center, 1999. Available: www.nedcc.org/home.php

Acquiring is only the first step in collection management. The volumes held in both special and general collections must be housed, handled, and, when necessary, repaired or restored. Preservation is an essential part of the library's responsibility for its collections. The books on disaster preparedness, water damage, and preservation are full of information to help librarians deal with the protection of their collections. The Northeast Document Conservation Center has produced a Web site that includes leaflets on specific topics that are freely available to all.

Rare book librarianship has many facets because of the great variety of formats collected in history of medicine libraries. Users of the collections are also varied as individuals interested in history and historical research range from students to scholars, laymen to health professionals, historians of medicine to those in different disciplines.

Good overviews of the kinds of work expected from rare book/history librarians as well as the wide range of resources needed can be found in the series of handbooks published by the Medical Library Association. The titles given in the "Readings" section below will acquaint librarians with background and guidelines.

The electronic world in which we work with and for the users in our libraries offers endless resources undreamed of by our predecessors. With the click of a mouse the librarian can retrieve medical and health-related books and journals that range from antiquity to the present. Susan E. Lederer writes that the craft of the historian (and I would add of the librarian) "has many parallels with the craft of the diagnostician. History, like diagnostics, is an interpretive activity in which one attempts to construct an intelligible narrative, based on elements from diverse possible choices." She goes on to say that historical narrative, like the physician's diagnosis is always subject to change. Just as an expert diagnostician incorporates cues from the patient's words, affect, and clothes, the historian "uses texts, films, literature, and the visual arts to elucidate and describe the past [3].

References

1. Gnudi MT. Building a medical history collection. *Bull Med Libr Assoc* 1975; 63(1):42–46.
2. Overmier JA. History sources. In: Roper FW, Boorkman JA, eds. *Introduction to reference sources in the health sciences.* 3rd ed. Metuchen, NJ: Scarecrow Press, 1994:257–270.
3. Lederer, SE. Medical history in the undergraduate medical curriculum. *Acad Med* 1995; 70(9):771.

Readings

1. Annan GL. Rare books and the history of medicine. In: Doe J, ed. *A handbook of medical library practice*. Chicago, IL: American Library Association, 1943:256–370.
2. Cavanagh GST. Rare books, archives, and the history of medicine. In: Annan GL, Felter JW, eds. *Handbook of medical library practice*. 3rd ed. Chicago, IL: Medical Library Association, 1970:254–283.
3. Zinn NW. Special collections: history of health science collections, oral history, archives, and manuscripts. In: Darling L, ed. *Handbook of medical library practice*. 4th ed. Chicago, IL: Medical Library Association, 1988:469–572.

CHAPTER 14

Grant Sources

Jo Anne Boorkman and Tom Flemming

Health professionals and institutions must increasingly seek grants to meet their funding needs. This funding can range from support for a research project or a travel grant to "bricks and mortar" funding for a major construction project or seed money to start a new program. The health sciences librarian can play an important role in this endeavor. In order to offer effective service, the librarian must be familiar with the complex structure of the grant-making world, along with the equally complex array of information sources in this area.

The sources available on grantmaking organizations vary in terms of funding sectors included, comprehensiveness, level of specificity, format, disciplines covered, and the frequency with which they are updated. The grant seeker's primary goal is to locate appropriate funding agencies likely to be interested in a specific project. This task will involve surveying federal programs in the relevant field and if advisable, examining the foundation and corporate arenas through a geographic or subject approach to identify likely contributors. The grant seeker will need to determine how closely the proposed project matches a foundation's or agency's interests and funding patterns.

Three types of publications will be useful in this process, regardless of which sector the applicant ends up approaching: grantsmanship guides, directories, and indexes. This chapter will concentrate on directories that include sources of both government and private funding.

Multisector Directories

14.1 *Annual Register of Grant Support.* New Medford, NJ: Information Today, 1969–. Annual. Continues: *Grant Data Quarterly.* Los Angeles, CA: Academic Media, 1967–68. Available: www.infotoday.com

Now in its 40th edition (2006), this multidisciplinary directory covers more than 3,500 support programs and fellowships of government agencies, public and private foundations, corporations, community trusts, unions, educational and professional associations, and special interest organizations. While not comprehensive, this directory contains entries for various special interest organizations, such as the American Diabetes Association, that are not found in some of the other major sources. It provides a good place to start. The directory has a classified arrangement organized by 11 major subject areas with 61 subcategories and four indexes: subject, organization and program, geographic, and personnel. The introduction discusses types of grant-supporting organizations, and there is a chapter on program planning and proposal writing. The "Life Sciences" chapter includes medicine and other health sciences specialties.

14.2   *Directory of Biomedical and Health Care Grants.* Phoenix, AZ: Oryx Press, 1985–. Annual.

The *Directory of Biomedical and Health Care Grants* lists slightly more than 2,700 funding programs in the areas of ''human health and biomedicine''. Now in its 20th edition (2006), the *Directory* includes:

> (1) the sponsor's update of previously published program statements included in prior editions of GRANTS publications; (2) questionnaires sent to sponsors whose programs were not included in previous editions; (3) other materials published by the sponsor and furnished by Oryx; or the sponsor's Web site. Updated information for U.S. government programs includes new and revised program information published in the latest edition of the *Catalog of Federal Domestic Assistance*; *the GIS Local/State Funding Report* ... the *Federal Register*; the *NIH Guide* ... and the *NSF E-Bulletin*. (Introduction).

Web addresses are listed for sponsoring organizations when available. Citations feature grant title requirements, sample awards, contact information and sponsor information. Four indexes provide access by subject, sponsoring organization, grants by program type (e.g., curriculum development/teacher training, faculty/professional development, seed grants, and so forth) and geographic. An informative introductory piece, "A Guide to Proposal Planning and Writing," by Jeremy Miner and Lynn Miner is included. It is also available on the Web at: www.wm.edu/grants/PROP/miner.pdf. The *Directory* is available through the GRANTS database online by subscription.

Federal Funding Sources

One caveat for grant seekers is that sources of federal funding should be explored before turning to foundations. This sequence is necessary because foundations tend to avoid duplicating federal programs and because the federal government still plays a major role in the total funding picture, in spite of well-publicized federal spending cutbacks.

The grant seeker will find some significant differences between the application process for private and federal funds. Federal agencies usually have standardized application forms, whereas foundations tend to provide the grant writer with only general application guidelines allowing more flexibility in the proposal. Furthermore, as a matter of public policy, all federal grant opportunities are announced in advance, while printed material about foundation and corporate giving may be scarce—especially for small grant-making organizations.

Because two major, comprehensive government publications on federal support exist, reference service in this area of funding could be viewed as a deceptively simple enterprise: For contract opportunities, one would consult the *Commerce Business Daily (CBD)*, which is now available on the Web as CBDNet (cbdnet.access.gpo.gov/) and for grants, the hefty *Catalog of Federal Domestic Assistance (CFDA)*, which is also available on the Web (www.cfda. gov). However, this approach discounts the fact that government programs are in a constant state of flux with changing funding levels, program status, and application procedures prevailing. Furthermore, a variety of materials published by individual federal grant-making agencies supplement program information in the *CFDA*. Then, too, the commercially-produced sources on government funding should be consulted. Some of these publications are informative and help the grant seeker cope with the changing federal scene; others simply duplicate government publications being sold at inflated prices.

Effective information service in the federal funding arena begins with a basic knowledge of the agency supporting biomedical projects. The Health Service supports the bulk of biomedical investigations. There are a number of major grant-making agencies within the Office of Public Health and Science, United States Department of Health and Human Services (www.hhs.gov/grants/index.shtml). These include:

- Administration for Children and Families (ACF)
- Administration on Aging (AOA)
- Agency for Healthcare Research and Quality (AHRQ)

- Agency for Toxic Substances and Disease Registry (ATSDR)
- Centers for Disease Control and Prevention (CDC)
- Centers for Medicare & Medicaid Services (CMS)
- Food and Drug Administration (FDA)
- Health Resources and Services Administration (HRSA)
- Indian Health Service (IHS)
- National Institutes of Health (NIH)
- Office of the Secretary (OS) Divisions
  - Assistant Secretary for Planning and Evaluation (ASPE)
  - Center for Faith-Based and Community Initiatives (CFBCI)
  - Office of Public Health and Sciences (OPHS)
    - Office of Minority Health Resource Center (OMHRC)
    - Office of Population Affairs (OPA)
- Substance Abuse and Mental Health Services Administration (SAMHSA)

With the mission to improve human health through research, the National Institutes of Health programs provide a broad array of opportunities for funding research oriented toward basic and applied scientific inquiry related to the cause, diagnosis, prevention, treatment, and rehabilitation of human diseases and disabilities; the fundamental biological processes of growth, development, and aging; and the biological effects of the environment. In addition, the National Science Foundation and the Environmental Protection Agency both administer funding programs of potential interest to the health sciences professional.

14.3　*NIH Guide for Grants and Contracts.* Available: grants2.nih.gov/ grants/guide/index.html

14.4　*Computer Retrieval of Information on Scientific Projects (CRISP).* 1972–. Available: crisp.cit.nih.gov/

Now available on the Web, *NIH Guide for Grants and Contracts* is the primary source for NIH awards. It contains relevant NIH policy information as well as new program announcements. It is easily searchable using keywords or phrases by active funding opportunities, recent notices or both. Advanced searching is also available. Requests for Active funding opportunities may be browsed for Requests for Applications (RFAs), Program Announcements (PAs) and Parent Announcements (unsolicited applications). Recent Policies and Guidelines from the most recent 12 months are also browsable. Historical

NIH Guide Publications 1970–1992 are available as PDFs. William Gerin has recently written a helpful publication, *Writing the NIH Grant Proposal: A Step-by-Step Guide* that can assist a first-time grant writer to navigate the process [1].

The CRISP database provides information on grants and contracts awarded by the National Institutes of Health (NIH), the Office of Substance Abuse and Mental Health Services (SAMHSA), Health Resources and Services Administration (SRSA), Food and Drug Administration (FDA), Centers for Disease Control and Prevention (CDC), Agency for Health Care Research and Quality (AHRQ), and Office of Assistant Secretary of Health (OASH). It provides another means for determining which agency to approach with a proposal. Basic and advanced searching is possible and instructions are provided for searching by key words or fields. The database is updated weekly. This information was formerly published in *Biomedical Index to PHS-supported Research* (National Institutes of Health, Divisions of Research. Washington, DC, U.S. Government Printing Office, 1988–. Annual. Formerly: National Institutes of Health. *Research Awards Index*. Washington, DC, U.S. Government Printing Office, 1976–1987.

Foundation Funding

A private foundation is a nongovernmental, nonprofit organization with funds usually coming from a single source such as an individual family or corporation. These funds are managed by the foundation's directors or trustees to "maintain or aid educational, social, charitable, religious, or other activities serving the common welfare primarily by making grants to other nonprofit organizations" [2]. In the United States, there are approximately 22,500 private foundations falling into four basic categories: independent, company-sponsored, operating, and community. Briefly, independent foundations award grants from an endowment established by a single donor or family, and giving may or may not be restricted by geographic or subject area.

Company-sponsored foundations manage funds provided by a profit-making corporation and are inclined to make awards in the neighboring communities of the sponsoring company. An operating foundation usually makes few external grants; instead it uses endowment funds to conduct its own research or social welfare programs. As the name implies, community foundations are publicly supported and make grants to charitable organization in the local community.

Unlike the federal government, which generates a constant stream of funding announcements, foundations do not usually issue lists of grants to be awarded in the upcoming months. In fact, depending on the size of the foundation, it may be difficult to locate any specifics at all about an organization's giving priorities.

Tracking down appropriate foundations is not a trivial exercise. No matter what the requirements of a particular proposal, the Foundation Center publications are the most highly-recommended resources in the area of grantsmanship. Located in New York City, the Foundation Center's mission is to collect information on private foundations and distribute this information through its publications and library collections. For reference purposes, the librarian should be aware of this organization's nationwide network of reference libraries where extensive grant information collections are maintained and open to public use. A list of these cooperating collections may be found in any of the Foundation Center reference tools.

14.5   *Foundation Directory.* New York, The Foundation Center, 1960–. Annual. Available: www.fdncenter.org

The *Foundation Directory* is one of many publications from the Foundation Center. The 29th edition (2006) lists the 10,000 largest grant-making foundations of nonprofit, nongovernmental organizations that have private financial backing that ranges from $1 million to $10 million in assets (Introduction). A second volume is also available with the 10,000 next largest grant-making foundations. This edition provides information on over 39,000 grants. This directory is especially useful for individuals seeking funds for research and education. Entries are arranged by state and include the address, date of establishment, donors, trustees, and purpose of the foundation, as well as its fields of interest and financial assets. Also included is grant application information. Indexes provide access by:

1. Names of persons associated with the foundations, such as donors, trustees, and administrators.
2. Geographic location.
3. Types of support, e.g., annual campaigns, building funds, conferences and seminars.
4. Subject.
5. Foundations new to the edition.
6. Foundation names.

The Foundation Directory Online is searchable on a fee-based service with varying subscription levels available. The entire database, representing over 70,000 grant-makers with over 200,000 grants, can be searched in its entirety by subject, foundation name or grant type. More focused searching of the 20,000 or 10,000 largest foundations is also available. The database is updated bi-weekly and has links to free Web resources.

Corporate Funding

In addition to the independent company-sponsored foundations, corporations also distribute funds through direct giving programs. Since 1935, the Internal Revenue Service has allowed a charitable deduction for corporate contributions up to 5 percent of net income. Due to the nature of direct corporate giving and the lack of published reference resources in this area, fundraising from the business sector depends heavily on personal contact.

Given the idiosyncratic nature of corporate philanthropy and the scarcity of published information about corporate giving policies, fundraising from the business sector is at least as challenging as tracking the small foundation grant. It is common knowledge that most corporations do not employ professionals to systematically operate the company giving program, nor do they have well-defined philanthropic objectives or procedures for grant applications. Companies offer various reasons for this lack of definition in corporate grant programs, ranging from a reluctance to violate corporate confidentiality to the fear of a deluge of applications.

Grant seekers should be aware that even company-sponsored foundations have little autonomy and exist merely to carry out the philanthropic objectives of their sponsoring corporations. No matter how vague or nonexistent their published charitable giving guidelines, corporations tend to fund organizations serving company employees, communities in which the company operates, research in related fields, or projects that will bolster the company's public image [3]. The company's financial outlook and the special interests of the organization's principal officers also play a part in the contributions. The burden of proof is clearly on the grant seeker to demonstrate how a project is related to the company's products and services, or how the company's customers, employees, or public image could benefit from funding the proposal. The specialized directories discussed in this section are particularly suited to the corporate funding environment.

14.6   *Corporate Foundation Profiles.* New York, The Foundation Center, 1980–2002. Irregular.

Compiled by the Foundation Center, *Corporate Foundation Profiles* appeared in its 12th and final edition in 2002. It provides detailed profiles 181 of the largest company-sponsored foundations that have made annual contributions over $1 billion. Each foundation profile is divided into three sections: a Foundation Portrait with basic information about the foundation, including the purpose, giving limitations and application guidelines; Grant Analysis, providing detailed information on the foundation's grant program; and Sample Grants, where recently-awarded grants are listed. An appendix provides additional information on 1,131 corporate foundations that provided at least $66,000 annually in grants.

Canadian Granting Agencies

14.7   *Canadian Institutes of Health Research (CIHR)/Instituts de recherche en santé du Canada (IRSC).* Available: www.cihr-irsc. gc.ca/

CIHR/IRSC is the federal government's lead funding agency for health research in Canada. In addition to providing grant money which funds research in all health-related disciplines, the agency provides support for re-search infrastructure at postsecondary educational institutions and research hospitals and fosters commercialization, helping to move research discoveries into the marketplace. In 2005–2006, the CIHR/IRSC had a budget of $700 million (Canadian); approximately 70 percent of this money was disbursed through peer-reviewed open competitions to investigator-driven research projects. Nearly 30 percent of its budget is reserved by the CIHR/IRSC for strategic initiatives targeted at major health challenges, also selected by peer review, which are developed by its 13 virtual institutes.

The CIHR/IRSC Web site provides information about the 13 constituent institutes (which deal with Aboriginal Peoples; Aging; Cancer; Circulatory and Respiratory Health; Gender; Genetics; Health Services and Policy Research; Human Development, Child and Youth Health; Infection and Immunity; Musculoskeletal Health and Arthritis; Neurosciences, Mental Health and Addiction; Nutrition, Metabolism and Diabetes; and Population and Public Health) and their activities. The section on "Funding Health Research" lists current and archived funding opportunities available from the CIHR/IRSC (both the open and strategic competitions) as well as from some external organizations which have chosen to be listed on the CIHR/IRSC Web site. All the information and the forms necessary to make application for CIHR/IRSC funding are accessible in this section. There is information, also, regarding the funding policy of the agency and its peer review process. The site also provides access to lists of current and archived funding decisions and to funding-related databases of relevant organizations. There are also sections of the Web site dealing with and explaining "Knowledge Translation and Commercialization," "Partnerships," "Major Strategic Initiatives," "International Cooperation," and "Ethics." All information on the site is available in Canada's two official languages: French and English.

14.8   *Canada Foundation for Innovation/Fondation canadienne pour l'innovation.* Available: www.innovation.ca/

The Canada Foundation for Innovation (CFI) is an independent corporation established by the Government of Canada in 1997 to strengthen research infrastructure in Canadian universities, colleges, research hospitals and other not-for-profit institutions so as to carry out world-class research and technology development that benefits Canadians. The CFI works by forming partnerships with institutions in which both partners put up money to fund new programs, the acquisition of equipment or the creation of new facilities to support research initiatives in the public, private and voluntary sectors. The CFI normally funds up to 40 percent of the infrastructure of successful projects out of the $3.65 billion (Canadian) it has been given by the Government of Canada since 1997.

The CFI Web site offers information about the programs funded, new initiatives, and the funds available for exploitation and provides everything necessary to make application for any of them. Information about the assessment of applications and critical dates is available to applicants. Foundation publications can be downloaded from the site in PDF format. Partner institutions can login to obtain institutional reports and gain access to financial information. As is common with sites supported by the federal government, all information is equally available in both official languages.

14.9   *Social Sciences and Humanities Research Council (SSHRC)/Conseil de recherches en sciences humains du Canada (CRSH).* Available: www.sshrc-crsh.gc.ca/

The Social Sciences and Humanities Research Council (SSHRC) is a federal funding agency at "arm's length" from the Canadian government. It funds university-based research and training in the social sciences and humanities and promotes "innovative thinking about real life issues, including the economy, education, health care, the environment, immigration," etc. SSHRC/CRSH is not likely to fund clinical research, but does support nursing research that makes a contribution to the social sciences and humanities. It also includes the disciplines of psychology and educational psychology, which sometimes are closely allied to health and health care.

The Web site for this agency contains a section which helps those in highly interdisciplinary pursuits to choose a funding agency appropriate to their interests and likely to grant them funding. Once again, there are the usual sections for information about the programs supported by SSHRC, the funding available, applying for funding and how to manage your grant, if you are a successful applicant.

14.10 *Natural Sciences and Engineering Research Council (NSERC)/ Conseil de recherches en sciences naturelles et en génie du Canada (CRSNG).* Available: www.nserc-crsng.gc.ca/

The Natural Sciences and Engineering Research Council (NSERC) supports basic university research in science and technology as well as the training of highly qualified researchers. Like SSHRC above, the interests of the NSERC do not actually include clinical research, but many of the funded projects involve basic sciences in the health care arena: pathology, anatomy, biochemistry, biology, and psychology, among others.

The NSERC Web site offers access to standard information about awards administered by the council for various types of applicants with application guidelines and forms. There are tutorials (in the form of PowerPoint presentations) which instruct the applicant how to use the NSERC system and guides that help applicants write successful proposals. There are also lists of awards made for the past several years.

In addition to the very helpful "navigation block," Canadian government Web sites all display at the top of each screen, this site has a left navigation bar which helps visitors to the site find material of specific interest to them. You can choose among: "For Professors," "For Students," "For Industry," "For Institutions," "For Media." In addition, you can find items such as program guides, eligibility criteria, and award holders' guides for each type of visitor pulled out of the welter of information and made readily available by user type.

14.11 *National Cancer Institute of Canada/Institut national du cancer du Canada.* Available: www.ncic.cancer.ca/

The National Cancer Institute of Canada (NCIC) is funded by the Canadian Cancer Society and the Terry Fox Foundation to provide support for cancer research and related programs undertaken at Canadian universities, hospitals and other research institutions. In 2006, the NCIC provided $67 million (Canadian) to support programs (research grants to individuals, projects, trainees, workshops, and symposia.) around the country.

The Web site offers access to information on NCIC programs and policies in its *Support for Research and Training Manual*, which is updated annually. All the forms necessary for application are available on the site, as are lists of new grants and awards by competition for the past three years. A section on "Cancer Control" indicates how the NCIC works with other agencies and partners to prevent and cure cancer and to increase survival and quality of life for those afflicted by cancer. This section offers a collection of statistical summaries on cancer in Canada. Like other sites of this sort, the NCIC site also offers access to promotional material; including relevant news and award recipients.

Canadian Foundation Sources

14.12 *Heart and Stroke Foundation of Canada/Fondation des maladies du coeur, Research Programs/Programmes de recherché*. Available: www.hsf.ca/research/

The mission of the Heart and Stroke Foundation of Canada/Fondation des maladies du coeur, as stated on its main site (ww2.heartandstroke.ca/) is "to improve the health of Canadians by preventing and reducing disability and death from heart disease and stroke through research, health promotion and advocacy."

The research site of the Heart and Stroke Foundation is separate from the main site, which is intended for the public, and is totally directed to the researcher. The "Research Programs" site provides access to information about funding opportunities in both national and provincial programs, the HSF Research Fund, peer review and the results of previous competitions. Guidelines, application forms and information about deadlines are available on the site. The site also provides access to a searchable database of over 900 researchers in Canada with interest and expertise in heart disease, stroke and related diseases who have received grants from the HSF. All information is available in both French and English.

14.13 *Canadian Directory to Foundations and Grants*. Toronto: Imagine Canada, 1996–. Available: www.imaginecanada.ca

Imagine Canada is the result of the 2003 merger of the Canadian Centre for Philanthropy and the Coalition of National Voluntary Organizations. More than 1,200 charities, foundations, corporations and governments across Canada come together in this organization to advance the role and interests of the charitable sector for the benefit of Canadian communities. It maintains publication of the print source mentioned above, the *Canadian Directory to Foundations and Grants*, and offers subscription-based online access to a directory of the same name via its Web site.

The 20th edition (2006) of the *Canadian Directory to Foundations and Grants* has grown to over 2,150 pages. It is still paperbound with a glossy paper cover, but now appears in two volumes. It offers a list of over 3,100 grant-making foundations whose funds are disbursed to a variety of individuals and organizations, including a special list of U.S. foundations with a history of granting in Canada. The entries for each foundation provide basic contact information, skeletal histories, information about purpose of the foundation, funding interests and types of support offered, as well as restrictions on support or funding, some financial data, names of officers and directors, and a recent history of grants larger than $1,000.00 (where the information is available). There is a geographic analysis of the size and scope of the foundations listed and their funding, useful in a country as regionalized and as large as Canada. There are excellent indexes and lists of the top 100 foundations by assets, government foundations (CIHR, SSHRC, NSERC and the like are not included, as they are not foundations), the top family foundations, community foundations, and corporate foundations. There is also a useful list of foundation Web sites.

The preliminary material also provides help in understanding what a foundation is and how it operates so that the applicant will stand a better chance of developing a successful proposal. There is detailed information for foundations about fundraising, and similar advice and assistance for individuals wanting to develop proposals to present to foundations. There are also lists of grant recipients by name and location.

As the only Canadian source in this list that offers information about multiple funding sources, this fat volume from Imagine Canada is invaluable. It is most likely, however, to be useful to the investigator looking for relatively small amounts of money to support research. Although some of the foundations listed offer as much as $15,000,000.00 (Canadian) in grants, the majority of the foundations appearing here have far less money to offer than is needed to support major health sciences research.

Subscribers to the online product can access the foundations and corporations information together or separately, but the print source named above lists only the foundations information found in the online database. Various useful online search capacities are described on the Web site as being available in the database, and charities and non-profit organizations with revenues of less than $100,000.00 per year are eligible to use a "starter kit," which provides limited information from the database free of charge.

Grants to Individuals

14.14 *Foundation Grants to Individuals.* New York: The Foundation Center, 1977–2003. Biennial; Annual, 2005–. Available: gtionline. fdncenter.org/

14.15 *Grants Register.* New York, London, Palgrave Macmillan, Annual, 1969/70; Biennial, 1971/73—1995/97; Annual, 2005–.

14.16 *GrantsNet.* Available: www.sciencemag.org/

Foundation Grants to Individuals contains programs arranged by grant type, including such categories as scholarships and loans, fellowships, grants for foreign individuals, general welfare and medical assistance, and grants restricted to company employees. This resource is well indexed and provides the usual descriptive information in each entry, along with lists of sample grants awarded. In addition, two informative articles appear in *Foundation Grants to Individuals*—an analysis of federal laws pertaining to this area of grantsmanship and an essay and extensive bibliography covering further sources of information on grants to individuals. Like other databases from the Foundation Center, online access is available with one-month, three-month and annual subscription options.

The *Grants Register* moved from a biennial to an annual publication in 2005 and is broader in scope than the *Foundation Grants to Individuals*, listing information on more than 4,500 awards and grants from government agencies as well as international, national, and private organizations. Over 80 countries are represented. Compiled for students at or above the graduate level and for others requiring further professional training, this directory includes scholarships and fellowships plus research and travel grants. While this publication emphasizes individuals in need, some of the programs make awards only through sponsoring institutions. Section six of the subject index is devoted to medical and health sciences.

Sponsored by the Howard Hughes Medical Institute (HHMI) and American Association for the Advancement of Science (AAAS), GrantsNet is available at no charge from the Web site for the journal *Science*. It has a section called ScienceCareers.org (sciencecareers.sciencemag.org/), which provides access to information about funding sources for training and research for students, postdocs, and junior faculty in science, medicine, math, engineering and technology in a very flexible manner. Clicking the Funding tab at the top of the web page in ScienceCareers.org provides access to GrantsNet, a database of information about sources of funding. There is a monthly *Funding News* note, providing information on the most recent updates to the database and highlighting new sources of funding for undergraduates, graduate students and faculty. The *International Grants and Fellowships Index* is included in GrantsNet and provides access to information about funding sources in Europe, Asia and the Americas. By clicking on the Career Development tab at the top of the screen in ScienceCareers.org, you can also choose to look specifically at funding sources in particular regions of the world. It is possible to explore jobs and funding in Canada, for instance, or in the U.K. and many other regions around the world, through this section of the Web site. Funding information can be accessed by career stage, work sector and discipline in addition to geographic region of the world. There is also a Minority Scientists Network and a posting of jobs available in different regions. This site is especially directed at those in the early stages of their career or in preparation for a career in science, an area of endeavour where funding is both important and often very hard to find.

Institutional Databases

14.17 *Community of Science (COS)*. Available: www.cos.com/

14.18 *Illinois Researcher Information Service (IRIS)*. Available: library.uiuc.edu/iris/

Available by institutional subscription, these databases provide opportunities for researchers to manage their profiles for identifying funding sources, identifying researchers doing similar work and being alerted to forthcoming funding opportunities.

The Community of Science makes its enormously useful, subscription-based COS Funding Opportunities database available on its own Web site and through the CSA platform. On its own site, the "Funding Opportunities" database is augmented with a suite of other databases and electronic tools in a package optimized for large research organizations such as universities and independent research organizations. On this site, the Community of Science offers COS Expertise, a searchable database of profiles of researchers, scholars and experts at universities, government agencies and other R&D institutions around the world. This database of researcher profiles can be used to publicize research externally, locate peer reviewers and collaborators, and to improve communication between personnel working in related disciplines.

The COS Funding Opportunities database is probably the world's largest and most comprehensive database of funding opportunities; it offers more than 22,000 records for organizations throughout the world making available over $33 billion in funding. The funding opportunities included are not restricted to competitions for basic research. There are opportunities for collaboration, travel, curriculum development, conferences, fellowships and postdoctoral positions, equipment and capital as well as operating expenses. It is possible to do free-text, simple searches, as well as to use Boolean logic with a small selection of useful controlled vocabulary terms, or to use a Search Wizard, which prompts you to choose key concepts from groups of related terms in order to build a very relevant search. You can limit a search to funding agencies in a particular country, or funding available to citizens of any country; a variety of other practical limits are also possible.

Also included in the package of research tools available on its home site, the Community of Science offers tools to create and manage researcher profiles, to create CVs from these profiles, and to manage alerts of new funding opportunities based on the profiles (COS Workbench). Another tool, called the COS Abstract Management System, permits collaborative online authoring and submission, peer reviewing, meeting management and personal itinerary planning. A final component of the Community of Science package is a module providing access to a series of reference databases; GeoRef, Medline, U.S. Patents, AGRICOLA, and the Federal Register are among those offered.

A service of the University of Illinois at Urbana-Champaign Library, the IRIS database provides information on funding opportunities in 25 subject areas, including selected items from the *Commerce Business Daily/FedBizOpps* and *Federal Register*. While designed for the University of Illinois community, other institutions can subscribe as well. Profiles can be set up for the IRIS Alert Service.

References

1. Gerin, W. *Writing the NIH grant proposal: a step-by-step guide*. Thousand Oaks, CA: Sage, 2006.
2. "Introduction." In: *The Foundation directory*. 14th ed. New York: The Foundation Center, 1992.
3. Kurzig CM. *Foundation fundamentals*. Rev. ed. New York: The Foundation Center, 1981:4.

Index